The Software Arts

Software Studies

Matthew Fuller, Lev Manovich, and Noah Wardrip-Fruin, editors

Expressive Processing: Digital Fictions, Computer Games, and Software Studies, Noah Wardrip-Fruin, 2009

Code/Space: Software and Everyday Life, Rob Kitchin and Martin Dodge, 2011

Programmed Visions: Software and Memory, Wendy Hui Kyong Chun, 2011

Speaking Code: Coding as Aesthetic and Political Expression, Geoff Cox and Alex McClean, 2012

10 PRINT CHR$(205.5+RND(1));: GOTO 10, Nick Montfort, Patsy Baudoin, John Bell, Ian Bogost, Jeremy Douglass, Mark Marino, Michael Mateas, Casey Reas, Mark Sample, and Noah Vawter, 2012

The Imaginary App, Paul D. Miller and Svitlana Matviyenko, 2014

The Stack: On Software and Sovereignty, Benjamin H. Bratton, 2015

Coding Literacy: How Computer Programming Is Changing Writing, Annette Vee, 2017

The Software Arts, Warren Sack, 2019

The Software Arts

Warren Sack

The MIT Press
Cambridge, Massachusetts
London, England

This book was set in ITC Stone Serif Std Medium by Westchester Publishing Services. Printed and bound in the United States of America.

Library of Congress Cataloging-in-Publication Data

Names: Sack, Warren, author.
Title: The software arts / Warren Sack.
Description: Cambridge, MA : The MIT Press, [2019] | Series: Software studies |
    Includes bibliographical references and index.
Identifiers: LCCN 2018032131 | ISBN 9780262039703 (hardcover : alk. paper)
Subjects: LCSH: Electronic data processing—Popular works. | Computer software—
    Popular works.
Classification: LCC QA76 .S2164 2019 | DDC 005.3—dc23
LC record available at https://lccn.loc.gov/2018032131

10 9 8 7 6 5 4 3 2 1

For Jennifer

Contents

Series Foreword

Software is deeply woven into contemporary life—economically, culturally, creatively, politically—in manners both obvious and nearly invisible. Yet while much is written about how software is used, and the activities that it supports and shapes, thinking about software itself has remained largely technical for much of its history. Increasingly, however, artists, scientists, engineers, hackers, designers, and scholars in the humanities and social sciences are finding that for the questions they face, and the things they need to build, an expanded understanding of software is necessary. For such understanding they can call upon a strand of texts in the history of computing and new media, they can take part in the rich implicit culture of software, and they also can take part in the development of an emerging, fundamentally transdisciplinary computational literacy. These provide the foundation for Software Studies.

Software Studies uses and develops cultural, theoretical, and practice-oriented approaches to make critical, historical, and experimental accounts of (and interventions via) the objects and processes of software. The field engages and contributes to the research of computer scientists, the work of software designers and engineers, and the creations of software artists. It tracks how software is substantially integrated into the processes of contemporary culture and society, reformulating processes, ideas, institutions, and cultural objects around their closeness to algorithmic and formal description and action. Software Studies proposes histories of computational cultures and works with the intellectual resources of computing to develop reflexive thinking about its entanglements and possibilities. It does this both in the scholarly modes of the humanities and social sciences and in the software creation/research modes of computer science, the arts, and design.

The Software Studies book series, published by the MIT Press, aims to publish the best new work in a critical and experimental field that is at once culturally and technically literate, reflecting the reality of today's software culture.

Foreword: Software as a Mode of Thinking—An Introduction

John Rajchman

The modern digital computer is the invention of two distinguished mathematicians, Alan Turing and John von Neumann, working in the heyday of a rich debate about numbers and logic and a grand search for the "laws of thought," which they then tried to introduce—perhaps it would be better to say "translate"—into the workings of a new kind of machine, the computer.

The story of this invention has often been told, that of Bletchy Park and The Institute for Advanced Study. Born of the urgencies of war, often elaborated in secrecy in government facilities against a formidable foe, and mobilizing its own science-tech sector, the invention would assume new forms after the war. It would become part of an ever-expanding "military industrial complex," with us now as much as ever, with our giant global Internet companies, surveillance, hacktivism, cybersecurity, smart cities, and infrastructures. In the process, "platforms" themselves would pass from mainframe to PC to smartphone, increasing in speed, efficiency, and reach, and leading to the operations of our great number-crunching algorithms in finance, politics, and social media. The invention of the computer by these two great mathematicians, carried on in military secrecy, in short, has led to an enormous complex in government and economics alike, touching on many aspects of the ways we think and live.

But what role did actual programming play in this history? How did the "translations" of various activities into this complex itself evolve, assuming new forms and functions? What role might programming yet play in the matter of "digital intelligence" today? Such is the complex problem this new study of the origins and nature of software sets out to raise and, in the first place, to formulate. How can we do the history of software itself: What exactly is it? How should we study it? In particular, what ever happened to the great logicist dream of discovering "laws of thought," which inspired Turing and von Neumann, extended at the time in striking ways by Gödel and Hilbert? In what ways did this logicist background help foster a picture of thinking or "smartness" itself, conceived as a matter of following rules in a finite number of steps, independent of human interaction of any kind—a picture still very much alive today in digital culture, popular as well as more sophisticated? What would it mean to see programming instead, from the start, as belonging to a different, more materially rooted history—more like cooking up ways of doing things, inventing "recipes" for integrating our smart machines into the larger demands of politics, war, finance, commerce, and everyday life? What role in particular might the arts play in this expanded history? What would it mean to see the "digitalization" of artistic media as part of it? Could we adapt what Bruno Latour calls "translation" for these purposes, challenging the idea, already found with "the computer," that digital intelligence arises by simply creating artificial forms for human activities? How then does such transformative translation work in the case of software? In what ways do the translations that software helps bring about introduce something new, for which no human model previously existed, challenging our very ideas of natural or nonartificial human activity? What role, in short, has software played in the ways we talk about and see things—and therefore act?

In fact, even to talk about the translations effectuated by computer programming, we often lack a preexisting vocabulary. The very words we are accustomed to using— "computer," "program," even "algorithm"—of necessity draw on predigital languages and practices, in genealogies we can now retrospectively examine. We see this, for example, in the case of "media" and "media studies" of the sort exemplified by Lev Manovich, part of the larger disciplinary framework through which we talk about and see digitalization. The terms "media" and "medium" were in fact drawn from the arts and journalism, then television, areas that themselves are being transformed by the rise of smart machines. In the arts today, for example, we see a movement away from the very ideas of media and medium, still important for a group like Radical Software, in favor of something more like "ecology of images." How might we start to chart these developments, studying software as a complex, evolving mode of thinking, within divisions of knowledge and artistic practices? Raising all these questions at once, this patient study, six years in the making, becomes a search for method and a plea for new ways of thinking, and the role that software practice might yet play in them.

What, then, is software as a mode of thinking? *The Software Arts* exposes an apparent paradox. While the grand logicist dream that led to the invention of the computer has long lost its philosophical hold on us, in many ways its ghost lives on in digital culture, in the very idea of smartness it helped introduce, in ways Warren Sack starts to trace: Turing machines, artificial intelligence, "cognitivism." He finds one turning point in Noam Chomsky, whose search for innate syntactic structures in language would lead to attempts to relocate such logic in the brain, or universal "neural cognition." To see software instead as a mode of thinking is to reverse the question—not whether our brains work like computers but how the ways our computers are in fact programmed end up programming our brains to fit their operations. If, then, more generally the aura of mathematical logic still hangs over our very idea of digital smartness, it is precisely there that it matters to question it. The dream of the "laws of thought" today is to be found not so much in the realm of language, where it was once hotly debated, as in the digital world in which we now live and think, and the problem it poses is not about language alone but also about artifice and nature, fact and fiction, cognition and labor. To see software as a complex mode of thinking, to exorcise the ghost of logicism in our picture of it, in short, is to insert its operations into a larger history of such questions.

We see this in the sorts of historical approaches to which Warren Sack turns in his search for methods. In looking back to grammar or rhetoric as precursors of "software thinking," he draws more or less explicitly on Foucault's attempt to analyze the great philosophical preoccupation of his day with language as a complex "discursive event," which helps change our very image and manner of thought. But in adapting this approach to software studies, he shifts from a focus on linguistic form toward practical questions of intervening in environments at once artificial and natural, or where the two are interrelated in new ways. He thus encounters a later phase in Foucault's own work—his genealogy of bio-power, administration, and the role of numbers in it. How, then, has software or software thinking figured in that? In his discussions of big data and the very idea of an algorithm, Sack turns to these matters.

Ian Hacking went on to develop Foucault's study of bio-power in a striking way, pointedly asking how to do the "history of statistics." Warren Sack's question—how to do the history of software—might be seen as one continuation, which in effect asks how and where the two histories of statistical administration and software as a mode of thinking came together in the big data number crunching of today. Hacking distinguished between "styles of reasoning" and "methods of inference." More than a simple logic of inference, statistics is a materially rooted style of reasoning, with many unforeseen consequences, in particular for the very ideas of law and chance, and the new roles they would start to have in arts and letters. Numbers and numbering would play a key role in this new practice. Hacking talks of an "avalanche of numbers," which would pose new questions about who "counts" in society and who does the counting. The role of numbers in this manner of reasoning is of course quite different from their role in the methods of logic, famously posed by Frege and Russell, or even later by Wittgenstein. Hacking thinks it marks a shift from a mechanical universe (a clock wound up by God) to a "stochastic" universe, where probability replaces certainty and the "game of thought" starts to be played in the new ways, which came to be associated in France with Nietzsche and Mallarmé's search for an "untamed" chance that no roll of the dice can ever abolish.

How, then, did computers or computing enter into this administrative territory, introducing a new "translation" in it? What role does it play, for example, in Cambridge Analytica and Facebook's "commercial surveillance"? When we look back, for example, at the opening of the Stasi files in what was thought to be postcommunist Germany, we see a predigital phase of administration—bureaus, paper files, archives—which now seems quite quaint. Today's "bureaus" are all increasingly on our screens. But does this shift—this software translation—also introduce something new, a sort of shift in administrative reason? The East German case, of course, was part of the sort of Soviet "brainwashing" Orwell feared might be coming to Britain. But in our current "post–Cold War" situation, are we confronted with something new that neither Orwell nor even Foucault lived to see? What role does software play in it? What makes data big is not sheer quantity but rather the invention of software enabling inventories at great speed that extract certain kinds of information (or facts) about us—our "friends" and "likes," our buying and voting habits—as well as the rise and fall of stocks. Perhaps, to talk like Foucault, we could look at how such software thinking helps "constitute" us as buyers, voters, or stockholders, in the process turning electoral politics into a new domain of manipulation and interference. Using a term from Peirce, Sack proposes to see in big data a sort of algorithmic "abduction." But, in some ways, Peirce still belongs to the earlier nineteenth-century universe of chance, as Ian Hacking argues in his book on the topic. Perhaps our problem is no longer Hacking's shift from a mechanical to a stochastic universe, to which artists and thinkers responded at the end of the nineteenth century; perhaps now, in an age of big data, we need new analyses and new forms of artistic intervention.

What, then, is software as a mode of thinking? How should we do its history, and how might this history contribute to the larger questions of digital intelligence today? We come to the last aspect of this enterprise. To further such study, to pose such questions, Sack argues, we need to overcome entrenched divisions in knowledge itself, dividing "humanistic" from "technical" or "scientific" culture, finding new ways of drawing from each and initiating new kinds of collaboration. His own itinerary offers one example. After studying with Donna Haraway at Santa Cruz, he would pursue his studies at the Media Lab at MIT, where he started work as well with Visual Arts and the History of Technology. For his thesis, he would write code to visualize large-scale Internet "conversations," arguing that they worked in ways that go beyond anything found in linguistic theories of speakers or speaking—a project that already showed an ambition to go beyond the more lucrative military or commercial uses of software usually undertaken at the Media Lab, instead using software to participate in a larger debate, artistic and philosophical, crossing academic boundaries.

This new space of exchange and analysis across the arts and sciences is one that must itself be invented. That is the suggestion that emerges from this study. It is not simply a matter of getting the two "communities," intellectual-artistic and military-commercial, to talk more with each other, but rather to encourage the creation of a new space of discussion, for the problem of digital intelligence today is not simply one of the two cultures, scientific and humanistic. (It is not clear that the "intelligence" of software nerds is very mathematical at all; it is in fact drawn from many other sources.) The question it poses is not in the first place a matter of machines and us, artifice and nature, regarding who is in control. (The history of software is a history of modes of thinking that are at once artificial and natural, scientific and artistic.) The problem of digital intelligence is rather how to invent new ways of working together, outside the confines within which our thinking is now kept, and for that no simple return to a bookish "humanities" will suffice. The workings of our smart machines need to be analyzed at once in the arts and the sciences in ways and through methods and means that help create new relations between them. Only then will the reigning idea of smartness be replaced by something more like a kind of collective intelligence, working and thinking together across many domains and disciplines. The force and originality of this study is to show how software—software as a mode of thinking—has a key role to play in this process.

Acknowledgments

This book has been written in Santa Cruz, California, and Paris, France. At the University of California, Santa Cruz (UCSC), I would like to thank the faculty, staff, and students in the Film + Digital Media Department, the Digital Arts & New Media MFA Program, the History of Art and Visual Culture Department, the History of Consciousness Department, the Computational Media Department, the Center for Cultural Studies, the Science and Justice Research Center, and the Center for Games and Playable Media. I have also benefited from logistical and financial support offered to me for this book by the staff and the Dean of the Arts.

The American Council of Learned Societies granted me an ACLS Digital Innovation Fellowship that allowed me to begin writing this book in Paris, hosted by Bruno Latour at the Médialab of Sciences Po and by Françoise Detienne at the Département Sciences Economiques et Sociales of Télécom ParisTech. I am deeply grateful for financial support from the ACLS and for the collegial and institutional support Bruno and Françoise and their respective networks offered me that year.

Also in Paris, I offer my thanks to Bernard Stiegler and Vincent Puig of the Institut de recherche et de l'innovation (IRI) at the Centre Georges Pompidou, where I have been invited to speak to and learn from them and our colleagues of the Digital Studies network. I am equally grateful to Samuel Bianchini and Emmanuel Mahé at EnsadLab of l'École des Arts Décoratifs (EnsAD) for the many interactions I have enjoyed with them and their doctoral students.

Most recently, my institutional home in Paris has been at the Paris Institute for Advanced Study (IAS), where this book and I benefited from a fellowship with the financial support of the French State program Investissements d'avenir, managed by the Agence Nationale de la Recherche (ANR-11-LABX-0027-01 Labex RFIEA+). I was a fellow at the Paris IAS during the fall of 2015 and the fall of 2016, housed in the spectacular Hôtel de Lauzun. Director Gretty Mirdal has created an extraordinarily productive interdisciplinary exchange. Simon Luck, the scientific coordinator, kept me connected to many research communities in and around Paris. Librarian Geneviève Marmin helped me navigate the libraries and archives of the ENS, MSH, the Sorbonne, Jussieu, and the CNAM.

Over the course of my two stays at the Paris IAS, I got to know forty other fellows. Each fellow made a contribution to my writing and thinking through our weekly colloquia and our daily lunches. I would like to thank Keith Baker, Sean Takats, and Charles Walton for providing me with suggestions about what to read and what to consider as my research began to move more deeply into the specifics of the eighteenth-century *Encyclopédie* of Diderot and d'Alembert. When I was working on the chapter on algorithms, Carlos Gonçalves generously offered his expert insights into ancient Mesopotamian mathematics. And I was very influenced by Nachum Dershowitz's approach to his research, in which he integrates both historical and technical details of computer science. Nachum and I also co-produced a workshop with our Parisian colleagues on the topic of software and the digital humanities, and we both contributed to a celebration of Ada Lovelace organized by Director Mirdal. For my IAS colloquium presentations, I was honored to have my Parisian colleagues Patrice Maniglier, Bernard Stiegler, and Jean-Gabriel Ganascia as my respondents.

This book has benefited from several other workshops in which my friends and colleagues reviewed the draft manuscript.

In March of 2013, Matthew Fuller and Noortje Marres hosted a workshop for me at Goldsmiths College, University of London. I would like to thank them, Olga Goriunova, Nina Wakeford, and the then-doctoral students—Beatrice Fazi, Ana Gross, Rosa Menkman, and David Moats—for the rigorous yet generous readings they gave to the manuscript.

In June of 2013, I hosted an ACLS-sponsored workshop in Paris that brought together colleagues from the Médialab, Télécom, and other research centers. Participants included Michael Baker, Audrey Baneyx, Valérie Beaudouin, Samuel Bianchini, Dominique Cunin, Jérôme Denis, Françoise Detienne, Dana Dimenescu, Paul Edwards, Annie Gentes, Marie Gil, Paul Girard, Jennifer González, Mathieu Jacomy, Benjamin Loveluck, Patrice Maniglier, Dominique Pasquier, Jean-Christophe Plantin, Serge Proulx, Vincent Puig, Everardo Reyes-García, and Tommaso Venturini.

In July of 2013, Richard Rogers of the University of Amsterdam invited me to speak at the Digital Methods Summer School about what, ultimately, became chapter 6 of this book, on the topic of rhetoric.

The ACLS fellowship allowed me to carry over funds from my fellowship to hold a workshop at UCSC in June of 2014. I wish to thank the following participants: Sophie Bargues-Rollins, David Bates, Jon Beller, Alan Christy, Chris Connery, Joe Dumit, Shelly Errington, Carla Freccero, Elaine Gan, Jennifer González, John Kadvany, Deirdra

"Squinky" Kiai, Dilan Mahendran, Michael Mateas, Soraya Murray, Abram "Aphid" Stern, Mike Travers, Lyle Troxell, and Noah Wardrip-Fruin. Now, listening to the recordings of our discussions, I am impressed with how our free-ranging discussion ultimately gave the book a much sharper focus.

During my last couple of stays in Paris, Patrice Maniglier included me in the "Sémiomaths" (semiology of mathematics) working group he co-organizes with Juan Luis Gastaldi and David Rabouin. I thank them for letting me join some of their meetings and for devoting a meeting in 2015 and another in 2018 to a discussion of my book manuscript.

I am deeply grateful to Doug Sery, my editor at the MIT Press, who has encouraged and supported this project since 2012. I thank the external reviewers for detailed and insightful analyses of the manuscript. When revising the text, I also had the good fortune to work with the remarkable developmental editor Kathryn Chetkovich, whose clarity and thoughtfulness significantly improved the final result.

My motivation for writing this book has been vitally connected to my role as a teacher. Hundreds of undergraduate students in my recent offerings of a large lecture course at UCSC, Introduction to Digital Media, have wrangled with earlier versions of this text. It has also benefited from the readings and comments of my current and former PhD and MFA students who have been teaching assistants for the undergraduate course; taken some version of my doctoral seminar, Software Studies; or my graduate course, Introduction to Programming for the Arts; or have decided to take a qualifying examination with me in software studies; or conducted research with me on Open Source Software development. I would especially like to acknowledge the following former and current graduate students for their insights and support over the years: Nicolas Ducheneaut, Elaine Gan, Fabiola Hanna, Nik Hanselmann, Meredith Hoy, Chris Kerich, Nick Lally, Dylan Lederle-Ensign, Dilan Mahendran, Michael McCarrin, Karl Mendonca, Abram "Aphid" Stern, and Lindsay Weinberg.

Many of the ideas in this book had their beginnings years ago when I was a member of the feminist studies of science and technology (STS) reading group that met in the basement of the Yale Computer Science Department in the 1980s; a Chateaubriand Fellow at the Department of Computer Science of the University of Paris 8 (St. Denis); an unofficial member of the STS Research Cluster of the Center for Cultural Studies at UCSC that was organized by Donna Haraway's graduate students in the late 1980s and early 1990s; a co-organizer of the Narrative Intelligence Reading Group that met in the basement of the MIT Media Lab in the 1990s; a visitor at the Center on Organizational Innovation at Columbia University; and a visitor at the Centre de sociologie de l'innovation at Mines ParisTech. I would like to thank past and present members of these inspiring communities.

Many of the pages I have written have been composed next to the Centre Pompidou at the Café Beaubourg in Paris and on Pacific Avenue in Santa Cruz at Lulu Carpenter's. I thank the respective owners and staff of these two cafés for their hospitality and for their production of third places with food, drink, and just the right balance of social interaction and isolation.

All of my colleagues have been generous with the time, attention, and resources they have given to me for this project, but some have been especially so, including David Bates, Sawad Brooks, Samuel Bianchini, Alan Christy, Wendy Hui Kyong Chun, Dominique Cunin, Françoise Detienne, Dana Diminescu, Joe Dumit, Matthew Fuller, Juan Luis Gastaldi, Annie Gentes, Jennifer González, Olga Goriunova, Donna Haraway, Yuk Hui, John Kadvany, Patrice Maniglier, Michael Mateas, Armand Mattelart, Hélène Mialet, Michel Moos, John Rajchman, Jenny Reardon, Everardo Reyes-García, Bernard Stiegler, Lyle Troxell, and Noah Wardrip-Fruin.

This project has been possible only with the love of my family. I am grateful for the confidence, support, and love given to me by my parents, Ronald and Margaret Sack, and my sister, Leslie Sack. I thank my sister-in-law and brother-in-law, Consuelo González and Richard Middleton, and my nephew, Karl Dyer, for their many forms of love, hospitality, and creative invention. Crispin and Kirsten González, my father-in-law and mother-in-law, have given me love and a home away from home from the first time I met them. I owe so much to my son, Felix, who has made frequent and enormous sacrifices for his dad's book, foregoing too many afternoons and weekends of play with his parents, and moving to and from Paris to accommodate my needs and desires to be there. Jennifer González, my life partner, has given me love, emotional support, practical advice, intellectual insight, and inspiration. Many of my thoughts on the topics of this book were produced in the years of conversations we have shared on art, philosophy, and technology. I dedicate this book to Jennifer.

Warren Sack
Santa Cruz, California
July 2018

1   Introduction

Computers are language machines.
—Paul N. Edwards

The computer revolution can be envisioned as a rewriting of the world. This book is an examination of computerization as a work of rewriting or, more specifically, as translation. Increasingly, in academia, industry, and government, ideas are exchanged as software rather than as printed prose documents. Software now constitutes a new form of logic, rhetoric, and grammar, a new means of thinking, arguing, and interpreting.

This book argues that computing grew out of the arts. This argument will be a provocation for some, especially for those who see a bright line dividing the "two cultures"[1] of the arts and the sciences. For others, the argument will not seem provocative at all. Important computer scientists have argued that computing is not a science, software is a literature, and computer programming is a kind of essay writing. For those who see no clear distinction between the arts and the sciences, this book will be an old saw with some new teeth.

Prior to the "scientific revolution"[2] of the seventeenth century, there were no scientists in Europe. There were no professional organizations of science. Most studies that we would now identify as scientific were conducted under the name of "natural philosophy." Natural philosophers most frequently published their works in Latin, in which the word "scientia" meant something broader than the modern cognate of "science," something more like the general term "knowledge." The professionalization of engineering occurred even later. At that time and before, education and inquiry were carried out in the mechanical arts and in the liberal arts. This book argues that the software arts—like science and engineering—are the fruit of a coupling of the liberal and the mechanical arts. To demonstrate this argument, the approach taken is partly historical. By tracing the genealogy of computing back to events before or during the initial professionalization of science and engineering, it becomes clear that computing grew out of the arts.

The Software Arts is also a reading of the texts of computing—code, algorithms, and technical papers—that emphasizes continuities between prose and programs.[3] Historically, it is possible to say that this position was first sketched out in the seventeenth century in proposals to develop artificial, philosophical languages that were used to knit together the liberal arts (e.g., logic, grammar, and rhetoric, the liberal arts of language) and the mechanical arts (e.g., those practiced by artisans in workshops producing pins, stockings, locks, guns, and jewelry).[4] In brief, these artificial languages became what we know today as computer programming languages. The claim is that contemporary, artificial languages have shaped and been shaped by the arts and have rearticulated the relationship between the liberal arts and the mechanical arts—an assembly we currently call art, design, the humanities, and technology.

Programming languages are the offspring of an effort to describe the mechanical arts in the languages of the liberal arts. Writing software is a practice of writing akin to the activity of novelists, playwrights, screenwriters, speechwriters, essayists, and academics in the arts and the humanities. Consequently, contemporary education, research, industry, and technology development all need to change to better recognize how the arts sit at the center of computing.

Apple's Artists

In 1995, Apple cofounder Steve Jobs said, "Part of what made the Macintosh great was that the people working on it were musicians, poets and artists and zoologists and historians who also happened to be the best computer scientists in the world.... And they brought with them, we all brought to this effort, a very liberal arts attitude."[5] Long after the introduction of the original Macintosh computer, Jobs was still describing the liberal arts as an Apple competitive advantage. At the launch of a new model of the iPad tablet computer, Jobs said, "It is in Apple's DNA that technology alone is not enough—it's technology married with liberal arts, married with the humanities, that yields us the results that make our heart sing."[6] In this book, I will argue that Jobs was right: the arts and the humanities are at the heart of computing.[7]

In the United States, Jobs's comments are remarkable today, when the arts and humanities are under siege with demands that students receive preprofessional training instead of a fine arts or liberal arts education.[8] The increasing disregard for a liberal arts education is misguided.[9] If Jobs was right, education needs to change. Computing education needs to be redesigned to recognize its rightful place in the liberal arts, and the humanities disciplines of the contemporary liberal arts need to be extended to acknowledge their position at the heart of the computer revolution.[10]

If Jobs was right, it also becomes possible to imagine how computing research and development can be pursued as forms of arts research and humanities scholarship. With this insight, the path to the next "insanely great"[11] computer technology widens to become a great expressway accommodating a much larger and more diverse group of fellow travelers.

To emphasize the centrality of the arts would almost certainly help the computer industry with its long-standing diversity problems. At least that is the thinking that drove the summer 2014 diversity campaign in which Apple described itself this way: "From the very beginning, we have been a collective of individuals. Different kinds of people from different kinds of places. Artists, designers, engineers and scientists, thinkers and dreamers. An intersection of technology and the liberal arts. Diverse backgrounds, all working together."[12]

Computing and the Arts

Beyond Steve Jobs and Apple are a number of important computer scientists who have also put the arts at the center of computing. For example, Harold Abelson, Gerald Sussman, and Julie Sussman wrote a programming textbook for their undergraduate students at the Massachusetts Institute of Technology. Their textbook, *The Structure and Interpretation of Computer Programs*, embodies this alternative vision of computing. The authors state in their introduction:

> Underlying our approach to this subject is our conviction that "computer science" is not a science and that its significance has little to do with computers. The computer revolution is a revolution in the way we think and in the way we express what we think. The essence of this change is the emergence of what might best be called procedural epistemology—the study of the structure of knowledge from an imperative point of view, as opposed to the more declarative point of view taken by classical mathematical subjects. Mathematics provides a framework for dealing precisely with notions of "what is." Computation provides a framework for dealing precisely with notions of "how to."[13]

By distinguishing classical mathematics from computation—"what is" as distinguished from "how to"—the authors articulate a position of "procedural epistemology," but rather than coining the new phrase "procedural epistemology," they could simply have said that computing is an art. "Art" in its original sense means how-to knowledge—as used in phrases such as "martial arts" and "arts and crafts."

In their book, Abelson, Sussman, and Sussman emphasize one aspect of epistemology: that computing constitutes a new way of thinking. Computer scientist Edsger Dijkstra stated the case like this: "[Computers] have had a great impact on our society in their capacity of tools, but in that capacity their influence will be but a ripple on the surface of our culture, compared with the much more profound influence they will have in their capacity of intellectual challenge without precedent in the cultural history of mankind."[14]

This form of research and education, with a focus on the implications for cultural history, has been pursued with a mixture of methods that weave together ideas from the arts, the humanities, and mathematics. Donald Knuth, Professor Emeritus of the Art of Computer Programming at Stanford University, advocates a method he calls "literate programming": "Let us change our traditional attitude to the construction of programs: Instead of imagining that our main task is to instruct a computer what to do, let us concentrate rather on explaining to human beings what we want a computer to do.... The practitioner of literate programming can be regarded as an essayist, whose main concern is with exposition and excellence of style."[15]

Knuth sees programming as an art and as literature. Practitioners of "literate programming" and "procedural epistemology" are essayists, writers, and expositors. For Steve Jobs, Donald Knuth, Edsger Dijkstra, Harold Abelson, Gerald Sussman, and many other important computer scientists in the world (e.g., many who have won the Turing Award, the analog of the Nobel Prize for computer science), computing is part and parcel with the liberal arts. By arguing that the arts are at the heart of computing, I am arguing neither a radical nor a marginal point.

Computing and Engineering

Unfortunately, even though this argument has been made repeatedly and with great authority, it remains institutionally marginalized and generally unpopular. Institutionally—in both education and industry—the winning arguments have positioned computing either within the sciences or as a form of engineering. As a result, in universities, most computing departments are positioned in schools of science or engineering and away from schools of the arts and humanities.

While these "winning" arguments have been reified in the shaping of institutions, if we look closely at the arguments as originally stated and as pursued to date, we see that they are based on undefined terms and nonobvious and unstable analogies between computing and the subjects and objects studied and produced by science and engineering disciplines. Casting computing in a new disciplinary mold is frequently, at least initially, not commonsensical. For example, in a remark at the first Software Engineering Conference, convened in 1968 by the North Atlantic Treaty Organization (NATO) Science Committee, an analogy was drawn between software production and engineering: "The phrase 'software engineering' was deliberately chosen as being provocative, in implying the need for software manufacture to be based on the types of theoretical foundations and practical disciplines that are traditional in the established branches of engineering."[16]

In an article on the history of software engineering, Michael Mahoney writes the following about this opening gambit of the conference:

> The phrase was indeed provocative, if only because it left all the crucial terms undefined. What does it mean to "manufacture" software? Is that a goal or current practice? What, precisely, are the "theoretical foundations and practical disciplines" that underpin the "established branches of engineering"? What roles did they play in the formation of the engineering disciplines? Is the story the same in each case? The reference to "traditional" makes the answer to that question a matter of history—analyzing how the fields of engineering took their present form and searching for historical precedents, or what we have come to refer to as "roots."[17]

As Mahoney goes on to show in this article and subsequent scholarship, these terms remain undefined, decades after this first conference.[18]

One of the participants at the first Software Engineering Conference of 1968, Alexander D'Agapeyeff, had the following complaint: "Programming is still too much of an artistic endeavor."[19] The presupposition inherent in this complaint is, of course, that programming is already an art but that the aspiring software engineers would like it to be otherwise.

Indeed, "software engineering" remains an unrealized goal despite its current institutional success. Software engineers would like their discipline to be accepted as a form of engineering, but they are repeatedly unsure that it is. As Mahoney wrote in the introduction to his article, "It is … not hard to find doubts about whether its current practice meets those criteria and, indeed, whether it is an engineering discipline at all.… [It has been declared that] 'Software engineering is not yet a true engineering discipline, but it has the potential to become one.' From the outset, software engineering conferences have routinely begun with a keynote address that asks, 'Are we there yet?'"[20]

Is Computing a Science?

In 1967, a year before the first Software Engineering Conference, Allen Newell, Alan Perlis, and Herbert Simon published a letter in the journal *Science* arguing that computing is not (just) engineering but is also a science: "Professors of computer science are often asked: 'Is there such a thing as computer science, and if there is, what is it?' The questions have a simple answer: Wherever there are phenomena, there can be a science to describe and explain those phenomena. Thus, the simplest (and correct) answer to 'What is botany?' is, 'Botany is the study of plants.' And zoology is the study of animals, astronomy the study of stars, and so on. Phenomena breed sciences. There are computers. Ergo, computer science is the study of computers."[21]

This letter had tremendous persuasive power and, arguably, launched the founding of many university computer science departments. It incorporates a number of tropes—rhetorical techniques—to press the case. Consider, for instance, the opening statement, "Professors of computer science are often asked...." In 1967, there were very few professors of computer science, because the first university computer science department had been founded only five years earlier, in 1962, at Purdue University.[22] All three of the letter writers were affiliated with Carnegie Mellon University (then called Carnegie Institute of Technology), where one of the first computer science departments in the country, after Purdue's, was founded in 1965 by the letter writers. Indeed, Alan Perlis had moved to Carnegie Tech from Purdue and was the first head of its Computer Science Department.[23] So, at the time, their opening line would have been akin to three of the first astronauts writing "astronauts are often asked...."

While this letter may have been the first word on the topic, it was hardly the last. In their 1976 Turing Award lecture, "Computer Science as Empirical Inquiry," Allen Newell and Herbert Simon group together geology, astronomy, and economics as "empirical disciplines" and then compare them as a group to computer science.[24] But geology, astronomy, and economics are not similar in any obvious way. Moreover, their intersection certainly does not provide a clear set comparable to an emerging fourth discipline, like computer science.

Newell and Simon elaborate on these unlikely comparisons with further far-fetched analogies: "Each program that is built is an experiment. It poses a question to nature, and its behavior offers clues to an answer."[25] Unaddressed by Newell and Simon is the poetic license they employ to anthropomorphize "nature" (a term they capitalize later in the article) into a being that can answer questions; the metaphorical notion that textual productions, like programs, are "built" rather than written; and the copular statement that makes building into a form of experimenting. That these kinds of loose and fanciful analogies carried the day and convinced many that the study of computing is a science may be puzzling but was—and, undeniably, still is—a winning rhetoric: "computer science" is more than analogical apposition; it is a large, growing, and well-funded discipline.

Simon tried to write the definitive word on this by publishing a book on the topic, *Sciences of the Artificial* (with three editions, in 1969, 1981, and 1996), but he never definitively settles the question, Can a science focus on phenomena and objects that are not naturally occurring?

Computational Thinking as the Science of All Sciences

Some have even argued that computing is not just *a* science but *the* science of all sciences. This cadre of computer scientists has been influential in promoting the belief that computer science—or what they call "computational thinking"—is the queen of the sciences, as philosophy and mathematics once were.[26]

"Computational thinking," promoted by the US National Science Foundation;[27] the website code.org, supported by a coalition of largely corporate concerns;[28] and other educational initiatives deploy a discourse of computation-as-thinking so abstract that it seems to apply to everything but refers to nothing in particular.

Nevertheless, thinking is always thinking about something, and it is always thinking with other people.[29] One might even do well to question the very notion of thinking in general. So, we need to ask, with whom is "computational thinking" done and about what? Science studies scholar Bruno Latour exhorts us to rethink thinking as work, co-work. "We neither think nor reason," Latour writes, "Rather, we work on fragile materials—texts, inscriptions, traces, or paints—with other people."[30] So, what is the work of "computational thinking"? Who does it? And for whose benefit?

Gender Diversity

Even if we could resolve these questions about "computational thinking," it is clear that it should not be taught as computer science is taught today. Diversity is one of the most important motivations for a new approach. Unfortunately, computer science—as a field—has largely failed in its efforts at inclusion and diversity. According to one of the leading professional organizations for computer science, the Computing Research Association, women constituted only 14 percent of graduates receiving bachelor's degrees from American computer science departments in 2013.[31] These figures are especially worrisome because they appear to be headed in the wrong direction. For example, according to the US Department of Education, 37 percent of the computer science graduates in 1984 were women.[32] In other words, women used to make up over one-third of each year's computer science graduates, and thirty years later they represented only one-seventh.[33]

The problems of diversity in education can only be exacerbating the diversity problems of industry. Recent surveys of gender and ethnic diversity at the top computer technology companies show that only 20–40 percent of the workforces of the most powerful computer technology companies are made up of women and that the vast majority of employees are white.[34] Disclosures by large technology companies concerning the diversity of their workforce are relatively new, but year-to-year data (e.g., from 2014 to 2015) show almost no progress.[35]

The fine arts, design, and the liberal arts—at least in the university—do not have the same diversity problems as science and engineering. I am motivated by the vision that computing can be taught and practiced as an art (or a set of arts). Pursuit of the software arts could reveal new horizons by opening the field to those in the arts and the humanities who now only think of themselves as users and not as makers of software.

Peter Denning, the former president of the main professional organization for computer science, the Association for Computing Machinery (ACM), wrote an article in 2013 that starts like this: "Computer science has for decades been ripped by an old saw: Any field that calls itself a science, cannot be science. The implied criticisms that we lack substance or hawk dubious results have been repeatedly refuted. And yet the criticism keeps coming up in contexts that matter to us."[36] What is appalling about Denning's opening line is not the idea that computing might not be a science but rather the presupposition that anything that is not a science must be a field that produces dubious results and lacks substance. Perhaps computing is not a science but nevertheless is a field of substance that produces rigorous, solid results!

Computing and Numbers

Common sense has it that—at their core—computers are made of numbers: ones and zeros. But consider an irrational number like the square root of two or, worse yet, a transcendental number like π. We can choose to represent π with a procedure that never terminates or as an infinite series of digits that begins 3.1415926....[37] For the computer, we are obliged to truncate this infinite series; we must decide how many bits of memory will be devoted to it.

If numbers were "native" to computers, we would not have to worry about how to approximate them. But, in actual practice, even if extremely precise calculations are needed, we tend to represent these infinite series with only 128 bits of computer memory.[38] Certainly, in principle, one could fill the entire disk and memory of a given computer with just the digits of one number, but even then we would be approximating an infinite series with a finite set of bits. Instead, an entire subdiscipline of computer science—numerical analysis—has been developed over the course of decades to address the problems of representing numbers and of calculating numbers with computers.[39]

If numbers were "native" to computers, no such computer science specialty would be necessary.[40]

My point is that although numbers and operations on numbers—such as arithmetic—can be approximated with a computer, computers are not numerical machines. They are language machines, and numbers are just a very common domain of application. Imagining computers only as powerful calculators confuses the machine itself with a single important application of computer technology.

Let me underline this pitfall with an absurd example. If I use the microwave oven in my kitchen mostly as a means to make popcorn, does that mean that the microwave is essentially a "popcorn machine"?

My point is controversial because it is, of course, a counternarrative to the most commonly told history, in which computers are figured as information technologies and are thus tied to information, quantification, and mathematics. In contrast, in the story I want to tell, computers are a coupling of the liberal arts and the mechanical arts—what today we would call the knowledge of artisans, artists, humanists, and designers. In the first story, computers are the materialization of mathematics and science. In the second story, computers are the manifestation of methods and theories from the arts and humanities.

Computing and the Liberal Arts

If computing can be conceived of as something other than just science or just engineering, what are the alternatives? Ironically, or perhaps characteristically, Alan Perlis—who, as mentioned earlier, argued in 1967 that computing *is* a science and, as a participant at the first Conference of Software Engineering in 1968, helped to articulate a vision of software production as engineering—described, in 1962, how computer programming should be integrated into a liberal arts education.[41] This third approach, computing as an intrinsic part of a liberal arts education, also advanced by Perlis, has more recently been revived by, for example, computational media theorists and practitioners Michael Mateas[42] and Ian Bogost in their respective advocacies for a "procedural literacy." Bogost specifically turns to an examination of the teaching of the language arts, the trivium, in his exploration of what a procedural literacy could mean for education and learning.[43]

Perlis's third path, the idea that computing research and education can be pursued within the liberal arts, is comfortable for computer scientists who are programming language designers, since they find it quite natural to imagine that computing is primarily about the creation and use of language. Alan Perlis was one of the designers of the ALGOL language.[44] Gerald Sussman, cited earlier, was co-designer of the Scheme programming language.[45] Casey Reas and Ben Fry designed Processing, a programming language to help artists and designers learn how to program.[46] Those who have been especially articulate about computing-as-language-art have included the designers of programming languages produced to teach children and novices to program. Alan Kay co-invented—originally for children—the object-oriented programming language Smalltalk.[47] Mitchel Resnick's Scratch programming language has transformed computing education for young children.[48] Resnick's mentor, Seymour Papert, was the co-designer of a programming language for children called LOGO.[49] Papert was pivotal in tearing down the walls between the language arts, science, and mathematics. In his book *Mindstorms*, Papert put it like this: "Plato wrote over his door, 'Let only geometers enter.' Times have changed. Most who now seek to enter Plato's intellectual world neither know mathematics nor sense the least contradiction in their disregard for his injunction. Our culture's schizophrenic split between 'humanities' and 'science' supports their sense of security. Plato was a philosopher, and a philosopher belongs to the humanities as surely as mathematics belongs to the sciences."[50]

Papert's comments make us recall that the traditional liberal arts, as studied and practiced in the early modern era of Europe, included both the trivium (the arts of language) and the quadrivium (the arts of number). At that time, there was no strict boundary to be drawn between what today we call the arts and the humanities and the sciences.

A Short History of the Liberal Arts

What might a recasting of computing as part of the liberal arts look like? A short history of the liberal arts will show that they have been expanding and diversifying for centuries and that the design of programming languages, the languages of software, are the latest version of a very old dream of the liberal arts—to find just the right words, just the right language.

What are the liberal arts? The *Oxford English Dictionary* (*OED*) defines the liberal arts as:

> Originally: the seven subjects of the trivium (grammar, rhetoric, and logic) and quadrivium (arithmetic, geometry, music, and astronomy) considered collectively (now historical).

American Catholic nun Miriam Joseph wrote a widely read college textbook in which she defined the seven liberal arts as follows:

> The *trivium* includes those aspects of the liberal arts that pertain to mind, and the *quadrivium*, those aspects of the liberal arts that pertain to matter. Logic, grammar, and rhetoric constitute

the *trivium*; and arithmetic, music, geometry, and astronomy constitute the *quadrivium*. Logic is the art of thinking; grammar, the art of inventing symbols and combining them to express thought; and rhetoric, the art of communicating thought from one mind to another, the adaption of language to circumstance. Arithmetic, the theory of number, and music, an application of the theory of number (the measurement of discrete quantities in motion), are the arts of discrete quantity or number. Geometry, the theory of space, and astronomy, an application of the theory of space, are the arts of continuous quantity or extension.... These arts of reading, writing, and reckoning have formed the traditional basis of liberal education, each constituting a field of knowledge and the technique to acquire that knowledge. The degree bachelor of arts is awarded to those who demonstrate the requisite proficiency in these arts, and the degree master of arts, to those who have demonstrated a greater proficiency.[51]

Many others summarize the trivium as the arts of language and the quadrivium as the arts of number.

Media scholar Marshall McLuhan wrote his dissertation on a history of three of the liberal arts, specifically the trivium.[52] He emphasized the historical centrality and continuity of the liberal arts, citing A. F. Leach: "It is hardly an exaggeration to say that the subjects and the methods of education remained the same from the days of Quintilian to the days of Arnold, from the first century to the mid-nineteenth century of the Christian era."[53] Arguably, in much of Europe, the liberal arts were at the heart of education for a millennium. Yet, as McLuhan's history makes clear, the static picture of the liberal arts projected by Sister Joseph was only a snapshot of a specific historical period. The definition of the arts and their relationships to each other changed dramatically from one era to the next, and thus "grammar," "logic," and "rhetoric" today are not necessarily the same as their historical precedents.

In the United States, many elite institutions are still called liberal arts colleges. Yet, what is called a "liberal arts education" today is no longer the Aristotelian endeavor outlined by Sister Joseph in 1948; nor is it exactly the silhouette A. F. Leach saw in 1911. In early modern Europe, the liberal arts were distinguished from mechanical or manual arts.[54] Today, in some countries, such as the United States, liberal arts colleges do include the fine arts. Elsewhere, however—for example, in France and Germany— art colleges and technical schools are separate from the university. But A. F. Leach's choice of the mid-nineteenth century as a critical moment for the transformation and expansion of the liberal arts throughout Europe and the United States is compelling, because it was then that both industrialization and the rise of the humanities changed the liberal arts by integrating them with the mechanical arts.

The contemporary definition of the liberal arts puts them in opposition to science and technology. I elided from the *OED* citation earlier this crucial sentence: "In later use more generally: arts subjects as opposed to science and technology (now chiefly

North American)." What happened in nineteenth-century American education that seems to have made technology and the liberal arts antonyms but at the same time paradoxically expanded a liberal arts education to include the mechanical arts, engineering, and technology?

In 1936, Henry Seidel Canby wrote a memoir set in the American college, specifically centered on his experience at Yale College. In *Alma Mater: The Gothic Age of the American College*,[55] Canby pointed out that the college had been radically transformed between 1870 and 1910. Industrialization, the rise of the corporation, and the invention of the American research university all played a part in changing college.

Before 1870, college was for an elite few. In the United States of 1870, there were about 50,000 undergraduates.[56] By 1920, there were an order of magnitude more undergraduates, over half a million. Before 1870, undergraduates enrolled in college were primarily pursuing a liberal arts education prior to entry into one of three specialties: divinity, law, or medicine. But during this period of industrialization, new, specialized forms of knowledge were developed to deal with the introduction of a myriad of emerging machines and new forms of production and distribution. Thus, for many, after 1870 a college education was no longer synonymous with a traditional liberal arts education.

The first federal aid for higher education in the United States was the 1862 Morrill Land Grant College Act: "An Act Donating public lands to the several States [and Territories] which may provide colleges for the benefit of agriculture and the Mechanic arts…in order to promote the liberal and practical education of the industrial classes in the several pursuits and professions in life."[57] The Morrill Act provided the founding financial support for many of the great public (and some private) universities of the United States, including the University of California, Berkeley; Purdue (later the site of the first computer science department); University of Wisconsin–Madison; University of Maryland, College Park; Massachusetts Institute of Technology; and Cornell. At the time, it was argued that the industrial era required a new form of college education incorporating "utilitarian" and "democratic" forms of knowledge.[58] Where previously a select group of gentlemen were instructed in the liberal arts before starting careers as clergymen, lawyers, or medical doctors, the Morrill Act signaled that a larger population needed to be educated in some hybrid of the mechanical and the liberal arts so that they might become accountants, engineers, and technical experts of the many, increasingly specialized, disciplines important for industrial capitalism. These new universities created by the Morrill Act were minted in a very different die than the older, originally ecclesiastical, colleges of early America, such as Harvard, Yale, and Princeton.

This thread of change—the expansion of college education to concern new forms of technical expertise[59]—was intertwined with another: the rise of the research university in the nineteenth century.[60] Prior to the nineteenth century, universities were primarily teaching institutions where professors were paid to teach an established canon of knowledge, not to develop new forms of knowledge and technology. In the nineteenth century, the research university was invented in Germany, especially Prussia. This new model of the university was imported to the United States by then-new universities, such as Johns Hopkins and the University of Chicago, and, after that, was adapted by long-standing institutions, such as Yale. Central to this new model of the university—and a departure from the older models—was the emphasis on empirical scientific research; the change in the duties of professors to pursue research in addition to teaching; and the increasing investment in secular forms of knowledge.[61]

As McLuhan demonstrates in his history of the trivium—the three liberal arts devoted to language—a liberal arts education was, for centuries, tantamount to a Christian religious education. Nevertheless, since this form of education properly started in ancient Greece, even during the early modern period it combined ancient Greek philosophy (especially Aristotelian philosophy) with teachings of the Catholic Church (especially those of Thomas Aquinas). So, the liberal arts have always been interdisciplinary.

The emergence of the humanities from the liberal arts arose from a secularization of this body of knowledge. This third strand of change—secularization—was woven with the influence that the increasing ubiquity of technologies of industrialization and the rise of the research university had on education. Secularization displaced the sacred and, in its stead, centralized the study of the human.

In the introduction to their text *Digital_Humanities*, Anne Burdick, Johanna Drucker, Peter Lunenfeld, Todd Presner, and Jeffrey Schnapp encapsulate this history in one paragraph:

> While the foundations of humanistic inquiry and the liberal arts can be traced back in the West to the medieval *trivium* and *quadrivium*, the modern human sciences are rooted in the Renaissance shift from a medieval, church-dominated, theocratic worldview to a human-centered one.... The wellsprings of humanism were fed by many sources, but the meticulous (and, sometimes, not-so-meticulous) transcription, translation, editing, and annotation of texts were their legacy. The printing press enabled the standardization and dissemination of humanistic cultural corpora while promoting the further development and refinement of editorial techniques. Along with many other scholars, we suggest that the migration of cultural materials into digital media is a process analogous to the flowering of Renaissance and post-Renaissance print culture.[62]

What is left unstated in their paragraph is that the "post-Renaissance" lasted a long time. At Yale College, for instance, nontheological topics of study, especially science, did not become important until the nineteenth century, and even then they had to be carefully negotiated with the clerical community in charge of the university.[63] Furthermore, the reigning "science" of the time was philology—the study of texts, especially ancient ones. Philology provided the model for newer sciences such as evolutionary biology.[64]

As sketched earlier—despite the assertion of the *Oxford English Dictionary* that the liberal arts are seen to be in opposition to science and technology—we find it difficult to narrate the emergence of contemporary disciplines and forms of knowledge without stumbling on the intertwining of the secular and the theological, the ancient and the modern, the coevolution of the humanities and the sciences, the liberal arts and the mechanical arts. Even a short historical review shows that the opposition between the liberal arts and science and technology is just a prejudice or a political strategy of marginalization to sideline the arts. The real story is instead a story of how cultural, economic, and technological changes arose already entangled with the arts.

Translation and the Liberal Arts

The liberal arts are not a static formation. They have always been constituted and reconfigured through the movement—the translation—of textual knowledge from one form into another. In Rome and then later throughout Europe, the development of the liberal arts was dependent on new practices of translation. Texts from Greek, Arabic, and Hebrew were translated into Latin starting, especially, with Jerome, who was born in 347 CE in contemporary Ljubljana, educated in Rome, and died in Bethlehem in 420 CE. As philosopher Barbara Cassin and the editors of the *Dictionary of Untranslatables* state in their entry "On Translation": "The notion of *translatio* is truly the confluence of the arts of language (grammar, logic, rhetoric) and of theology. In its widest acceptance of meaning, the term *translatio* designates a transfer of meaning, a displacement of signification, from a proper usage to an improper usage."[65]

As the confluence of the liberal arts of language (the trivium) and its primary practice (the translation and interpretation of primary texts in other languages), translation will be both the object of study and the method of analysis pursued in this book. We will examine contemporary forms of translation and how they have been employed to develop new metaphors, new equivalences, and even new identities. Contemporary forms of translation are tied up in various forms of computation, so we will refer to these new practices as the software arts. The software arts are a practice of computing that emerges from a coupling of the liberal arts and the mechanical arts. Just as it is possible to understand science and engineering as practices that emerged from artisans' workshops,[66] the software arts is an understanding of computing as a practice that emerged from the arts and the humanities.

Translation and Information Technologies

Previously, translation, as a practice of the liberal arts, meant a transformation that would, unavoidably, take away or add information to a text or message. In contrast, today's information and communication technologies are frequently developed with the ideal that messages can be moved or translated with no information lost or added. In their conception and design, information and communication technologies are meant to exactly reproduce that which was produced at the other end of the transmission line. In their foundational text *A Mathematical Theory of Communication*, Warren Weaver and Claude Shannon stated the issue like this: "The fundamental problem of communication is that of reproducing at one point either exactly or approximately a message selected at another point."[67] Elsewhere in the same book, Weaver and Shannon point out that, according to their theory, information is accorded no meaning.[68] In short, from an engineering perspective, what we are engaged in when we send email or use the web is a meaningless reproduction that pays no attention to its social and political environment. This meaningless mimicry is considered the fundamental problem of communication.

In engineering terms, information and communication technologies are evaluated according to their ability to push bits losslessly across a fixed-capacity channel, repeating what was recorded at one end of the "wire" exactly and without reference to environment on the other end of the "wire." In classical philosophy, there is a name for this kind of exact repetition. Repetition without knowledge of meaning, context, or association is called "imitation" or, more specifically, "mimicry," or "sophistry" in the writings of Plato. In his Socratic dialogue titled the *Sophist*, Plato states: "Some mimics know the thing they are impersonating; others do not.... [F]or the purposes of distinction let us call mimicry guided by opinion 'conceit mimicry,' and the sort guided by knowledge 'mimicry by acquaintance.'... The art of contradiction making, descended from an insincere kind of conceit mimicry, of the semblance-making breed, derived from image making, ...—such are the blood and lineage which can, with perfect truth, be assigned to the authentic Sophist."[69]

In other words, the criteria for success articulated in information and communication theory are exactly Plato's criteria for the worst kind of ethical and aesthetic failure. They are, according to Plato, the worst behavior of sophistry taken as a virtue, indeed taken to be the fundamental virtue of a working technology.[70] For these reasons, contemporary theories and technologies of information, communication, and computation can be called "sophisticated," a point I will elaborate on in my discussion of rhetoric in chapter 6.

The connection between communication theory and translation's radical transformation under the conditions of computation was already apparent in Warren Weaver's 1949 report titled "Translation."[71] Weaver's purpose was to explore the idea that one might design a computer program to translate texts from one language into another. Those familiar with Shannon and Weaver's text on the theory of communication will not find the following too surprising, but any bilingual person is likely to find Weaver's understanding of translation fantastical. Weaver wrote: "When I look at an article in Russian, I say, 'This is really written in English, but it has been coded in some strange symbols. I will now proceed to decode.'" Weaver wrote this shortly after World War II, when protocomputers were first applied—with great success—to the problem of breaking Germany's military communication codes. In short, for Weaver, it was clear that computers were good for the tasks of decryption, so if a problem could be reconceptualized to look like a decryption problem, then it was probably something a computer could do. Despite skepticism voiced by scientific luminaries of the day,[72] Weaver's "Translation" essay was enormously influential[73] and, arguably, still informs computer scientists' approaches to translation. For example, the statistical approach to decoding that Weaver outlined in his essay constitutes the core of popular work in contemporary machine translation.

Two points of Weaver's text from 1949 are notable. First is the previously unusual idea that machines—specifically computers—can be used to translate texts from one language into another. Second is the radical translation of the very word "translation" that his text performs: Weaver equates translation with the operations of (information lossless) encryption and decryption. These two points will serve as points of contention for our exploration of the software arts.

Any bilingual person with access to the web can go online and test the current viability of Weaver's assertion that translation is just a form of decryption. For instance, find Google's online translation service[74] and try translating a text from one language into another. Unless the text is incredibly simple, the automatic machine translation will be riddled with errors, even gross mistakes. Certainly machine translation has improved dramatically since its inception in 1949, but there is still a gap between machine translation and good translation. Furthermore, there is not just a gap but a chasm between machine translation and transformation of a text in one language into a text in another language without loss or gain of information (i.e., a perfect translation as conceptualized by Weaver and other information theorists).

One of the problematics central to the software arts is to grapple with how computers and networks have come to incorporate this untenable idea of lossless translation and to pursue this by exercising older understandings of translation as they have been developed by scholars of the liberal arts and the humanities.

Translation and Science and Technology Studies

Historian and philosopher of science Michel Serres, in his book *Hermès III: La Traduction*, developed an approach to studying science and technology by means of translation.[75] Serres's method was then extended under the rubric of a "sociology of translation," alternatively, and more commonly, called "actor-network theory" or just ANT.[76]

Philosopher and science studies scholar Bruno Latour regrets the more recent and popular name "actor-network theory":

> At the time [the late 1970s and early 1980s], the word network, like Deleuze's and Guattari's term rhizome, clearly meant a series of transformations—translations, transductions—which could not be captured by any of the traditional terms of social theory. With the new popularization of the word network, it now means transport without deformation, an instantaneous, unmediated access to every piece of information. That is exactly the opposite of what we meant. What I would like to call "double click information" has killed the last bit of the critical cutting edge of the notion of network. I don't think we should use it anymore at least not to mean the type of transformations and translations that we want now to explore.[77]

Readers of Latour's more recent work know that his previous mention of "double click information" was far from casual.[78] In a recent book, he identifies "double click" as one of the fifteen "modes of existence" examined and strongly distinguishes it from other modes of existence, including what he calls the "mode of networks."

A sociology of translation is appropriate to an analysis of software, since computer scientists describe much of their work as translation. Beyond the problematics of machine translation (from one natural language into another), many practical problems are called "translations" in software design and engineering, including those translations alternatively labeled, in computer science, "compilations" or "interpretations" (as in the translation from a high-level programming language into a lower-level language) and "implementations" (as in the translation of an abstract system specification into a piece of working software).

Translation—as we know it in the arts and humanities—is always a force of change. Each translation involves either the loss or the addition of information, or both. Consequently, the result of any translation is not the same as the text translated—it is different. But translation—as it is known in computer science and information theory—is ideally lossless. From this perspective, a perfect translation from the source text to the target is one in which information is neither lost nor gained. A humanities scholar is likely to find the computer science approach to translation naive or idealistic. The computer scientist, conversely, might view the humanities approach as self-defeating since, if a translation can only be a deformation, degradation, or elaboration of the source text, then an accurate translation is always out of reach. But humanists do not believe translation is impossible, only that any given translation can always be improved. This book explores the clashes that emerge from these differing perspectives on translation.

The Software Arts and the Liberal Arts of Language

Historian of science and technology Paul Edwards, commenting on a famous essay about computer historiography by Michael Mahoney (cited earlier),[79] explained that computer histories generally fall into a very small set of story types. Edwards wrote, "The first genre is an intellectual history in which computers function primarily as the embodiment of ideas about information, symbols, and logic." He continues: "The standard lineage here runs from Plato's investigations of the foundations of knowledge and belief, through Leibniz's rationalism, to Lady Lovelace's notes on Charles Babbage's Analytical Engine and Boole's *Laws of Thought* in the nineteenth century."[80] The lineage runs through the twentieth century and includes Alan Turing's machines, Norbert Wiener's cybernetic theory, the McCulloch-Pitts theory of neurons, and John von Neumann's collaborative work on computers. It is a history I retell in this book, but I retell it here in tension with two other less popular narratives: computer-as-rhetoric and computer-as-grammar.

This book is structured around the trivium, the three language arts of logic, rhetoric, and grammar. As Edwards and Mahoney point out, many computer histories tell the computer-as-logic story. In contrast, the computer-as-rhetoric history is one that emphasizes the role of computer software as a means of persuasion. Computer graphics and computer simulations are two forms of software widely deployed as forms of rhetoric. In contrast with the computer-as-logic and computer-as-rhetoric histories is the narrative of computer-as-grammar. Grammar concerns the rules of language. Grammar rules have long been considered by some to be machines. The story of computer-as-grammar came into focus in the mid-twentieth century, when it was ventured that the rules of language are machines or devices of software. By spinning together these three separate histories of computation, a clear picture can be woven of computing as a coproduction of the liberal arts of language.

The computer-as-logic, computer-as-rhetoric, and computer-as-grammar stories are three different interpretations of computing. These stories intersect somewhat but are also quite different. Their differences are partly explicable by the historical differences between logic, rhetoric, and grammar as three separate fields of study.

Our contemporary usage of the terms "grammar," "logic," and "rhetoric" is symptomatic of an old rivalry between them. As McLuhan describes in his history of the trivium from ancient Greece to about the time of William Shakespeare, each of these areas of knowledge has been in competition with the others for millennia. When we praise someone for their logic and deride another for their rhetoric, we are voicing the current state of this competition. Clearly, today, logicians are accorded more respect than rhetoricians, since phrases like "empty logic" and "sound rhetoric" seem almost oxymoronic; the adjectives "logical" and "rhetorical" are laudatory and derogatory, respectively. Grammarians are now the leaders in this three-way rivalry, since grammar is institutionalized to the extent that we think nothing of sending our children to grammar school or having them learn grammar from their earliest years in school. We would be inhabiting a very different world if children were sent to rhetoric or logic school—rather than to grammar school—at age seven. Since rhetoric, logic, and grammar have been in a rivalry for ascendancy for centuries, the triptych painted in this book—of computer-as-logic, computer-as-rhetoric, computer-as-grammar—will expose some raw edges between them.

Stakes and Claims

The stakes of this book are threefold: pedagogical, industrial, and epistemological. First, if software is an art, then education needs to change to integrate it into the liberal arts. What do we teach? What do we learn? These are old questions that need to be posed once again in a world where basic literacy is not just a matter of English, Latin, and Greek but also of software. Second, if software can be written in the manner of an artist/humanist, then new avenues of software production beyond engineering and mathematics may be possible—avenues that some, like Steve Jobs, have already traveled. Third, if software is the new lingua franca, then there are a series of ethical and moral questions that must be pursued in conjunction with this epistemological transformation. What counts as knowledge, for whom, and at what cost?[81]

The most general claim of this book is that the software arts is a new name for something that has been going on for centuries: the pursuit of methods to invent and interrogate statements of connection, equivalence, and identity. Today, writing software is essential to both science and engineering. Yes, writing programs is very different from writing prose. Yes, computer languages are distinctively different from natural languages. But, regardless of whether we call software "machines" or "instructions," "objects" or "rules," regardless of whether we call the production of software "building" or "writing," "construction" or "composition," our names for software and its production are metaphors, and once we are working with metaphors, we are working as artists. I argue, along with Steve Jobs, that the arts are at the center of software.

History, Philosophy, and the Software Arts

I have tried to substantiate the constitution of the software arts both historically and philosophically. In what follows, I trace a more detailed history that runs from Denis Diderot, to Adam Smith, to Gaspard de Prony, to Charles Babbage, to Ada Lovelace, to Alan Turing, to today. When Denis Diderot and his collaborators on the eighteenth-century *Encyclopédie* were faced with the task of describing, in some standard manner, all of the processes, operations, and gestures employed in the studios and workshops of diverse artists and artisans throughout France, they needed to forge a language accept-able to the liberal arts and adequately descriptive of the mechanical arts. The ency-clopedists did this by first listening to the artists and artisans to learn the language they used to describe their work practices and the machines they employed in their productions. In chapter 3, I call language like this "work and machine language." Then, the encyclopedists had to translate these various work and machine languages into a uniform lexicon and syntax for the *Encyclopédie* entries and a uniform visual language for the images that illustrated the entries. The language of the *Encyclopédie* had to cover everything from the making of stockings to the manufacture of pins. I argue that the encyclopedists' translation between the mechanical arts and the liberal arts eventually constituted the basis for what we know today as programming languages.

Philosophically, the substantiation of the software arts is entwined with this history. Francis Bacon, Gottfried Wilhelm Leibniz, and others were, in the words of semiotician, novelist, and historian Umberto Eco, engaged in a "search for the perfect language": a philosophical language, a "universal characteristic" with which all types of knowledge could be articulated. But none of them attempted a full-scale encyclopedia of knowl-edge. However, Diderot et al. did attempt such a full-scale catalog and did so with an understanding of how their project responded to Bacon's and Leibniz's aspirations.

The software arts continue with the encyclopedists' efforts to translate the mechani-cal arts into a language of the liberal arts and vice versa. The lingua francas forged for this project are now programming languages, forms of inscription liminally positioned between prose and machines.

On the Limits of Translation

Programming languages are limited in comparison with natural languages because they, and the programs they comprise, are imperative, independent, impersonal, infin-itesimal, inscrutable, and instantaneous in ways that no previous forms of language are or have been. For example, in a programming language, one can "conjugate" only in the imperative ("fetch," "return," "assign," etc.) and the conditional ("if this then do that"). The subjunctive, even the past tense, is beyond expression in a programming language. Programming languages are "languages" and yet they are "machines."

Given this picture of programming languages, it does not seem too difficult to imagine that translating an analog process into a piece of software is frequently like forcing a large, round peg into a small, square hole. Like any translation, even one between spoken and written languages, a translation into a programming language is an exercise in loss, change, and addition. Stuff gets broken and has to be mended and amended in the process. In the words of the Italian proverb, "tradurre è tradire"; that is, "translation is betrayal."

As elaborated in chapter 2, this understanding of translation—that it is always "lossy," always an agent of change—is commonsensical to most polyglots and to those in the arts and humanities more generally. In a translation between a source language and a target language, there is always some "je ne sais quoi" in the source language text that is impossible to phrase in the target language, so there is always something that needs to be made up and inserted into the target-language text that has no counterpart in the source-language text.

Problems with Perfect Languages

The search for the perfect language, however, carries with it a fantasy of the "lossless" translation. This fantasy is the conviction that we can design a perfect language into which anything and everything can be translated without loss, addition, or change. This fantasy has persisted in mathematics and logic, and it now animates programming language design.

Here then is the spark for a repeated drama. Believers in a perfect language translate X, in a source language, into Y, a text in a "perfect" target language. The believers then declare that "X is Y." But to declare "X is Y," one must either overlook some "je ne sais quoi" that differentiates X from Y or one must deem this difference insignificant. This drama recurs in many of the other chapters.

Once it is declared that "X is Y," there will always be a nonbeliever, someone who does not believe in the perfect language and who will dispute the idea that the difference between X and Y can be overlooked or who will argue that the difference between X and Y is a significant difference. Today, the posited perfect language is frequently a computer programming language; Y is some piece of software written in that language; the believers are computer scientists or software engineers; and the nonbelievers are former stakeholders in X who have now lost control of X because Y has displaced it.

For example, let us imagine that X is the book publishing, distribution, and retailing business as it previously existed and Y is Amazon.com, especially the software that runs the website, but also the various internal software systems that predict readership demand, organize warehouses, route boxes of books between warehouses and from warehouses to customers' houses, and other operations. The nonbelievers in this scenario include the former local bookstore owner and her former regular customers who used to love her reading knowledge and her ability to always have a book they wanted, even before they knew of the book.

When X is a long-standing institution—like the book business—then Y is, in the vernacular of Silicon Valley, an attempt to "disrupt" that institution and replace it with a new institution configured around a piece of software. Amazon.com is an example of this; so is Uber's "disruption" of the taxi business. Bitcoin is an effort to disrupt banking and monetary currencies, Netflix has upended television, and there are many other examples. When many of our social, cultural, economic, and political institutions are configured around software, I say we live under "computational conditions," or, more simply, that our life is a "digital life."

When X is an idea, an area of research and teaching—such as biology, sociology, or physics—then Y is an attempt to replace some key intellectual construct; Y could be a model, a simulation, the "search" in "research," even a theory. The genetic code, for example, is often investigated as if it was a computer code.

Ideologies and Equalities

I consider a set of equivalences and inequalities as constituting a system of ideas or, more concisely, an "ideology" (with no pejorative sense of the term intended). When the set of equivalences and inequalities concerns software, or computers more generally, I call this a "digital ideology." When Y is a piece of software and can be considered a "theory," we have arrived at a strange new place where knowledge can be phrased as a computer program. I call this place a "computational episteme" and interrogate its implications in chapter 7.

Translation of a big idea or a big institution cannot be done with a little piece of software and a grand statement of equivalence, even though it has been tried. When computers were first introduced in the 1950s, journalists naively called them "electronic brains." This ideology of 1950s journalism and popular culture included the assertion "computers=brains." In contrast, in rigorous intellectual climates and in demanding industries, large equivalences need to be substantiated with a large collection of smaller equivalences. To constitute such a collection entails translating many smaller ideas or institutions into many smaller pieces of software.

So, before one asserts that the computer is a brain, one might want to investigate, as Warren McCulloch and Walter Pitts did in "A Logical Calculus of Ideas Immanent in Nervous Activity," published in 1943, whether neural activities can be modeled as a set of logic circuits. If one wants to call a small computer a "smartphone," there is a large set of smaller equivalences that need to be established, for example to render and operationalize "buttons" for dialing a number as a graphical object on a touch screen. Equivalences between two unlike entities are established by translating one into the other.

These translations are frequently predicated on an older set of equivalences established through earlier translation efforts. Thus, for instance, McCulloch and Pitts's logical calculus was based on earlier efforts to translate all of mathematics into logic (e.g., the work of Bertrand Russell and Alfred North Whitehead). These earlier efforts, in turn, developed partially from translations attempted in the converse direction, such as George Boole's nineteenth-century efforts to render Aristotelian logic as a form of algebra or arithmetic.

There are many techniques and methods, especially from mathematical logic and the theory of computation, to equate objects and processes with software and to "prove" or "disprove" an equivalence between one piece of software and another and/or between a piece of digital software and an analog entity. Yet, from the perspective of the arts and the humanities, "proofs" of equivalence are not irrefutable but rather are only arguments or demonstrations that a translation was done rigorously. In chapter 6, on rhetoric, various forms of demonstration with computation are examined.

If we think of these equivalences as "proved" and thus settled once and for all, we are unlikely to think of alternatives or innovate further. If instead we think of these equivalences as the result of a translation effort, we can always ask, "What got lost in translation?" For example, even though Claude Shannon "proved" in his master's thesis that Boolean logic and Boolean circuits are the same thing, if we persist in asking how they are different, we quickly unearth a set of problems circuits have that written logics do not; for example, while designing circuits, we have to worry about heat produced by the electrical current running through the circuit. While modern computers need fans to keep them cool, George Boole's nineteenth-century arithmetic of logic never needed a fan! Differences in materiality are significant differences. This example is discussed in detail in chapter 5, on logic.

Translation as Imperfect

To take this liberal arts attitude about the messiness of translation into the technical literature entails closely rereading pivotal papers of science, mathematics, and engineering to find and evaluate what got lost in translation. Given a proposed equivalence

X = Y, what link was established between X and Y; how was X translated into Y and Y into X? What had to be put to the side or ignored in order to establish the equivalence? Chapter 2, on translation, is essentially a chapter on methodology—an interpretation of actor-network theory—and its employment in following such chains of equivalence in the texts of software.

Bruno Latour wrote a small philosophical work, *Irreductions*, that starts with a declaration as far afield from a digital ideology as one can find. Latour asks, "What happens when nothing is reduced to anything else?...Nothing is, by itself, either reducible or irreducible to anything else. I will call this the 'principle of irreducibility,' but it is a prince that does not govern since that would be a self-contradiction."[82] While a digital ideology might include a myriad of reductions showing how life, the universe, and everything can be digitized or reduced to some form of computer program, Latour's declaration establishes an alternative and opposing manifesto: everything and everyone is singular, nothing is equivalent to anything else, everything is irreducible. However, even if that is the case, things can still be connected or linked together. With enough links between things, we have a network, thus "actor-network theory."

Under the theory of ideology exercised in this book, inspired by Algirdas Julien Greimas, an ideology can be analyzed as a set of equivalences between a number of ideas and/or identities. These equivalences and/or inequalities can be stated in a number of ways, including copular statements (X is Y), equations (X = Y), and—especially important for the digital—assignment statements (X := Y; i.e., X is assigned the value of Y) and rewrite rules (X → Y; i.e., X is rewritten as Y). To do actor-network theory on an ideology is to question its equivalences: to ask whether they are really definitional or are provisional. In a sense, it is akin to what Socrates did in the agora of Athens by flipping the copular assertions of common sense and turning them into questions of definition: What is courage? What is truth?

Actor-Network Theory and Software Studies

Two independent inspirations for ANT were Greimasian semiotics[83] and sociologist Harold Garfinkel's ethnomethodology.[84] The work of ethnomethodologists has been dominated by ethnographic concerns and methods—observing and writing down the oral and physical interactions between people. In contrast, Greimasian semiotics was originally developed to study texts of literature.

ANT has been applied to the equations and equivalences of many areas of science and technology but only rarely to the texts of software. When they have been interested in software, the way that ANT practitioners, in particular, and STS researchers, more generally, have pursued the study of computer science and software engineering has been heavy on ethnography and light on semiotics. Consequently, there are a number of wonderful ethnographic studies of various software development projects in which we learn a lot about the programmers and how they interact, but these studies tend to leave out of focus the texts of software: What exactly was the code being written by the programmers? What were the technical papers being read and written by the project group members, and how did the ideas proposed in the papers make their way—or not—into the goals and accomplishments of the programmers' productions, the code and its commentary?

This book illustrates how ANT, the sociology of translation, can be used as a method for looking at the texts of software (including code and technical papers). It is a necessary complement to the STS work that has been done to understand the people producing the software; that is, to, as one of Bruno Latour's books is subtitled, "follow scientists and engineers through society."[85] We need to study the texts of software as well as follow the people who produce it.

One would think that computer historians would have already written a lot about software, but much of computer history has focused on hardware, and only recently has software become an object of study. One might equally imagine that philosophers and historians of logic would have written a lot about software, but they rarely investigate contemporary software texts. Thus, in the lacunae of STS, computer history, and the history and philosophy of logic, there is an opening for a new kind of scholarship that focuses on the texts of software. This new kind of scholarship is the emerging field of software studies, and this book can be seen as a contribution to it.

Close Readings

Simply put, this book is a close reading of key texts of computer science and its history. For example, in chapter 4, when we read closely Donald Knuth's features of an algorithm—perhaps the key term for computer science—we find a circularity and several logical inconsistencies; for example, Knuth claims that algorithms can be defined independently of any programming language, yet all of his algorithms are defined in terms of a specific programming language of his own design. In chapter 2, reading Alan Turing's paper on the definition of Turing machines and papers by his students and colleagues popularizing the idea, we find that central to Turing's original paper is a negative result—that there are tasks that the computer cannot be programmed to perform. Yet, in its popular reception, we find an enthusiasm for the idea that a computer can be programmed to do anything and everything. In chapter 5, by closely reading texts on logic and computation, we find—directly at the roots of software—a long-standing and strangely circular project to make logic into arithmetic and arithmetic into logic. This circular project has profoundly reshaped logic and has shaped computing since its inception. In chapter 6, on rhetoric, we follow the radical transformation of what it used to mean to demonstrate a point in a rigorous argument into the very different "demos" of today, the demos we see in Silicon Valley and in the arguments of "big data" practitioners. I call these demos "abductive demonstrations" and contrast them with the previously dominant forms of deductive and inductive demonstrations. In chapter 7, in an examination of the work of Noam Chomsky—as well as his teachers, colleagues, and students—we encounter the nascence of the notion that theories can be "devices," specifically devices rendered in software. When theories become devices, we do not ask *why* questions, we ask *how* questions: we ask whether the theories work. But we should also ask for whom they work and at what cost.

In sum, when we read the technical texts of software closely, we frequently find their popularizations are miles away from what the original texts actually say. Culturally, economically, politically, socially, and technically, this would not matter if software were a marginal concern left to a few specialists with no power and no influence, but today software looms large in research and teaching and in the everyday lives of people all over the world.

The Organization of the Book

The proposal of this book is that we read and write software as an extension of the liberal arts, specifically the trivium, the three language arts of the liberal arts. Logic, grammar, and rhetoric (in the guise of the "demo") are all instantly recognizable as intrinsic to software and central to computer science. The book is organized around these three liberal arts but with the first four chapters—this introductory chapter and then chapters on translation, language, and algorithms—devoted to introductory materials. In chapter 5, the first of the trivium, logic, is examined. Following that is a chapter on rhetoric, and then a chapter on grammar.

The composition of the book is self-similar, with the same kind of arguments made for the book as a whole and also at the scale of the chapter. I closely read a piece of computer science, looking for its instabilities and contradictions and seeking clues to its historical precedents. I then chase down those historical precedents to see what lost or neglected alternatives existed that could serve as improvements or correctives to the computer science of today. The instabilities and contradictions usually result from efforts to reduce everything to mathematics or logic or, more specifically, to digitize, to turn everything into a form of arithmetic, to collapse it into a concern of calculation. In contrast, the historical alternatives I have found come from the arts and the humanities.

I have been writing this book with two readerships in mind. One is a set of cultural workers, artists, and scholars of culture interested in examining what software might have to offer in terms of theories, methods, or tools. The other is a group of computer scientists and software engineers whose work is bound up with cultural production—game design, social media, or streaming video. My message to all readers is that culture and computing are knotted together, and one way we can understand their entanglements is by closely reading the texts of software—code and technical books and papers. For each chapter of the book, I have a hope for the reader.

To begin, if this chapter, the introduction, has worked as I wished, the reader is willing to entertain the possibility that although computing can be seen as science (e.g., computer science) and as engineering (e.g., software engineering), it can also be seen as an art, or a collection of arts: the software arts.

Chapter 2, on translation, is offered as a "methods" chapter. Translation is known to the scholar and to the computer scientist, but each is familiar with a very different flavor of it. The main example discussed in the chapter is a set of texts from the beginnings of the theory of computation, concerning Alan Turing's machines, Alonzo Church's lambda-calculus, and popularizations of the Church-Turing thesis that claim that there are no limits to what a computer can do. This popularization is not true. Turing's original publication shows definitively that computers do have limits. By reading popularizations of the texts of software as a series of translations—from the most technical to the most popular—I show how the popular reception of a technical text can result in a fantasy that contradicts the findings of the original publication. My hope is that the reader will see how to reframe a popularization as a series of translations from the technical literature "out" into the wilds of popular culture and then back again—into the technical literature. The methodology presented is an amendment and an extension to actor-network theory, also well known in the field of science and technology studies as the sociology of translation. This contribution to actor-network theory (or ANT for short) is the main methodological contribution of the book.

In chapter 3, on language, I argue that computers are not information technologies and that the operations of computing are not the functions of mathematics. To expand on these assertions, I narrate a history of programming languages that starts in the artisans' workshops of eighteenth-century France. I trace a history of the division of labor as it was practiced in these studios and workshops; as it was transcribed by economist Adam Smith in the first chapter of his book *The Wealth of Nations*; as Gaspard Prony revised Smith's ideas to organize large-scale calculations with human computers for postrevolutionary France; and as Charles Babbage devised a machine to embody Prony's methods in his Analytical Engine. Ada Lovelace, who in 1843 used the operations of the Analytical Engine to write the first computer program, called this a "science of operations" and contrasted it with mathematical logic. Lovelace wrote, "The science of operations... is a science of itself, and has its own abstract truth and value; just as logic has its own peculiar truth and value, independently of the subjects to which we may apply its reasonings and processes."[86] My hope is that through this history the reader will come to understand the huge gap that separates logic and mathematics from computation, and the affinities shared between computation and the kind of work that is accomplished in the arts.

In their original form, algorithms, the topic of chapter 4, were simply a new way to do arithmetic, which arrived in Europe when merchant capitalism was a dominant force. With the rise of industrial capitalism and in today's age of financial and linguistic capitalism, arithmetic has gone from being economically important to becoming the beating heart of the economy. Concomitant with this rise of arithmetic in commerce and industry was its transformation into a hegemonic form of knowledge from a circumscribed liberal art where it was one of the quadrivium, the arts of number, which also includes geometry, astronomy, and music. Originally spurred by the challenges of mathematics, over the course of the twentieth century, mathematicians, linguists, logicians, and economists reduced huge swaths of intellectual terrain to arithmetic, to calculation, in a move called "arithmetization." Arithmetization presaged what we now call "digitization" and "convergence." These moves to centralize calculation have been environmental disasters for many fields—as calamitous for thought as monocrop agriculture has been to the Earth's air, water, and soil. The hope for this chapter is that the reader, by following a history of the algorithm from early modern Venice to the computer algorithms of today, will be given the means to stop marveling at the power of algorithms and instead begin to think beyond the current ideological limits of algorithms. To do this, one needs to understand the industrial and intellectual forces that have been applied for well over a century to translate the language arts into the liberal art of arithmetic and, once understood, to reverse these translations.

The focus of chapter 5 is the liberal art of logic. The computer-as-logic story is often told to emphasize the many contributions of the language art of logic to the development of the computer. I, too, retell that story, but I include two details that are frequently occluded: materiality and history. It complicates the computer-as-logic story if one admits that computers of today—with power supplies, screens, and circuits—are materially very different from older works of logic printed on paper, so material details are usually sidelined when telling the computer-as-logic story. Historical specificity is also usually marginalized in the common narrative because logic, as it is articulated today in technical venues, is not very old. First-order predicate logic is an invention of the twentieth century. Consequently, narrating how logic begat computers becomes too complicated if one acknowledges that the logic of yesterday was a completely different animal than the logics of today. By examining a history of logic, the material specificity of logic circuits, and some of the software design techniques of logic programming, my hope is that the reader will gain insights into how one can take a seemingly unitary, monolithic, technical topic—logic—and break it down into its many disparate parts. There is no such thing as Logic, with a capital "L," only a multitude of logics, all spelled with lowercase letters.

Chapter 6 is on the second art of the trivium: rhetoric. Aristotle tells us that the strongest rhetoric is closely tied to logical demonstration. This chapter traces a history of demonstration. The history of the "demo" starts in ancient Greece, when definitive demonstration was a matter of deduction as practiced in geometry. Euclid's demonstration or deductive demonstration is displaced by inductive demonstration in the seventeenth century, during the "scientific revolution." Inductive demonstration, which we can call Robert Boyle's demonstration, was made necessary when arguments began to be based on empirical data and not just derived from statements taken to be obviously true. Today, arguments are made on the basis of so much data—"big data"—that no one person could possibly read it all, much less observe its collection. This has necessitated the invention of yet another form of argumentation, which I term "abductive demonstration" or, alternatively, Solomonoff's and Kolmogorov's demonstration. The latest form of rhetorical demonstration is actually a kind of data compression, otherwise known as machine learning. My point is concordant with media theorist Jonathan Sterne's idea that we should now be concerned with compression rather than representation.[87] One could say that the founding document of contemporary machine learning was Ray Solomonoff's 1960 publication "A Preliminary Report on a General Theory of Inductive Inference."[88] Employing a theorem in Solomonoff's paper, Soviet mathematician Andrey Kolmogorov articulated a theory of complexity. The Kolmogorov measure of complexity of a collection of data is the length of the shortest computer program that can generate the data as output. Machine-learning algorithms are designed to accept a collection of data and then search the space of computer programs to find the shortest one that is applicable. We are led to believe that big data sets are aptly characterized by the outputs produced by machine-learning algorithms, but we have no way of checking the data, so I call this an abductive demonstration because philosopher Charles Peirce, who first articulated abduction in its contemporary sense, said that abduction is a form of guessing. Alternatively, we might say that abduction is a form of interpretation, a practice well known to the arts and the humanities. The chapter proceeds from older means of making a point to the newest forms of persuasion. I hope to provide the reader with ways to both question and compose software-based arguments.

Chapter 7 is on the third of the three liberal arts of language: grammar. For a long time, grammar was a political project prosecuted as pedagogy in order to homogenize written and spoken language of empires. Later, it was deployed in an analogous manner to consolidate nation-states. Grammar was initially predominantly prescriptive. Then, in the late nineteenth and early twentieth centuries, grammar was reframed by linguists desiring to describe how language is actually used. With linguist and semiotician Ferdinand de Saussure, grammar became descriptive. When it did, its locus moved from textbooks into machines—both mechanical and imagined mechanisms of the brain. By the mid-twentieth century, linguistics had joined forces with the mathematical formalism championed by David Hilbert. This resulted in a transformation of linguistics to exclude meaning from its object of study. In the words of Noam Chomsky, "The study of meaning and reference and of the use of language should be excluded from the field of linguistics."[89] Instead, Chomsky and his followers pursue linguistics in the form of meaningless syntactic manipulations ultimately articulated as computer programs. After Chomsky, grammar machines became software, and claims were made that software could constitute a theory of language. This represented a huge shift in intellectual culture. When a computer program, a piece of software, can be a theory, we have entered what I will call the "computational episteme." In a computational episteme, software is taken for theoretical insight, and meaning is pushed to the margins. These conditions are strange and challenging. I hope that the reader will see that one way to make sense in a computational episteme—to revive meaning—is to act as an artist, to engage in the software arts.

2   Translation

The first part of this chapter is an open-ended discussion of translation and its uses in several areas of study, especially its relevance and definition in the arts, the humanities, science and technology studies (STS), and computer science. In STS, the analysis of translation is frequently pursued under the rubric of "actor-network theory" (ANT) and employed to study a diverse range of scientific fields and technical objects. We will see how the ANT methodology can be amended and extended for the study of software.

The second part of the chapter focuses on a detailed example pivotal for the foundations of computer science and now central to popular opinion: David Hilbert's "decision problem" and its analysis by Alan Turing and Alonzo Church. Through a close reading of some key texts that address Hilbert's decision problem, I will illustrate how to use the methods of ANT to scrutinize the formal mathematical/logical proofs of this technical literature. I focus on the specific means—the techniques of translation—deployed by Turing, Church, and others to assign identities and equivalences, especially those that assert that computers are like, or the same thing as, people. My point is that there are always gaps that separate the computer from whatever or whoever it is rhetorically equated with. I implore you—as do signs on the platforms of London Tube stations—to mind the gap!

After examining how equivalences are forged in the more technical language of the foundations of computer science, I will pursue Hilbert's decision problem as it emerges from the technical literature and gets translated into larger, more popular venues where false assertions are made, such as "computers can be programmed to simulate anything." A reworking of the ANT methodology provides the tools we need to understand how the popularization of the texts of software establishes stronger and weaker links between the technical works and everyday common sense about the limits of computing.

Assignments and Simulations

In Pedro Almodóvar's 2011 film *The Skin I Live In*,[1] Robert Ledgard, a plastic surgeon, tracks down a young man, Vincente Piñeiro, holds him hostage, and—over the course of six years—subjects him to a series of operations that transform him into a simulation of Robert's late wife, Vera Cruz. When one of Robert's colleagues accuses him of performing Vincente's sex-reassignment surgery without Vincente's consent, Vincente attests that s/he has been a willing participant, but when Robert tries to have what initially seems to be consensual sex with Vera/Vincente and s/he takes Robert's gun, kills him, and escapes, we realize that, like Robert, we have been outsmarted by Vincente's skills as a simulator. Vincente never identified with Vera and never bonded with his captor, Robert. Rather, Vincente just plotted strategically and waited for the right moment to strike back. At the end of the film, Vincente returns to his mother to reclaim his identity as her son.

Robert's surgeries make Vincente into a simulation. After six years of cutting and grafting, s/he looks and sounds like Robert's late wife—but is not. Almodóvar's movie tells us that the essentials of identity are more than skin deep. In the fiction, Vincente is certainly not Vera; he is a simulator who only pretends to accept the role of Vera. The crucial plot point pivots on the critical difference that, inside, Vincente is not and never can be Vera. Robert cannot cut and stitch together his late wife from the flesh of Vincente, because he can never take the memories and suffering of the man out of the woman.

A simulation can never be its model. Most contemporary simulations are digital productions—not heinous crimes of the flesh. Nevertheless, just as Vincente is crucially different from Vera, any digital simulation always incorporates a set of crucial differences that separates it from its model.

In fiction, Almodóvar's monstrous simulation is more the rule than the exception. Since at least Mary Shelley's *Frankenstein*,[2] the simulation that falls short of its model has been a frequently told story. These stories scare us by making the familiar unfamiliar: Vincente looks like Vera but is not. Dr. Frankenstein's creature looks like a man but is a monster. In philosophical aesthetics, there is a word for this kind of scariness. Sigmund Freud called it the "uncanny."[3]

Fetishism and Disavowal

But what happens if we recognize the crucial difference between the simulation and the model yet act as if no substantial difference exists? Freud has another term for this condition: "fetishism."[4] The fetishist is able to know the difference between simulation and model and, simultaneously, believes them to be the same. The fetishist says, I know very well the differences, yet I will overlook them. It is a condition that, according to Freud, is closely linked to disavowal, in which we refuse to recognize a traumatic event. Robert is a fetishist. He knows very well that Vincente is not Vera, but he disavows his traumatic criminal and surgical interventions in order to live in a fantasy where he imagines his former wife, Vera, to be reincarnated.

Those who create or perform simulations were accused of immoral behavior long before Freud's time. In ancient Greece, Plato accused the rival Sophists of being practitioners of simulation because of the way they practiced rhetoric as a form of false representation. "Simulation" was a dirty word for thousands of years before it became what it is now: a respectable pursuit in science, engineering, and mathematics.

Certainly in Robert's case, the simulation of Vera through Vincente is immoral and criminal, although not all simulations are immoral constructs and not all fetishists are criminals. This state of disavowal is the norm of contemporary life, and most of us are indeed nonviolent fetishists. We know very well that the digital simulations of our everyday life are not the same as the models they are based on. Our email, our smartphones, our streaming movies and videos, our social-networking "friends," and even the synthesized voices and the digitally filtered vocalists we hear on the "radio" are all digital now but based on precomputer models, media, and institutions of the past. We treat these simulations as though they were essentially equivalent to their respective models. This is everyday digital life. It is reproduced with hype, disavowal, and ignorance.

I use the term "model" in a manner analogous to the way biomedical researchers use the term. For example, a cancer researcher can use mice as a model organism to test out a new drug because mice share enough similarities with humans to illustrate how the drug might perform on humans. Models, in this sense, are not closer to some ideal than simulations are. Thus, when I assert that a simulation can never be its model, I am not saying that simulations are "virtual" and models are "real." Nor am I expressing nostalgic sentiments imagining that models are "authentic" and simulations are "fake." Mice are neither more real nor less authentic than anything else. Rather, for the purposes of biomedical research, mice make viable models because they resemble humans in some important ways and, obviously, are quite different in other ways.

I posit that there is no ordering on models and simulations: neither is closer to the real than the other. In contrast, as we will see in chapter 6, on rhetoric, others, like Plato, posit that simulations are much further away from the real.

Identity, Equality, and Assignment

On her 1982 hit album *Big Science*,[5] Laurie Anderson sang, "I met this guy—and he looked like he might have been a hat check clerk at an ice rink. Which, in fact, he turned out to be. And I said: Oh boy. Right again. Let $X = X$." Anderson's quirky humor here ties her to a long tradition in philosophy. Let $X = X$ is a statement of the law of identity, the first of the three classical laws of thought, originally written by Plato and subsequently elaborated by many philosophers.

As any computer programmer knows, assignment is not a declaration of identity. Assignment is a form of coercion that is time dependent. In mathematics, $X = Y$ is a declaration of identity that means X is Y and always will be, and equality is commutative: writing $X = Y$ means the same thing as writing $Y = X$. Unlike in mathematics, in computer programming, $X := Y$ is an assignment that means X becomes Y after a certain moment in time. Assignment is normally not commutative: writing $X := Y$ usually means something entirely different than writing $Y := X$.[6]

As a statement, $X := Y$ hardly seems as if it could function as the kernel of a compelling story, but of course the dramatic potential of identity is more in the suspense around its assignment than in its declaration. Assignment can be dramatic under conditions when it is not warranted, not wanted, or not expected. In Almodóvar's movie, when Vincente is surgically reassigned to be Vera, it is done under conditions of extreme physical and psychological violence. To reassign Vincente's identity, Robert must exercise tyrannical and terrible power.

A major concern of this book is assignment and its entanglements with identity and equivalence. Specifically, the focus here is digital assignment. How and by what means are computers used to assert that different things—the model and the simulation—are the same?

The computer's role in contemporary questions of assignment and identity is a starring one, but there are many other players, too, especially us. In acknowledging our role, I am not making claims about "us" like those made by writers who want to argue that the younger generation are "digital natives"[7] or that computers are making us stupid.[8] Instead, at issue are the specific computational means deployed to assign identities and equivalences, a means that I refer to more generally as simply "translation."

I do not yearn for a predigital, authentic time. Rather, my motivation comes from a belief in education even though the hype and disavowal of our contemporary digital conditions cannot be addressed with education. Even well-educated people fall for hype and indulge in disavowal. However, I do think the third factor of digital fetishism— ignorance—can be treated educationally. Thus, my hope is that a careful analysis of the workings of computers can at least help us understand what we are doing when we disavow the mode of digital production and fetishize its products: Oh! How I love my new smartphone!

Between Models and Simulations Are Gaps

Nevertheless, I am not entreating you, as some have, to enjoy your symptom![9] Instead, I implore you to—as the signs on the platforms of London Tube stations advise—mind the gap! My interest is in how the differences between models and digital simulations are addressed. Just as Robert made a thousand cuts and stitches in an attempt to make Vincente into Vera, big digital equivalences require a myriad of smaller technical arrangements for their assignment. These smaller technical arrangements are frequently also digital assignments.

For example, how does one make one's computer perform like a phone or a television? At the core of this process is coding, the production of software. Software is a special kind of text, and the production of software is a special kind of writing. At the heart of every smartphone is a computer. To make a computer operate as a smartphone is an effort to substantiate thousands of smaller equivalences that make it possible for me, in everyday life, to use the computer as a phone. The gap that separates the computer from the phone is filled with software. We will mind that gap.

Digital Convergence and the Power to Assign Equivalences

The power to assign equivalences is central to an essay Michel Callon and Bruno Latour wrote to explain both politics and science as forms of translation. Callon and Latour wrote, "He or she who holds the equivalences holds the secret of power."[10] In science and politics—even in play—asserting an equivalence is not enough, however; an equivalence always needs to be demonstrated and then distributed widely through a set of translations that move us to believe the identity asserted.

In the eighteenth century, Antoine-Laurent de Lavoisier (1743–1794) determined that water was a combination of hydrogen and oxygen. In order for this equivalence to be believed, he had to demonstrate the decomposition of water (H_2O) into two gases (hydrogen and oxygen).[11] An equivalence that was nonsense before Lavoisier is now common sense after repeated demonstrations in laboratories and classrooms around the world.[12] In science studies and political philosophy, carefully examining the process of a translation like this is an approach known as the "sociology of translation" or, more commonly, "actor-network theory" (ANT).[13]

We are in the midst of a rewriting of the world in which many of our important political, economic, social, and cultural institutions are being translated into software, the vernacular of computers and networks. Commonly, these translations are understood to be a "convergence" in which digitization is accomplished by reducing music, video, text, money, friendship—almost everything—into bits, into ones and zeros.

Convergence is actually a matter of language and only marginally a matter of number. To understand the increasing importance of computers, we need to understand computers as a language technology and digitization and computerization as processes of translation, equivalence, and identity.

Translation into the Perfect (Programming) Language

Digital assignment (X:= Y) is a form of translation, but translation is a general term employed in computer science to talk about how software written in one programming language is rendered automatically into another, "lower level" language. Thus, one might say that a compiler translates the high-level programming language JavaScript into a low-level assembly language.

German media theorist and historian Claus Pias wrote, "To translate—at least in the starry heights of computer-scientific abstraction—is to convert the data structures of one system of order (the source language) into the data structures of another system of order (the target language). Unfortunately, natural languages are of course full of ambiguities—be they of a lexical, syntactical, or referential sort. Such ambiguities manifest themselves through remote relations, ellipses, paraphrases, implicit knowledge, or through unbridgeable 'translation gaps.'"[14]

What are the roots of the computer science ideal of language and translation? As Mark Priestley convincingly narrates in his 2011 book *A Science of Operations*,[15] computer programming can be understood as the fruit of two long-standing efforts: one, to give a mechanical account of language; and the other, to provide a linguistic account of machines. According to Priestley, these histories start with Francis Bacon's seventeenth-century efforts to remake the sciences with the means of the mechanical arts both by introducing machines and experiments into science and by eliminating the errors and illusions of natural language through the design and use of an artificial language. Bacon proposed that a universal, artificial, philosophical language could be devised with a precise and unambiguous vocabulary. Subsequently, John Wilkins, bishop of Chester and cofounder of the Royal Society, among others, attempted to devise such a Baconian, philosophical language—a project that also came to be called the creation of a "real" or "universal" character. The most renowned thinker to become engaged with this project was philosopher and mathematician Gottfried Leibniz, who was also the co-inventor (with Isaac Newton) of the calculus.

Many highly readable books of computer history draw a direct lineage from Leibniz to today by passing through some of the major figures of mathematical logic. For example, Martin Davis's excellent book *The Universal Computer: The Road from Leibniz to Turing*[16] jumps from Gottfried Leibniz (seventeenth century) to George Boole (nineteenth century) and then on to Gottlob Frege, Georg Cantor, David Hilbert, Kurt Gödel, and, finally, Alan Turing (twentieth century).[17] When the inventor of cybernetics, Norbert Wiener, named Leibniz the "patron saint" of cybernetics,[18] he was telegraphing this now frequently told history of the efforts made, from Leibniz to Turing, to craft a Baconian, artificial language tantamount to a machine. How can language work like a machine? How can a machine do the work of language? Any answers to these questions depend on an understanding of how Leibniz and his successors approached the problems of translation—for example, the problem of translating logic into a machine.

Today, computer science has answers to these questions. The Leibnizian/Baconian artificial language has become a programming language. The linguistic expression that is tantamount to a machine is software, and the means of translating from language to machine is alternatively called, in contemporary computer science, "compilation" or "interpretation" of a programming language.

The roots of the computer science ideal of (information) lossless translation can be described as Leibnizian, and, from the perspective of this tradition, Warren Weaver's fantasy of translation as decryption (mentioned in the introduction) seems no more fantastical than the idea that computer programs written in a programming language can be translated into a machine or, more specifically, into electrical currents in the circuits of a computer.

French logician, mathematician, and linguist Louis Couturat noted that Leibniz "thus conceived logic, in turn, in the form of an arithmetic, an algebra, a geometry, even a mechanism. Each, moreover, entirely symbolic and constitutive of concrete expressions of the same abstract science. The imaginative idea of so transposing logic and casting it into mathematical forms stemmed from, on the one hand, his desire to render reason tangible and palpable and from, on the other hand, his deeply held conviction in the harmony between all rational sciences that, according to his favorite expression, must 'symbolize' between them."[19] The translations Leibniz was able to effect—for example, from the operations of arithmetic to the mechanical operations of a machine—seem sensible and circumscribed. Leibniz's successors have managed much grander translations, but this intellectual tradition demands very careful proof for each translation claimed, so even these grand successes are carefully circumscribed.

Digital Ideology and Digital Life

More precisely, such translations are *usually* carefully circumscribed. A counterexample can be seen in the claim by the Turing Award winners and cofounders of the field of artificial intelligence, Allen Newell and Herbert Simon, that humans and computers are equivalent because both are "symbol systems." They attempted to demonstrate this equivalence by implementation: they tried to write software that could think like humans.

Newell and Simon are far from lonely in a cohort of computer scientists who have made hyperbolic claims about what computers are or what computers can or cannot do. Notoriously, many artificial intelligence researchers have been promising for decades that human-level, even superhuman-level, intelligence is just around the corner—and they continue to do so today. There is a huge body of literature that is, essentially, science fiction published not as entertainment but as purported scientific fact. Included in this literature of science fiction are claims that people are computers, that our brains are computers, that the entire physical universe is a big computer, and on and on. Each of these "scientific" claims has fictional precedents in which writers have envisioned, for example, sentient, conscious robots.

Bordering this territory of science fiction is a set of statements framed as scientific hypotheses about the translation of various phenomena into computational terms. For instance, Howard Gardner, in his overview and introduction to cognitive science, states that one of the paramount features of cognitive science is this belief: "There is the faith that central to any understanding of the human mind is the electronic computer. Not only are computers indispensable for carrying out studies of various sorts, but, more crucially, the computer also serves as the most viable model of how the human mind functions."[20]

So, for some cognitive scientists, the human mind is a computer; for many molecular biologists, the genetic code is a computer code; and so forth. These are not fanciful leaps of faith but rather beliefs held by large groups of scientists who publish in peer-reviewed journals. Let us lump this together with the science fiction and label the lot "digital ideology" to distinguish these beliefs in computation from something far more pervasive: "digital life."

Digital life moves outside of professional circles and beyond the technical vocabularies of specialists' dialogues. Digital life is everyday life in a society that enacts a digital ideology by replacing everyday institutions (e.g., the mail system, the cinema, banking, etc.) with technologies that incorporate computers in a manner that makes them indispensable. For example, what would be left of your personal photo collection if you lost the digitalized, electronic archive? Do you have paper backups?

Digital life is lived with a belief in the equivalences of digital ideology. Digital ideology is founded on very many assertions of equivalence; among these assertions are that the brain is a computer or that digital video is just like older forms of film. In the scientific literature, digital ideology is usually elaborated in very careful, tightly circumscribed, and rigorously argued equivalences ultimately presented as identities: $X = Y$. These equivalences take the form of technical claims. In the technical literature, one cannot easily claim, for instance, that logic is a form of arithmetic. Rather, such a claim has to be substantiated using a set of techniques of scientific and/or mathematical demonstration; that is, techniques of translation to prove the equivalence of two entities.

Yet even if the equivalences, the identities, established through the translations of science and technology are correct, they are not perfect. We will show how the technical equivalences established by computer science are imperfect, and we will describe what is lost or added when these equivalences are established as identities.

The Computational Condition = Digital Ideology + Digital Life

In his 1979 diagnosis of the current state of knowledge for the government of Quebec, French philosopher Jean-François Lyotard predicted an immediate future in which "the direction of new research will be dictated by the possibility of its eventual results being translated into computer language. The 'producers' and users of knowledge must now, and will have to, possess the means of translating into these languages whatever they want to learn."[21] Lyotard labeled his diagnosis—that we have turned away from other languages (especially narrative language) to computer languages—the "postmodern condition." Lyotard's postmodern condition might be more precisely called a computational condition, a condition that encompasses both digital ideology and digital life. In my phrase "computational condition," I expect humanities scholars will hear the echo of both Jean-François Lyotard's "postmodern condition" and Hannah Arendt's "human condition."[22] A computational condition is a state of knowledge in which scientifically and technically established equivalences are taken to be perfect identities without loss or gain on either side of the translation. They are equivalences taken for identities and therefore sound like absurd tautologies when they are said together: May I have a glass of H_2O water?

The equivalences of digital ideology are taken to be culturally conditioned common sense if, once demonstrated, they are repeated widely and often enough. According to this conception of ideology and common sense, common sense is dynamic and subject to change as new ideas and technologies become popular. In the words of philosopher

Antonio Gramsci, "Every social stratum has its own 'common sense' and its own 'good sense,' which are basically the most widespread conception of life and of men. Every philosophical current leaves behind a sedimentation of 'common sense': this is the document of its historical effectiveness. Common sense is not something rigid and immobile, but is continually transforming itself, enriching itself with scientific ideas and with philosophical opinions which have entered ordinary life.... Common sense creates the folklore of the future, that is as a relatively rigid phase of popular knowledge at a given place and time."[23]

Digital ideology is employed in everyday digital life when narrow, technical, circumscribed equivalences are loosened and expanded. For example, those of us who live in a computational condition see no contradiction in treating an email to our family as the same thing as a written letter sent through the postal service and delivered by hand. When we watch a movie on a streaming video service, we say we have seen the movie, even if the small-screen experience and the former conditions of cinema-going (popcorn, crowds, paper tickets) are quite different. More subtly, it is now unclear what we have done—a digital act or a physical act—when we say we have been "searching" for someone or something or when we say we are "friends" with someone.

From Media Studies to Actor-Network Theory

So how do the equivalences of digital ideology come to be used, loosened, and expanded into digital life? Some forms of science and media studies and newer forms of social media analysis employ a model of "diffusion" of ideas or envision the movement of ideas with the metaphors of epidemiology or genetics.[24] Ideas are said to "spread like a virus"[25] (thus the phrase "viral media") or to move like genes through reproduction and evolution (thus the notion of "memes").[26]

Many older schools of communication and media studies also trope people as physical or mechanical systems. For example, the regnant metaphor of mass communications is the "mass" or physical system. This metaphor allows the researcher to ask questions like, "What is the *impact* of a given message on an audience?"[27]

In the 1940s, Robert Merton and Paul Lazarsfeld[28] advanced a program of research in which social structures were seen to be stable or unstable, in equilibrium or disequilibrium, according to group dynamics and the media messages that influence the members of a group. The metaphor of people as a thermodynamic system engenders questions about the production and breakdown of social order.

All the metaphors of old and new media studies intended to explain how ideas move are inaccurate and mildly insulting because, ironically, they implicitly assume that people do not have language—that people do not speak, listen, read, or write. These notions of diffusion, contagion, spreading, impact, equilibrium, and evolution all figure people as mute, nonhuman animals, organic or inorganic materials. Obviously, people are not inert masses moved only by Newtonian mechanics. Nor are they exclusively porous materials through which ideas are "diffused," vectors for viral "contagions," or breeding animals restricted to reproducing their "genes" or "memes"! In contrast to these old and new schools of communication and media study, let us start with the much more reasonable assumption that people think and speak.

Developers and practitioners of actor-network theory—the sociology of translation— have shown quite definitively why these other approaches are inadequate to the task of explaining how ideas become a part of everyday life and common sense. Instead of this pack of metaphors, actor-network theory hypothesizes that the bridge from ideology to everyday life is a set of cognitively, culturally, and materially specific practices of translation that are employed rhetorically and technologically to convince people of equivalences, differences, and identities.

Interestingly, with few exceptions, actor-network theorists have not studied software.[29] When science studies researchers have focused on software, they have not examined the texts themselves—code and technical articles from the literature of computer science. Rather, they have followed the people who produce and use software.[30]

This lack of attention to the texts of software is surprising because actor-network theory is said to combine the concerns of ethnography and ethnomethodology with insights from semiotics, the humanistic study of meaning and meaning making, a set of methods developed especially for textual analysis. I will employ an understanding of translation that is deeply indebted to actor-network theory, but to supplement ANT for the purposes of studying the texts of software, I will need to draw from the even deeper well of translation as it has been practiced in the humanities.

Translation and the "Ductions" of Michel Serres

Philosopher and historian of science Michel Serres wrote, "We only understand something according to the transformations that can be performed on it. There are at least four such transformations: deduction in the area of logic and mathematics; induction in fields of empirical experimentation; production in domains of practice; translation [traduction] in the space of texts. It is not unexpected that they all incorporate the same root word. There is no philosophy except for that of "duction"—with a variety of prefixes. A lifetime might be spent trying to clarify this state of affairs."[31] This quotation is from the beginning of Serres's book on translation, *Hermès III: La Traduction*, a text that inspired and deeply influenced the developers of ANT. The quotation is difficult to translate into English because the French word for "translation" is "traduction" and Serres's point in this passage is that all of these terms for transformation—deduction, induction, production, and translation (traduction)—incorporate the Latin root "dūcĕre," a word that means "to lead."

Each of the prefixes prepended to "dūcĕre" indicate a direction. "De-," for instance, means "down" or "down from." So, "deduce" connotes "to lead down." "In-" means "into" or "in." Thus, in Latin, "induce" means "to lead into," and "introduction" is a "leading-into." "Produce" is "to lead out," "to lead forth," "to bring forward." "Re-" is the prefix for "back" or "again," so to "reduce" is "to lead back (again)."

"Translate" in English can be unpacked in the same way. Note that "translāt-" is the Latin participial stem of "transferre," which can be broken into the prefix "trans-," meaning "across," and "ferre," meaning "to carry" or "to bring" (instead of, as is the case in French, "to lead"). The English word "ferry" is a contemporary form of "ferre." All of these terms—deduction, induction, production, reduction, translation—imply movement or travel. Each indicates, however, that the reader or listener will be led or carried in a particular direction: down, into, out, or across.

What Serres does in his book, and what the actor-network theorists (like Bruno Latour and others) do in following him, is to make "translation" the more general term. In this manner, we can understand all of these words as denoting different kinds of translation. Therefore, they differ according to which direction a translation is intended to take us, the reading subjects, or the objects of its operation—down, into, or out.

Once alerted by Serres to four kinds of translation, we quickly find others, since "down," "into," and "out" do not exhaust the list of possible prepositions. "Conduction" is a kind of translation that brings two things together. "Abduction" is a translation that leads us away. If "induction" leads something into something else, "introduction" brings the reader in. "Seduce" compounds the prefix "se-," meaning "without" or "away," with "dūcĕre" meaning, then, that a phrase like "to seduce someone away from someone else" is redundant, since the roots of the word imply that seduction is an act of leading away. Then, if we compound prefixes—like "re-" and "pro-"—the forms of translation multiply. Thus, "reproduce" means "to bring forth again." "Irreduction" means "to not bring back (again)."

Of course, Serres's suggestion to use the Latin root word "duction" to orient our navigation of various forms of translation is a notational convenience since it is metaphorical and not historical. Metaphorically, I can employ the word "deduction" to mean a far wider array of operations than just those that contemporary logicians would admit as deduction.

In contrast, historically, one can narrate a story about the word and technique of deduction as it has developed over the past several thousand years in logic and mathematics. Reviel Netz's book *The Shaping of Deduction in Greek Mathematics*[32] is a marvelous telling of the beginnings of this story. Analogously, the other words in this list—induction, abduction, conduction, production, and others—each have their own etymologies, most of which traverse the technical lexicons of science, mathematics, and engineering. I use these words both historically—for example, to try to understand how "deduction" came to have the meaning it has today—and metaphorically/etymologically, in the spirit of Serres's suggestion, in order to differentiate one sort of translation from another and to indicate in which direction a given translation is intended to lead us.

Translation and Actor-Network Theory

The translations I am most concerned with are not translations of isolated words, single lexemes, like the ones one might find in a bilingual dictionary: "eau" for "water," for example. Instead, what I am primarily concerned with are statements, especially statements of equivalence, difference, and identity—for example, equations, assignment statements, or copular statements like "Water is H_2O."

In argument, proof, or demonstration, statements of equivalence are frequently developed in sequence, as a chain leading from a first statement and ending in a final equivalence or identity. Translations are thus rarely one-step operations. Bruno Latour describes translation in his work "Irreductions": "All reasoning is of the same form; one sentence follows another. Then a third asserts these are identical even though they do not resemble one another. Thenceforth the second is used in place of the first, and a fifth affirms that the second and the fourth are identical, even though … and so on, until one sentence is displaced while pretending not to have moved, and translated while pretending to have stayed faithful."[33]

Latour's explanation of translation assumes that each step leads toward the next and away from the last, and it describes the repeated application of a single form of translation in which we are led directly, linearly, from the first statement to the last. More typically, multiple forms of translation constitute an argument or demonstration so we are led, for instance, away from an initial statement, toward an intermediary, and then, perhaps, back to the first statement.

Latour's DNA and the Double Helix

Latour illustrates this more complex version with a comic strip in his book *Science in Action: How to Follow Scientists and Engineers through Society*.[34] The comic strip depicts the fate of a statement about deoxyribonucleic acid (DNA) in, at the beginning, reverse chronological order, and then, at the end, in chronological order. In sum, it shows how we can question scientific facts by looking at their earlier formulations and then shows how those earlier, conditional formulations are developed into definitive, textbook statements of equivalence.

In the first frame of the comic strip is written: "The DNA molecule has the shape of a double helix." Latour writes,

> To sketch the general shape of this book, it is best to picture the following comic strip: we start with a textbook sentence which is devoid of any trace of fabrication, construction or ownership; we then put it in quotation marks ["The DNA molecule has the shape of a double helix"], surround it with a bubble, place it in the mouth of someone who speaks; then we add to this speaking character another character to whom this character is speaking; then we place all of them in a specific situation, somewhere in time and place, surrounded by equipment, machines, colleagues; [First Colleague: "Why don't you guys do something serious?" Second Colleague: "Maybe it is a triple helix." Third Colleague: "It is not a helix at all." Watson to Crick: "If it had the shape of a double helix ..." Crick to Watson: "... this would explain Chargaff ..." Watson: "... and it would be pretty."] then when the controversy heats up a bit we look at where the disputing people go and what sort of new elements they fetch, recruit or seduce [note Latour's use of "se-duce," a term also preferred by Serres] in order to convince their colleagues; then we see how the people being convinced stop discussing one another; situations, localizations, even people start being slowly erased; [Colleague to several other colleagues: "They say Watson and Crick have shown that DNA is a double helix." In the penultimate frame of the comic strip, no people are shown, just a book with this sentence highlighted in it: "Watson and Crick have shown that DNA is a double helix."] in the last picture we see a new sentence, without any quotation marks, written in a textbook similar to the one we started with in the first picture. This is the general movement of what we will study over and over again in the course of this book, penetrating science from the outside, following controversies and accompanying scientists up to the end, being slowly led out of science in the making.[35]

With this comic strip and this paragraph, Latour explains how he plans to lead us, the readers of the book—first from the outside to the inside of science, and then, once inside, to lead us by following the scientists. He then tells us that we will be "slowly led out of science in the making." To move from within science in the making to the outside is to move, for instance, from scientific journals with a small readership to textbooks with a large readership. In a metaphorical/etymological sense, we can say that Latour's text and comic strip describes first an "introduction," a translation that leads us into science, and then a "production," a translation that leads us out and brings something forward.

That something that is produced is, of course, a new fact. The clue of a fact's production is also in its etymology, since the Latin "factum" is the neuter past participle of "facere," "to make." Examining discourse as a series of translations is a means for understanding how facts are produced.

Translations of Hilbert's Decision Problem into and out of Computer Science

How does this approach work for the texts of software? Let us follow one of the key cases of computer science, starting first from the "outside," moving "into" a closer examination of the technical texts, and then moving "out" again. In other words, our tour of this case will follow the same trajectory as Latour's trajectory through the introduction and then the production of the fact that DNA is a double helix.

We, too, will start with a textbook statement. In a book by David Hilbert and Wilhelm Ackermann, *Grundzüge der Theoretischen Logik* (Berlin: Springer, 1928), the statement concerns the "decision problem" (or in German, "das Entscheidungsproblem"). Hilbert and Ackermann wrote, "The decision problem is solved when we know a procedure with a finite number of operations that determines the validity or satisfiability of any given expression.... The decision problem must be considered the main problem of mathematical logic."[36]

Twenty-three-year-old Cambridge mathematics student Alan Turing likely encountered this statement while he was following a course on the foundations of mathematics given by professor M. H. A. Newman during the spring term of 1935. Professor Newman had attended the 1928 mathematics conference where David Hilbert reiterated the decision problem to the mathematics community.[37] Hilbert had first stated a version of the problem when he gave what is perhaps the most influential speech in the history of mathematics at the 1900 International Congress of Mathematicians in Paris. In his address, Hilbert posed twenty-three open problems, many of which became key sites of inquiry for twentieth-century mathematics. Hilbert's tenth problem introduced into mathematics what was subsequently called the "decision problem."

> 10. Determination of the solvability of a diophantine equation: Given a diophantine equation with any number of unknown quantities and with rational integral numerical coefficients: to devise a process according to which it can be determined by a finite number of operations whether the equation is solvable in rational integers.

This question, as it was later taken up by other logicians and mathematicians, quickly exceeded the boundaries of integers and diophantine equations.[38] Instead, intensive scrutiny was devoted to the phrase immediately following the last colon: "to devise a process according to which it can be determined by a finite number of operations." Today, we would summarize Hilbert's tenth problem as a search for an algorithm, a step-by-step procedure to determine whether a certain kind of equation can be solved. However, as we will see, the word "algorithm," as we know it today, only gained currency in the decades after Hilbert's address.[39]

So, in 1936, when Alan Turing published a paper on the "decision problem,"[40] it was a long-standing and well-known challenge in the mathematics community and, as we will see in chapter 7, on grammar, Hilbert's research program was influential beyond mathematics, especially in the field of linguistics. In section 11 of his publication, Turing cites Hilbert and Ackermann's textbook formulation of the problem. In a sense, Turing did solve Hilbert's problem, but his answer was negative: no algorithm can be found that determines for all possible problems whether they are solvable. However, in his paper, Turing introduced what became known as a general model for computers— and what we refer to today, in the theory of computation, as "Turing machines." It is that aspect of the paper that still fires the contemporary popular imagination.

A crucial first step in Turing's 1936 paper is a formalization that starts as a rough analogy. To understand how this analogy might have been interpreted in 1936, you need to know that, at the time, computers were not machines; computers were people.[41] More specifically, computing was a job held by people, frequently women and young men. Employed to calculate large tables of numbers (e.g., the values of trigonometric functions used in ballistics and astronomy), computers worked in teams for large governmental and corporate concerns. Consequently, hearing the word "computer" in 1936, one would think of a person, not a machine. Turing's 1936 paper is based on an extended analogy between the work of a human computer and the working of a machine. Essentially, he formalizes the computer's job into very exact operations susceptible to formal analysis and proof.

In section 1, "Computing Machines," Turing writes, "We may compare a man in the process of computing a real number to a machine which is only capable of a finite number of conditions."[42] Turing was very canny to equate the process envisioned by Hilbert with the process followed by human computers of the day. The brilliance of Turing's insight is clouded today by the ubiquity of computers, but it was strikingly clear then.

To begin to see what his contemporaries saw in him, we can compare Turing's theoretical machine (Turing machine) with another that appeared just prior to Turing's publication. In 1936, both Turing and Alonzo Church, then a professor at Princeton (in fact, later Turing's adviser for his doctoral degree), independently invented new, but distinct, technical definitions of computation. Church called his formalism the "lambda-calculus."[43] Shortly thereafter, Turing demonstrated that expressions written in the lambda-calculus could be translated into Turing machines and vice versa.[44] Thus, it was declared that their two different formalisms were equivalent insofar as any algorithm written in one could be directly translated into the other.

Turing's equivalence proof (between his machines and Church's lambda-calculus) is a translation of conduction because each formalism was thereafter understood to have the standing of the other: each is seen to have the limits and the possibilities of the other. So, if it is possible to write a process as a Turing machine, it should be possible to write the same process in the lambda-calculus. If, on the other hand, there are intrinsic limits or weaknesses of Turing machines, those same limits and weaknesses must also apply to the lambda-calculus.

Even Church himself, in his review of Turing's paper, seemed to like Turing's formulation better than his own: "Of these [formulations] ... [Turing's] has the advantage of making the identification with effectiveness in the ordinary (not explicitly defined) sense evident immediately."[45] The famous philosopher and Cambridge professor Ludwig Wittgenstein (who also later became one of Turing's professors) was very succinct about what made Turing's formulation so striking: "These machines," said Wittgenstein, "are humans who calculate."[46]

Like Latour's narrative about DNA, our story starts with a reading of a textbook (Turing's reading of Hilbert and Ackermann) and moves us into the technical exchanges between specialists (including Turing, Church, and their students). What is the metaphorical "distance traveled" between Hilbert's textbook statement of the decision problem and Turing's 1936 paper? Remarkably, even today, Turing's accomplishment in 1936 and its comparison to Church's is still under close scrutiny and interpretation. We can thus turn to contemporary specialists' comments to try to understand Turing's accomplishment and thereby the metaphorical "distance" between Hilbert's textbook and Turing's published paper.

Robin Gandy (Turing's friend, colleague, and sole doctoral student at the University of Cambridge, who graduated in 1953, the year before Turing's death) has commented on the philosophical significance of Turing's analysis. Gandy writes, "Turing's work is a paradigm of philosophical analysis: it shows that what appears to be a vague intuitive notion has in fact a unique meaning which can be stated with complete precision."[47] University of Chicago professor of logic and mathematics Robert Soare used terms analogous to Gandy's when he put it like this in 1996: "It was Turing alone who ... gave the first convincing formal definition of a computable function ... [and] proved that the informal notion coincided with this formal one."[48]

Note that both Gandy and Soare characterize Turing's accomplishment as demonstrating an equivalence between an "informal" or "vague intuitive notion" and a "formal" or precise one. Gandy's and Soare's statements are symptomatic of how mathematical logicians have understood Turing's contribution. However, paradoxically, they are not statements of mathematical logic. That is to say, a turn of phrase like "vague intuitive notion" or "informal notion" is not a locution proper and exclusive to the specialized field of mathematical logic. These characterizations of Turing's work implicitly make a claim about translation—specifically, that an informal notion can be translated into a formal definition (i.e., a logical, mathematical definition) that is unique and precise.

Under what circumstances can you imagine that an informal notion can be translated into a succinct and precise text with one and only one meaning? Gandy's answer to this question is presupposed in his assessment of Turing's work: "It shows that what appears to be a vague intuitive notion has in fact a unique meaning." Gandy's argument is essentially that Turing's work concerns a confusion of categories; namely, we used to think something was a vague intuitive notion but in fact we were mistaken, and Turing's work set us straight. The vague notion "has in fact a unique meaning which can be stated with complete precision."

Gandy's answer to my question prompts another question: What was the vague intuitive notion that was so confusing before Turing's publication? The pivotal consideration leads us back to Wittgenstein's comment that Turing's "machines are humans who calculate." Earlier in his paper, Gandy writes, "[Turing] considers the actions of an abstract human being who is making a calculation; he pictures him as working on squared papers as in 'a child's arithmetic book.' ... Turing easily shows that the behavior of the *computor* [Gandy's neologism for a human computer] can be exactly simulated by a Turing machine."[49] But doesn't Gandy's description contradict his own conclusion? Turing, according to Gandy, did not render a vague intuitive notion into a precise definition. Rather, Turing's starting point, according to Gandy, is not intuitive but instead abstract, specifically "an abstract human being."

To interpret Gandy's claim, even if we are not mathematical logicians, we need to consider whether Turing's abstraction matches our intuition, our informal notion, since indeed, by their very definition, informal and intuitive notions do not have a priori formal definitions, do they? Well, they do if you subscribe to certain schools of philosophy, especially Plato's school, where everyday forms and ideas are just inaccurate reproductions of perfect, abstract forms. In other words, for those who subscribe to Plato, there is no contradiction in the idea that an informal notion and a formal definition can be proved—by induction or deduction—to be equivalent.

This, then, is one of the major frictions that will be confronted. How can anyone engaged in the practical work of translation believe that an informal notion can be translated without loss or addition into a precise formal definition? Such a belief requires a second belief, a belief that a "perfect language"[50] exists, a language in which only necessary, sufficient, and true definitions can be given.

From this perspective, translations into the "perfect language" clarify a notion even if translations between imperfect languages do not. A number of "perfect languages" have been considered throughout history, including Leibniz's "real character," mathematics more generally, and the original language thought to have been spoken by Adam as recounted in the first book of the Bible.

My point is that the arguments of Gandy and Soare are nonsense if one is not a believer in a perfect language, but I will not argue against the existence of a perfect language. Instead, I want to illustrate how this worldview, this ideology, clashes with other worldviews that do not admit a perfect language. I also want to propose that there are new hybrid forms of thought that do not fit so neatly into the boxes of this binary opposition. My purpose is prescriptive and comparative, not proscriptive; my aim is to be productive, to allow us to better invent and innovate.

A Definition of Ideology

In order to compare worldviews, I offer a relatively simple description of "ideology." After the French Revolution, Antoine Destutt de Tracy coined the term and the practice of "ideology" to critically examine the ideas of postrevolutionary France.[51] At the moment of its invention ideology was not a pejorative term. Rather, by ideology, de Tracy meant the science or study of ideas, just as, for example, we understand sociology to be a social science or understand biology to be a life science. We need to study ideas, specifically in their digital, especially software, inflections. We will examine some of the pivotal ideas of the "computer revolution" without endorsing them. If this approach worked after the French Revolution, perhaps it can work for the "computer revolution," too.

Today, of course, the term "ideology" is often used as a bad word. When one says, "Oh, that's just ideology," often one could just as well have said, "That's untrue," "That's a distorted picture of the world," or "That's unscientific." Even within the specialized humanities literature on ideology, the word is often meant to denote "false consciousness." However, there exist a variety of other useful definitions of ideology.[52]

I will use a definition of ideology-as-semiotic-closure, a theory discussed by, among others, literary theorist Fredric Jameson.[53] According to this definition, ideology is a special kind of system of ideas about social, economic, and political relations—the ideas that regulate and represent individuals, institutions, groups, and the relationships among them. Thus, in principle, any idea could be a part of an ideology, because any idea might affect some relationship. As many historians of science have shown, even ideas about obscure scientific technicalities can be shown to be ideological. However, in practice, only a subset of all ideas is of significance in a given study of ideology. Which ideas are of interest depends on the individuals, institutions, and groups studied. Thus, beliefs about the number and type of subatomic particles might clearly partition, via controversy, some set of physicists at a given historical juncture but would be of no use in exploring the social structure of another group—for example, a group of professional baseball players—at the same moment in history.

In a discussion of ideology as semiotic closure, Fredric Jameson explores the development of equivalent terms but also, especially, various forms of nonequivalence that are a larger set of relations than just binary opposition. Jameson employs in his discussion a diagram known as the Greimasian square of opposition—after the French-Lithuanian semiotician and literary theorist Algirdas Julien Greimas, who developed the kind of semiotics employed in actor-network theory. The square is also referred to as an Aristotelian square. It maps various forms of opposition between four propositions.

The square distinguishes between two different kinds of nonequivalence—the contrary and the contradictory. If we start with an adjective—say, white—its contradictory is its negation, not white, but its contrary might be black. The contradiction and contrary are not the same thing. For example, while not white as a category includes black, it is not equivalent to black and only black.

There are more subtleties in the use of these squares, and Jameson's discussion teases them out.[54] For our purposes, however, the crucial point is that just as there exist multiple forms of equivalence, one can enumerate multiple forms of nonequivalence, and, as a representation of ideology-as-semiotic-closure, the square illustrates how a system of ideas encapsulates both a set of equivalent and nonequivalent terms and a means for enumerating them—a means that is hard, if not impossible, to think beyond.

Just as I did in my introduction of Michel Serres's various terms of "duction" and translation, here, too, I must insist on differentiating the metaphorical and the historical uses of a square of oppositions. Historically, Aristotle's square of oppositions and, more generally, his system of logic have long been overwritten by various other forms of logic, some of which we will see later in this book. In today's technical language, it would be more correct to say that Aristotle's logic is limited to *propositions*, while my discussion will engage with statements that would require a more sophisticated logic of *predicates* to model them. Consequently, I will employ the notion of ideology-as-square-of-oppositions not as a model but as a metaphor.

As a metaphor, this figure of ideology crystallizes several key questions. Within a given ideology, what counts as equivalent, equal, or identical to what? What is in opposition to what? How are equivalences and oppositions reduced and produced—translated—in general? In comparing and contrasting one ideology with another, special attention will be paid to equivalences in one that are oppositions in another.

The In(tro)duction: On Being Led into Science

Let us now return from this interlude on ideology to our story-in-progress. Remember that both Gandy and Soare were of the opinion that an informal notion could be equivalent to a formal, mathematical definition and, further, that the method of translation from one to the other was a mathematical proof, namely Turing's 1936 paper. This is a characterization of the first half of the story, the part of the story that moves from "outside" science to "inside" science, from the informal to the formal and precise. Characterized as a "move," those of a certain philosophical bent will say that Turing's work was not a move or a translation at all, since the formal definition was always already intrinsic to the informal notion.

Others will disagree, saying, for instance, that a flesh-and-blood human in the act of calculation is an entirely different entity than a silicon-based electronic computer, and thus Turing's translation constitutes a radical attempt to bridge the yawning gap between these two entities.[55] Depending on one's philosophical predispositions, then, the first half of the story, which takes us from outside of science into science-in-the-making, either moves us well beyond Turing's starting place or leaves us not so far away, very much in the neighborhood where Turing started. The latter position is Platonic: it implies a belief in a perfect language. But there are multiple positions within this Platonic space, some modest about the powers of Turing machines, others immodest or even grandiose.

Gandy takes a very modest stance. He claims the following about where Turing's work of 1936 leads: "Any function which can be calculated by a human being can be computed by a Turing machine."[56] It is hardly the stuff of headlines to say that a human working at the highly circumscribed job of computer—basically grinding through a bunch of arithmetic problems—can be replaced by a machine.

This very modest assessment of Turing's accomplishment was reflected in Turing's own words when in 1948 he said, "A man provided with paper, pencil, and rubber,

and subject to strict discipline, is in effect a universal machine."[57] Turing also emphasized this interpretation when elaborating on its implications—not just for the powers
of his theoretical construct, Turing machines, but also for its implications for the ACE,
the electronic computer he built at the National Physical Laboratory in London: "The
class of problems capable of solution by the machine [the ACE] can be defined fairly
specifically. They are [a subset of] those problems which can be solved by human clerical labour, working to fixed rules, and without understanding."[58]

It seems clear that for Gandy, Soare, and Turing, the formally defined Turing machine
is equivalent to the informal notion of what a low-level clerk can do strictly within his
or her highly circumscribed job specifications. Using this modest interpretation, people
in general, even those with just a slightly more expansive job specification than computer, are working beyond the capacities of a Turing machine.

Gandy elaborates on this by distinguishing the work mathematicians do when they
calculate from the work they do when they speculate or conjecture. Gandy wrote, "It is
not necessary to the argument, as Turing already indicated, to suppose that mathematicians always work in a deterministic manner.... What is required is to realize that when
they are calculating (not when they are speculating or conjecturing) they are following
a given routine—a fixed set of instructions."[59]

This distinction between the "high-level" speculating and conjecturing work of
mathematics and the "low-level" work of calculation is a long-standing division that
can be seen in centuries of commentary by inventors of calculating machinery. Philosopher and mathematician Gottfried Leibniz (1646–1716) was also the designer of one
of the first mechanical calculators and explained the division of labor like this: "It is
unworthy of excellent men to lose hours like slaves in the labor of calculation which
could safely be relegated to anyone else if the machine were used."[60]

Leibniz's comments are like those made by Vannevar Bush, inventor (among many
other accomplishments) of a seminal analog computer. In 1945, Bush wrote, "For
mature thought there is no mechanical substitute. But creative thought and essentially
repetitive thought are very different things. For the latter there are, and may be, powerful mechanical aids. Adding a column of figures is a repetitive thought process, and it
was long ago properly relegated to the machine."[61]

Decentering this denigrating attitude toward the work of calculation (as something
to be relegated to slaves), Turing was seen by his contemporaries to be both revolutionary and his machines as the most satisfying response to Hilbert. Turing's brilliance
and perspicuity were ultimately the result of his audacious invention—his machines—
which put the "low-level" work of calculation into the center of the "high-level" work

of mathematics. In a phrase to be defined in chapter 3 of this book, Turing broke the "Aristotelian barrier."[62]

From the start of the story, we have traveled from outside of science (i.e., from Turing's reading of Hilbert's textbook) to inside via the vehicle of Turing's 1936 paper. The modest interpretation, like Gandy's, sees the distance traveled as relatively small. The immodest interpretation—which we will see soon—argues that the distance traveled is enormous. Even before we review the immodest position, it should be clear that the distance traveled and the destination at which one arrives via Turing's 1936 paper are both still being argued about some eighty years later. Nevertheless, both the modest and the immodest camps largely agree that there is a name for the destination: the Church-Turing thesis.

Actually, as we will see, the Church-Turing thesis is not so much the destination for our trip but instead the turnaround point. Analogous to Latour's story about DNA, we have been led into science-in-the-making, and now we are going to make the trip back out. The first steps of our story take us to the Church-Turing thesis. The rest will lead us back out.

Popularization or Production: On Being Led Out of Science

Narratively speaking, we can ride the Church-Turing thesis all the way back out of science on the waves of popular culture since, although it refers to the important papers of Church's lambda-calculus and Turing's machines, the thesis is employed rhetorically to support a huge range of opinions on all sorts of topics.

Church's text on the lambda-calculus, Turing's text on his machines, and Turing's text arguing for an equivalence between functions of the lambda-calculus and Turing machines all were popularized first by the authors, Church and Turing, then by their colleagues, and then, as computer technology became more and more important, by a huge number of other people.

Turing's popularization is referred to as "Turing's thesis," and he stated it like this in 1948: "[Turing machines] can do anything that could be described as 'rule of thumb' or 'purely mechanical.'"[63]

Church had his own popularization, called "Church's thesis." Turing's and Church's colleague Stephen Kleene (both Kleene, in 1934, and later Turing, in 1938, earned their doctoral degrees from Princeton with Church as dissertation adviser) seems to have been the first to adjoin these theses, writing, "So Turing's and Church's theses are equivalent. We shall usually refer to them both as Church's thesis, or in connection with one of its…versions which deals with 'Turing machines' as the Church-Turing thesis."[64]

Note that what Turing rigorously proved to fellow logicians in the *Journal of Symbolic Logic* was an equivalence between Turing machines and the lambda-calculus. However, what Turing's thesis claims is much larger. It is not simply a claim about an equivalence between two formal systems but a claim about the equivalence between these systems (of Church and Turing) and "anything that could be described as…'purely mechanical.'" This is, needless to say, a considerable widening of the claim from "Turing machines are equivalent to the lambda-calculus" to "Turing machines are equivalent to anything mechanical"! How well Turing machines perform as motorcycles, radial arm saws, or washing machines has not, unfortunately, been tested.[65]

Subsequently, the Church-Turing thesis was expanded far beyond even Turing's widened claim. Popularizers of the thesis tend to return to a section of Turing's 1936 paper in which he shows that there is a Turing machine that can simulate all other Turing machines.[66] In the paper, Turing calls this specific machine a "universal machine" not because he claims it can simulate all machines (as is implied by the Church-Turing thesis) but rather because it can simulate all machines defined by the formalism introduced in the paper. However, subsequent popularizers conjoin this section of Turing's 1936 paper with the Church-Turing thesis to arrive at the conclusion that the 1936 paper shows that machines of any sort—regardless of whether they have been rendered as a Turing machine or in the lambda-calculus—can be simulated by a Turing machine. Neither Turing nor Church proved that all machines could be rendered in their formalisms. Such a claim is not a proven claim but is instead an open question. Nevertheless, this popularization is repeated again and again as a proven fact and not as an open question. For example, Mark Priestley's book *A Science of Operations*, cited earlier, is for the most part a carefully argued history of computing but includes this in its first pages:

> The very ubiquity of computers might make us reflect, and ask how it is that one device can fulfill such a dazzling array of roles. The answer, of course, is that the computer is a universal device, in a sense made precise by the British mathematician Alan Turing in the 1930s. Unlike, say, a washing machine, which is designed to perform one specific function, a computer has the potential to perform an unlimited range of tasks. For example, one and the same machine might be used to process text or financial data, to act as a communication device across the global networks, to play games, music or movies, or to simulate other devices.…Computers possess this flexibility because of the great range of programs that can be run on them. A program is a set of instructions telling a computer how to perform a particular task: the flexibility of the computer is therefore limited only by the ingenuity of its programmers in describing complex activities in a way that can be interpreted by the machine.[67]

Priestley's hyperbole is a repetition of contemporary common sense: "A computer has the potential to perform an unlimited range of tasks." Yet if one reads Turing's 1936 paper, one sees that its main result was a negative result showing, definitively, that there are tasks that a computer cannot do! In other words, what Turing did in this famous paper was to introduce a formalism tantamount to a computer and then demonstrate its limits.[68]

While Priestley writes that "the flexibility of the computer is therefore limited only by the ingenuity of its programmers," what Turing showed—in the very paper Priestley cites—is actually the opposite: the flexibility of the computer is limited in ways unconnected to the ingenuity of its programmers. Priestley and other popularizers are in the immodest camp, the group that imagines that Turing machines can do anything. They are not in the modest camp, which includes Gandy and others, who think that Turing machines perform only the relatively restrictive operations of calculation. What is so paradoxical about the writings of most popularizers of the Church-Turing thesis is that, as Priestley does here, the popularizers assert that there are no limits to what computers might be programmed to do, while Turing showed the opposite—that computers do have limits.[69]

The popularizations of the Church-Turing thesis illustrate a truism: popularizations are simplifications or distortions of technical knowledge. Yet, as science studies scholar Stephen Hilgartner has pointed out, this truism is, recursively, a distorted or simplified view of popularization.[70] Instead, as Hilgartner discusses, we can view popularization with the tools of actor-network theory and understand it as the collective transformation of a set of statements made in a scientific or mathematical language into a set of statements in a common or vernacular language. Popularization is thus to be seen as just another translation and, like all translations, will of course entail both the loss of and the addition of information to the original set of statements.

By referring to all of these losses and additions of information as "distortions" or "simplifications," critics of popularization imply that a lossless, perfect translation is possible. Instead, one might distinguish between the deployment of the rhetorically loaded terms "distortion" and "simplification" to critique all popularizations in contrast with their use to critique a particular one. Certainly, some popularizations are bad translations, but some are not. Yet all of them, inevitably, entail some change to the original texts.

Popularizations of technical texts are inevitable if for no other reason than that the research specialist has a life that extends well beyond the confines of a technical discipline. Researchers are accountable to—and so must explain themselves to—family, friends, granting agencies, bosses, students, and colleagues with different specialties.

As soon as Turing and Church had to write for an audience other than the readership of specialized journals of mathematics and logic, they needed to make their results
known in a vocabulary that differed from the one they used in their original scientific
papers. Precisely, they needed to translate their results. All scientists face this imperative of translation when they write a proposal to a granting agency, when they write a
textbook or teach an introductory course in their area of specialization, when they give
a talk to an audience that includes those who do not study what they do, or when they
engage in interdisciplinary research to investigate whether their results have implications for other fields. Turing himself also did pioneering work in cryptography, biology,
and artificial intelligence.

We can understand this second half of the story that leads us out of science-in-the-
making as a tale of popularization, but the wisdom of Michel Serres's choice of words
provides us with an alternative term: production. This second half is more precisely a
production, a leading out, because it is not, necessarily, just a translation of the work
to make it understandable to a large audience. Unlike a popularization, a production
can be any translation that makes the original scientific results accessible to a different
audience—even if that different audience is a small one.

It is more typical that technical results are used elsewhere, not that they are used
everywhere. Thus, the facts produced in one field are integrated into another. We see
this especially in interdisciplinary work. For instance, physician and neuroscientist
Warren McCulloch declared in a forum of popular science in 1955, referring to a scientific paper of his published in 1943, "[Walter] Pitts and I showed that brains were
Turing machines, and that any Turing machine could be made out of neurons."[71] Here
we see an example of how one part of Turing's 1936 paper (i.e., the "positive" part
describing machines, not the "negative" part proving what the machines could not do)
is taken up in an entirely different area of study as the intersection of mathematical
logic and brain science. Moreover, McCulloch's claim is that his main object of study—
the brain—is identical to Turing machines. McCulloch's claim participates in a system
of ideas—that is, an ideology—based on a set of equivalences anchored in the technical
literature of the foundations of computing. I call this specific ideology a digital ideology, an ideology now tied tightly to the technical texts of computer science and logic,
an area that we will unpack further in chapter 5.

3 Language

The authors of the eighteenth-century French *Encyclopédie* midwifed the birth of a language to describe artisans' work and their machines, and, over the course of centuries, this became the ancestor of what we know today as programming languages. By printing as text and diagrams what the artisans spoke in the workshop, the encyclopedists paired the mechanical arts and the liberal arts. This coupling was a radical intervention at a time and place where the two had been kept separate for centuries. The French encyclopedists translated the everyday language of the workshop, a language of the mechanical arts, into a language of literature and learned discourse, the language of the liberal arts.

Like all remarkable translators, the encyclopedists had to invent new language. Specifically, they invented what I will call a "work language" and another I will term a "machine language." I define "work language" to mean the language—the text and talk—employed to describe the processes and products of work. A "machine language" is a work language employed in the design and analysis of machines. When a machine is designed to replace a human in a work process, the actions performed by the human must be translated into a machine language.

At the center of computing is the work language and machine language of operations, birthed in the eighteenth-century workshops of the French artists, designers, and artisans. A century after the publication of the *Encyclopédie*, Charles Babbage and Ada Lovelace together were able to translate a work language of operations into a machine language in an endeavor Lovelace called a "science of operations." Even now, the operations of computing are confused with the functions of mathematics, but there is a huge gap between the artisans' operations of computing and the functions of mathematics. Many careers have been devoted to trying to bridge that gap—to make computing a form of pure or applied mathematics—yet no perfect translation between the two has been found. Consequently, computing remains an art and a craft quite unlike mathematics and not at all a science written in functions, despite Lovelace's wishful phrase of a "science of operations."

Bacon's *Organum*

Lord Chancellor Francis Bacon was one year away from political disgrace and a fall from power and was six years away from his death when he published the *Novum Organum Scientiarum* (New Instrument of Science), considered the founding document of empirical science and the first description of a form of logical induction subsequently named the "scientific method."

The "organum," the "instrument," in his title refers to Aristotle's writings on logic collected under the title *Organum*. Bacon understood the study of nature, under the influence of Aristotelian philosophers, to have been stalled for two thousand years. His book was a critique of the Aristotelians and was a proposal to refound the study of nature by, among other things, patterning it after and enlisting the aid of the mechanical arts.

According to Bacon, compared to the mechanical arts, the liberal arts had made almost no progress in the previous two millennia. Bacon attributes various "discoveries" to the mechanical arts, including printing, gunpowder, and the compass: "For these three have changed the appearance and state of the whole world: first in literature, then in warfare, and lastly in navigation; and innumerable changes have been thence derived, so that no empire, sect, or star, appears to have exercised a greater power and influence on human affairs than these mechanical discoveries."[1]

Like many writers of the era, Bacon figured nature as feminine and consequently described the study of nature in terms of gender, sex, and reproduction. For instance, he writes of the "womb of nature." If nature-as-woman were a loose or rare metaphor in Bacon's writings, one might pay it no heed, but, as historian and philosopher of science Evelyn Fox Keller writes in a chapter titled "Baconian Science: The Arts of Mastery and Obedience,"[2] Bacon's sexual imagery was systematic, ubiquitous to his writings about science and thus not at all casual. Bacon's aim was for man to attain mastery over nature for his purposes, just as in seventeenth-century England a husband was thought to be within his rights to gain mastery over and require obedience from his wife.

At first, Bacon's prescription for the reinvigoration of the sciences seems like a call for domestic abuse made by a cuckold,[3] hardly a positive role model for the scientist. But further on in the *Novum Organum*, Bacon moves to several positive ideas for reinvigorating the sciences: "The plan to be pursued is this: all the mechanical, and even the liberal arts (as far as they are practical), should be visited and thoroughly examined, and thence there should be formed a compilation or particular history of the great masterpieces, or most finished works in each, as well as of the mode of carrying them into effect."[4]

The Encyclopedists as Midwives

Many, including German mathematician and philosopher Gottfried Leibniz, were subsequently inspired by this plan for a compilation of the masterworks of the arts—mechanical and liberal. A century after the publication of Bacon's book, the compilation was undertaken as a large-scale project conducted by philosopher and writer Denis Diderot, mathematician Jean Le Rond d'Alembert, and their colleagues, who together produced the multivolume *Encyclopédie*.

However, the encyclopedists did not figure their role as being akin to the role of man over nature or husband over wife. Rather, they saw themselves in a very different role, remarkably that of midwife; not literally a midwife but "literately" a midwife—one who could put the inchoate, oral descriptions of artists and artisans into a printable, literate language.

They saw this as a necessary role because the artisan—like the artist and the designer of today—was frequently assumed to be a taciturn intuitive worker able to operate and practice but unable to articulate or interrogate machines, instruments, and processes of production and manufacturing. In the "Preliminary Discourse" to the *Encyclopédie*, Jean Le Rond d'Alembert wrote, "Most of those who engage in the mechanical arts have embraced them only by necessity and work only by instinct. Hardly a dozen among a thousand can be found who are in a position to express themselves with some clarity upon the instrument they use and the things they manufacture. We have seen some workers who have worked for forty years without knowing anything about their machines."[5]

Yet d'Alembert, reporting on work that was directed primarily by his co-editor Diderot—the son of an artisan, a cutler—wrote, "We approached the most capable of them in Paris and in the realm. We took the trouble of going into their shops, of questioning them, of writing at their dictation, of developing their thoughts and of drawing therefrom the terms peculiar to their professions, of setting up tables of these terms and of working out definitions for them, of conversing with those from whom we obtained memoranda, and (an almost indispensable precaution) of correcting through long and frequent conversations with others what some of them imperfectly, obscurely, and sometimes unreliably had explained."[6] He summarized by saying, "With [the artisans], it was necessary to exercise the function in which Socrates gloried, the painful and delicate function of being midwife of the mind, *obstetrix animorum*."[7]

I will argue that Diderot, d'Alembert, and the encyclopedists did indeed midwife the birth of a language to describe artisans' work and their machines and that, over the course of the centuries, this became the root of what we know today as programming languages. By printing as text and diagrams what the artisans usually just spoke in the workshop, the encyclopedists paired the mechanical arts and the liberal arts. This pairing was a radical intervention at a time and place where the two had been kept separate for centuries.

The Aristotelian Barrier

We can call this traditional separation the "Aristotelian barrier." In the words of historian of science Pamela Long, "Aristotle delineated three areas of human activity: first, material and technical production (*techne*); second, action (*praxis*), such as political or military action, that requires judgment in contingent or uncertain situations (*phronesis*); and third, theoretical knowledge or knowledge of unchanging things (*episteme*). Aristotle's separation of material production from action and from theoretical knowledge presupposed a hierarchy with *techne* at the bottom and *episteme*, or theoretical knowledge, at the top."[8]

These epistemological divisions led to divisions in the educational system, where the liberal arts were taught separately from the mechanical arts. To this day, the Aristotelian barrier separates language that belongs to the liberal arts (specifically the language arts of the trivium) from machines that belong to the mechanical arts.

Given a social context in which this barrier is accepted, d'Alembert's comments about inarticulate artisans seem quite natural, but notice also how self-contradictory d'Alembert's declaration is when he states that he was "writing at their [the artisans'] dictation." So, the artisans could not express themselves in words, yet the words written about their various crafts are the words dictated by the artisans themselves!?

Obviously, the artisans could communicate their craft; they just could not do it in the then-current languages of the liberal arts. Put more plainly, the workingman's language needed to be translated into the upper-class language of the liberal arts before it could be printed in the *Encyclopédie*. Diderot and d'Alembert's accomplishment, thus phrased, is an accomplishment of translation, a translation across class divides.

Breaking the Aristotelian barrier was an imperative for Bacon and then for Diderot and d'Alembert, and it continues to be an imperative even today. Pamela Long's own research emphasizes the important role of artisans in the history of science. Breaking the Aristotelian barrier in the history of astronomy, for instance, might lead us to investigate the role of the artisan who made Galileo's telescope. Are Galileo's astronomical discoveries to be credited to Galileo or/and to the artisans who made the discoveries possible?

Breaking the Aristotelian barrier also remains one of the most pressing issues in contemporary philosophy. Philosopher Bernard Stiegler both highlighted and broke this barrier in the first volume of his book *Technics and Time*, where he wrote, "At the beginning of its history philosophy separates *tekhné* from *épistème*.... The separation is determined by a political context, one in which the philosopher accuses the Sophist of instrumentalizing the *logos* as rhetoric and logography, that is, as both an instrument of power and a renunciation of knowledge. It is in the inheritance of this conflict—in which the philosophical *épistème* is pitched against the sophistic *tekhné*, whereby all technical knowledge is devalued—that the essence of the technical entities is conceived."[9]

As industrial capitalism came to dominate the economy, the Aristotelian barrier was an impediment for the upper classes to understand the sources of their wealth. Writing almost a century after Diderot, in the preface to his book *On the Economy of Machinery and Manufactures*,[10] Charles Babbage admonishes his peers—those who have wealth, leisure, and a liberal arts education—for being ignorant of the mechanical arts. He writes, "Those who possess rank in a manufacturing country, can scarcely be excused if they are entirely ignorant of principles, whose development has produced its greatness. The possessors of wealth can scarcely be indifferent to processes which, nearly or remotely have been the fertile source of their possessions. Those who enjoy leisure can scarcely find a more interesting and instructive pursuit than the examination of the workshops of their own country, which contain within them a rich mine of knowledge, too generally neglected by the wealthier classes."[11] Moreover, Babbage tells his peers that learning something about the sources of their wealth will not be too difficult: "The difficulty of understanding the processes of manufactures has unfortunately been greatly overrated. To examine them with the eye of a manufacturer, so as to be able to direct others to repeat them, does undoubtedly require much skill and previous acquaintance with the subject; but merely to apprehend their general principles and mutual relations, is within the power of almost every person possessing a tolerable education."[12]

With these statements, Babbage clearly indicates that his perspective is one from the berth/birth of the upper class; he also assures his readers that the mechanical arts can in fact be translated into the languages of the liberal arts since, at the time, "a tolerable education" was, axiomatically, for the upper class, a liberal arts education.

Dramatis Personae

Possible and desirable though it may be, breaking the Aristotelian barrier entailed—and still necessitates—a move beyond one's education and upbringing, since we are all circumscribed by social, political, economic, and cultural conditions that govern who knows what and who does what. Moreover, generally speaking, most educational institutions preserve the Aristotelian barrier. As d'Alembert pointed out, those apprenticed in an artisan's workshop do not necessarily know how to write. Conversely, even today, those who get a liberal arts education are not trained to become automobile mechanics. Concisely, race, class, gender, sexuality, occupation, and education are performed within roles that are not easily refused. To find alternatives to our assigned roles, we need to imagine dramatis personae that blend, divide, or diverge from conventional roles. This is a suggestion inspired by philosopher Gilles Deleuze.[13]

If we look carefully at the dramatis personae proposed respectively by d'Alembert and Babbage, we can see that they were catalytic in the creation of new institutions of knowledge and practice. D'Alembert acknowledges that the image of philosopher-as-midwife is at least as old as Socrates, yet even now, Socratic dialogue is explosive, if not revolutionary. As it was performed by Socrates, midwifery was a practice of intensively questioning someone's common sense, thereby birthing a new understanding of self.

Babbage's preface to *On the Economy of Machinery and Manufactures* evokes what at first glance seems to be a much less demanding role. Babbage seems to be describing a "gentleman mechanic" akin to the "gentleman farmer"—a persona that would require the gentleman to have some knowledge about how his wealth was produced but to acquire this knowledge as a form of leisure, not as a matter of necessity.

Babbage's preface tells his gentleman reader that he will reveal an entertaining diversion for his leisure time and, simultaneously, that the principles of the mechanical arts to be explained are not at all a diversion for him (Babbage) but rather should be seen as the very foundation of his intellectual life and the probable source of wealth for anyone who will benefit from the industrial revolution.[14] Babbage's aspirations exceed entertainment. He wants to inspire his gentleman reader to become a manufacturer.

In a different essay, Babbage explicitly names the role he would have for his gentleman and all men: "It is not a bad definition of man to describe him as a tool-making animal."[15] Babbage's dramatis persona is not *Homo sapiens*, the wise, rational, intelligent man. Neither is he what cultural historian Johan Huizinga has called *Homo ludens*, the man of leisure, man the player.[16] Babbage's dramatis persona is *Homo faber*, man the maker.

Many philosophers, political theorists, and economists have elaborated on the cultural, social, economic, and political consequences of an ideology that places the persona of *Homo faber* at its center. This trope can be elaborated by distinguishing between seemingly close variants. If we say that "man the maker" is a pivotal figure, we are pressed to consider just what it is that these men make and what kind of work they must engage in to make what they do. For instance, is the agricultural laborer fundamentally different from the construction worker, the factory worker, the office worker, or the researcher who tills the fields of knowledge? If so, is the distinction made according to how the work is done or according to what is made?

Using the definition of ideology discussed in chapter 2, it is possible to examine Baconian science, the arts and sciences of the *Encyclopédie*, and Babbage's "science of operations" as distinct ideologies elaborated around their respective dramatis persona: husband, midwife, *Homo faber*.

Analogously, we can consider the brilliance and perspicuity of Turing's 1936 article as resulting from his audacious move to put the modest dramatis persona of human computer at the center of a rethinking of mathematical work. Turing's machines put the "low-level" work of calculation into the center of the "high-level" work of mathematics. In a phrase, Turing—like Bacon, Diderot, and Babbage before him—broke the "Aristotelian barrier."

Homo faber and Work versus *Homo laborans* and Labor

Many languages include at least two words for "work." In English, we have "labor" and "work." In French, the analogous terms are "travailler" and "oeuvrer." In her book *The Human Condition*, philosopher Hannah Arendt points out that this double term exists not only in English and French but also in many other languages, including German, Greek, and Latin.[17] Arendt hinges one of the main arguments of her book on this repeated difference, which philosopher John Locke references in his *Second Treatise of Civil Government*, where he writes about "the labour of our body and the work of our hands" (section 26).

Arendt points out that in ancient Greece labor was shunned and work was esteemed. This valuation lingers on in our everyday locutions, where we can talk about, for example, a "work of art" but not a "labor of art," or, in English, borrowing from French, where an artist's work can be referred to as the artist's "oeuvre" but not the artist's "travail" (which in English would mean laborious or painful effort).

According to Arendt, in ancient Greece, labor included those efforts made by women, slaves, and domestic animals to sustain and reproduce life and the necessities of life. Work was the production of free men in public for public, rather than private, purposes. The private realm was considered a position of privation, and labor was considered the activity that took place in private. Work was an act of honor and renown that took place in public. Arendt's distinction describes the circumstances in which some forms of effort, production, and reproduction are unseemly or hidden from view and other forms of work are highlighted, highly valued, and given center stage. Furthermore, class and gender strictly regulated the differences between labor and work, private and public. Arendt refers to those men engaged in work as *Homo faber*. Those engaged in labor are *Homo laborans* or, following Arendt, *Animal laborans*.

Arendt contrasts this ancient Greek valuation of work over labor (and thus workers over laborers) with political economist Karl Marx's idea that labor (and thus laborers) should be central to and thus at the top of all valuation.[18] So one can see that entire ideologies can be elaborated around images of work and who does what kind of work.

Work Languages and Machine Languages

To articulate various kinds of work and who or what does what kind of work (or labor), I introduce two constructs of my own design. One I call "work languages," and the other I term "machine languages." I define "work language" to mean the language—the text and talk—employed to describe the processes and products of work. So, for instance, one might scrutinize Benjamin Franklin's writings about work—"Early to bed and early to rise makes a man healthy, wealthy, and wise"[19]—in order to argue that contemporary business practices (e.g., as inscribed in documents of corporate mission, legal contracts, legislation, or employee manuals) are still tied to Protestant ethics in a variety of ways.[20] Each age, each culture, each industry, and each economy has one or more work languages. By examining differences and similarities between these languages, one can interrogate what work is here and now and how it contrasts with work as it was there and then.

Central to today's work are the almost performative qualities of "machine languages," a subset of work languages employed in the design and analysis of machines. To adequately describe how a machine works is tantamount to demonstrating the work to be done in exacting detail. When a machine is designed to replace a human in a work process, when work is automated, the actions performed by the human must be translated into a machine language.

Two work languages are central to this chapter. The first is a work language of physics that begins as a language of construction and evolves into a language of information. This first work language is descriptive of what Arendt calls "labor." The second is a work language of the arts that eventually becomes a language of computation. The second is descriptive of some of the activities that Arendt calls "work." The two languages are closely related but distinct.

A Work Language of Construction, Physics, and Information

The work language of physics is a language of calculation developed in the eighteenth century by a network of Enlightenment engineers, scientists, philosophers, and mathematicians, including French mathematician and scientist André-Marie Ampère (1775–1836), Swiss scientist and mathematician Daniel Bernoulli (1700–1782), French engineer and scientist Charles-Augustin de Coulomb (1736–1806), German scientist and mathematician Georg Simon Ohm (1789–1854), Italian scientist Alessandro Giuseppe Volta (1745–1827), and Scottish inventor James Watt (1736–1819). Originally, their work language was used to measure the activity of men and machines as heat or electrical charge. Thus, we have the quantitative measures of the watt, the joule, and the coulomb—all still used today.

French fortifications engineer Charles-Augustin de Coulomb stated at the beginning of his 1775 treatise (republished in 1821) what he took to be the fundamental unit of work. He uses this unit to compare the work of machines and the work of men: "We have just seen that the effect of a machine can always be measured according to a weight multiplied by the height to which it has been raised."[21] This measure of work—weight multiplied by the height to which it is raised—is still central to contemporary physics and engineering. It reduces what might be a set of very complicated movements to a single number labeled with a unit; specifically, the unit of foot-pounds. In Arendt's terms, this is properly a language of labor and not a language of work, but in contemporary technical terms, a foot-pound force is defined to be a unit of energy or work, so in this section we will persist in calling it a work language.

The formalization of this language is defined in the unit of work named after James Prescott Joule (1818–1889), an English scientist and beer brewer.[22] The definition of a joule in turn relates together the eponymous units of many of the participants of the network listed earlier—and also includes units named for Isaac Newton (1643–1727) and Blaise Pascal (1623–1662). One joule, usually written as J, is a unit of work equal to the expenditure of energy necessary to apply one newton—that is, to accelerate one kilogram of mass at the rate of one meter per second squared—through a distance of one meter. Alternatively, a joule can be defined as passing an electric current of one ampere—that is, one coulomb per second—through a resistance of one ohm for one second. We can also understand a joule to be the heat required to raise the temperature of one gram of water by 0.24 kelvin, a measure of temperature named after British physicist and engineer Lord Kelvin (1824–1907). This definition can be written as an algebraic equation:[23]

$$J = \frac{kg \times m^2}{s^2} = N \times m = Pa \times m^3 = W \times s = C \times V$$

This equation does far more than Coulomb's sentences of 1775. It succinctly relates not just weight and height but also heat and electricity, mechanics, thermodynamics, and electrodynamics—many of the fluxes and flows investigated independently in the eighteenth century.

This line of research was continued through the nineteenth century as thermodynamics, with practical application to, among other things, Joule's business of brewing beer, the construction of steam engines, and, eventually, internal combustion engines. The unit of one joule divided by kelvin (that is, a measure of work or energy divided by temperature) turned out to be pivotal for the development of thermodynamics: J/K is the unit of *entropy*, the measure of (dis)order! Who could have foreseen such a direct connection between work and disorder? Entropy is a measure of the number of ways in which a system may be arranged; that is, its measurement in a system is proportional to the number of possible states of the system.

In the middle of the twentieth century, Claude Shannon created a formal definition of information based on this definition of entropy. According to Shannon, entropy is equal to the average amount of information contained in a message.[24] This we know today as the basis for information theory.

This definition of information has its origins in the eighteenth-century problem of measuring how much work a common laborer accomplishes lifting and carrying loads at a construction site. Using Arendt's terms, one could say that the language of physics and information is a formalization of what is done by *Homo laborans*. Clearly, this language and its earlier formulations are apt for work in mechanics, thermodynamics, and electrodynamics, but they are not the languages of the arts and computation. They are inadequate when used to analyze the work of *Homo faber*. In Arendt's terms, the language of physics and information is the language of labor; in contrast, the language of computation is the language of skilled work.[25]

Work Languages Have Limits

Clearly, the work language of physics and information has many uses and has been at the center of many innovations. Nevertheless, each work language has its limits when applied to activities for which it was not developed. Consequently, it is not surprising that many students of introductory physics have been struck by the limits of its work language.

For example, let us imagine that you are a house builder's apprentice. Your name is "Sisyphus." In the morning, your duty is to take the builder's toolbox out of the truck and open it up. The builder climbs to the second floor of the house under construction. Whenever he calls for a tool—"Sisyphus, bring me a hammer!"—your job is to get it out of the toolbox, climb the ladder, give it to him, wait until he finishes the task for which he needed the tool, and then climb down the ladder again and put the tool in the tool-box.[26] According to the definition of work used in physics, at the end of the day, if you have performed your job well and returned all of the tools back to the box, you have done no work! You lifted certain weights in the form of tools to certain heights at the top of the ladder; that constitutes work. But you returned those same weights back to the toolbox on the ground; that constitutes negative work. Therefore, the total work completed by you is zero! Poor Sisyphus!

A Work Language of the Arts

To better describe the activities of Sisyphus and the house builder, one needs to use a work language of the arts. This work language is not the language of physics and infor-mation. Its origins can be seen in Diderot and d'Alembert's *Encyclopédie.*

Let us look at the *Encyclopédie*'s plates depicting the work of artisan pin makers (see figures 3.1, 3.2, and 3.3). Do you see men and machines lifting a lot of weight? No, right? So, even if the work language of physics and information is the right one for describing the labor of coal mining and construction sites, it is not the right one for describing the work of the mechanical arts. In fact, it is absurd when employed in the artisan's workshop.

What is the appropriate work language for describing what artisans, designers, and art-ists do? As it happens, a second work language was developed in the eighteenth century, and, curiously, this history starts at the same place with some of the same people as in the history of the joule. Unlike the work language of physics, this second language does not reduce the description of work to a single number (of joules). Rather, the work lan-guage of the arts can be employed to describe *how work is done.* The work language of the arts anticipates what we know today as computer programming languages.

Its history is referred to within the literature of computer science but rarely told in full. For example, one of the founders of the field of computer science, Herbert Simon, quipped in 1958 that "Physicists and engineers had little to do with the invention of the digital computer.... The real inventor was the economist Adam Smith."[27]

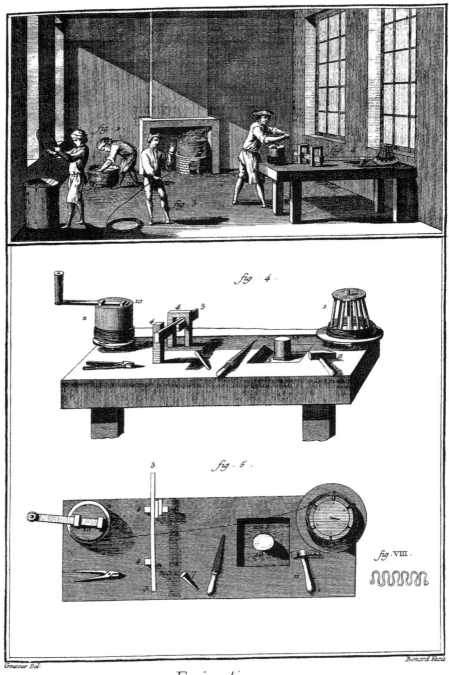

Figure 3.1
Plate I of the *Encyclopédie* entry for "Pinmaker."

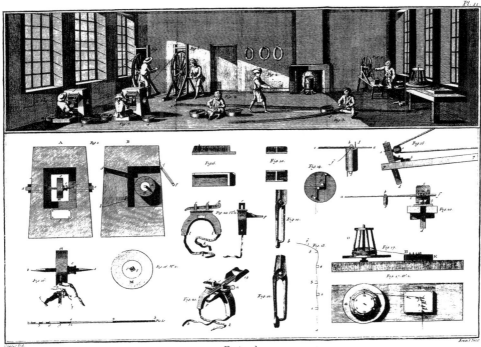

Figure 3.2
Plate II of the *Encyclopédie* entry for "Pinmaker."

What is Simon referring to here? Recall that book 1, chapter 1, of Adam Smith's best-known work, *The Wealth of Nations* (1776), is on the division of labor, specifically in the production of pins. Smith wrote, "The greatest improvements in the productive power of labor, and the greater part of the skill, dexterity, and judgement with which it is any where directed, or applied, seem to have been the effects of the division of labor." A division of labor is an organization of collaboration in which the work to be done is distributed between different people using a number of tools and machines. Herbert Simon is suggesting that we examine how work and the division of labor are at the core of the computer.

If we want to maintain some fidelity to the philosophical language of Arendt, we would say that when Smith describes a division of labor he is, in Arendtian terms, describing a division of work. This is because Smith's description—as we will see—draws on an entirely different kind of language than the work language of physics just

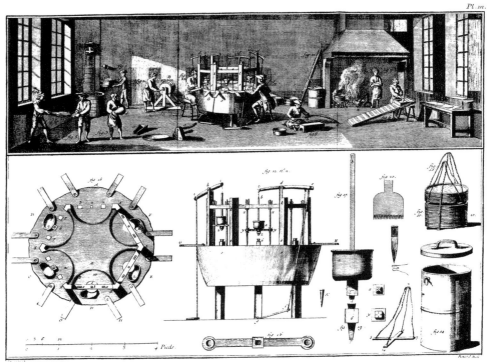

Figure. 3.3
Plate III of the *Encyclopédie* entry for "Pinmaker."

described. Adam Smith's work language has its beginnings in a set of drawings detailing a workshop producing pins in a little town in Normandy: Laigle, France.

Engineer Jean-Rudolphe Perronet did the original observational work at this site. Let us call the observational work—anachronistically—ethnographic work, so that we can be reminded of the importance of contemporary human scientists', especially ethnographers', contributions to the design of software and hardware.[28] Trained in civil engineering, mathematics, and mechanics, Perronet joined the engineering corps of the Ponts et Chaussées in 1735.[29] Soon thereafter, he was appointed the chief engineer for the district of Alençon and was primarily concerned with the construction and paving of roads.

During the same period, however, Perronet also studied the workshops of artisans and craftsmen and wrote two manuscripts on the manufacture of pins at a workshop in the nearby town of Laigle.[30] While neither of these manuscripts was published immediately, Perronet contributed to the entry for "Pin" (Épingle) in Diderot and d'Alembert's *Encyclopédie*.[31] Moreover, Perronet's detailed descriptions of how the crafts-men manufactured the pins, how they used their machines, and how the machines were designed anticipated the work language of the *Encyclopédie*, a collection that incorporated many articles on contemporary methods of the mechanical arts.

Design historian Antoine Picon discusses the three main terms of this work lan-guage of the *Encyclopédie*—gestures, operations, and processes: "The common threads that connect the different articles devoted to the arts and crafts are the description of elementary gestures of production, how these movements are integrated and thereby define aggregate technical operations, and the logic of chaining together these opera-tions to form processes organized according to a division of labor.... From individual movement to process chain, the thread that weaves them together is analogous to the overall aim of Diderot, D'Alembert, and their *Encyclopédie* collaborators: the integration of all forms of knowledge."[32]

For example, here are some extracts from the four-page *Encyclopédie* entry for "Pinmaker." It summarizes in eighteen steps how straight pins were made: "A pin under-goes eighteen operations before it becomes a commercial commodity. 1. one yellows the brass wire... 2. one pulls the wire around the bobble... 3. one draws out the wire... 4. one cuts the wire... 5. one puts a point on it...."[33] Note that this looks like a recipe for making pins. Figures 3.1, 3.2, and 3.3 are the illustration plates for the entry. As we will see in chapter 4, on algorithms, algorithms are frequently compared to recipes. One might say that the *Encyclopédie* includes a set of recipes for making not just food but all kinds of different things.[34]

Adam Smith's example of pin making was inspired by his reading of d'Alembert and Diderot's *Encyclopédie*.[35] A few years later, in 1791, Gaspard Prony—charged by the French government with producing a set of enormous and detailed logarithmic and trigonometric tables—borrowed back from Adam Smith this image of the division of labor, citing Smith and claiming he "could manufacture logarithms as easily as one manufactures pins."[36] Prony organized a great number of working-class nonmathema-ticians to perform as a set of "computers" in order to calculate the tables.

There is, however, some sort of oedipal perversity in Prony's claim that he was inspired by Smith, because, as we have seen, Smith's source was Diderot's *Encyclopédie*, to which Perronet contributed. And Perronet was not just Prony's professor, mentor, supervisor, and eventual collaborator but also his predecessor as the first director of the École des Ponts et Chaussées. Prony succeeded him as director in 1798.

We might say instead that the real inventors of the computer were Perronet, Prony, and the encyclopedists and that, contrary to Herbert Simon's attribution, the only contribution Adam Smith made was to copy from the *Encyclopédie* so that it was ulti-mately cited by Prony. My point is that Prony could have received his information about the division of work and the production of pins directly from Perronet and that Smith was just an unlikely middleman. But this unlikely detour through Scotland—through the writings of Adam Smith—that connects the genealogy of computing from Perronet to Prony is the source of computer scientist and Nobel Prize–winning econo-mist Herbert Simon's quip that Smith was the inventor of the computer.

Babbage and the Translation from Manual to Machine Operations

A few years after Prony's achievement, British mathematician, philosopher, and engi-neer Charles Babbage noted how Prony's division of work could be incorporated as a machine. In my preferred terms, Babbage thus translated the work language of the *Ency-clopédie* into a machine language. He achieved this in plan but not in physical form; his Analytical Engine was not completed in his lifetime.[37] Nevertheless, even on the draw-ing board, it became clear that the machine language he forged out of the *Encyclopédie's* work language was from a very different family than logic or mathematics.

The differences appear clearly in Babbage's drawings. Historian Mark Priestley tells us, "In the course of this work, Babbage found that the traditional method of using drawings to describe machinery was inadequate. A drawing could only represent the state of a machine at one instant, and so provided little assistance in understanding the sequences of movements involved in a complex mechanism or in working out the appropriate timing of the movements of its interacting parts."[38] Consequently, Bab-bage was driven to invent new graphical notation for machines that combined textual annotation and the illustration of the structure of the parts of the machine with a novel means to describe the succession of movements that were to take place in the machine. (See figure 3.4.) In the terms of the *Encyclopédie*, Babbage had to develop a new means to diagram the gestures, operations, and sequences of movements and operations—that is, processes.[39]

As Picon points out, operations were at the semantic foundations of the *Encyclo-pédie's* work language. Soon after Babbage completed his design, it became clear that oper-ations were central to his machine language, too. English mathematician Ada Lovelace argued, in elucidating the differences between the operations of Babbage's machine and the functions of arithmetic and calculus, that Babbage's machine would require a new field of research beyond mathematics, a field she called "a science of opera-tions": "The science of operations…is a science of itself, and has its own abstract truth and value; just as logic has its own peculiar truth and value, independently of the

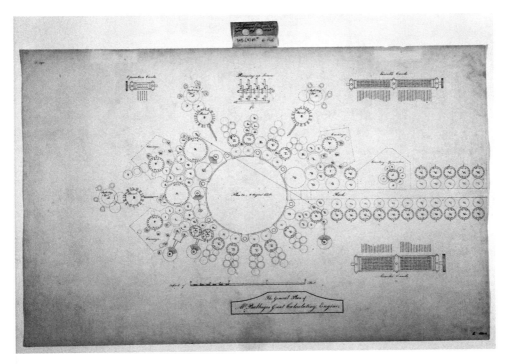

Figure 3.4
The general plan of Mr. Babbage's Great Calculating Engine,1840. Reproduced with permission
from Science Museum Archive/Science and Society
Picture Library: SSPL Image 10303657.

subjects to which we may apply its reasonings and processes."[40] Because of her writings
on Babbage's machine, Lovelace is acknowledged to be the first computer programmer,
the first software designer *avant la lettre*, and indeed, key issues she identified in 1843
concerning the rendering and execution of operations are still concerns of computer
science today.

Functions versus Operations

The language of labor, the language of physics, described previously, is a language of
functions. In contrast, this second language is a work language of operations, the language of the arts. In other words, the latter is a work language of operations and not of
mathematical functions. To underline Lovelace's point, computing is not mathematics.

What is the difference between a function and an operation? One can see, in the *Oxford English Dictionary (OED)* that prior to Leibniz, the term "function" was a very general term meaning, for example, "official duties" or "the kind of action proper to a person as belonging to a particular class." These are quite general definitions applicable to all kinds of work.

After Leibniz, however, according to the *OED*, a new, more specialized and specifically mathematical definition is introduced: "A variable quantity regarded in its relation to one or more other variables in terms of which it may be expressed,...This use of the Latin *functio* is due to Leibniz and his associates." Thus, the language of labor quantified in joules (or joules per kelvin) is part and parcel of the eighteenth-century movement in engineering to recast engineering analysis and design into the language of Leibniz's and Newton's calculus.

Looking to the *OED* again for the definition of "operation," we see that it, too, was—and still is—a general term applicable to the description of all kinds of work: definition 1.a. is "The exertion of force or influence; working, activity; a manner of working, the way in which a thing works." "Operation" thus contrasts with mathematical "function."[41] As Antoine Picon emphasizes, "One must observe that although quantification and mathematical calculation could be considered as the quintessence of analysis, the analytical method [of the *Encyclopédie*] could very well remain purely qualitative."[42] In other words, the work language of functions is quantitative; the work language of operations can be purely qualitative.

The Work Language of the *Encyclopédie* Anticipates Computer Programming Languages

> The *Encyclopédie* constantly testifies to a tale of matter, but this is also in a certain way a tale of "mind": for the encyclopedist, the trajectory of matter is the progression of reasoning: the images of the plates have a logical function....Here we find prophetically the very principle of cybernetic assemblages; the image of the machine depicted in the plate is in its own way a "brain"; in it one can see where matter is input and the organization of a "program."[43]

Let us now rush this history forward about a century (this time skipping Turing) to 1947, when Herman Goldstine and John von Neumann published *Planning and Coding for an Electronic Instrument*, a text that we might read today as the first-ever computer programming manual. Goldstine and von Neumann were trying to describe coding—that is, programming—for a readership that was completely unfamiliar with the notion.

They defined programming as the task of translating mathematical formulas into the language of the computer but were not entirely comfortable with the notion that it was a form of translation. They seemed to feel that the rewriting of mathematical formulas into computer language was much more difficult than translating from one language into another. They wrote, "The relation of the coded instruction sequence to the mathematically conceived procedure of (numerical) solution is not a statical one, that of a translation, but highly dynamical: A coded order stands not simply for its present contents at its present location, but more fully for any succession of passages...through it."[44] In other words, here is yet another difference between these operations and mathematical functions: the operations can change their order, their number, or their kind as execution of the program proceeds.

The exposition of Goldstine and von Neumann hinges on their development of the then-newest graphical means of diagramming a machine: the flow diagram.[45] Software is still frequently designed in a graphical notation that bears a strong resemblance to Goldstine and von Neumann's flow diagrams. (See figure 3.5.) As in theirs,

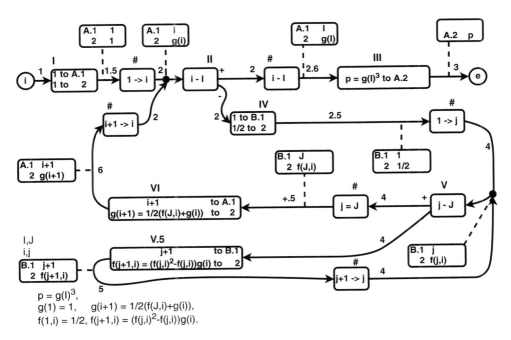

Figure 3.5
This flow chart was modeled on figure 7.2 from Herman Goldstine and John von Neumann, *Planning and Coding for an Electronic Instrument* (1947).

in contemporary flow diagrams, boxes describe operations and arrows denote the sequence in which the operations are to be performed.

There are no people depicted in Babbage's notations, nor are there any in Goldstine and von Neumann's flow diagrams. When we compare them to the *Encyclopédie*'s engravings, this lack of people is striking.[46] Flow diagrams are a picture of work without workers. This picture is at the vanishing point of automation, where all workers have been ejected from the workshop and replaced by machines.

Something of the work language of operations was lost as it was translated through the centuries from Perronet, to Smith, to Prony, to Babbage, and then to von Neumann and Goldstine. What was lost in the language was the facility to include people; or, more specifically, what was lost in translation was an articulation of the interactions between people and between people and machines. As we will see in chapter 4, on algorithms, the loss of people was not by accident but rather by design. Babbage and then later von Neumann and others were especially keen to get people out of the loop.

Recall Antoine Picon's discussion of the three main terms of the work language of the *Encyclopédie*: gestures, operations, and processes. When one looks for the materialization of these three terms in contemporary computing, operations and processes are easy to see, because they constitute central terms or constructions in most modern computer programming languages. To see gestures in software, however, takes more effort.

Gesture recognition and gesture-based computing are, nevertheless, foundationally important to today's mobile platforms and game controllers. Microsoft's Kinect provides game designers with tools for automatically recognizing a large repertoire of human gestures and movements using techniques from machine vision.[47] Equally familiar to any regular user of Apple's iPhone or similar products are the embedded computational techniques deployed in the hardware of touchscreens and accelerometers; with handheld devices, we the users swipe, tap, tilt, and shake the mobile phone or tablet computer.[48] So, in some sense, gestures are a central construct for today's interface and user-experience designers.

But there is an apposite site in which gestures can be seen in contemporary computing: the site of the division of work. People began to disappear from the workshops of artisans and designers and then from factories and offices because their jobs had become automated. Automating a job entails breaking it down into component parts, dividing mental operations and physical gestures into tiny movements until they are so small or trivial that they can be performed by a machine. But this act of breaking down entails more than the phrase "division of work" communicates.

Division is, of course, an operation of arithmetic, but dividing work or labor is much more complicated than just plain arithmetic. It is not so much a question of finding a division of work as it is a matter of finding a grammar of work,[49] a grammar that includes complexities like doing operations again and again (iteratively or recursively); of chaining together sequences of operations—processes—and nesting them into powerful "black boxes" that have simple inputs and outputs even if they hide very complicated machines inside them; and of articulating together, in network topologies, these black boxes so that they mimic the relationships between workers we glimpsed in the workshop illustrated in the *Encyclopédie*.[50]

Decomposing operations into complex assemblages of smaller operations requires more than division; it requires a grammar. Compare division to an ax, and compare grammar to a whole toolkit. An ax is a fine tool for splitting wood, but a carpenter needs a large array of tools to both cut and join wood in many diverse assemblages. For these reasons and others, I will follow a number of other theorists, especially Bernard Stiegler, and refer to grammars of work and efforts to distribute work into complex, recomposable, and reconfigurable units as efforts of "grammatization." Grammar and grammatization will be more fully explored in chapter 7.

4   Algorithm

The digital rewriting of the world has resulted in the translation of existing ideas, institutions, operations, and processes into algorithms, but what is an algorithm?

The story of algorithms is entangled with the history of arithmetic. Before the early modern period, shopkeepers did arithmetic with an abacus. At the birth of merchant capitalism, the arithmetic of shopkeepers became a matter of algorithms rather than of the abacus. The shopkeeper's algorithms were operations of pen applied to paper to perform calculations using the then-new system of Hindu, decimal, fixed-point arithmetic.

Centuries later, arithmetic became even more important to the rise of industrial capitalism. In this period, two changes to arithmetic were seminal. First, the recasting of work in a format that allowed it to be measured and estimated in quantitative terms was essential to spelling out how labor and capital could be connected through money. How much would it cost to have a given piece of work done? Would it be worth the cost for the capitalist to invest in expensive machinery to replace human laborers? Second was not just an industrial but also an intellectual shift that put extended forms of arithmetic at the center of many previously distinct disciplines of knowledge.

In the history of mathematics and logic, this shift is referred to as "arithmetization," a research program in the foundations of mathematics. Can all of mathematics be translated into a form of arithmetic, into essentially a set of algorithms? The rising industrial and intellectual importance of arithmetical calculation led Charles Babbage to wonder if it could be done by machine and thus more quickly and with fewer errors than if done by hand.

Paradoxically, the push to automate people out of the picture cemented an image from the history of algorithms into their contemporary foundations. Alan Turing and Donald Knuth both based algorithms on an image of a man with paper and pen that could have been taken from a fourteenth-century Venetian reckoning school.

Algorithms of today are, consequently, intrinsically anthropomorphized, based on what their designers imagine people might be able to do with pen and paper. Consequently, for example, even some of the most technical writings seriously consider how machines can "learn," or be "smart" or "intelligent." The newest forms of capitalism—such as financial capitalism—are dependent on cutting-edge algorithms, like those for machine "learning." But, as we will see in this chapter, even machine-learning algorithms are just advanced forms of counting and arithmetic.

As arithmetic has become increasingly important to capitalism (from merchant, to industrial, to financial), more and more activities far beyond the previous boundaries of mathematics—activities such as learning—have been rewritten as essentially algorithms of arithmetic, and central to them is an image of a "typical man" with pen and paper. We must ask, as philosopher Herbert Marcuse once did regarding industrial capitalism, who is this one-dimensional man—so devoid of critical thought and oppositional action—sitting right at the center of contemporary capitalism and its algorithms?

Knuth's Analysis of Algorithms

Algorithms are now familiar to us as step-by-step procedures designed to solve well-defined problems, but historically they were introduced as the operations of pen applied to paper to perform calculations using the then-new system of Hindu, decimal, fixed-point arithmetic. Only much later did "algorithm" come to have a more expansive meaning—beyond simple arithmetic—after the arithmetization of mathematics and the development of theoretical and then electronic computers.

Arguably, the meaning of "algorithm" did not really settle around the composition of software until the 1960s, when Donald Knuth started to publish *The Art of Computer Programming*, his multivolume work on the analysis of algorithms. According to Knuth, there are five important features of algorithms:

(1) Finiteness: An algorithm must always terminate after a finite number of steps.... A procedure which has all the characteristics of an algorithm except that it possibly lacks finiteness may be called a "computational method."

(2) Definiteness: Each step of an algorithm must be precisely defined; the actions to be carried out must be rigorously and unambiguously specified for each case.... [F]ormally defined programming languages or computer languages are designed for specifying algorithms, in which every statement has a very definite meaning.

(3) Input: ... quantities which are given to it initially before the algorithm begins.

(4) Output: ... quantities which have a specified relation to the inputs.

Algorithm   81

(5) Effectiveness:...all of the operations performed in the algorithm must be sufficiently basic that they can in principle be done exactly and in a finite length of
time by a man using pencil and paper.[1]

Note that Knuth's first feature, finiteness, implies that most of what we use computers
for today can be called "computational methods" but not "algorithms." Operating systems, web servers, smartphone apps, Facebook, Google—in general, most systems—are
not algorithms according to Knuth, because they are not designed to stop after a finite
number of operations.

In computer science, algorithms are distinguished from systems. They are considered two different subfields, taught in university programs by different sets of professors. Why? Because they name two different sets of problems.

Algorithms concern the set of difficulties one faces in implementing a particular
process or operation of calculation irrespective of the computing environment (e.g.,
the computer hardware, the specifics of network latency and capacity, the other software built as "layers" below the software defining the algorithm, or the kinds of people
who use the software). But—as we will soon see—implementation-independent algorithms are an impossible idealization.

In contrast, systems address issues of interface, interaction, scale, and infrastructure.
System problems normally come after the algorithm questions have been addressed.
After that, any problem that prevents a piece of software from performing as it should
perform might be a system problem.

I would not mention this basic distinction except that algorithms and systems are
frequently confused in the digital humanities and social science literatures about "algorithms." In a short article on the keyword "algorithm" as used by social scientists,
sociologist Tarleton Gillespie defends how sociologists and journalists employ the word
"algorithm" as a rhetorical synecdoche to refer to many different parts of software
and hardware systems, including "model, target goal, data, training data, application,
[and] hardware."[2] The approach of Gillespie and others is problematic because if we
approach the eclectic concerns of system design as though they could all be addressed
by concentrating on algorithms, we will be repeatedly getting lost in the wrong details.
It is like that aphorism about how if the only tool you have is a hammer, you will treat
everything as if it were a nail. Not everything that is software is an algorithm! Moreover, most non–computer scientists writing about algorithms today seem to want to
address system questions.[3]

Knuth's second feature of algorithms, what he terms "definiteness," has become
orthodoxy in computer science, but it introduces a contradiction into the technical literature. On the one hand, Knuth's analysis of algorithms is supposed to be free of the

contextual details of a given implementation. Yet, in his own description of "definiteness," he tells us that it can be assured if the algorithm can be defined (i.e., coded) in a programming language, and in his multivolume work, Knuth uses a specific programming language of his own design, MIXAL, to define algorithms.[4] He chose not to use an existing language for fear that the books would have to be reedited every time the programming language changed. Nevertheless, indicative of the changing context of computing, years later Knuth felt compelled to "update" his invented language (from MIXAL to MMIXAL) to better match contemporary computers.[5] Ironically, despite his dependence on a very specific programming language to state algorithms, Knuth disavowed this approach in a journal article he published just prior to the publication of *The Art of Computer Programming* itself. In short, his articulation is tantamount to saying that algorithms are computer programs. However, elsewhere Knuth explicitly states that algorithms are not computer programs but rather something more abstract and completely independent of programming languages.[6]

Knuth's fifth criterion damns the definition of "algorithm" to the same slippery slope of semiosis suffered by any and all nontechnical language. Knuth defines algorithms as effective methods, but, in the theory of computing, there is a strong tradition of doing the logical converse—defining effective methods as precisely those methods that have algorithms for their solution. We see this in, for example, Alonzo Church's writings: "For every function of positive integers which is effectively calculable in the sense just defined, there exists an algorithm for the calculation of its values."[7] Knuth's statement therefore completes a circle: algorithms are computational methods that are effective and—via Church—effective methods are those that have algorithms.[8]

Finally, note that in his definition of effectiveness, Knuth states that "the operations performed in the algorithm must be sufficiently basic that they can in principle be done … by a man using pencil and paper." The motivation for this is perfectly clear: Knuth means to exclude impossible steps from algorithms; for example, first invent a perpetual motion machine and then fly through the air like Superman. Such a list of steps, even if they are clear, are impossible and thus do not constitute the steps of an algorithm.

However, only by consulting the history of computing can we understand specifically what Knuth means by operations done "by a man using pencil and paper." He does not mean a man like Rembrandt or Shakespeare. Rather, he means some "typical" man. Specifically, he implicitly connotes the men and women who worked as computers for centuries before the invention of computing machinery: the men—but usually women—who worked in teams to produce laborious arithmetical calculations. As discussed in chapter 2, these people who performed the job of computer were referenced

Algorithm   83

by Turing in his 1936 paper.[9] In fact, it should be noted that Knuth's employment of "effectiveness" propels him into the same contradictions discussed in chapter 2 concerning the writings of Church, Turing, Gandy, and other theorists of computation. By tying the definition of "algorithm" to what a man can do with pencil and paper, Knuth puts the technical literature of algorithms on a very vague and imprecise foundation. Any well-trained humanities scholar would want more precision on this point. What does Knuth mean by "a man"? Which man? Or does he mean woman? Working under what conditions? In which historical period? With what kind of educational background?

One can understand the ambiguities inherent in Knuth's definition of "algorithm" by seeing that he has provided a contemporary translation for a term that has had a very circumscribed and historically contingent etymology. Knuth's definition of algorithm is self-contradictory insofar as he holds both that it is dependent on coding in computer programming languages and is entirely independent of the same. His definition is circular insofar as algorithms are defined in terms of effective methods, which are defined in terms of algorithms. His definition is highly restricted insofar as algorithms are supposed to be finite—terminate after a finite number of steps—yet most of what we use computers for today involves systems that are designed to run endlessly, to never terminate, and therefore are not algorithms according to Knuth. Finally, Knuth's definition of "algorithm" smuggles in a highly circumscribed and yet ambiguous form of human subjectivity when he ties it to what an undefined man can do with a pencil and paper.

Despite his frequent use of historical examples, Knuth's definition is ahistorical. Knuth begins his book with a discussion of "Euclid's algorithm," an iterative method for finding the greatest common divisor of two numbers. It appears in Euclid's *Elements*, Book VII, propositions 1 and 2. The ancient Greek mathematician Euclid lived in the mid-fourth century BCE, but the algorithm attributed to him can be easily written in one line of a contemporary programming language like JavaScript:

```
function gcd(m,n) {if (n==0) return(m); else return(gcd(n,m%n));}
```

Euclid's method has been called an "algorithm" for a long time and was so called well before Knuth started writing his books. However, when Euclid devised this method, it certainly was not called an algorithm, because the word "algorithm" did not exist in ancient Greek.[10]

algorithm, *n.*

Origin: A borrowing from Latin. Etymon: Latin *algorithmus*.

Etymology: post-classical Latin *algorithmus* (15th cent.), alteration of *algorismus*[11]

According to the *Oxford English Dictionary*, the closest term in ancient Greek was "ἀριθμός," which meant number. The ancient Greeks also had words for rational approximation and reckoning, but "algorithm" stems from postclassical Latin. Consequently, it is anachronistic to call Euclid's method an algorithm. The only way we can call it that is to forget all of the works of transcription and translation that eventually rendered propositions 1 and 2 of Book VII of Euclid's text into a form that can be compared to what we now call algorithms and to what can be written out so simply in one line of code.

Analogously, we may call eighteenth-century horse-drawn carriages "early automobiles," but to do so we need to acknowledge the historical and technological contexts that make possible this highly idiosyncratic interpretation of eighteenth-century vehicles. But perhaps most importantly, by calling an old technique or technology by a new name, we need to admit that we do so at the risk of exporting to it a teleology and a set of values and intentions from our own time.

I propose that we examine how older methods can be or have been translated into algorithms and, furthermore, how the very definition of "algorithm" has changed over time. This proposal is intended to be in contrast with Knuth's flawed—but nevertheless influential—definition and anachronistic application of the term "algorithm." Knuth's axiomatization of "algorithm" elides the messiness of history, context, and interpretation.

Knuth's efforts are aimed at trying to make algorithms into a kind of mathematics or logic. But, a priori, algorithms are not mathematics, so, unsurprisingly, the analysis of algorithms is a very difficult discipline.

Algorithms as Recipes

So, if algorithms are not mathematics or logic, then what are they? Algorithms are part and parcel with what historian of science Pamela Long describes as the long history of writings from and about the mechanical arts, including "ancient writings related to technical production, such as Hellenistic engineering books, as well as writings tied to political and military praxis, including Xenophon's *Oeconomicus* and Roman agricultural writings."[12] This tradition includes medieval guild regulations and continues on into today's language of patent law and how-to books, and, crucially, this tradition of the mechanical arts also includes recipes and cookbooks.

Knuth recognizes this direct connection to the arts but does not pursue it with any rigor. In chapter 1 of the first volume of *The Art of Computer Programming*, Knuth compares algorithms to recipes, asserts that "a computer programmer can learn much by

Algorithm   85

studying a good recipe book," and then admits that "the author has barely resisted the temptation to name the present volume 'The Programmer's Cookbook.' Perhaps someday he will attempt a book called 'Algorithms for the Kitchen.'"[13]

Knuth is hardly alone in comparing algorithms to recipes. The practice continues to be idiomatic. Princeton computer science professor and specialist in the analysis of algorithms Bernard Chazelle wrote the following in his 2006 essay "The Algorithm: Idiom of Modern Science": "Algorithms are often compared to recipes. As clichés go, a little shopworn perhaps, but remember: no metaphor that appeals to one's stomach can be truly bad. Furthermore, the literary analogy is spot-on. Algorithms are—and should be understood as—works of literature."[14]

This tussle between mathematics and the mechanical arts, between Knuth's ventured axioms of algorithms and cookbooks of recipes, is emblematic of almost every controversy I recount in this book. Frequently, as is the case here with the respective writings of Knuth and Chazelle, the two sides of the controversy are authored by the same famous computer scientists. In a noetic register, they try to subsume software under mathematical logic. In a poetic register, they pull it back into the kitchen, the workshop, or the studio of the mechanical arts. However, as can be seen in the quotations here, when a computer scientist calls computing an art, it is usually done in jest, or at least is done flippantly and without any rigor. But what would happen if we took these flippant quips seriously? What is software if it is indeed an art?

In chapter 3, on language, I pursued this question by starting with an examination of the craft "recipes" of eighteenth-century France, but let us revisit this insight, keeping in mind Knuth's features of algorithms.

First, consider the condition of definiteness. Let us say you visit a restaurant for the first time and have a love-at-first-bite experience with the signature dish of the chef. You are in London at Le Gavroche, the chef is Michel Roux, and the signature dish is his Soufflé Suissesse. You ask your waiter if it would be possible to compliment the chef in person. M. Roux has a spare minute in the kitchen, so you are lucky enough to get to talk with him. After thanking him profusely, you boldly ask him for the recipe. To your surprise, M. Roux says, "There is no secret to this dish! It is simply a cheese soufflé baked on double cream. You can find the full recipe in *Le Gavroche Cookbook*, which I published in 2001."

You hurry home, download the cookbook, and immediately set to work. You are very excited. You have all the ingredients. You have the step-by-step instructions. Everything is going fine until you try this step: "Whisk the egg whites with a pinch of salt until they form firm, not stiff, peaks." You ask yourself, "What's the difference between firm and stiff peaks, and how do I do the whisking to get them one way and not the other?" The problem is that the devil is in the details. The recipe (or algorithm) seems to contain all you need to know, but—no matter how detailed it is—there is always some crucial detail missing. In other words, definiteness is not a feature but rather an impossible ideal for algorithms.

The condition of effectiveness is an exacerbated version of the problem of definiteness. What is possible for a "typical" man to do exactly and in a finite length of time with simple tools (paper and pencil, whisk and bowl, etc.)? Let us imagine a future in which Le Gavroche has closed and M. Roux's cookbook is out of print. You are trying to recreate the Soufflé Suissesse a century from now. Kitchen technology has changed radically, and ingredients common to the early twenty-first century are now rare. Perhaps the humble whisk is extinct and the practices of industrial chicken farming came to be considered too cruel to continue, or some future variant of avian influenza decimated the bird population so a single egg now costs roughly half one's annual salary. The devil is in the details but also in the context. "Effectiveness" of one historical moment with one demographic is not necessarily the same condition for a different set of people at a different moment in time.

Analogous problems have been addressed by computer scientists. In algorithms as in recipes, not every detail is spelled out. Only the crucial details are included, and those details are predicated on the assumption of an existing context of almost-ubiquitous hardware and software: programming languages, operating systems, and network protocols.

Recipes and algorithms are equally imprecise and context dependent. To take the analogy seriously is to admit that the theories and methods of the cultural or intellectual historian—as they might be applied to a study of food and recipes[15]—are applicable to the study of algorithms.

Histories of Arithmetics

The history of the algorithm is entangled with the history of arithmetic. In its earliest form, the algorithm was just a form of arithmetic. However, by saying this, I do not mean to imply that this is a simple history. "Arithmetization," a reexamination of arithmetic, is at the foundation of contemporary mathematics and computation and was a forerunner of what is discussed today under the rubric of "digital convergence." Arithmetization was both a search for the logical foundations of number and arithmetic and conversely the search for the arithmetical foundations of logic. We can understand this circular search as what historian Hayden White called an "emplotment."[16]

Algorithm   87

Arithmetic, calculation—computation in general—is not just one kind of work but many. That there are multiple kinds of arithmetic has been discussed in philosophy for thousands of years. Plato describes at least two.[17] The first is arithmetic for military leaders:

Socrates: Can we deny that a warrior should have a knowledge of arithmetic?

Glaucon: Certainly he should, if he is to have the smallest understanding of military tactics, or indeed, I should rather say, if he is to be a man at all.

According to Plato, without knowing arithmetic, one cannot become a leader; moreover, a boy cannot even become a man.[18] But there is a twist, as revealed in the subsequent dialogue between Socrates and Glaucon. Apparently, the calculations of warriors and philosophers are not to be confused with the arithmetic of the shopkeeper.[19]

Socrates: I must add how charming the science is! And in how many ways it conduces to our desired end, if pursued in the spirit of a philosopher, and not of a shopkeeper!

Glaucon: How do you mean?

Socrates: I mean, as I was saying, that arithmetic has a very great and elevating effect, compelling the soul to reason about abstract number, and rebelling against the introduction of visible or tangible objects into the argument.

How are we to understand this? That is, how are we to understand Plato's notion that arithmetic done as a philosopher or military tactician is an entirely different pursuit than arithmetic done as a shopkeeper?[20]

Chapter 4 of volume 2 of Donald Knuth's *The Art of Computer Programming* is devoted to arithmetic. Knuth begins with a short history of arithmetic, and it is here, in his history, that one can find a forerunner to Plato's distinction between the arithmetic of shopkeepers and that of philosophers. According to Knuth, cuneiform tablets show that by 1750 BCE, the Babylonians had two distinct systems of number representation.[21] One system was used by, among others, shopkeepers involved in everyday business transactions where large numbers were seldom required. The second system was a positional notation developed for and by mathematicians that was especially convenient for multiplication and division. Greek astronomers (and, presumably, other sorts of natural philosophers) employed the latter system of the Babylonian mathematicians. Greek shopkeepers, in contrast, employed an early form of the abacus using sand and pebbles on a slab for their day-to-day business.

The word "abacus" is derived from the Greek word "abax," meaning "slab," and the Hebrew word for dust, "abhaq."[22] So, in ancient Greece, calculating as a philosopher would have entailed an entirely different set of activities than doing arithmetic as a shopkeeper, who, with an abacus, would have thus used "visible or tangible objects"—as Plato noted with distaste.[23]

For Plato, then, there is a distinction between one kind of arithmetic and another, depending on who is doing it, how, and with what. Thus, depending on the institution that contextualizes it, arithmetic is either "high-level" work of the kind performed by philosophers or "low-level" work of the sort performed by shopkeepers. This distinction between the high-level and low-level forms of calculation persisted for over a thousand years. In fifteenth-century Europe, one could learn the former at a university and the latter at a special school run by a master of commercial arithmetic.[24] Within the community of merchants in fifteenth-century Venice, there emerged a rivalry between the masters of arithmetic who used the abacus and those who employed the new algorithms of arithmetic, which allowed calculations to be performed with pen and paper (see figure 4.1).

The algorithms had arrived in Europe with the translation of texts of Muslim scholarship about the Hindu system of numbers. Among these texts was the arithmetic primer on decimal numbers and their computational schemes written by the Persian scholar Muḥammad ibn Mūsā al-Khwārizmī (780–850 CE), whose last name constitutes the etymological origin of the word "algorithm." Al-Khwārizmī's book on arithmetic was collected in Spain and translated into Latin by an Englishman, Robert of Chester, who gave it the title *Algoritmi de numero indorum*[25] (meaning "Algoritmi on the numbers of the Indians," where "Algoritmi" is the name "al-Khwārizmī" as translated by Chester).

The then-new Hindu representation of numbers was what we know today as the ubiquitous everyday decimal system. Recall that the previous representation was the Roman system: I, II, III, IV, V, VI, VII, VIII, IX, X, etc.[26] Adoption of the decimal system made arithmetic simpler and less error-prone. Consider, for instance, multiplying a number by ten in the Roman system; for example, IV times X equals XL. Doing the same in decimal, fixed-point positional notation is trivial in comparison: $4 \times 10 = 40$. In the decimal system, all that needs to be done is to put a zero to the right of the integer to be multiplied by ten. In contrast, in the Roman system, all operations of arithmetic entail grouping, arranging, and then rewriting.

At the birth of mercantile capitalism, the arithmetic of shopkeepers became a matter of algorithms rather than the abacus, and thus, ultimately, the advantages of the algorithms of the decimal system overtook the perceived powers of the abacus. Young men from throughout Europe came to Venice to learn the new algorithms essential to capitalism. As these algorithms became ever more popular, reckoning schools were established in many cities beyond Venice. In 1338, Florence had six such schools; by 1613, the city of Nuremberg had forty-eight.[27]

Algorithm 89

Figure 4.1
Illustration from Gregor Reisch's textbook *Margarita Philosophica*, 1508.

Well into the nineteenth century, what was considered essential to the definition of "algorithm" was the employment of the decimal representation of numbers. This is documented in the *Oxford English Dictionary*, where the first definition under the entry for "algorithm" is "the Arabic system of numbering, characterized by a zero." The second definition is "Mathematics and Computing. A procedure or set of rules used in calculation and problem-solving; ... a precisely defined set of mathematical or logical operations for the performance of a particular task." Examples of the second definition are found beginning in texts of the nineteenth century.[28]

From a historical point of view, it should be clear that arithmetic changed from Plato's time, to fifteenth-century Venice, to the nineteenth century, and then again to the twentieth century, with the development of hardware and software for arithmetical operations. Furthermore, even at any given historical moment, we can find two or more different kinds of operations for doing arithmetic.

While arithmetic was essential to mercantile capitalism, it became even more important to the rise of industrial capitalism in the nineteenth century. In this period, two changes to arithmetic were seminal. First, the recasting of work and labor in a format that allowed it to be measured and estimated in quantitative terms was essential to spelling out how labor and capital could be connected through money. How much would it cost to have a given piece of work done? Would it be worth the cost for the capitalist to invest in expensive machinery to replace human laborers? This recasting of labor into a quantitative form, a form that boils it down to just one number, is the work/labor language of construction, steam engines, and information technologies described in chapter 3.

Second was not just an industrial but also an epistemological shift that put extended forms of arithmetic at the center of many previously distinct disciplines of knowledge. In the history of mathematics and logic, this shift is referred to as "arithmetization," a research program in the foundations of mathematics.[29] "Arithmetization" largely shaped many important developments of twentieth-century mathematics and logic, including Turing's 1936 paper.

Arithmetization

What does it mean for a discipline of knowledge to undergo "arithmetization"? The result of such a translation is twofold: arithmetic is enlarged; and a topic previously unrelated to mathematics is brought under the aegis of mathematics.

Mathematician George Boole's work on turning logic into arithmetic provides a good illustration of how a discipline can be rewritten—translated—into arithmetic. In his 1854 work *An Investigation of the Laws of Thought on Which Are Founded the Mathematical*

Algorithm   91

Theories of Logic and Probabilities, Boole proposes a means to write logical expressions in a form of arithmetic or algebra.[30] Boolean logic operates on the assumption that the value of every expression is either zero (i.e., "false") or one (i.e., "true"). Expressions of Boolean logic can include variables (e.g., a, b, c), the sign of identity (=; i.e., equality), and translations of three of the arithmetic operators (+: addition; –: subtraction; and ×: multiplication).

According to Boole, if a denotes "all things white" and b denotes "all sheep," a multiplied by b denotes "all white sheep" and can be written as ab or ba, since $ab=ba$. If a represents "men" and b represents "women," then $a+b$ can be understood to mean "men and women" or "men or women." If c stands for "European," then $c(a+b)=ca+cb$. In other words, the distributive law of multiplication is translated for logic so that stating "European men and women" is the same thing as saying "European men and European women." Analogously, the expression $a-c$ can be read as "all men who are not European." Boole states: "'The class of things not in a' can be written $(1-a)$. If, again, a denotes 'men,' then the equation $a(1-a)$ will represent the class whose members are at once 'men,' and 'not men,' and…thus express the principle, that a class whose members are at the same time men and not men does not exist. In other words, that it is impossible for the same individual to be at the same time a man and not a man."

Boole continues,

Now let the meaning of the symbol a be extended from the representing of "men," to that of any class of beings characterized by the possession of any quality whatever; and the equation $a(1-a)=0$ will then express that it is impossible for a being to possess a quality and not to possess that quality at the same time. But this is identically that "principle of contradiction" which Aristotle has described as the fundamental axiom of all philosophy. "It is impossible that the same quality should both belong and not belong to the same thing.…This is the most certain of all principles.…Wherefore they who demonstrate refer to this as an ultimate opinion. For it is by nature the source of all the other axioms" (*Metaphysica*, III, 3).[31]

Aristotle's "principle of contradiction" is conventionally the second of his three "laws of thought." The others are the first law, the law of identity: everything is the same as itself $a=a$; and the third law, the law of excluded middle: everything either has a given quality or the negation of that quality, stated in Boole's notation as $a+(1-a)=1$. Note further that Boole's algebraic notation allows one to rewrite a conditional statement— "if a then b"—as a polynomial: $a(1-b)=0$.

Long before Boole, Leibniz had translated certain logical statements into an algebra, including $a=a$; *if a is b and b is c, then a is c*; $a=$ *not not a*; and *a is b=not a is not b*. But Boole completed Leibniz's logic by translating the whole of Aristotelian logic into arithmetical polynomials (i.e., formulas with variables combined with the operators of arithmetic: +, –, ×, and =). Boole's polynomials evaluate to either 1 or 0.[32]

If we accept Boole's translation of logic into arithmetic, we can see how this has enlarged the very definition of arithmetic. Before Boole, it was perfectly clear that by performing the operations of arithmetic, one was calculating; one was said to be, for instance, adding or multiplying numbers. After Boole, in performing exactly the same sorts of calculations, one might alternatively be said to be making logical inferences. Similarly, we can see how Boole's translation displaces logic into mathematics, since logic is thereby seen to be a form of arithmetic and thus, by definition, a concern of mathematics and not a concern akin to the language arts of rhetoric and grammar. After Boole, using the language art of logic is seen to be one and the same thing as calculating, a double surprise. We know that someone is calculating because they are using a certain form of language! We know that someone is using this language because they are calculating!

Wittgenstein on the Foundations of Mathematics

Boole's work on logic and arithmetic was central to a research program on the foundations of mathematics that extended from the nineteenth century well into the twentieth. Characteristic of this work was the increasing influence of arithmetic in the definition of logic and mathematics. As arithmetic became regnant, it became difficult to understand what was not calculation. Is all thought and action just arithmetic?

In 1939, during the Lent and Easter terms at Cambridge University, philosopher Ludwig Wittgenstein discussed these questions in his course on the foundations of mathematics. Although Wittgenstein lectured without a written text, his students took thorough notes that were later collated and edited together to form a record of Wittgenstein's statements and the seminar discussion. Apparently, there were thirteen or fourteen regular attendees, including Alan Turing, who had recently returned to Cambridge after his doctoral work at Princeton.

According to his students' notes, Wittgenstein posed the following question in his lecture: "But—and this is an important point—how do we know that a phenomenon which we observe when we are observing human beings is what we ought to call a language? Or what we should call calculating?"[33]

At first, Wittgenstein's question seems very strange. How complicated can it be to recognize whether someone is calculating? Wittgenstein pursues this unlikely difficulty with another set of questions. What do we observe when we see someone calculating? "If I see someone with a piece of paper making marks in a certain sort of way, I may say, 'He is calculating.'"[34] But can we be certain that someone is calculating just by watching that person make marks on paper? Later, Wittgenstein says, "If you do this, we wouldn't call it calculating. Is $4+5 = \{\}$—where you write down anything which

Algorithm   93

comes into your head for {}—an arithmetical operation? Call it what you like. It misses out some of the most essential points of a calculus."[35]

Elsewhere in the lecture notes, Turing is recorded as commenting that one might compare calculation and experimentation. Wittgenstein uses this comparison to open a discussion: "Let us go back to Turing's comparison of an experiment in physics with a mathematical calculation. Suppose that one invents one's arithmetic in such a way that $2+2=4$ is proved by putting two bits and then two more bits in one scale pan and four bits in the other and seeing that neither pan goes down. In what circumstances should we call this an experiment and in what circumstances should we call this a calculation?"[36] This is an entirely different image of calculation. We can imagine calculation as making specific marks on paper or as taking place with the help of physical bits (i.e., weights) and a scale. What counts as calculation? What does not?

In Wittgenstein's lectures on the foundations of mathematics, he frequently turns to Turing to pose a question or to produce an example. With respect to these discussions on the nature of calculation, this is hardly surprising since we can understand Turing's 1936 article (discussed in chapter 2) as defining the essentials of calculation.

Part of Turing's achievement was to formulate what is taken to be a general description of calculation or computation based on an analogy to arithmetic.[37] Nevertheless, Wittgenstein posed these questions about calculation after the publication of Turing's paper and, in fact, was posing these questions not just to anyone but to Turing himself. Why? What still needed to be cleared up after Turing's definitive answer?

When Computers Were Human

To understand the instability of the image of calculation, we will return to Wittgenstein's observation (discussed in chapter 2) that Turing's "machines" were people, humans doing arithmetic with pencil and gridded paper.

Because arithmetic became so important to so many areas of thought and work, its ubiquity engendered a new form of work that was denigrated as labor. As noted in chapter 2, this new form of labor was already apparent to Leibniz in the seventeenth century. He wrote that "it is unworthy of excellent men to lose hours like slaves in the labor of calculation which could safely be relegated to anyone else if the machine were used." This new form of labor was what Leibniz called the labor of calculation. As the algorithms of arithmetic spread through business, science, engineering, and government, the job of human computer was invented to execute these now numerous calculations.

Probably the best history of calculation as human labor is David Grier's book *When Computers Were Human*. Grier starts his history with the return of Halley's comet in 1758. Isaac Newton's "followers have, from his principles, ventured even to predict the returns of several [comets]," wrote Scottish philosopher Adam Smith (1723–1790), "particularly of one which is to make its appearance in 1758."[38] Unfortunately, Newton's calculus had no straightforward way of stating or solving a three-body problem. In this case, the three bodies thought to have the most influence on the comet's trajectory were the sun, Jupiter, and Saturn. To predict the date of the return of Halley's comet, the astronomers were reduced to slicing the data from observations of the movement into small steps, at each step analyzing the influence of the three bodies on the movement of the comet, and then integrating all of these step-by-step analyses together. As one astronomer of the time put it, "What immense labor, what geometrical knowledge did not this task require?"[39]

Actually, the labor was not geometrical but arithmetical; it entailed an immense number of calculations. French mathematician Alexis-Claude Clairaut decided to undertake the task by enlisting two astronomer friends to do the calculations with him: Nicole-Reine Étable de la Brière Lepaute (notably a woman, since few women were astronomers at the time) and Joseph-Jérôme Le Français de Lalande. According to Grier, "The three friends began their computations of Halley's comet in June 1757. They worked at a common table in the Palais Luxembourg using goose-quill pens and heavy linen paper. Lalande and Lepaute worked at one side of the table and handed their results to Clairaut."[40]

They worked on these calculations together until late September, and in early November they reported to the Academie des Sciences their estimate that Halley's comet would return sometime between mid-March and mid-April of 1758. The comet reached its perihelion on March 13.

The calculation was an enormous effort. Joseph Lalande later wrote that "as a result of this hard work, I acquired an illness which, for the rest of my life, shall be with me."

Despite the essential success of these laborious calculations, the mathematician and co-editor of the *Encyclopédie*, Jean Le Rond d'Alembert, denounced what he saw as an emerging "spirit of calculation" and computation specifically as more "laborious than deep."[41] This set in motion an acrimonious debate between d'Alembert and Clairaut. On the one hand, this debate was to be expected, since clearly—in the terms discussed in chapter 3—the arithmetical calculations done by Clairaut and his two colleagues were labor, the kind of "low-level" work that Leibniz complained only slaves should be assigned. But it was perhaps surprising that the one taking this stand and thereby attacking Clairaut was d'Alembert.

Recall that d'Alembert's co-editor of the *Encyclopédie* was Diderot: Diderot, the son of an artisan and the analyst, expositor, and champion of the principles of the division of labor in the productions of the workshops of France! For these calculations,

Algorithm   95

Clairaut's accomplishment was, among other things, the application of the division of labor to a new task, the task of astronomical calculations. In this accomplishment are the origins of computation and especially the invention of the human job of computer: the job—the work—that Turing eventually formalized in his 1936 paper.[42]

With this eighteenth-century invention of the human computer, there also came a realization of the nitty-gritty of the job. The job was not only one of executing a myriad of arithmetical operations but also one of detecting and correcting errors. Each calculation done to simulate the orbit of Halley's comet was dependent on all of the previous calculations. Consequently, especially in the early stages of the calculation, any error made could invalidate the whole enterprise.

A disdain for the labor of arithmetical calculation, along with an acknowledgment of the precariousness of the results because of the possible or probable introduction of human error, persisted throughout the following two hundred years, in which human computers were the primary means of performing large-scale computations. These two considerations of intensive labor and likelihood of error, coupled with a third, the increasing importance, in industry and science, of calculations in the dawning age of industrial capitalism, formed the troika that pressed Charles Babbage to invent a machine to replace the labor of the human computers.

When Computers Became Machines

In their excellent introduction to an edited collection of Babbage's writings, Philip and Emily Morrison write that Babbage's thinking about a machine for calculation was sparked when he was an undergraduate at Cambridge, when he and his friend John Herschel set about checking some calculations done by human computers for the Astronomical Society. Babbage is said to have exclaimed in the tedium of the moment, "I wish to God these calculations had been executed by steam." Herschel replied by hypothesizing that it would be possible to have a machine to do the calculations.[43]

Many years later, Babbage, in a letter to Sir Humphrey Davy, president of the Royal Society, wrote: "The intolerable labor and fatiguing monotony of a continued repetition of similar arithmetical calculations, first excited the desire, and afterwards suggested the idea, of a machine, which, by the aid of gravity or any other moving power, should become a substitute for one of the lowest operations of human intellect."[44] Notice the deep disdain even Babbage held for this kind of labor.

Babbage articulated the purpose of his machines as a means to economize. As communicated to and then reported by General Luigi Federico Menabrea (later prime minister of Italy), Babbage was concerned with three economies: (1) an *economy of accuracy*, to be achieved by eliminating human error through the creation of a fully automatic machine of calculation; (2) an *economy of time*, to be achieved because the machine could perform arithmetic much more quickly than human computers; and (3) an *economy of intelligence*, essentially a reiteration of Leibniz's concern that the intellectual labor of excellent men be spared from calculation so that they might be engaged in higher forms of thinking.[45]

Clearly, these three economies would demand that humans be moved "above" or "outside" of the labor of calculation because humans are considered too error-prone, too slow, and too precious for the work. These three economies motivated Babbage and others to orchestrate people out of the picture, as discussed at the end of chapter 3. These three economies are what motivated the disappearance of people from computation.

By the nineteenth century, the arithmetization of important areas of research, such as logic and astronomy, made the problems of arithmetical calculation central to many areas of teaching and research. The need for large-scale calculations also made arithmetic central to government (e.g., the national census), the military (e.g., for the purposes of ballistics), business (e.g., actuarial tables for life insurance), and industry—in many forms of engineering (e.g., construction, mechanics, and the thermodynamics of steam engines).

Given this historical context, Babbage's efforts to make calculations "by steam" are understandable, and we can also better understand Wittgenstein's comments on the changing nature of calculation. Wittgenstein asks us to consider what calculation looks like. Before the introduction of algorithms, calculation looked like a human moving beads on an abacus. Before the introduction of calculating machines, calculation looked like the performance, by a human, of certain algorithms with the aid of pen and paper. Despite these many transformations of the activity of calculation, all of them involved a human. But with Babbage's aim of eliminating human error, we are essentially being asked to imagine calculation without a human. We are asked to imagine that "calculating" looks like a running machine with no one in sight.

Error versus Instrumentality

Babbage's conceived machines, and all computing machines that followed, of course, still required a person to set them up, start them, and, when they stop, read the calculated results. Human error, then—even in Babbage's conceptualization—is still possible at several sites: in the design of the machine, in the maintenance and setup of the machine (e.g., keying in data or the operations to be performed), and even in recording the calculated results. At best, with the automation of calculation, human error cannot

Algorithm   97

be eliminated but rather only displaced or translated to another site or into another form.

As historian Michael Mahoney has illustrated, while it took years for this problem to be recognized, it remains even today and was one of the motivations for the creation of that discipline now known as software engineering: How can time and human error be managed and minimized?[46] Discussing Mahoney's historical work and her own readings of the foundational documents of software engineering (from the seminal 1968 conference held in Garmisch, Germany), philosopher Federica Frabetti concludes that the automation of algorithms—their materialization as software—was not widely recognized as a possible site of error until almost a century after Babbage's work: "With the Garmisch conference, software began to be conceptualized as a problem—and the 'software crisis' was constituted as a point of origin for the discipline of software engineering."[47]

In her reading of software, Frabetti draws from Bernard Stiegler's rereading of Jacques Derrida's writings on opacity and technology.[48] Key to this approach is an understanding that algorithms exceed the instrumental. When we assume that software or other forms of automated calculation are just instruments or tools, we forget that machines can produce unexpected results in the form of errors, "bugs," or calculations that cannot be anticipated in any way other than through step-by-step computation. For example, with Leibniz and Newton's calculus, we cannot anticipate the results of a simulation of a three-body problem, much less a simulation of global climate change. Algorithms have unanticipated implications, unexpected consequences.

Thus, for Frabetti, "To think of technology…we must first and foremost remember that technology cannot be thought from within the conceptual framework of calculability and instrumentality."[49] Frabetti labels her approach "deconstructive." She writes, "A deconstructive reading of software is the opposite of a functional reading. For a computer professional, the point where the system 'undoes itself' is a malfunction, something that needs to be fixed. From the perspective of deconstruction, in turn, it is a point of revelation, one in which the conceptual system underlying the software is clarified."[50] According to both Frabetti and software engineering professionals, if algorithms are just as much problems as they are solutions (what Derrida and Stiegler might call a "pharmakon"—both a medicine and a poison), then we need to understand errors and not just attempt to build machines that avoid them.

Frabetti's deconstructive approach is deeply resonant with other areas of the humanities that consider human error to be intrinsic to the human condition.[51] Thus, for example, Sigmund Freud examines errors of memory, physical action, and speech, "slips of the tongue"—what he calls "parapraxes"—as symptomatic of other simultaneous, parallel forms of cognitive, precognitive, and noncognitive processing. In his book

Jokes and Their Relation to the Unconscious (1905), Freud analyzes a set of humorous slips of the tongue. The first example of the book is this:

> [The German poet and essayist Heinrich] Heine introduces the delightful figure…Hirsch-Hyacinth…who boasts to the poet of his relations with the wealthy Baron Rothschild, and finally says: "And, as true as God shall grant me all good things, Doctor, I sat beside Salomon Rothschild and he treated me quite as his equal—quite *famillionairely*." …The process which has converted the thought into a joke can then be represented in the following manner, which may at first sight seem fantastic, but nevertheless produces precisely the outcome that is really before us: "R. treated me quite *familiär*, that is, so far as a *Millionär* can." Let us now imagine that a compressing force is brought to bear on these sentences and that for some reason the second is the less resistant one. It is thereupon made to disappear, while its most important constituent, the word "*Millionär*," which has succeeded in rebelling against being suppressed, is, as it were, pushed up against the first sentence, and fused with the element of that sentence which is so much like it—"*familiar*."[52]

Freud attributes to a process this "slip," this production of the word "famillionaire." The process he imagines is mechanical or thermodynamic: he describes it as including a "compressing force" on two presupposed (but unspoken) sentences. In this book, what Freud conjured over a century ago is a visualization of a "possibility space" of statements that are moved—translated—from one into, or onto, another according to a set of processes.[53]

Freud's image of human error is one of translation: human productions of speech, gesture, or action can be translated into or condensed together with others. Error, then, is not random but rather is motivated and symptomatic of the interaction between several processes. From this perspective, diagnosing and understanding human error entails the identification of the interacting or interfering processes that produced the error.

Errors as Movements in a Space of Algorithms

The phrase "Freudian slip" communicates well the idea that errors are movements or translations within a larger space of possible actions.[54] Consider again Wittgenstein's comment on what could be taken for an error in arithmetic: "Is $4+5=\{\}$—where you write down anything which comes into your head for {}—an arithmetical operation? Call it what you like. It misses out some of the most essential points of a calculus." As each symbol is written, a choice needs to be made as to what comes next: first "4," then "+," then "5," then "=." Instead of writing "+," we might have chosen to write "−." Instead of "5," we might have chosen "6." Through the point at which "=" is written, this is correct; no human error has been introduced. But now writing, say, "45" ("$4+5=45$") introduces an error. If the whole string of symbols from "4" to "45" is

Algorithm   99

considered a path through a possibility space of a larger set of choices, then a similar path is imaginable—say, one that ends in "9" rather than in "45." Imagining human action as a series of choices in a larger space of possibilities allows us to visualize human error as one or more movements or missteps along a path.

Educational research has demonstrated that this is an insightful imaginary for children's arithmetic errors. Educational technologists and artificial intelligence experts John Seely Brown and Kurt VanLehn pictured arithmetic as a space of rules in which errors are made when a child invents an incorrect rule or employs a correct rule at the wrong moment in the process of doing a sum or a difference. For example, in a multicolumn subtraction process, at certain points in the computation, it is necessary to "borrow" from the column to the left of the current column of numbers. Novices might "borrow" but fail to decrement the number in the column to the left or, to avoid subtracting a larger digit from a smaller one, if the digit in the lower row is the larger one, they might flip the digits in the lower and upper rows and then subtract.

Brown and VanLehn claim "that all bugs of a procedural skill can be derived by a highly constrained form of problem solving acting on incomplete procedures. These procedures are characterized by formal deletion operations that model incomplete learning and forgetting."[55] They propose that we imagine the algorithms of arithmetic as being embedded in a much larger possibility space of algorithms, some correct and others incorrect for a given task. Each algorithm is composed of a set of rules, so "moving" or "translating" from one of these algorithms to another is, in their framing, a matter of deleting or, more generally, editing a rule (or series of rules) in the algorithm. Human error—and also human learning[56]—in arithmetic is, for Brown and VanLehn, the navigation of a large space of rule sets.

That the algorithms of arithmetic are part of a much larger space of algorithms helps us better understand issues of error, learning, and why Wittgenstein seemed to think that calculation was an unstable, shifting target. I want to elaborate on this crucial issue of arithmetic and algorithms by describing more specifically what a "space of algorithms" might look like. While, in principle, it would be possible to do this with the notation for rules that Brown and VanLehn used, I think their notation was unnecessarily complicated. Instead, I propose to write the rules of arithmetic as black and white squares.

Figure 4.2 depicts one possible way of representing the rules of binary addition in black and white squares.[57] Each rule of the algorithm is written with five squares. The top three match a column of the sum in process. The bottom two squares are used to rewrite two squares of the result as it is recorded in the final row. One can think of the first three squares as a pattern that must be matched before the rule is invoked: a precondition. The second two squares are written to the result if the rule is invoked: a postcondition. In other words, each of the rules can be read as *if…then* statements: if the

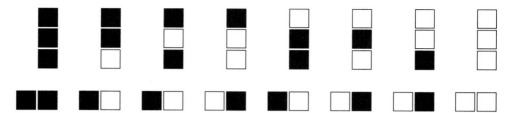

Figure 4.2
Rules of addition for binary numbers.

first three squares match the current column of the addition problem, then rewrite two of the squares of the result as shown. The right-hand square of each rule consequence is used to record one bit of the final result. The left-hand square is used as a "carry bit."

Just as students are asked to learn how to "carry the 1" in decimal arithmetic when the sum of two single digits results in a two-digit number, the left-hand squares of these rules encode when a 1 (i.e., a black square) should be carried into the next column. Thus, in general, if two or more black squares are in one column, one needs to carry a black square into the column to the left (because, in binary addition, remember that $1 + 1 = 10$).

Figure 4.3 shows the binary equivalent of the addition problem $87 + 56 =?$ The first row is the binary equivalent of 87 (i.e., 01010111); the second row codes 56 (i.e., 00111000); and the third row starts empty and will hold the sum after all the matched rules have been applied. The rules are applied first to the rightmost column, then to the column to the left of that, and so on.

So, the first rule that matches has a black square on top and two white squares underneath. It rewrites the column so that the first digit of the sum is written in the last row and the last column of figure 4.4, and after the rules have been applied to all of the columns of the sum, the result appears in the third row of figure 4.5. In decimal form, the whole of figure 4.5 reads like this: $87 + 56 = 143$.[58]

Look again at the rules for addition as shown in figure 4.2. The rules are ordered according to their preconditions; that is, according to patterns in the top three squares of the rules. In the leftmost rule, all of the precondition's squares are black. In the rightmost rule, all of the precondition's squares are white. If we turn all of the preconditions on their side, so that they can be examined horizontally rather than vertically, and if we then compare these triplets to the representation of binary numbers (as black and white squares), we can see that the sequence of black and white squares "spells out," from right to left (or top to bottom if you have in fact turned the page counterclockwise ninety degrees, horizontally, as suggested earlier), 0, 1, 2, 3, 4, 5, 6, 7.

Algorithm   101

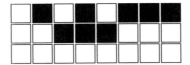

Figure 4.3
The initial state of the addition of two binary numbers.

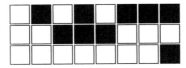

Figure 4.4
The addition of two binary numbers in process.

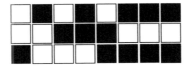

Figure 4.5
The final state of the addition of two binary numbers.

In the decimal system, one can write a maximum of one thousand different integers with three digits (i.e., {0 ... 999}). In a binary system, with three digits one can only write eight different integers (i.e., {0, 1, 10, 11, 100, 101, 110, 111}). We can make it a convention to always arrange the rules of a rule set as a sequence of eight wherein the leftmost precondition is the one in which all of the squares are black (i.e., it codes the binary representation for 7: 111). The rightmost precondition contains three white squares (i.e., 000).

In figure 4.6, for example, is a rule set for subtraction. Compare it to the rule set for addition and you will find the preconditions in the same order, but it is clear that the postconditions (the bottom two squares of each rule in the set) are different. In this case, the left-hand square of each postcondition represents a "borrow bit" (analogous to the rules for borrowing we employ in conventional subtraction) rather than—as was the case in the rule set for addition—a "carry bit."

Once we have adopted the ordering convention to always arrange the rules according to the numbers represented by their preconditions, it is possible to write any rule

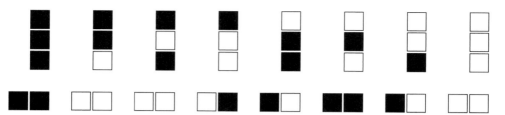

Figure 4.6
Rules of subtraction for binary numbers.

set by just writing its postconditions, since we know that its preconditions will always just be the sequence 7 … 0 (in binary format). Furthermore, because we know that each postcondition is two bits long (i.e., that each postcondition comprises two squares), it is possible to write a rule set as a single number by concatenating all of the postconditions of the set together. Thus, the binary, 1s and 0s, equivalent of the subtraction rule set is just this: 1100000110111000. In short, the rule set can be abbreviated as a sixteen-digit binary number.

The decimal equivalent of this binary number is 49592. The decimal representation of the sixteen-bit binary number that comprises the postconditions of the addition rule set, discussed earlier, is 59796.

One can well imagine, for instance, that within the space of all possible rule sets there is a rule set that is simply this: 0000000000000000. Such a rule set is quite boring in its execution: any and all combinations of black and white squares result in a final row having cells that are all white. There is a similarly simple rule set that is just sixteen ones: 1111111111111111. This rule set, applied to any two arbitrary rows of black and white squares, results in a third row of squares, all of which are black. Since it is possible to write 65536 unique numbers using sixteen digits in a binary format, there are therefore 65536 possible rule sets in this particular representation.

Rule set 0 (i.e., rule set 0000000000000000) is quite boring: it maps everything to white squares. Rule set 65535 (i.e., rule set 1111111111111111) is equally boring: it maps everything to black squares. But rule set 49592 is a representation of subtraction, and rule set 59796 is a representation of addition. What about the two rule sets that are right next to addition in an enumeration of rule sets: 59795 and 59797? Are they just erroneous forms of addition? Or what about the procedures quite distant in this enumeration; for example, rule set 34567? Do they, too, code a procedure, an algorithm, that can produce new true statements given two facts? In other words, are they, too, objects of a centuries-long history of philosophical inquiry into methods, procedures, and algorithms? Or

Algorithm   103

might they be a part of that genealogy and yet remained unexamined? Or are they just boring rule sets that represent methods of no particular interest?

Once one has developed a means of systematically enumerating a series of rule sets, one has the means to ask questions about a large space of algorithms rather than seeing each as a singularity. For example, one might ask, given this representation of algorithms, is rule set 59796 the only one that constitutes an effective procedure for binary addition? Is there another set that does so? Or are there perhaps dozens of rule sets for addition?

Using this enumeration of a space of algorithms that includes those of addition and subtraction, we can revisit Brown and VanLehn's hypotheses about children's arithmetic errors. For example, if one were to employ rule set 59797 (instead of rule set 59796) to do addition, one would manage to do it well most of the time, except in cases where one was using the incorrect rule (i.e., namely the last rule, which in the correct set states that $0+0=0$ with 0 carried but in the incorrect rule set, 59797, states that $0+0=1$ with 0 carried). In this way, one could visualize a set of systematic arithmetic errors as a translation: a slight movement in the space of enumerated algorithms from rule set 59796 to rule set 59797.

Machine Learning

An enumerable space of rule sets is also the key ingredient in most "machine-learning" algorithms. The simplest machine-learning algorithm is "generate-and-test." Let us imagine that the goal is to have the computer "learn" how to do addition. The machine-learning algorithm is given (a) an enumerable space of rule sets and (b) a set of examples, namely a list of worked sums (e.g., $0+0=0$; $1+1=2$; $87+56=143$; $50+50=100$; etc.). A generate-and-test procedure could then start with rule set 0, note that it works just fine for one example ($0+0=0$), but find that it does not produce the correct answer for any of the other examples. It would continue with rule set 1, then rule set 2, and so forth, finally reaching rule set 59796, at which point the machine-learning algorithm would note that the entire list of worked sums could be reproduced.

So, after trying out almost 60,000 rule sets, the procedure would then be said to have "learned" arithmetic. Machine-learning algorithms more sophisticated than generate-and-test are designed to traverse the space of all possible rule sets in a manner that is more efficient than simple enumeration. For example, note that rule set 1 encodes, as its rightmost rule, the incorrect sum $0+0=1$. Thus, the machine-learning algorithm could note, after checking rule set 1, that the rightmost rule of rule set 1 does not work on any of the examples and then, if any subsequent rule sets contain that rule, it could skip them without checking them against the worked sums. In that manner, each of the rules in a rule set can be checked independently and entire rule sets excluded if they contain one or more rules that have been determined to be incorrect.

This is a form of machine learning called "induction," defining a set of procedures that we will revisit again in chapter 5, on logic; in chapter 6, on rhetoric; and in chapter 7, on grammar. In subsequent work, VanLehn tried to substantiate the idea that students learned arithmetic by using a procedure like one that can be implemented as an inductive machine-learning algorithm.[59] While it is possible to say that, even with a simple generate-and-test algorithm, a procedure might, eventually, output a rule set that can perform addition, it seems a wild leap of faith to claim, as VanLehn does, that this form of induction has anything in common with what schoolchildren do when they learn arithmetic. In my opinion, machine learning is very feebly equated to human learning and might in fact have nothing in common with what we do when we learn something.

But VanLehn is hardly alone in making the claim that human learning can be understood as analogous to machine learning (and vice versa). Both in science fiction about software (e.g., the beloved program "Samantha" in the film *Her*[60]) and in the technical literature of computer science, computer programs are said to improve by "learning." In the film, "Samantha" tells the protagonist that she has been "learning" by reading books. By this we are led to believe that software learns the way humans do, but if we consult the contemporary computer science literature on machine learning, we can see how distant machine learning is from human learning; for example, one of the leading textbooks on artificial intelligence summarizes a set of algorithms for machine learning and states that most of these algorithms take as input a vector of attribute values (e.g., a long list of numbers) and output either a decimal or an integer.[61]

Algorithms as Imperfect Imitations

The current enthusiasm in business, science, and government for "big data" is based on the idea that computers "learn," whereas what they actually do is find correlations between attribute values of the input vectors. This conflation of the vernacular understanding of learning with a set of algorithms is a useful conceit in science-fiction storytelling and has seduced some into seeing data as a social and economic panacea,[62] but it has been bad for human learning and educational institutions.

For instance, many believe that specialists in machine learning are the ones who know the most about education. They are thus sold on online "learning" that, taken

Algorithm 105

as a replacement for face-to-face education, is at best a risky bet for students.[63] Current forms of online learning (e.g., MOOCs) amplify the worst of university education—large, anonymous lectures—and leave out the best approach to pedagogy: small tutorials.

Brown and VanLehn's work shows how human error in arithmetic can be conceptualized as movements between rule sets in a space of algorithms, like the space enumerable with these arrangements of black and white squares. However, we need to admit that Brown and VanLehn's representation of arithmetic errors is at best partial. In the terms introduced in chapter 3, the "work language" of arithmetic—for example, the language human computers or their organizers, such as Prony—used to describe and do the labor of calculation is certainly much larger and more encompassing than the black and white squares used here as a "machine language." For example, to describe the working conditions of a human computer, one would be obliged to describe the tools of the trade (pencils, gridded paper), the seating arrangements, the reporting structure (who will check the results), the hours of work (lunchtime, quitting time), and so on. Consequently, some human errors might be explicable as translations between rule sets in the space of algorithms enumerated in the machine language, while other human errors—and the larger labor of human computation—are lost in translation from the work language to the machine language.

These losses accrued in the translation from a work language to a machine language are a possible model for ideological limitations or, specifically, semiotic closure, as discussed in chapter 2. That is to say, even though the articulation of a machine language—like that of the black and white squares just discussed—allows us a means to visualize errors and limitations (via, for instance, enumeration of all possible algorithms in a space of algorithms), it also circumscribes what can be imagined.

Brown and VanLehn again provide us with a clear illustration of what is at stake. They write, "Given a procedural skill, [our theory] predicts which systematic errors…will occur in the behavior of students learning the skill."[64] But consider the following example of how systematic errors can fall beyond a machine language and thus beyond the predictive powers of Brown and VanLehn's theory. Imagine a large construction project right across the street from a classroom. During the construction, a huge noise periodically makes the classroom windows shudder and renders the students temporarily deaf. Across the street, walls are ripped down, pilings are pounded, and power tools rend the air. If these noises systematically disturb some of the students and, as a result, they make errors in their arithmetic worksheets, are these systematic errors beyond Brown and VanLehn's theory to explain? What about systematic errors made by students who are sleep deprived or who never have a proper breakfast?[65]

Brown and Van Lehn claim that their theory can predict all systematic errors in all procedural skills, yet these situations fall beyond their theory. Their claim is too broad and, by being too broad, exhibits the symptoms of semiotic closure. Their machine language is not expressive enough to describe many of the possible working conditions of human computation, so neither is it expressive enough to describe all possible systematic errors in the performance of arithmetic.

My claim, then, is that—even in the seemingly simple area of arithmetic—the translations between work languages and machine languages can expose gaps in digital ideologies. Though it may seem that the definitions of "arithmetic," "calculation," and "algorithm" are all settled now that they have been so closely tied to software and computers, in fact their definitions are still unstable. Just as Wittgenstein's comments and questions from 1939 hint, Turing's 1936 paper did not resolve the debates. Historically, the changing material conditions of arithmetic (from, for example, the abacus to pen-and-paper methods of algorithms and on to the use of computers) have redefined what it means to calculate. We can understand algorithms by visualizing them in an enormous possibility space, such as I demonstrated with the rule sets or algorithms written in black and white squares. Even then, however, such a conceptualization has ideological limits or semiotic closures like those illustrated by the work of Brown and VanLehn on errors: a work language will always be riven with details, contexts, and opacities that cannot be sutured with a machine language. If we think of a machine language as a "grammar" (as will be elaborated in chapter 7), overall my point in this chapter is akin to the pronouncement of anthropologist-linguist Edward Sapir (1884–1939): "all grammars leak."[66]

5 Logic

Many see a direct line of development from nineteenth-century mathematical logic to the twentieth-century creation of the electronic digital computer. The computer-born-from-logic story is frequently told and often starts with the work mathematician George Boole did to make logic into an algebra, an arithmetic of three logical operations: AND, OR, and NOT. If we follow this story, we can see that, by the late 1930s, logic was translated into algebraic/arithmetic equations; logic equations were translated into circuits and vice versa; and logic equations could also be translated into tables. The computer-born-from-logic story emphasizes continuity between these different forms of logic. We are meant to be convinced that, for example, Boole's algebraic equations from the nineteenth century have been seamlessly, losslessly translated into the Boolean circuits now ubiquitous in the hardware of all contemporary digital computers.

In contrast to this narrative, this chapter will illustrate how each translation of logic—from Aristotle, to Boole, to Peirce, to Wittgenstein, to Shannon, to today—entails, like all translations, both losses and gains. So, all of these things—equations and circuits alike—have been glossed as "logic," but in fact they are all operationally and materially quite different.

Ever since Boole, logic has branched off into thousands of different formalisms and many different materialities, none of which are exactly equivalent. The argument is that many very different kinds of operations are now taken to be equivalent to logic; in digital ideologies, a diverse assortment of techniques and technologies are grouped under the name of "logic." Perhaps yesterday there was one "Logic," but today there is not. Rather, there are many special logics, many special-purpose artificial languages that are all called "logics." The belief in "Logic" as a universal omnipotent foundation for the definition or implementation of computing and human thought is long-standing and unwarranted.

For centuries, "logic" and "dialectic" were treated as synonyms. Even now, in the *Oxford English Dictionary* (*OED*), definition 1.a. of "dialectic" is "logic, reasoning." Yet, if we read further in the *OED* and notice the etymologies of each term, we see "logic" in ancient Greek was "λόγος word, oration, reasoning, reason." In contrast, in ancient Greek, "dialectic" was "ἡδιαλεκτική the dialectic art, the art of discussion or debate." This chapter begins with an exploration of the history of dialectic and logic. When did they separate, and why did they become two very different arts?

After this short history, we will question the commonsensical notion that computers are logic machines. The origin myth from computer history is one in which, once logic parts company with dialectic to become more "precise," more "mathematical," it then develops into the computer. In other words, the myth is that the computer is an outgrowth of logic. The actual history is much more complex and much more interesting. If, for example, one looks at the testimony of those who made some of the first digital computers, one sees that the main motivation driving their development was to create a machine to perform numerical calculations, not logical inferences.[1] Moreover, even in 1950, well after the invention of the digital computer, the scientific literature on logic machines was distinct from the literature on computer design.[2]

Starting in the 1950s, projects were initiated to simulate logic machines in software.[3] While logical operations did come to be written in software as a special-purpose application, these operations remain a small subset of what a computer can do. To demonstrate that computers are not only logic machines, the second part of this chapter will examine some key attributes that distinguish computers from logic; for example, it examines what distinguishes Boolean logic from the "logic circuits" of digital computers.

In the third and final part of this chapter, we take a closer look at how logic is implemented in software as special-purpose applications through a quick overview of two areas. One is the area of logic circuit simulation in software, the kinds of software tools employed in the design of computer hardware. The second area is "logic programming," a set of programming techniques and languages that are said to have logic at their core.

The Beginnings of Dialectic

In his book *A Preface to Plato*, Eric Havelock, a scholar of ancient Greece, asks us to imagine what teaching, learning, and knowledge were like before literacy. Long stories like the *Iliad* and the *Odyssey* were repeated from memory by generations of poets. These poems, these stories, counted not just as entertainment but, most importantly, as wisdom and know-how. They constituted, according to Havelock, an encyclopedia—"pedia" being related to the ancient Greek term for upbringing or learning: "παιδεία" or "paideía." Cultural ideals of courage and honor were embodied in characters like Achilles; moral codes were enacted in the exchanges between men and women, children and adults, enemies and friends, gods and men; and specific practices were detailed in these poems, such as how to make war, how to worship the gods, how to run a household, how to be a host, how to be a guest, how to navigate the sea, and how to fight in battle.

Prior to the age of literacy, a performance of these poems was one of the primary means by which a new generation learned the knowledge of the older generations. The formulaic verbal clichés, rhythm, and meter of the poems made them memorable. Havelock points out that, consequently, a performance of such poetry is not one in which the audience is encouraged to ask questions and thus both disrupt the flow of the story and distract the poet. Rather, at such a performance, "learning" was a matter of listening intently, memorizing as much as possible, and identifying with the characters.

So, at about the moment of the widespread adoption of writing in ancient Greece, the entrance of dialectic into this still-persistent state of orality was disruptive if not downright seditious. Havelock writes,

> This was the method of dialectic, ... the original device in its simplest form, which consisted in asking a speaker to repeat himself and explain what he had meant....Now, the statement in question, if it concerned important matters of cultural tradition and morals, would be a poet-ised one, using the imagery and often the rhythms of poetry. [T]o say, "What do you mean? Say that again," abruptly disturbed the pleasurable complacency felt in the poetic formula or the image. It meant using different words and these equivalent words would fail to be poetic; they would be prosaic....In short, the dialectic ... was a weapon for arousing the consciousness from its dream language and stimulating it to think abstractly. As it did this, the conception of "me thinking about Achilles" rather than "me identifying with Achilles" was born.[4]

Even though dialectic was originally a technique of conversation,[5] Havelock reminds us that it was seen, from the beginning, as a dangerous weapon, a means to interrupt not just the poet but also the social order, because poetry was intrinsic to the production and reproduction of the social order.

Ultimately, however, what was most suspect about dialectic was its development as a method that could be employed by anyone.[6] It was at the time outrageous to imagine that knowledge could emerge from a line of questioning by anyone—even someone who professed to know nothing about a subject.[7]

That this notion was folly was amply illustrated by those who, unprepared in mind, nevertheless asked questions of the oracle of Delphi. For example, in 560 BCE, according to Herodotus, Croesus of Lydia asked if he should go to war with the Persians. The oracle responded that if he did so, a mighty empire would be destroyed. Only at the conclusion of the war did it become clear which empire: it was Croesus's, not the empire of the Persians, that was destroyed by the war.[8] Oops!

In an oral society, dialectic is a speech practice—an art of conversation—that disrupts the recitation of poetry. As an oral practice, however, dialectic cannot replace poetry, because dialectic drives discourse into the prosaic and therefore makes what is said forgettable. As such, dialectic is only sustainable in a literate society where things to be remembered can be written down. In this manner, dialectic spurs political, social, and cultural institutions out of poetry and into written prose.

Distinguishing Dialectic from Logic

After a society moves from orality to literacy, writing becomes intrinsic to argumentation. Medievalist Walter Ong explains this consequent tangling of mind and material world:

> Philosophy and all the sciences and "arts" (analytic studies of procedures, such as Aristotle's *Art of Rhetoric*) depend for their existence on writing, which is to say they are produced not by the unaided human mind but by the mind making use of a technology that has been deeply interiorized, incorporated into mental processes themselves. The mind interacts with the material world around it more profoundly and creatively than has hitherto been thought. Philosophy, it seems, should be reflectively aware of itself as a technological product—which is to say a special kind of very human product. Logic itself emerges from the technology of writing.[9]

So the principal characteristic that differentiates logic from dialectic is that logic is a practice of writing and dialectic is a practice of oral conversation.

In *The Art of Controversy*, philosopher Arthur Schopenhauer (1788–1860) distinguishes logic from dialectic along lines complementary to Ong's:

> It is clear, then, that Logic deals with a subject of a purely *a priori* character, separable in definition from experience, namely, the laws of thought, the process of reason or the *logos*, the laws, that is, which reason follows when it is left to itself and not hindered, as in the case of solitary thought on the part of a rational being who is in no way misled. Dialectic, on the other hand, would treat of the intercourse between two rational beings who, because they are rational, ought to think in common, but who, as soon as they cease to agree like two clocks keeping exactly the same time, create a disputation, or intellectual contest.[10]

Schopenhauer's distinction between logic, which is the solitary thought of one person, and dialectic, which is conversational exchange between two, is complementary to Ong's, since writing is a solitary activity and oral conversation an interaction between people. But Schopenhauer adds another distinction between these two when he writes, "Logic deals with a subject of a purely *a priori* character."

The work of Marshall McLuhan, who was a colleague of both Walter Ong and Eric Havelock, can be understood as an elaboration to Schopenhauer's distinction that employs the category of the a priori: "Since Aristotle it is easy to see that logic and dialectic are distinct in that the former is demonstrative and the latter probable in the mode of proof; and that this is owing to matters with which they are concerned."[11]

Within such a framework, then, the distinction between logic and dialectic is not a matter of how they are done or how many people do them. Rather, the distinction hinges on the kind of knowledge on which they are performed. Thus, according to this definition, when we are dealing with certain knowledge—for example, Euclid's axioms of geometry—then we are properly in the realm of logic. If, on the other hand, we are considering opinions, then we are in the realm of dialectic.

McLuhan further considers the outrage stirred up by medieval Christian dialecticians when they were seen to be misapplying dialectic to the certain knowledge of God's word. Ultimately, this outrage ended in dialectic's disgrace, a fall from academic and theological grace that endured well into the eighteenth century, as we will soon see.

Understandably, in a culture of theological absolutes—like the one inhabited by the medieval European scholastics and ruled by the Catholic Church—such a procedure could not be applied without danger to statements asserted to be true by the Church. If, for example, one is led via the dialectical procedure to both "God exists" and "God does not exist" as equally probable statements, one has been led astray, from the perspective of Catholic doctrine.

Even long before the medieval scholastics, however, dialectic was considered a dangerous weapon because of the way it instrumentalized language, making it into a tool that even those without wisdom could use to dismantle common sense. This was how Socrates and the Sophists deployed dialectic.

Zeno's Dialectic

As cited earlier, Havelock explains that dialectic, in its original form, was simply an interruption, a question posed to a singer or a poet in the middle of recitation. Shortly thereafter, however, "dialectic" came to be used to refer to a much more precise method of questioning, said to have been invented by Zeno of Elea. McLuhan cites the French classicist Léon Robin to narrate this shift.

> Zeno's method, defined with such exact precision, is what, since Aristotle, has been called the "dialectical." With reference to a given question, from a "probable" answer—that is, one approved by an imaginary interlocutor, or by some philosopher, or by some common opinion—you deduce the consequences which it entails, and you show that these consequences contradict each other and the initial thesis and lead to an opposite thesis no less "probable" than the first.... To his method we owe, if not the application of dialogue to philosophical inquiry,

at least a certain way of disentangling and debating questions, which is equally found in the rhetoric of the Sophists and in Socratic philosophy.[12]

Zeno, the inventor of the method, is said to have developed a number of paradoxes that illustrate how dialectic can refute common sense. His best-known paradox is that of Achilles and the tortoise. As stated by Aristotle, "This is that the slowest runner never will be overtaken by the fastest; for it is necessary for the one chasing to come first to where the one fleeing started from, so that it is necessary for the slower runner always to be ahead some."[13]

The paradox has been repeatedly described with reference to two runners: one fast, Achilles; the other slow, the tortoise. Achilles and the tortoise are to race, and the tortoise is given a head start. Can Achilles catch the tortoise? Zeno argues that he cannot. Why? Let us say the tortoise is given a head start so that when Achilles starts, the tortoise is already some distance down the road. For illustration's sake, let us say the tortoise is a kilometer down the road. Running, Achilles will certainly cover a kilometer quickly, but in the amount of time Achilles is running there, the tortoise will have advanced farther than a kilometer, maybe a hundred meters. So, upon reaching the kilometer mark, Achilles will not have caught the tortoise because the tortoise will then be at the 1,100 meter mark. But then, to continue, by the time Achilles gets to the 1,100-meter mark, the tortoise will have advanced farther, let us say to the 1,110-meter mark, and so forth. Thus, Achilles will never catch the tortoise.

Zeno's argument seems flawless but obviously flies in the face of common sense. Of course the faster runner will eventually catch the slower runner! Incredible as it may seem, Zeno's paradox has been a matter of intense debate from Aristotle until now. Throughout the millennia, there have been skeptics who find that Zeno's paradox is not a paradox at all, and others who think the paradox has yet to be solved.

There are many "solutions" to Zeno's paradox. For example, "A Discrete Solution for the Paradox of Achilles and the Tortoise," a 2015 article by philosopher Vincent Ardourel,[14] argues that if one employs a discrete representation of time instead of a continuous one, one can show and calculate when Achilles will catch the tortoise. Ardourel's "solution" ultimately entails writing a computer program to "solve" Zeno's paradox.[15] A discrete representation of time is one that, at some level of granularity, is indivisible. For example, we might say that the unit is a "blink of the eye" and there is nothing smaller than that; that is, half a "blink of an eye" is not seen as a valid measure.

Clearly, Ardourel's solution will be of interest only to those who think the paradox is still unsolved. Anyone who does not care about the paradox will find any such "solution"—contemporary or ancient—useless or absurd for one of three reasons: (i) because any empirical investigation of the situation (e.g., setting up a series of foot races between a superb human runner and a tortoise) will show that the tortoise will always lose; (ii) because simple and early life experience predicts Achilles's victory; or (iii) because anyone, like Ardourel, who seeks to state and solve the problem as an abstract calculation is approaching the world from an orbit well outside of everyday common sense.[16]

Descartes's Method and the Cartesian Moment

The latter position is diagnostic of a mind-set that portends a digital ideology, a way of viewing the world in which access to truth is seen as a question of having the right method or, more specifically, making the correct calculation. There is a history of this mind-set that goes well beyond a history of Zeno's paradox to include the role of method in philosophy, mathematics, and science more generally. Why would one want to address a problem like Zeno's paradox by using a calculation—a method—rather than using one's common sense, trying it out empirically or through consultation and discussion with others?

Until roughly the seventeenth century, there was a belief that the truth was available only to those who prepared themselves physically, mentally, and spiritually. Philosopher Michel Foucault argues that a shift to the belief that truth is not predicated on the physical and spiritual preparation of the seeker of knowledge is a shift characteristic of the modern age. Foucault loosely dates this shift by naming it the "Cartesian moment," a reference to Descartes's belief that truth can be found through thinking ("I think therefore I am"), independent of spiritual and physical preparation. In particular, Descartes states his belief in a formal method, a method that we might call deduction or, more generally, logic.[17]

What Foucault names the "Cartesian moment" marked a radical shift in what counted as knowledge and who was understood to be capable of acquiring it. This belief after the Cartesian moment, that truth is a matter only of knowledge and that it can be found via a correct method or form of calculation, has become more complicated now—but only for those who manage to think beyond a digital ideology, such as feminist epistemologists.[18] Characteristic of a digital ideology is an absolute belief in method and calculation or, more precisely, calculation *as* method. Indeed, within today's digital ideology, truth is seen to be entirely independent of the subject and entirely dependent on methods of calculation.[19] This ideology allows one to talk—without irony—about "smartphones" and "intelligent machines." Now, after Foucault's modern age, many think that methods of calculation—data and algorithms—can lead to knowledge, with or without a knowing or prepared human subject at the helm. In addition, most perniciously, according to this ideology, although no particular subject need be in control of these algorithms, there is a widespread presupposition that these algorithms can only be developed by white men of industry, like the founder of Facebook, the founders of Microsoft, the founders of Google, and others.[20]

Logic in the *Encyclopédie*: Art or Science?

That Foucault was correct in dating a major epistemological shift to about the time of Descartes can be verified from eighteenth-century writings on logic shortly after those of Descartes, such as the entry for "logic" in Diderot and d'Alembert's *Encyclopédie*. The entry begins with a definition:

> Logic is the art of correct thinking, or that of employing thinking in a manner amenable to our rational faculties, for definition, division, and reason. The word is derived from the Greek term λόγος that, rendered into Latin, is *sermo* and in [English] is discourse. This is because thinking is a kind of interior, mental discourse in which the mind converses with itself. Logic is frequently called dialectic.... To think correctly it is necessary to perceive, to judge, to discourse, and to methodically link together one's ideas; it thus follows that perception, judgment, discourse, and method are the four fundamental aspects of the art of logic. It is our reflections on the four operations of the mind that comprise logic.... Lord Bacon divides logic in four parts, the same four that we here propose.[21]

The encyclopedists described logic in the work language of "operations," even though logic is presumably far afield from the artisans' workshops in which this work language was birthed. Such opening language would seem to indicate that logic was to be discussed as an art. But later in the same entry, the question is posed explicitly: Is logic a science or an art?

It would seem to be in keeping with the encyclopedists' regard for Bacon's work that they would declare, given Bacon's improvements, that logic should be called a science. As mentioned in chapter 3, Bacon's *Novum Organum* is considered to be the founding document of empirical science and the first description of a form of induction subsequently named the "scientific method." Bacon criticized the contemporary state of logic and proposed replacing it with his (grammatical) method of induction.[22]

But instead of simply calling logic a science, the encyclopedists make a case for its being an art: "But, is it an art?...It depends on what meaning you assign to the word 'art.' Some want to only call an art that which has as its object something material. Others are willing to call an art any acquired disposition with which operations are effected—be they spiritual or corporeal—by rules or reflections."[23] Insofar as logic can be described in the vocabulary of operations, it would seem to count as an art.

Whatever their differences with Bacon on the classification of logic as art or science, the encyclopedists join him in lamenting the sorry state of contemporary logic:

> It has fallen into a discredited state.... Logic was never more than an art of words which frequently had no sense but which were marvelously adept at hiding ignorance instead of perfecting judgment; for playing with reason instead of strengthening it; and for disfiguring the truth instead of clarifying it. It is claimed that its foundations were cast by Zeno of Elea.... It is known that the ancient Sophists proposed to never be caught short, to never be unprepared, but, with equal facility, to argue for and against all sorts of subjects. They found in dialectic immense resources for this facility and appropriated all of them for their own purposes. This ridiculous heritage did not remain fallow in the hands of the scholastics who enriched it further than their ancient predecessors. Universal categories and other learned trifles were the essence of logic and of all the reflections and disputes about it. Thus was the state of logic from its origins until the last century [the seventeenth century] and so did it fall into such disparagement that people still are not willing to return to it. And truly it must be admitted that the way in which logic is treated in schools today further contributes to the contempt that many people still have for this science.[24]

Nevertheless, the *Encyclopédie* entry notes an improvement in logic's reputation in the seventeenth century, an improvement they credit to Descartes:

> Descartes, the true restorer of reasoning, was the first to develop a new method of reasoning, much more valuable than even his philosophy, much of which is false or very uncertain, judged according to the very rules he developed and taught us. It is to him that we owe the precision and accuracy that prevails not only in physics and metaphysics, but also in religion, moral reasoning, and criticism. In general the principles and method of Descartes have been of great utility, accustoming us to accurately analyze words and ideas and, thereby, to conduct us on the road to truth.... The method of Descartes gave birth to logic, called the art of thinking.[25]

Thus the history of logic recounted in the *Encyclopédie* is one in which logic and dialectic have been synonyms for centuries and defined by a set of techniques of dialogue and reasoning that start (with Zeno), come to ruin, and then are revived by Descartes, who puts them on a sound footing. The history recounted in the entry is clearly partisan: the encyclopedists do not hide their disdain for Zeno's work ("this ridiculous heritage") or their reverence for Descartes ("the true restorer of reasoning").

Logic, Dialectic, and the Trivium as Schools of Thought

The *Encyclopédie* entry distinguishes dialectic from logic and attributes the founding of the former to Zeno and that of the latter to Descartes. This kind of lineage or genealogy is best contextualized with an understanding of what dialectic and logic were in the period before the Enlightenment—in the early modern age, during the time of the scholastics. At that time, the trivium—grammar, rhetoric, and dialectic—did not name three special topics of study. Rather, each was a powerful school of thought locking horns with the others in a competition of epistemology and politics.

Marshall McLuhan summarized the history of the competition between the three schools of the trivium. Dialectic had been in contention with rhetoric from the time of the Sophists, with Plato and Aristotle arguing that dialectic should dominate rhetoric. Grammar then gained hegemony until the revival of dialectic by Gerbert in the eleventh century. But then, in the fifteenth century, culminating in Erasmus's work, grammar and rhetoric regained dominance over dialectic. Nevertheless, the rivalry between dialectic and rhetoric continues, and the consequences of this rivalry resonate far beyond the confines of the schools. In McLuhan's words, "The war between these literary camps is basically the opposition between dialectic and rhetoric to control the modes of literary composition; and the ramifications of this opposition stretch into the realms of ethics and politics, both in antiquity and in the Renaissance."[26] McLuhan's history of the trivium ends at the time of Shakespeare, but the contests between dialectic, rhetoric, and grammar continued on into the eighteenth century, the era of the encyclopedists, and arguably continue even today.

The *Encyclopédie* entry in concert with a history of the trivium provides us with an exogenous means of distinguishing logic from dialectic: they can be seen as rival schools or intellectual traditions even if they were wrangling over the same terrain of language and literary composition. This exogenous distinction complements the several endogenous means of distinguishing logic from dialectic discussed earlier: (i) Walter Ong argues that dialectic is an oral practice, while logic is a practice made possible by literacy; (ii) Schopenhauer argues that logic is a form of solitary thought and dialectic is only possible with two or more people; (iii) McLuhan, relying on Aristotle, claims that the difference between the two primarily depends on the subject matter to which they are applied; (iv) Foucault's "Cartesian moment" and the obviously partisan, Cartesian *Encyclopédie* entry introduce a fourth possible distinction: logic is a sound method of calculation, while dialectic is an unprincipled form of rhetoric.

Stated in a less partisan manner, one might say that logic became a form of calculation and dialectic remained a form of conversation. Alternatively, to widen McLuhan's history from just the trivium (dialectic, rhetoric, and grammar) to also include the quadrivium (music, geometry, arithmetic, and astronomy), we might say that the "Cartesian moment" is the moment when logic and dialectic part ways: dialectic stays in the trivium, the arts of language; and logic attempts to cross the border into the quadrivium, the arts of number.

Historiographers of the human sciences point out that other arts—or techniques if you prefer—moved from the trivium to the quadrivium or vice versa. For instance, David Cram of Oxford University has argued that in the seventeenth century, music underwent a dramatic realignment from the quadrivium to the trivium; that is to say, music was formerly considered an art of number but then became a language art. Cram argues that "a radically different sort of musical analysis emerges at the turn of the sixteenth and seventeenth centuries, which explicitly places music within the framework of rhetorical theory, thus linking music to the other language arts of the *trivium*."[27] But Cram's analysis is a little more complicated than this observation of music's move from the number arts to the language arts. In his conclusion, he points out that what counts as a language changed between the seventeenth century and the eighteenth century.

Artificial and Natural Languages

In the seventeenth century, there were said to be "instituted languages," such as English, German, and French. These instituted languages were contrasted with the "natural languages" of, for example, gesture, facial expression, onomatopoeia, and what the Christian theologians referred to as the "Adamic language," the original language of Adam.

Then, in the eighteenth century, there was a switch: "natural languages" became the phrase used to refer to what in the seventeenth century had been called "instituted languages." After this switch, English, German, and French came to be considered not "instituted languages" but rather the canonical "natural languages," which were contrasted with the newly named "artificial languages."

According to Cram, it was the invention of artificial languages that effected this change in what counted as a natural language. These artificial languages included, notably, the work of Francis Lodwick (1619–1694), George Dalgarno (1616–1687), John Wilkins (1614–1672), and Gottfried Wilhelm Leibniz (1646–1716) to develop a "universal characteristic" in which signs were to stand not for words but for things. There is some excellent scholarship on these experiments in artificial languages, such as Jaap Maat's relatively recent work *Philosophical Languages in the Seventeenth Century: Dalgarno, Wilkins, Leibniz*[28] and the easy-to-read book by Umberto Eco *The Search for the Perfect Language*.[29]

As examples of artificial languages, Cram lists not only the seventeenth-century designs of Leibniz and others but also twentieth-century creations like Esperanto and computer languages like ALGOL, an invention of computer scientists (including Alan Perlis) in the 1960s. Cram's connection between the Enlightenment and the contemporary era can be interpreted in several ways.

Computer as Logic Machine

One interpretation is a Whiggish history that sees the development of logic at the core of the connection between old and new artificial languages. In this history, the story of computer-as-logic, told very accessibly by mathematical logician Martin Davis in his book *The Universal Computer: The Road from Leibniz to Turing*,[30] we are shown a trail from Leibniz's dissertation on a philosophical language, a "universal characteristic," through a series of chapters on George Boole (1815–1864), then Gottlob Frege (1848–1925), Georg Cantor (1845–1918), David Hilbert (1862–1943), Kurt Gödel (1906–1978), and on to Alan Turing (1912–1954) and thus to the modern computer.

Martin Davis's history is implicitly based in mathematical logic, a largely nineteenth- and twentieth-century invention that deftly moves logic out of the language arts and into the arts of number, effecting a movement opposite to the direction that music underwent. Alternatively, perhaps more importantly for my argument, it should be noted that mathematical logic effectively detached logic from the other language arts of rhetoric and grammar.

When logic and dialectic are taken as synonyms, their relationship to the other language arts of rhetoric and grammar is clear. However, when they are separated and logic is then taken to be a form of calculation and not a form of conversation, its moral and ethical aspects are difficult to discern. Thus, a rupture occurred that started during the "Cartesian moment" and exploded in the nineteenth century, at about the time of the inception of mathematical logic, separating critical thinking—for instance, Karl Marx's dialectical materialism—and mathematical logic, a logic that became concerned, almost exclusively, with the foundations of arithmetic, geometry, and other areas of mathematics.

So, certainly, one can agree with Martin Davis that computers are logic machines. But, more subtly, my argument is that they are machines of a logic rarely considered by computer historians bedazzled by the powers of mathematical logic. To underline this distinction, let me rephrase my earlier claim that computers are language machines by saying, more specifically, that computers are machines of rhetoric, grammar, logic, and dialectic.

Logic Collapses to Calculation

My story does not pivot exclusively on logic. It is one in which, in the nineteenth century, the twin siblings, logic and dialectic, are separated. Logic is then displaced from the trivium into the quadrivium—from the arts of language into the arts of number. In contrast, dialectic remains at home, in the arts of language. Each develops with almost no communication with the other. In logic, a method of reasoned argument becomes an operation of calculation. Dialectic develops, too, but its nature does not change too much: it becomes a sophisticated means for the pursuit of argumentation, conversation, and, ultimately, critical theory. Consequently, contemporary dialectic knows practically nothing about the latest developments of logic, the development of logic into computation. And the ignorance is mutual: logic knows practically nothing about the development of dialectic.

What went wrong with logic? How did it become a form of calculation instead of a technique of conversation? As we saw in chapter 4, on algorithms, it underwent a process of "arithmetization," thanks especially to the work of George Boole.

Once Boole made logic into arithmetic, strangely it became an imperative for mathematicians to formalize numbers and arithmetic as logic. One example of this project was the articulation by Giuseppe Peano (1858–1932) of a set of logically phrased axioms of numbers and arithmetic.[31] Peano's axioms were tightly tied to Boole's work; his formulation of logic was partly based on Boole's algebra. Peano's axioms are odd, as is the entire project of the logical formalization of mathematics, because it is circular or, perhaps more specifically, tautological. Think about it: Boole shows how logic can be translated into arithmetic, and then Peano shows how arithmetic can be rewritten as a form of logic. Taking Boole and Peano together, we find a proof, if you prefer that term, that equates arithmetic to logic based on work showing that logic is arithmetic!

This struck mathematician David Hilbert as a research program chasing its tail: "Arithmetic is often considered to be part of logic, and the traditional fundamental logical notions are usually presupposed when it is a question of establishing a foundation for arithmetic. If we observe attentively, however, we realize that in the traditional exposition of the laws of logic certain fundamental mental arithmetic notions are already used, for example, the notion of set and, to some extent, also that of number. Thus we already find ourselves turning in a circle."[32] If we were evaluating this endeavor a century or so ago, we might be tempted to just write the whole thing off as some kind of crazy exercise. But, as we now know, these moves in logical formalization and arithmetization led David Hilbert to challenge the mathematics community to prove mathematics complete, consistent, and decidable. In response, Kurt Gödel showed mathematics to be incomplete and inconsistent. Then, Alan Turing showed it to be undecidable, and—in the same paper—developed a theoretical machine tantamount to what we now call a computer or, more specifically, an algorithm.

Furthermore, every digital computer today has as a central component Boolean circuits implementing Boolean logic lithographed in silicon and gold. In other words, what was arguably a small branch of philosophy and mathematics in the nineteenth century has become the main trunk of computers and the contemporary computer industry. This branch of philosophy has become the hardware and software now entangled with so many of our social, cultural, political, and economic institutions.

Leibniz as Rhetorician

An objection to this position—the destination at which one arrives following what Martin Davis narrates as *The Road from Leibniz to Turing*—is voiced by philosopher Alain Badiou, who frames Peano's work as a form of sophistry.[33] In the same book, Badiou writes, "No one is obliged to be a Leibnizian, even if we must recognise in this philosophy the archetype of one of the … great orientations in thought."[34] Taken together, these two statements from Badiou are an accusation that Leibniz was a Sophist, a skilled rhetorician. If, as many historians of computing maintain, Leibniz is at the root of computers, then—via Badiou—here is a way to see that computers are also rhetoric machines.

As Cram describes, Leibniz was one of the first to try his hand at the invention of an artificial language. Why did Leibniz want an artificial language? In a phrase, he wanted one because he did not want to argue. Leibniz wrote, "This language will be the greatest instrument of reason [for] when there are disputes among persons, we can simply say: Let us calculate, without further ado, and see who is right."[35] What was Leibniz's intention? Was his ambition to invent an objective process of calculation that could fairly adjudicate any dispute?[36] That has been the predominant interpretation of this quotation. It puts Leibniz in a genealogy that leads back to Plato's efforts to find a more perfect form of rational argumentation, dialectic, that can be distinguished from the wilder, less rational moves of rhetoric. We will examine this more closely in chapter 6, when we read about the beginnings of deductive demonstration, a form of argumentation Plato borrows from the discourse of geometry.

Alternatively, was Leibniz intent on bringing a gun to a knife fight? That is to say, was Leibniz a Sophist, a rhetorician, who foresaw the possibility of bringing a calculating machine to an argument and thereby always winning the argument because calculation would become—perhaps has now become—the strongest of all forms of rhetoric?

One does not need to choose between the two interpretations. Leibniz was both a rhetorician and a logician. However, let us consider what kind of logic Leibniz was developing, regardless of whether this logic had anything to do with rhetoric and argumentation.

Logic Circuits

Thus far in this chapter, we have reviewed various ways in which logic was distinguished and then separated from dialectic. In chapter 4, on algorithms, we reviewed how the project of "arithmetization" translated Aristotle's relatively informal syllogisms into Boolean logic, defined as a sort of arithmetic. Leibniz's work on logic anticipated some of Boole's, so historians of mathematical logic, such as Martin Davis, see a direct line from Leibniz to Boole. Seen from this perspective, the trajectory from nineteenth-century Boolean logic to twentieth-century digital computing is equally direct. This connection is usually drawn between Boole and Claude Shannon, whose 1937 MIT master's degree thesis was on the topic of translating Boolean logic into electrical circuits, the Boolean circuits now ubiquitous in every digital computing device we use today.[37]

I want to point out first that the very notion of a "Boolean circuit" is what I have called a digital assignment statement, a symptom of a digital ideology. Boolean logic originally had nothing to do with circuits, but when Shannon showed how a Boolean circuit could be constructed, he asserted an equivalence between Boole's AND, OR, and NOT operators and electrical circuitry. This is an example of a set of digital assignment statements: a set of statements that claims an equivalence between nondigital expressions and a digital technology.

What needs to be forgotten or overlooked in order to translate Boolean logic into hardware and software? In some ways, this is simple to demonstrate by pointing to the many hurdles that computer chip designers and manufacturers face: the design of the circuits can be incorrect; the layout of the chip can cause unintended interference between different circuits that logically must work independently (e.g., when one tries to put too many transistors on too small a piece of silicon, a limit that chip manufacturing is running into now at the end of so-called Moore's law[38]); or there can be flaws in the materials used in the chip (e.g., the silicon might not be "doped" correctly and thus might not have the planned resistance). But, short of a long side trip into the territories of Intel and the other companies that make the insides of our computing devices, this point can be mapped out in a more general manner. Giving only minimal attention to the details of chip manufacturing, I will point out how a series of translations—from Boolean logic into Boolean circuits—results in the introduction of a very powerful difference between the two, a difference that can be identified as the introduction of a new form of time.

36 W 15th St.

New York, 1886 Dec. 30.

My dear Marquand:

... You spoke, when I saw you, as if disappointed with the reception your machine had met with. I wish I could see it.... I think electricity would be the best thing to rely on.

...

Let A, B, C be three keys or other points where the circuit may be open or closed. As in Fig. 1, there is a circuit only if all are closed; in Fig. 2, there is a circuit if any one is closed. This is like multiplication & addition in Logic.

Yours faithfully

C. S. Peirce[39]

When philosopher Charles Sanders Peirce wrote these words to art historian Allan Marquand, his former student, Marquand was building a machine to do logic, a machine that could calculate whether a logical expression is true or false. Marquand built the first version of his machine out of wood.[40] At the time (1886), there was already a long history of attempts to build logic machines,[41] but all of the previously constructed logic machines had been, like Marquand's, mechanical and thus built from levers, gears, or cables.[42] What is exceptional in Peirce's letter is the suggestion that the machine be built as an electrical device rather than as a mechanical device.

Peirce's letter with his hand-drawn diagrams is shown in figure 5.1. The first of Peirce's diagrams (the one he labeled "Fig. 1" in his letter) would be described—in contemporary terms—as a chain of switches (A, B, and C) connected in *series*. A, B, and C are *switches* because they can be either open or closed. (In the letter, Peirce uses the term "key" instead of switch.) The second diagram ("Fig. 2") depicts a chain of switches connected in *parallel*. Today, both chains (the one in series and the one in parallel) could be described as *logic blocks*, the basic building blocks of contemporary computers. The first figure is a schematic for a logic block that is known as *conjunction* or *AND*. Peirce refers to this as "multiplication" in logic. The second figure is a schematic for what is known as *disjunction* or *OR*. Peirce refers to this as "addition" in logic.

Peirce's letter was all but forgotten, and his design was reinvented, but not until a half century later.[43] As a graduate student at the Massachusetts Institute of Technology (MIT), Claude Shannon reinvented Boolean logic as electrical circuits.[44] He showed how a polynomial representing a statement in logic could be translated into a circuit and, inversely, how a circuit could be translated into a polynomial. In other words, while Peirce sketched out a translation from logic to circuits, Shannon created what

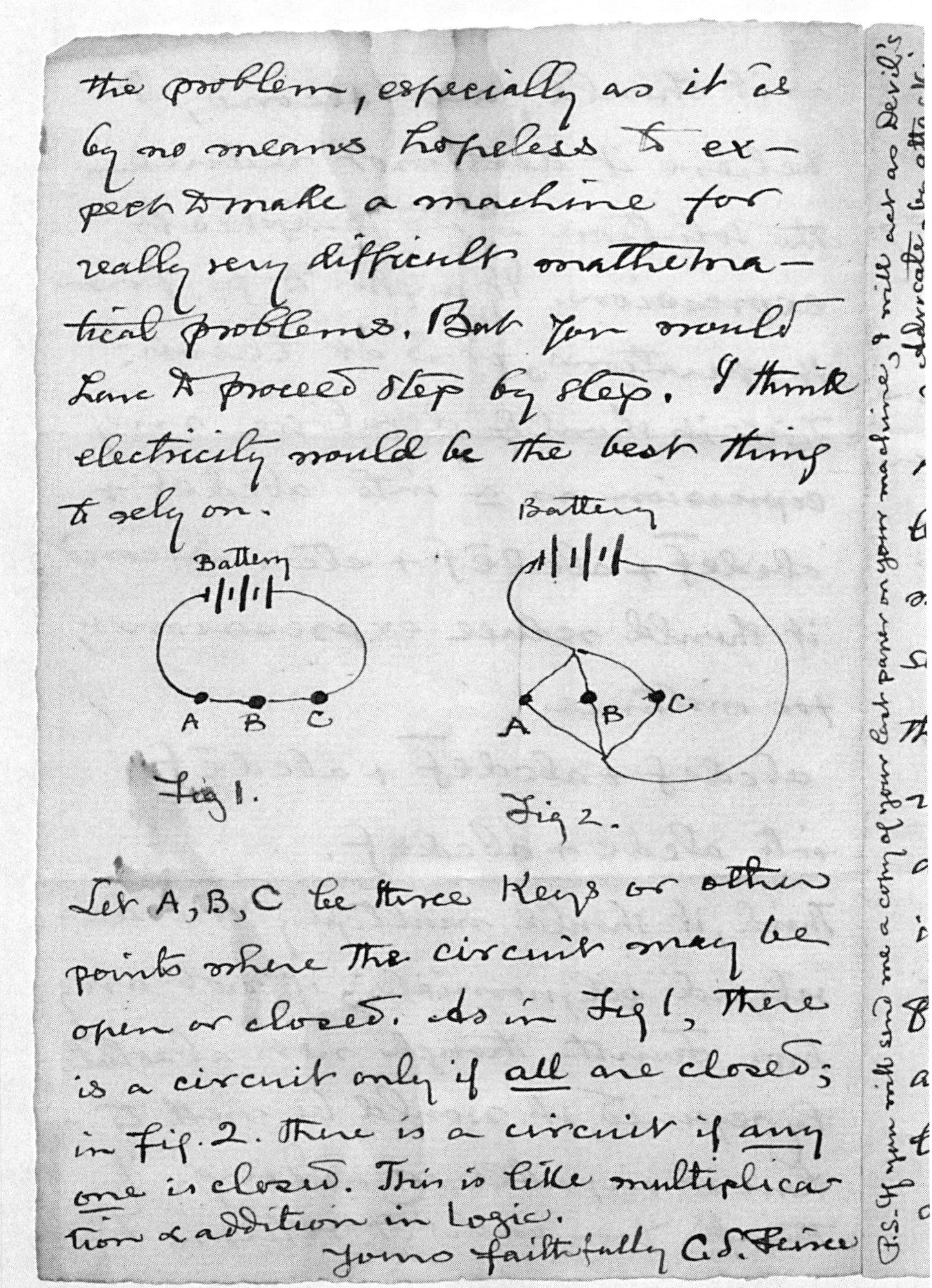

the problem, especially as it is by no means hopeless to expect to make a machine for really very difficult mathematical problems. But you would have to proceed step by step. I think electricity would be the best thing to rely on.

Battery

A B C

Fig 1.

Battery

A B C

Fig 2.

Let A, B, C be three keys or other points where the circuit may be open or closed. As in Fig 1, there is a circuit only if all are closed; in Fig. 2. there is a circuit if any one is closed. This is like multiplication & addition in Logic.

Yours faithfully C. S. Peirce

P.S. If you will send me a copy of your last paper on your machine, I will act as Devil's advocate,

Figure 5.1

Letter from Charles Sanders Peirce to Allan Marquand, 1886. Image reproduced with permission from the Princeton University Library, Allan Marquand Papers, Manuscripts Division, Department of Rare Books and Special Collections.

came to be widely accepted as an equivalence, a bidirectional translation, from logic to circuits and back again. The utility of the equivalence was and is in the design of circuits. A circuit can be translated into a polynomial and then reduced using various definitions in logic. The resultant reduced polynomial can then be translated back into a circuit of smaller size but with the same functionality as the original circuit.[45]

While the circuits for contemporary implementations of Boolean logic do look different from those that Peirce described (today they are not electrical but instead electronic, built with transistors), the essentials are the same. To implement the AND, all of the switches need to be closed (A AND B AND C) so that the electric charge flows from the power source (e.g., a battery) through the circuit and back to the power source. In comparison, to implement the OR, only one switch needs to be closed for the circuit to be complete (A OR B OR C).

Beyond the circuits for AND and OR, one more logic block is necessary to translate Boolean logic into circuits: an *inverter*. An inverter implements a NOT: if the input carries an electric current, the output does not; if the input does not carry an electric current, the output does.

Today, there are simplified graphical conventions to denote the logic blocks, or *logic gates*, that hide the details of their wiring. The AND and OR gates have one output and can have two or more inputs. Conventionally, they are diagrammed with two inputs (as compared to the three—A, B, and C—that Peirce used). The input side of the AND gate is a straight line; the output side is a curve. The input side of the OR gate is a curve; the output side comprises two curves that meet at a point. The NOT inverter has one input and one output. It is diagrammed as a small triangle with an even smaller circle on the output lead.

In figure 5.2, note the 1s and 0s at the ends of the input and output wires. A 1 conventionally denotes a voltage on the wire. A 0 means no voltage on the wire.

There are four possible input combinations for the AND and OR gates: (0, 0), (0, 1), (1, 0), and (1, 1). Both the AND and OR gates are diagrammed four times in the figure to show how each behaves with each possible pair of inputs. The NOT inverter is shown only twice since it accepts only one input—0 or 1.

Truth Tables

Years after Peirce wrote his letter to Marquand, philosopher Ludwig Wittgenstein described a compact graphical means for the input-output sets of a logic gate.[46] Truth tables can be written in three columns: first input, second input, and third output. Tables 5.1, 5.2, and 5.3 show the truth tables for AND, OR, and NOT.

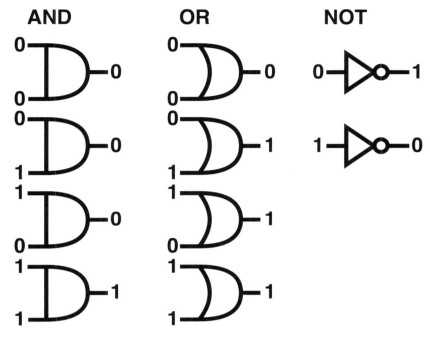

Figure 5.2
All possible inputs and outputs for AND, OR, and NOT gates.

Table 5.1
Truth table for AND.

A	B	A AND B
0	0	0
0	1	0
1	0	0
1	1	1

Table 5.2
Truth table for OR.

A	B	A OR B
0	0	0
0	1	1
1	0	1
1	1	1

Table 5.3
Truth table for NOT.

A	NOT A
0	1
1	0

Wittgenstein's tables portended yet another translation: a visual representation of logic functions. So, by the 1930s, logic could be translated into algebraic/arithmetic equations (via Boole); logic equations could be translated into circuits (via Peirce) and back again (via Shannon); and/or the equations could be translated into tables (via Wittgenstein). In fact, if we read Wittgenstein carefully, it is clear that, by 1939, he also understood—without reference to Peirce or Shannon—that logic could be translated into circuits, even if he apparently thought that doing so was just a bad simile.[47]

Tables and Circuits of Arithmetic

Translating a function of arithmetic into a Wittgensteinian "truth table" provides a straightforward means to compare it to known logic constructs (such as NOT, AND, and OR).

Table 5.4 is the truth table for binary addition. The ADD function almost looks like the OR, except for one row: $1 + 1 = 10$, rather than 1 OR $1 = 1$. This resemblance between the ADD table and the OR's truth table sparks a question: Can arithmetic be implemented with logic gates? In fact, yes, arithmetic can be wired as a series of logic gates. For example, figure 5.3 shows a *half-adder* that accepts two inputs and returns two outputs: a sum bit and a carry bit (for the case of $1 + 1$, when the result requires two bits rather than just one bit). In the diagram in figure 5.3, the wire for the sum bit is below the wire for the carry bit. The result depicted is $1 + 1 = 10$.

The half-adder shown in figure 5.3 uses five gates, three of them AND gates. But it could be redesigned with only two AND gates (and thus four gates in total) since the voltage for the carry bit can be read on the wire that is the input to the NOT gate. By designing a circuit that performs the same operation but with fewer gates (four instead of five), the circuit becomes cheaper to produce and easier to maintain.

If we understand Boole's achievement as the translation of Aristotelian logic into a form of arithmetic (algebra), then, in this circuit for a half-adder, we can see the sketch of the converse, something akin to Peano's axioms: the translation of arithmetic into logic. Via Boolean circuits, the identities described by combining the works of Boole

Table 5.4
Truth table for binary addition.

A	B	A + B
0	0	0
0	1	1
1	0	1
1	1	10

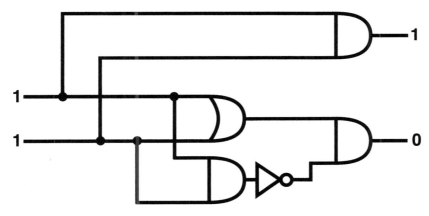

Figure 5.3
A half-adder with inputs 1 and 1, and output 10.

and Peano can be established in another way: arithmetic = logic; and logic = arithmetic. This equivalence, between logic and arithmetic, is established in a rigorous manner by means of algebra and electrical engineering.

There is tremendous utility in establishing this equivalence to, for instance, reduce the number of gates in a circuit by using methods of algebra or build a circuit that can add numbers. However, it is just as clear that this equivalence between logic and arithmetic can only be established by ignoring the graphical and material differences that distinguish algebraic formulas from electronic circuits.

Oscillators and Flip-Flops: Circuits and Tables with Feedback

Differences between these two "equivalents" become clear when something is "written" in one form that is difficult or impossible to translate into the other form. For example, what is the algebraic form of the circuit shown in figure 5.4? It is an inverter

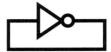

Figure 5.4
A looped inverter (oscillator or clock).

looped back on itself so that the wire from its output is connected back to the wire that is its input.

Consider what happens in the circuit in figure 5.4 if no voltage (i.e., a 0) is applied to the input of the inverter. Then, by definition and design, the output of the inverter will have a voltage; that is, the output will be 1. But just a moment later, since the output loops back to the input, the input to the inverter will be 1, soon thereafter the output will be 0, and so forth. Consequently, this circuit is called an "oscillator" or a "clock." As a digital clock, it constitutes the heart of a computer. Its "beat" synchronizes all of the operations of the computer.

The clock is both a perfectly valid Boolean circuit and an incredibly difficult-to-imagine expression in its algebraic or logical form. In that form, it just looks like a violation of all three of Aristotle's laws of thought: A = not(A).

Remember, however, that Aristotle's laws of thought cover only what can be true at a given moment in time, while the circuit diagram, in contrast, implicitly includes more than one moment of time. Thus, A = not(A) is an incorrect algebraic translation of the circuit diagram for an oscillator. Try to translate the circuit into a truth table and you will note, analogous to the algebraic notation, that neither does the truth table format have a way to express multiple moments of time.

Nevertheless, there *is* a way to express time in a table if we extend its conventions beyond the bounds that Wittgenstein laid out. Namely, we add one more column that notes the state of the machine. Table 5.5 is this kind of extended truth table for a circuit called a set-reset (or SR) *flip-flop* (or, alternatively, *latch*). Like a seesaw on a children's playground, the circuit has two stable states: one called *set*, the other called *reset*. The two inputs to the circuit are labeled S and R. The two outputs are Q and notQ. The intention is that when Q is 1, notQ will be 0; when notQ is 1, Q will be 0. Like a seesaw, when one side is up, the other side is down, and vice versa.

Note that table 5.5 is incomplete. Where is the entry for when both inputs are 1? Theoretically, this can happen, but the circuit is not intended to be used that way. Because the table does not encode all possible states, it implicitly describes pragmatics of use. A rule it leaves unwritten is that a flip-flop should not be incorporated into a

Table 5.5
Table for a set-reset (SR) flip-flop (or latch).

state	S	R	Q	notQ
set: Q gets 1	1	0	1	0
set: no change	0	0	1	0
reset: Q gets 0	0	1	0	1
reset: no change	0	0	0	1

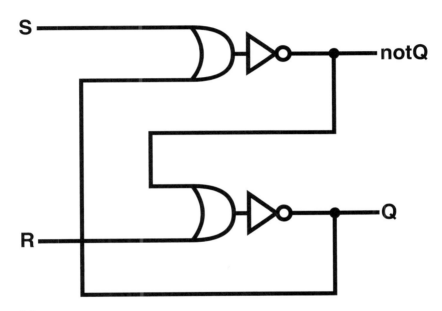

Figure 5.5
Boolean circuit for an SR flip-flop.

larger circuit that might put a voltage (i.e., a 1) on both the S and the R inputs. In other words, it should not be *set* and *reset* at the same time.

Figure 5.5 shows the Boolean circuit for an SR flip-flop. To use it, one might start by setting it; that is, by putting a voltage (a 1) on Q and none (a 0) on R. The output Q will then have a voltage (a 1), and the output notQ will have no voltage (a 0). Now, once the circuit has been set, Q and notQ will stay the same even if the voltage on S is turned off.

We can reset Q to 0 by setting the input R to 1. In the resultant state, "reset: Q gets 0," S is 0, R is 1, Q is 0, and notQ is 1. Reading from the fourth line in the table the values for the state titled "reset: no change," we can see, again, that neither Q nor notQ will change value if both inputs are subsequently turned off; that is, if both inputs are 0.

In other words, the values of Q and notQ are not solely dependent on the current values of S and R but also on their prior values: they are dependent on the last state of the circuit. This is the building block for computer memory. A flip-flop can store a bit—a 1 or a 0—and hold it between successive states of the circuit. This is done with feedback: one of the inputs to the OR gate on the top of the circuit comes from one of the outputs of the NOT gate on the bottom of the circuit, and vice versa.

Both the oscillator and the flip-flop circuits—the clock and the memory—incorporate feedback. In the circuit diagrams, feedback is easy to "write": an output of one component is wired to be the input of another (or the same) component. Feedback is impossible to write in Boole's algebraic notation; it lacks "inputs," "outputs," and "wires."

However, Wittgenstein's tables extended to include a column for states are perfectly adequate for defining feedback. By making one state dependent on a second state and the second state, recursively, dependent on the first state, feedback is defined in the table. The tables Turing used to define the computing machines in his 1936 paper were tables of this sort—ones in which states are named and inscribed into the tables.

Differences and Gaps

Nevertheless, tables are not exactly the same as circuits. To this point in the discussion, we have ignored one of the most important issues of circuit design: timing. Think of a simple circuit, such as an AND gate. Both inputs must be 1 for the output to be 1. Otherwise, the output is 0. Imagine if one of the inputs to the AND gate is wired to a switch on the other side of town, and the other input is a switch that sits right next to the AND gate. Even though electricity travels very quickly, it is nevertheless the case that an electrical current coming from the other side of town will take longer to reach the AND gate than the current that originates right next to the gate. So the issue of timing is this: When can the output of a gate be read?

Let us say that both inputs to the AND gate are on; that is, they are 1. But the output of the AND gate reads 0. Why? Because the electrical current coming from the switch closed all the way across town has yet to arrive at the input to the AND gate. We need to wait for its arrival before the AND gate registers a 1 on both its inputs and therefore changes its output to a 1.

Today most digital computers are built according to a (John) von Neumann architecture. This architecture incorporates the three kinds of circuits we have looked at here: (1) sets of AND, OR, and NOT gates to perform logical and arithmetical operations on data; (2) sets of flip-flops to store data; and (3) some form of looped inverter to serve as a clock. Synchronized to the clock, the digital computer performs its work by fetching, from the memory, the next operation in the process, decoding the operation, executing it, and then moving on to the subsequent operation. This is called the fetch-decode-execute (or FDX) cycle and is still built into the core of nearly every computer today.

If we compare this kind of work, the FDX cycle, with the definition of the joule (discussed in chapter 3, on work and machine languages), we see that while the joule incorporates time through the inclusion of gravity in its definition (via the use of mass and acceleration), the FDX cycle incorporates a very different kind of time. Its clock is "weightless," independent of gravity, and not so much a measuring device as a metronome that can be built, in its simplest form, as a looped inverter; that is, as a logic gate, specifically a gate that implements the NOT operator in which the wire that carries the output of the gate is looped back to the wire that is its input. Thus, a clock today is now a looped inverter and not a dial where the "hour hand" and the "minute hand" spin in circles.

Frequently, there are unintended consequences when the technology of clocks and calendars changes.[48] Thus, for instance, when the clock speed of computers (i.e., the FDX cycle governed by a digital clock, like the looped inverter) increased dramatically from megahertz (millions of cycles per second) to gigahertz (billions of cycles per second), new forms of financial transactions became possible and thus facilitated new market activities (e.g., high-frequency trading) and new forms of financial disasters (e.g., the May 6, 2010, "Flash Crash").

There are also unanticipated connections between older and newer forms of work and time. For example, neither the tables nor the circuit diagrams reveal the banal fact that computers need electrical power and that Boolean circuits produce joules of heat. And when they are employed billions of times per second, they produce a lot of heat; in fact, they produce so much heat that most computers have a fan incorporated into them, and technologies like cell phones that do not have a fan get perceptibly hot if they are performing a lot of calculations (as they do when, for instance, they are used to watch video). Power and heat are enormous problems for "cloud computing" giants like Amazon, Facebook, and Google, which consequently try to locate their server farms in places with cheap electrical power and in geographically cool places, like northern Sweden, because they thereby save so much on cooling costs.

In a nutshell, my point is that there exist enormous differences between computers and logic. Logic has no problems with timing, no need for fans or power supplies, and classically no notation for state or feedback. In contrast, we say that digital computers are built from Boolean circuits, but in fact they incorporate forms of time and work—such as the oscillator and the FDX cycle—that are measured in gigahertz, billionths of a second, a form of time outside the synchrony of Boolean logic.

Filling the Gap

Computer historian Michael Mahoney writes, "A theory of computation appositive to the electronic digital stored-program computer with random-access memory lay somewhere between the Turing machine and the switching circuit. Computer science arose out of the effort to fill that gap."[49] According to Mahoney, there is a gap between the logic of the Turing machine and the circuits of digital computers, and computer science as a whole is an attempt to fill that gap. In computer science, there is an attempt to fill that gap with software and other expressions in formal languages.

These formal languages are, for the most part, computer programming languages. In chapter 1, I cited a famous introductory textbook by Harold Abelson, Gerald Sussman, and Julie Sussman, *Structure and Interpretation of Computer Programs*, which argues that computer science is not a science. They call their approach "procedural epistemology," "the study of the structure of knowledge from an imperative point of view, as opposed to the more declarative point of view taken by classical mathematical subjects. Mathematics provides a framework for dealing precisely with notions of 'what is.' Computation provides a framework for dealing precisely with notions of 'how to.'"[50] The Abelson, Sussman, and Sussman text substantiates this approach by describing how all software design can be conceptualized as the design and implementation of special-purpose programming languages: "It is no exaggeration to regard this as the most fundamental idea in programming: the evaluator, which determines the meaning of expressions in a programming language, is just another program. To appreciate this point is to change our images of ourselves as programmers. We come to see ourselves as designers of languages, rather than only users of languages designed by others. In fact, we can regard almost any program as the evaluator for some language."[51] The bulk of their text is devoted to illustrating how one designs and implements different sorts of programming languages.

Abelson, Sussman, and Sussman's approach highlights a very direct link back to Bacon, Leibniz, and the eighteenth-century encyclopedists. That is to say, Abelson, Sussman, and Sussman place contemporary computation as the latest in the lineage of efforts to design artificial languages. As I argued in the introduction, the lineage I follow starts with Bacon's exhortations to combine the liberal arts with the mechanical arts and continues through Steve Jobs, when he explained that Apple's advantage is a combination of technology and the liberal arts. In Abelson, Sussman, and Sussman, we find not only able spokespersons for this genealogy but also an explicit methodology for pursuing this perspective—specifically, programming language design.

The Abelson, Sussman, and Sussman textbook was so well known in computer science circles that it was frequently referred to by its acronym, *SICP*. The programming examples in *SICP* are in the Scheme programming language. For the purposes of this book, I have taken one of their examples and translated it from Scheme into JavaScript so that it can be inspected with any modern web browser (because JavaScript—unlike Scheme—is natively supported in practically all browsers today). The example I will discuss is a translation of logic into software.

A Logic Circuit Simulator

Consider the problems of circuit design. Designers need a means of "sketching" their designs before they commit them to hardware, and usually the means for doing that is software. First, the circuits are designed using a software simulator, then refined and debugged before they are finalized in the materials of a chip. Almost every computer programming language natively supports the Boolean operators of AND, OR, and NOT, but for circuit designers this is not enough, because of all of the problems of timing discussed earlier: electricity is fast but not instantaneous, so any circuit simulator must incorporate some notion of how long a current will take to get from a to b, from the input of a logic gate to its output, and so on.

So, a circuit simulator must have the means to define a wire, a logic gate, and how the gates are connected together with the wires; furthermore, the simulator must provide a means to follow the flow of electricity through the wires and gates. The full text of my JavaScript program can be found on the website for this book.[52] In the pages that follow, I will focus primarily on some of the abstractions provided by the circuit simulator and less on the parts of the JavaScript code that implement the simulator.

Here is a little piece of code that sets up the simulator, defines an OR gate and the wires that lead into and out of the gate, puts a current on the wires going into the gate, and then runs the simulator. Comments on the code are preceded by "//."

```
// Create an instance of a circuit simulator, call it "cs."
var cs = makeCircuitSimulator();
// Create an instance of an agenda, call it "ag."
var ag = cs.getAgenda();
// Set up and run an OR gate.
// First define three wires: two input wires (a and b) and one output (c).
var a = cs.makeWire();
var b = cs.makeWire();
var c = cs.makeWire();
// Introduce a new instance of an OR gate into the simulator and attach the
```

```
// input and output wires to the gate.
cs.orGate(a,b,c);
// Put no current on the input wire a by setting its value to 0.
a.setValue(0);
// Put a current on the input wire b by setting its value to 1.
b.setValue(1);
// Now, put "probes" on all of the wires so that at every time step, the
// simulator prints out whether or not there is a current on each of the wires.
a.probe("wire a");
b.probe("wire b");
c.probe("wire c");
// Finally, turn on the simulator by propagating, via the agenda, the currents
// (i.e., the values 1 and 0) through the circuit.
ag.propagate();
// The "probes" will print out the following to the JavaScript console when the
// propagate() command is executed:
value for wire a @ time 0 is 0
value for wire b @ time 0 is 1
value for wire c @ time 0 is 0
value for wire c @ time 5 is 1
```

Note that at the start of the simulation (at time 0) the currents on the wires are either as defined (a is 0; b is 1) or as expected: c is 0 because the output from the OR gate has yet to be determined. A short time later (time 5), the c wire has a current because, as discussed earlier, the output from an OR gate is 1 if either or both of the inputs is 1.

Within the code that implements the circuit simulator, one can state how many increments of time it will take for a current to propagate through a given type of logic gate. In this case, I decided that the delay through an OR gate is 5 increments, that through an AND gate is 3, and that through a NOT gate, an inverter, is also 3. This is why the probe on the output wire for the OR gate does not report a value of 1 until time 5. While these delays can be easily changed in the code for the simulator, note that the ratio between the delays (5:3:3) needs to correspond with the ratio of delays one might observe in a hardware circuit—if the simulation is intended to resemble the performance of hardware.

In this translation of the circuit simulator, I did not provide a means for assigning a delay to a wire. All wires are idealized to work as if they could propagate a current with no delay at all. Clearly, one could change the simulator to allow wires to be assigned delays, as was done for the gates.

In writing a simulator like this, one makes a series of simplifying decisions. Here the wires are defined as propagating a current instantaneously, none of the gates need power, none of the gates produce heat, and the problem of layout is completely elided.

Layout is a major issue in the physical production of circuits: the gates need to be placed on a flat surface (usually a little piece of silicon) and then connected together with wires in such a way that the wires do not overlap and the delays of the gates are taken into account so that inputs arrive when they should and outputs are registered when they need to be.

Layout problems are exacerbated by timing problems, known as "race conditions." Imagine that a current from a very complicated circuit and the output of a very simple circuit are used as inputs to an AND gate. With all of the delays in the gates of the complicated circuit compared to the small number of delays in the simple circuit, the complicated circuit will output its result long after the simple circuit has stopped doing so. So, either some means must be devised to delay the arrival of the output from the simple circuit—so that it is in sync with the output of the complex circuit—or the reading of the output from the AND gate that depends on these two inputs is delayed until the complex circuit has finished.

Abelson, Sussman, and Sussman call their approach, which centers on the design and implementation of special-purpose programming languages, "metalinguistic abstraction."[53] The circuit simulator is an example of this approach. An abstraction is designed for each of the objects or subjects of interest—in this case, orGate, andGate, inverter, wire, and current (which is represented as simply a 1 or a 0). An abstraction is defined for each process of interest; in this case, the agenda is the abstraction that defines how currents are propagated through the wires and gates. Then, a means for composing the abstractions together is defined. In this case, the means are JavaScript "functions" and the definition of data structures in JavaScript, called "objects." Together, these abstractions and the means of composition constitute a special-purpose programming language for designing circuits. We can understand this circuit simulator as a special-purpose subset of the JavaScript language.

Here is another simple example of this special-purpose language in use. This defines an oscillator, a clock, as a looped inverter by connecting the same wire to the input and the output of the inverter.

```
var cs = makeCircuitSimulator();
var ag = cs.getAgenda();
var a = cs.makeWire();
cs.inverter(a,a); // The wire "a" is both the inverter's input and output
a.setValue(1);
```

a.probe("wire a");

ag.propagate();

// The simulator outputs the following trace. Remember that I have set the

// delay for inverters to be 3 time units.

value for wire a @ time 0 is 1

value for wire a @ time 3 is 0

value for wire a @ time 6 is 1

value for wire a @ time 9 is 0

With this special-purpose programming language, it is equally possible to define and simulate some of the other circuits discussed, including a half-adder, for example. But I want to emphasize again that the software of the circuit simulator is neither identical to actual circuitry (because of, among other things, the abstractions and simplifications listed earlier) nor equivalent to the Boolean logic it is modeled after (again because, for instance, there is an abstraction of time in the circuit simulator that is not present in Boolean logic). To paraphrase Michael Mahoney, software is neither logic nor circuitry, but the software arts provide a means to imperfectly translate between the two.

Logic Programming

> The theorem prover may be considered an "interpreter" for a high-level assertional or declarative language—logic.[54]

For decades, some computer scientists have dreamed of using logic as a programming language. In 1972, French computer scientists Alain Colmerauer and Philippe Roussel developed the Prolog programming language[55] with key assistance from a number of others, including Robert Kowalski.[56] "Prolog" stands for "programming in logic." According to Kowalski, "The driving force behind logic programming is the idea that a single formalism suffices for both logic and computation, and that logic subsumes computation."[57]

In the title of a 1979 paper, Kowalski telegraphs the difficulties inherent in developing this vision: "Algorithm = Logic + Control."[58] To render this idea in a slightly less laconic manner, one might say that while logic can be used to explain the relations that hold between the input and the output, one still needs control—a means of specifying how the input will be transformed into the output—in order to write a computer program.

We can rewrite Kowalski's title/equation to make the primary difference between logic and algorithm clearer by rearranging his equation to read Logic = Algorithm − Control. The dream has been to make Logic = Algorithm, and the work of decades of computer scientists with this dream has been to put control into logic. Obviously, to do so, one needs to either change what an algorithm is, change the very definition of logic, or both.

Arguably, both algorithms, as articulated in the theory of computation, and logic, as defined by professional logicians, have changed in response to each other. But, at the beginning of this dream—and perhaps, for some, even today—logic was defined as predicate logic.[59] Recall that in the preceding section, on logic and circuit simulation, the logic of concern was George Boole's translation of Aristotelian logic. But predicate logic is something else.

First-Order Predicate Logic

Until about the time of Boole, logic was primarily concerned with Aristotle's syllogisms. Boole began his work, as discussed in chapter 4, by translating examples of Aristotle's syllogisms into his new notation. Then, in the following century (mid-nineteenth to mid-twentieth), logic changed radically in response to the works of, among others, George Boole, Gottlob Frege, Charles Sanders Peirce, David Hilbert, Alfred North Whitehead, Kurt Gödel, and Rudolf Carnap. The result, according to a fascinating history of logic narrated by logician, philosopher, and historian José Ferreirós, was an expansion of logic to encompass a much wider field and then, after that, a relatively rapid narrowing and convergence on first-order predicate logic. Ferreirós writes, "Presenting in a nutshell the results of our quick historical overview, we can say that around 1900 logic was conceived as a theory of sentences, sets and relations; after World War I and as late as 1930 the exemplar for modern logic was a higher-order system, simple type theory; and only around 1940–1950 did the community of logicians as a whole come to agree that the paradigm logical system is FOL [first-order predicate logic]."[60]

Ferreirós's history explains how contemporary understandings of logic are historically and contextually contingent: "There is a tendency to think that logic is of a peculiarly clear and crystalline nature, but this is more a deceitful image than an evidence. I expect the foregoing arguments may have made (at least) plausible the conclusion that FOL is no natural unity, raising the impression that the notion of logic involves some obscurity or indeterminacy. But, if so, how and why have we come to modern first-order logic? Quite obviously, when first principles are insufficient, we must turn to historical contexts and traditions."[61] In other words, today, when logicians, mathematicians, philosophers, and computer scientists talk about "logic," they are referring to a very specific and relatively recent invention of the early twentieth century.[62]

Variables and Quantifiers

In the late nineteenth century, Frege and Peirce independently invented the two most important aspects that distinguish modern logic from its Aristotelian predecessor: predicates with variables and quantifiers.[63]

Why are predicates with variables such a big deal in logic? Consider that in propositional logic one can write something like this: "if A then B." A and B stand for propositions. Perhaps A stands for "Socrates is a man" and B stands for "Socrates is mortal." Thus, "if A then B" stands for "if Socrates is a man then Socrates is mortal."

That is fine if we are only interested in inferences about Socrates, but what if we are interested in inferences about Plato, Alcibiades—many men—and not just Socrates? The introduction of predicates with variables allows one to state a more general rule like this: "if man(x) then mortal(x)." A specific instance of the general rule, when the free variable x is bound to Socrates, looks like this: "if man(Socrates) then mortal(Socrates)." Predicates with variables allow one to state general rules like this, which are impossible to state concisely in a propositional logic.

Questions of quantification arrived in Peirce's and Frege's respective predicate calculi because, once a predicate with variables has been stated, one must consider what can be bound to the variables of the predicate. For example, is the predicate applicable to all men? Perhaps, but imagine you are a Christian. Does this ring true: "if man(Jesus) then mortal(Jesus)"? Theology aside, Frege and Peirce each saw a need to introduce universal and existential quantifiers to address questions of generality and specificity.

Today, the universal quantifier is usually written as an upside down "A," indicating "for ALL." So, one can write all men are mortal like this: "∀x(if man(x) then mortal(x))."

Today, the existential quantifier is usually written as a rotated "E," indicating "there EXISTS." So, one can write that there exists some man that is mortal like this: "∃x(if man(x) then mortal(x))." With an existentially quantified variable, the predicate is about some specific man, not all men.

Programming in Prolog

To return to Kowalski's driving motivation cited earlier, those who have developed logic programming aim to write statements in the notation of logic and have those statements run as computer programs. In the Prolog programming language, one can write predicates and assertions like this:[64]

man(socrates).
man(plato).
mortal(X):- man(X). % This means X is mortal if X is a man.

The Prolog interpreter allows us to query for statements that are asserted directly in the database, and it allows us to query for statements that can be deduced from the statements (usually called assertions) and the predicates in the database. Thus, a query like

?- man(Who)

would result in the variable "Who" being bound first to "socrates" and then to "plato." Similarly, because the predicate for "mortal" is defined, the query

?- mortal(Who)

also results in the same bindings: "Who" is first bound to "socrates," then to "plato." With this short example, one might conclude that Kowalski and his colleagues have accomplished their goal of programming in logic, but let us extend the example just a little bit to show how, as Kowalski expressed in the title of his 1979 paper, software renderings of algorithms include specifications of control that are not expressed in logic.

First we will add one more assertion:

man(jesus).

Next, we will define a predicate for "equal":

equal(Y,Y). % Two entities are equal if they are identical.

Now we will add one more conjunct to the predicate "mortal":

mortal(X):- man(X),not(equal(X,jesus)). % X is a man and X is not jesus.

With these small additions, the query

?- mortal(Who)

results in "Who" being first bound to "socrates" and then to "plato." In other words, because of the added condition in the predicate "mortal," mortal(jesus) cannot be deduced from the asserted statements and predicates.

Note that in first-order predicate logic, conjunction is commutative; for example, "man(X) and not(equal(X,jesus))" means the same thing as "not(equal(X,jesus)) and man(X)." But, in contrast to logic, in Prolog the ordering of the conjuncts does make a difference.

Consider that when the predicate for "mortal" is rewritten as

mortal(X):- not(equal(X,jesus)),man(X). % X is not jesus and X is a man.

the query

?- mortal(Who)

results in "Who" being bound to what? Actually, now the query fails. Prolog fails to identify any entities that can be proved to be mortal. (When a query fails, Prolog interpreters usually return "false" or just "no.")

There are two reasons why this query now fails. First, the conjunction operator "and" in Prolog is not commutative as it is in first-order predicate logic. Second, in Prolog, the negation operator "not" means something different from negation in logic. Moreover, even though this small example does not illustrate it, the other major logical operator, "or," also has very different semantics in Prolog than it does in logic. In other words, programming in Prolog, despite its name, is not at all like programming in logic, because conjunction ("and"), disjunction ("or"), and negation ("not") have very different meanings in Prolog than they do in first-order predicate logic.

Using the distinctions described in chapter 3, on work and machine languages, one could say that AND, OR, and NOT are mathematical functions in logic but are operators in Prolog. More specifically, one can say that in Prolog they are step-by-step procedures that operate on a database. Alternatively, in the terminology of the computer science literature on logic programming, Prolog code has a procedural meaning[65] that logic does not.

For instance, given the query

?- mortal(Who).

when the predicate is defined as

mortal(X):- man(X), not(equal(X,jesus)).

the Prolog interpreter does the following. First, it searches through the database for all the matches to the first conjunct, "man(Who)," and finds three such matches: man(socrates), man(plato), man(jesus). Next, the Prolog interpreter filters those results by running them through the second conjunct, "not(equal(Who,jesus))." The second conjunct eliminates one of these three matches, so Prolog then returns two results to the query: "mortal(socrates), mortal(plato)."

Now, consider what happens when the conjuncts are reversed as

mortal(X):- not(equal(X,jesus)),man(X).

and the query is again

?- mortal(Who).

Prolog tries the first conjunct, not(equal(Who,jesus)). This fails because "Who" is an unbound variable that can therefore be bound to anything in the database, including "jesus." "Who" can be unified with "jesus" so "equal(Who,jesus)" succeeds and then its negation—"not(equal(Who,jesus))"—fails.[66]

In logic programming, this interpretation of negation is referred to as "negation as failure." It is dependent on a "closed-world assumption": the assumption that everything that exists is in the database as an assertion or can be computed from the predicates and the assertions in the database.

To illustrate, let us use the Prolog database specified earlier and then pose the following query:

?- mortal(god).

The Prolog interpreter will respond to this query with "false" not because it somehow knows that God is immortal but rather because, when it runs the predicate that defines "mortal," it searches for an assertion of the form "man(god)" and finds no such assertion in the database. Thus the query fails.

What happens, however, if we pose this query:

?- not(mortal(god)).

The Prolog interpreter will respond to this query with "true" not because it somehow knows that God is immortal but rather because the query "mortal(god)" returns "false" and therefore the query "not(false)" returns "true." It will also return "true" for this query:

?- not(mortal(dog)).

Indeed, the only two entities that this database cannot "prove" to be not mortal are "socrates" and "plato," because they are the only ones that have been declared to be men and are not equal to "jesus." This is an illustration of both negation-as-failure and the closed-world assumption implicit in Prolog.[67]

In Prolog, "quantification" has been translated into a search through a database. In logic, when we use a universal quantifier—for example, "$\forall x$(if man(x) then mortal(x))"—it is supposed that x might be bound to absolutely anything in the universe. In contrast, Prolog's variables can only be bound to assertions found in a specific database, and the database is searched in a specific sequence. Consequently, even if they bear some family resemblance, Prolog's "and," "or," "not," variables and quantification are all quite different from their counterparts in first-order predicate logic.

Bringing Logic and Dialectic Back Together Again?

As narrated at the beginning of this chapter, over time, logic and dialectic sheared away from each other and became distinctly different arts. One might therefore be skeptical when told that—at least in the world of software—they are being sutured together again. Kowalski, one of the pioneers of Prolog, and others now claim that logic is not a form of calculation but rather a form of argumentation! Bondarenko et al. write, "The notions of argument, assumption, attack and defence are sufficient to reconstruct…most logic programming semantics."[68]

Others, in close dialogue with Kowalski, have attempted to show the converse: that argumentation, of all kinds, is simply a form of logic programming! Computer scientist Phan Minh Dung writes, "Though argumentation is a powerful method for problem solving, it turns out that it can be 'implemented' easily in logic programming. We demonstrate this by showing that argumentation can be viewed as logic programming with negation as failure."[69]

Recall that "negation as failure" is a standard "feature" of Prolog programming, the method used to translate negation into a search through a database. That this difference with negation in the first-order predicate logic is the key to turning logic back into a technique of conversation, of argumentation, seems unlikely. Dung continues, "This result shows that logic programming is the perfect tool for implementing argumentation systems. It seems necessary to point out again that our primary intention in this paper is not to study the relationship between logic programming and nonmonotonic reasoning though much light is shed on this relationship from our result that both of them are forms of argumentation. Our main goal is to give an analysis of the nature of human argumentation in its full generality."[70]

The translations of logic—into circuits, into software, into a kind of arithmetic, and so forth—have resulted in a huge variety of significantly different techniques and technologies. By tracing through some of these translations, I have tried to provide a means for understanding how claims like Dung's might be seen as absurd. How can there not be enormous and significant differences between logic programming and "the nature of human argumentation in its full generality"? In my opinion, one must be thinking within the bubble of a full-blown digital ideology to imagine that logic programming and human argumentation can be considered equivalent.

Doing Logic as a Form of Translation

The unwarranted, almost religious, belief in logic as a universal, omnipotent foundation for the definition or implementation of almost any form of thought is long-standing. Philosopher Bertrand Russell stated his belief in the foundational role of logic like this: "The fact that all Mathematics is Symbolic Logic is one of the greatest discoveries of our age; and when this fact has been established, the remainder of the principles of Mathematics consists in the analysis of Symbolic Logic itself."[71]

Russell's student, then colleague and rival, Ludwig Wittgenstein became a skeptic of this belief in logic. Wittgenstein wrote, "If Russell has connected mathematical procedures with logic, this might mean that he just *translates* [my emphasis] them into a new language. But it is misleading to think this is an explanation: to think that when we get down to predicates and predicative functions, we see what mathematics is really about,"[72] meaning "the idea that there is a science, namely logic, on which mathematics rests. I want to say in no way it rests on logic. And the fact that you can make logic formulae agree with it, in no way shows that it rests on logic."[73]

With these words, Wittgenstein articulates a position far afield from Russell's (and those of Kowalski and other believers in the omnipotence of logic). Tellingly, Wittgenstein points out that doing logic is a practice of translation into a different language and not necessarily into some ultimate form of language.

From Logical Calculation to Rhetorical Demonstration

"QED" is an acronym frequently employed at the end of a logical proof. It stands for "quod erat demonstrandum"—in English, "what was to be shown," or "thus it has been demonstrated." Implicitly, the acronym declares that the preceding set of logical inferences leads one to the final conclusion, which can be labeled QED.

But only an audience that can be led from statement to statement by logical inference will arrive at the labeled conclusion convinced of its truth. In Wittgenstein's critique of Russell, we find a skeptical audience: Wittgenstein is not a reader willing to be led by Russell's logic about mathematics. Or is Russell's logic not a logic but a form of rhetoric? In chapter 6, we will closely examine the boundary between logical and rhetorical forms of demonstration—especially deductive, inductive, and abductive demonstration.

Recall Michel Serres's observation, discussed in chapter 2, that many terms for translation—deduction, induction, abduction, and others—incorporate the Latin root "dūcĕre," a word that means "to lead." Each of the prefixes prepended to "dūcĕre" indicate a direction. "De-," for instance, means "down" or "down from." So, "deduce" connotes "to lead down." "In-" means "into" or "in." Thus, "induce," in Latin, means "to lead into." "Ab" is "away," so "abduce" means "to lead away," "to carry away," or "to draw away" someone or something. Each is a form of inference leading one from statement to statement.

Deduction is perhaps the most familiar of these logical vehicles of travel. Given a specific example and a general rule, one can deduce more specifics about the example. Thus, to repeat the example employed in the discussion of Prolog programming, imagine we know that Socrates is a man (the specific example) and know that all men are mortal (the general rule). Thereby it can be deduced that Socrates is mortal. But if the deductive inference is performed by a Prolog program, for whom is the conclusion demonstrated? Who is convinced by the inferences performed by the program?

Peirce made many contributions to logic, including his insight that Boolean logic could be translated into electrical circuits, discussed earlier in this chapter. In other works, Peirce discussed logical inferences of three forms: deductive, inductive, and abductive. All three have been given highly detailed meanings in software and programming; specifically, I refer to three forms of programming: deductive logic programming, such as Prolog,[74] inductive logic programming,[75] and abductive logic programming.[76] With respect to the latter, diagnostic reasoning[77] (e.g., for medicine), means-ends analysis[78] (e.g., also known as "planning," where there is a goal to reach and we need to infer what steps need to be taken to reach it), and a number of other forms of reasoning[79] have been considered as forms of abductive inference.

As programming language paradigms,[80] deductive, inductive, and abductive logic programming are effectively forms of calculation and not methods employed to convince people—even though one might be convinced of a result reached by a computer program. For example, the execution of a global climate simulation might be very persuasive rhetoric. Nevertheless, there are gaps between Peirce's descriptions of these "ductions" and their translations into software.

Through a discussion of some of the history of logic and dialectic and the explanation of several examples of how logic has been translated into computer hardware and software, this chapter examines some of these gaps and argues that logic has no single stable definition. Instead, logic is best understood as a language art that has undergone—and continues to undergo—many translations. It has sprouted, pullulating into a myriad of practices and materialities, the latest of which are software. In chapter 6, on rhetoric, we will examine more closely how such software has been employed as a means of persuasion.

6 Rhetoric

Digital rhetoric employs demonstrations to argue that an idea, institution, or practice can be translated into software. Computer simulations, "big data" visualizations, and computer "demos" are all examples of digital rhetoric.

This chapter recounts a history of the "demonstration," or the "demo," a practice that has put the arts at the center of the definitions of both rhetoric and logic. How does the ancient Greek demonstration become the Silicon Valley standard pitch of today? Answering such a question will move us closer to an understanding of contemporary rhetoric.

The history of the "demo" starts in ancient Greece, where definitive demonstration was a matter of deduction exemplified by demonstrations in geometry. Deductive demonstration was displaced by inductive demonstration in the seventeenth century, during the "scientific revolution." Inductive demonstration was made necessary when arguments began to be based on empirical data and not just derived from statements taken to be obviously true. For example, the remaking of alchemy into chemistry required the invention of a form of rigorous, inductive demonstration from empirical observations.

Today, arguments are made on the basis of so much data—"big data"—that no one person could possibly read it all, much less observe its collection. This has necessitated the invention of yet another form of argumentation, which I term "abductive demonstration." Silicon Valley "demos" are in the genus of abductive demonstrations. At the end of the chapter, we will carefully read an argument that employs simulation to claim that life, the universe, and everything is just a big computer. What is the contemporary form of rhetorical demonstration and digital ideology that makes such a claim seem plausible?

The Mother of All Demos

December 9, 1968, was a remarkable day in the history of computing. Douglas Engelbart presented what has been called the "mother of all demos" at the ACM/IEEE[1] Computer Society's Fall Joint Computer Conference in San Francisco.[2] Actually, there were two sites for the demo: San Francisco and Menlo Park, about 30 miles to the south in Silicon Valley. The sites were connected by microwave and telephone to establish a two-way video link and to allow Engelbart to connect from the stage in San Francisco to his computer at the Stanford Research Institute (SRI) in Menlo Park. Today, we think nothing of this kind of network connectivity, but it was almost unheard of in 1968.[3] For most of the computer professionals in the audience of the 2,000-seat auditorium, it was their first look at the future of the computer interface. Engelbart demonstrated a number of things that were remarkable then and are ubiquitous now, including the computer mouse, resizable windows, teleconferencing, hypertext, word processing, and collaborative editing.[4] His demo showed what we now know as personal computing.[5]

In 1994, journalist Steven Levy called Engelbart's 1968 event the "mother of all demos."[6] One might imagine that he did so because the technology Engelbart showed in 1968 was the mother of the personal computers so ubiquitous in 1994, but in this chapter I want to call attention not to what Engelbart was demonstrating but rather how—the form and practice of the demo.

Engelbart's demo borrowed a number of its forms from the 1960s American counterculture,[7] but by then, "demos" had already been in the American commercial landscape for decades.[8] A "demo" at a retail store, such as a car dealership, or at a professional trade show could be an example of the product for sale available for temporary use by the potential customer before buying the product. This form of demo still exists in many American retail situations: try before you buy. Alternatively, a "demo" was a step-by-step performance by a skilled technician or artisan to show a potential customer how to use a product. Thus, in contemporary American supermarkets, one will often find "demos" of new kinds of packaged foods cooked in front of the shoppers and available for tasting, or, in an appliance store, one can find "demos" of food processors, mixers, blenders, and barbecues operated by skilled cooks to convince the potential buyer how easy to use the appliance is and how marvelous the results of doing so can be. Both trial products and performances are demos aimed at persuading customers to heed a very simple message: "Buy it!"

Engelbart's "mother of all demos" was more complicated in its aims and its results than those usually pursued through commercial product demos. In no simple sense was

Engelbart's aim to get someone to buy what he was demonstrating. The United States Department of Defense Advanced Research Projects Agency (ARPA) had funded his research group, the Augmentation Research Center (ARC), for years, and would continue to fund it for several more years after the demo. In fact, it was his program director at ARPA who encouraged him to do the demo[9] even though ARPA had already "bought" the technology. Instead, what was being sold at Engelbart's demo was a vision of the future of knowledge work, as Engelbart outlined it in his published papers.

Furthermore, what Engelbart gained after the demo was not cash but rather a considerable reputation. He went from being the leader of an obscure project to being seen as a visionary who commanded the skills and resources to execute on that vision.[10] In some ways, the "mother of all demos" was less like an advertisement for a product and more like science fiction—a vision of the future.

Engelbart hired Stewart Brand to be the videographer of the 1968 demo. Brand was a former US Army parachutist and closely connected to military and industrial high-technology research labs like Engelbart's ARC. He was also, thanks to a lot of nomadic travel, a lively member of both the New York and California countercultures. As he puts it in his online autobiography, "[Brand] hung out with Ken Kesey, the Merry Pranksters, and early Acid Tests; designed and organized the 'Trips Festival,' a 3-day rock-light watershed event at Longshoreman's Hall in San Francisco; and, did sound and doorways for 'We Are All 1' at the Riverside Museum, New York City, with USCO (an artist/engineer team based in Garnerville, NY)."[11]

The kinds of drug, rock, and art installations Brand was involved with at the time were immersive environments not meant to communicate a single message but instead intended to get the participants to experience life and everyday phenomena with an altered consciousness.[12] These were "demos" of vision and life, not simple product demos.

Demos at MIT

Years later, after an extended residence at the Massachusetts Institute of Technology (MIT), Brand wrote a book where he remarked on the central role of the demo in the technological productions of the MIT Media Laboratory:

> Everything [at the MIT Media Laboratory] involves communication, empowers the individual, employs computers … and makes a flashy demonstration. Students and professors at the Media Laboratory write papers and books and publish them, but the byword in this grove of academe is not "Publish or Perish." In Lab parlance it's "Demo or Die"—make the case for your idea

with an unfaked performance of it working at least once, or let somebody else at the equipment.... [Visitors] see the demos and are suitably dazzled or puzzled, but what draws them here is that they've heard or sensed the Media Laboratory has a Vision, capital V.[13]

The subtitle of Brand's book on the MIT Media Lab is "Inventing the Future at MIT." Brand argues that the demos of the Media Lab, like Engelbart's "mother of all demos," are not commercial product demos but rather attempts to persuade visitors to buy into a vision of the future.[14]

While the MIT Media Lab was—and still is—well known for its demos, years earlier demos had become a mainstay at other laboratories, at least on the MIT campus. For instance, in 1970, Terry Winograd (now a professor emeritus of computer science at Stanford) completed his PhD while working at the MIT Artificial Intelligence Lab. Winograd's dissertation program, SHRDLU, could display a three-dimensional graphics picture of a set of children's blocks, accept English language questions and commands (e.g., "Put the green block on top of the small red one"), and reply by moving the blocks displayed onscreen and by responding with English sentences.[15] Winograd's SHRDLU program was hailed as a breakthrough in artificial intelligence and especially natural language understanding,[16] but in an interview twenty years later, it was obvious that he was uneasy about his famous demo exactly because it was, in Brand's terms, "an unfaked performance [that worked] at least once."

Winograd, in conversation with computer historian Arthur L. Norberg (of the Charles Babbage Institute, University of Minnesota), said the following about his demo and other demos at MIT:

> Implementation was always there as the coin of the realm. Implementation meant something you could show off. It didn't mean something that somebody else could use.... [M]y thesis was certainly that way.... [T]he famous dialogue with SHRDLU where you could pick up a block, and so on, I very carefully worked through, line by line. If you sat down in front of it, and asked it a question that wasn't in the dialogue, there was some probability it would answer it. I mean, if it was reasonably close to one of the questions that was there in form and in content, it would probably get it. But there was no attempt to get it to the point where you could actually hand it to somebody and they could use it to move blocks around. And there was no pressure for that whatsoever. Pressure was for something you could demo. Take a recent example, Negroponte's Media Lab, where instead of "perish or publish" it's "demo or die." I think that's a problem. I think AI [artificial intelligence] suffered from that a lot, because it led to "Potemkin villages," things which—for the things they actually did in the demo looked good, but when you looked behind that there wasn't enough structure to make it really work more generally.[17]

In this statement, Winograd articulates his unease with demos in multiple ways. His first concern is method. The method he employs to implement a demo is largely patterned on a method of theater: "the famous dialogue…I very carefully worked through, line by line." The second concern is probability. According to Winograd, unscripted interactions with the demo had a low probability of performing correctly: "There was some probability it would answer it." The third concern was practicality. The program was built more as a prop for a solo performance rather than as a tool to be shared with others: "You could [not] hand it to somebody [so] they could use it." The final concern was artifice. The demo was implemented as a kind of theater set and not as a structure meant to be in daily use; that is, it was a sort of "Potemkin village." Note that all of these reservations (about method, probability, practicality, and artifice) are standard features of theatrical plays and their performance. They are, analogously, desired features of scripts, scripted acting, props, and theater set design. Winograd's unease with the form of the demo reads as a discomfort with the demo's close proximity to theater.

The Imitation Game

Of course, this should not be a surprise: some theater professionals might take it as a compliment to have their work called "scientific," but most scientists would be offended to have their work called "theatrical." Winograd's citation of "Potemkin villages" is telling. When the governor-general of Russia's southern provinces, Grigory Potemkin, set out to fool Empress Catherine II by erecting a façade, a fake village, along the banks of the Dnieper River for her to see as she passed by on her way to Crimea, he was applying stagecraft—theatrical set design—offstage where it served not as theater but as dissimulation: a lie about the actual state of peasant villages. Thus, in politics, engineering, and science, the phrase "Potemkin village" is one of disapprobation. Winograd's unease with the demo is revealed to be a moral objection: he fears a demo is tantamount to dissimulation or is at best a bad imitation.

As will shortly be discussed, this unease with imitation has a long history in philosophy, going back at least as far as Plato. But it has been and continues to be a persistent sentiment and therefore has been voiced by many famous philosophers, mathematicians, and scientists through the millennia.

For example, Norbert Wiener, MIT professor and the founder of cybernetics, expressed his reservation about imitation in 1960, a decade before Terry Winograd's famous demo and twenty-five years before the founding of the MIT Media Lab: "If we use, to achieve our purposes, a mechanical agency with whose operation we cannot interfere effectively…we had better be quite sure that the purpose put into the machine is the purpose which we really desire and not merely a colorful imitation of it."[18] Wiener's remark makes it clear that the moral quandary is not with the mechanical imitation itself but rather with the power of the imitation should it be taken for the thing, or person, it is imitating. The danger therefore concerns a fear of forgery and impersonation or, worse yet, the uncanny terror that the imitation will usurp the actual thing or person.

In the conclusion of this book, I will elaborate on a 1950 essay by Alan Turing that has been considered the founding essay of artificial intelligence.[19] The essay is composed around a game of conversational interaction: Turing calls it the "imitation game." Turing's imitation game is in play with the longer philosophical discourse on imitation and simulation that is under examination in the present chapter.

As discussed in chapter 2, on translation, worries about bad imitations (both morally corrupt and poorly crafted) are worries about translation. To establish an equivalence between two a priori unlike entities (e.g., in Winograd's case, between a computer program and a verbally proficient child playing with blocks), one must enact some sort of translation so that the features and faults of one become those of the other. Ironically, historically, the way to rigorously establish an equivalence has been through "demonstration." Demonstration was central both to logic and to the kind of rhetoric that borrows heavily from logic.

Plato's Demonstrations

There have been many forms of demonstration practiced between the time of Plato and now. In sketching out a history of the "demo," we will see that, initially, demonstrations were patterned on a very narrow and constrained practice: the mathematical proofs of geometry. Geometrical demonstration was taken as the ideal way to prove a point and thereby win consensus without really arguing. Plato's and then Aristotle's peculiarity of borrowing from geometry persisted for thousands of years because Aristotle's writings stayed central to the teaching of the liberal arts. Theatrics is notably absent from the practice of the geometers. As can be seen in Plato's works, he disapproved of most of the arts of imitation, including poetry, theater, painting, and sculpture. In Winograd's unease, we hear echoes of Plato's reservations about the conjoining of mathematical proof and theater in the form of a rhetorical demonstration.

The ancient Greek geometry demonstration—Plato's and Aristotle's ideal form of argumentation—was designed to be a very intimate affair performed for a small circle of friends or colleagues knowledgeable about the topic of discussion. Rhetoric, on the other hand, is a form of argumentation pursued in front of large crowds peopled by many who know nothing about the topic and who are apathetic if not antagonistic.[20]

As philosopher and anthropologist Bruno Latour points out in his close reading of Plato's *Gorgias* dialogue, Plato's image of intimate dialogue in the form of mathematical demonstration as an ideal for public debate was at best unrealistic and at worst highly destructive to democracy and to the reputation of the Sophists, the artists, and the Athenian public, since the arts—especially the techniques of theater—are essential to any form of public performance, including demonstrations of rhetoric.[21] Today, demonstrations that venture beyond strict adherence to the form of mathematical proof, especially those demonstrations that might look like theater, are still viewed with suspicion by many philosophers, mathematicians, and scientists influenced, consciously or not, by these disastrous Platonic, antiart ideals.

Simulation and the Art of the Sophists

Plato's suspicions about rhetoric were personified by the Sophists, a group of highly skilled rhetoricians who set up schools in Athens to teach argumentation, persuasion, and techniques of imitation. Imitation was practiced in different ways in the different arts. Thus, a painter might create a highly realistic picture of a bunch of grapes, leading us to try to pick one.[22] But, according to Plato, the Sophists' art of rhetoric was the worst of the arts, because the Sophists were the most general kind of imitator, willing to impersonate anyone and imitate anything. So, in the Platonic dialogues, the Sophists are called "simulacra" (from the Latin *simulāre*, to make like).[23]

Plato pleaded that the Sophists' sins against Athens were twofold. First, the Sophists used rhetorical techniques well beyond (Plato's) acceptable limits of mathematical demonstration; that is, they argued in ways that did not resemble geometry proofs. Second, the Sophists had the temerity to argue any point for or against anyone's point of view. Plato thought the Sophists' methods and aims were false and that their credentials to play any role, to argue any position, were suspect.

In the nineteenth century, a series of attempts were made to redeem the Sophists' reputation from Plato's defamation, including those of philosopher Georg Wilhelm Friedrich Hegel (1770–1831), historian George Grote (1794–1871), and philosopher Friedrich Nietzsche (1844–1900). This redemption has been difficult to accomplish because much of what is known about the Sophists is known by way of Plato's writing about them. But redeeming the Sophists' reputation is not only a matter of documentation—that is, finding more writings about and by them. It is also a question of reschooling ourselves. Most likely, if you are reading this book, you have read Plato. But have you read Protagoras, Gorgias, or any of the other Sophists? Probably not, unless you are a scholar specializing in ancient Greece. Consequently, as a result of the kind of schooling most of us get even now, we tend to read with Plato, implicitly taking up Plato's slanderous position against the Sophists.

This project of redeeming the Sophists proceeded into the twentieth century and continues up to today. Following Nietzsche,[24] this project was continued by, among others, a number of European philosophers, including Hannah Arendt, Gilles Deleuze, Michel Foucault, Pierre Klossowski, Bruno Latour, and Jean-François Lyotard. These philosophers have worked to "queer" the term "simulacrum," to make a term of abuse into a term of praise, or at least one of value.[25]

What I will attempt to show in this chapter is how this old fight about argument and persuasion carries on today in the newest contests of rhetoric—computer simulations, "demos," and data visualizations. The demos of Engelbart, Winograd, and Negroponte would have been too theatrical—not sufficiently mathematical—for Plato. Yet, nascent in these demos were a set of rhetorical tropes of simulation that are very effective means of persuasion. Computer simulations are the newest addition to the art of rhetoric. At the end of this chapter, we will see the general form of argument-by-simulation by looking more closely at one sample argument from the fields of artificial life and cellular automata, at the intersection of biology and computer science.

Aristotle's Demonstrations

In the introduction to his book on rhetoric, Aristotle states, "Rhetorical study, in its strict sense, is concerned with the modes of persuasion. Persuasion is clearly a sort of demonstration, since we are most fully persuaded when we consider a thing to have been demonstrated. The orator's demonstration is an enthymeme, and this is, in general, the most effective of the modes of persuasion. The enthymeme is a sort of syllogism, and the consideration of syllogisms of all kinds, without distinction, is the business of dialectic."[26] Keeping in mind that a syllogism is a form of demonstration by logical deduction, we can see that Aristotle considers the heart of rhetoric as an extension—a translation—from dialectic: a translation from syllogisms to enthymemes.

In chapter 5, on logic and dialectics, we saw a common example of a syllogism: major premise: "all men are mortal"; minor premise: "Socrates is a man"; and conclusion: "therefore, Socrates is mortal." Aristotle's enthymemes are more or less a looser, nonrigorous form of syllogism. For example, one form of enthymeme leaves the major premise unstated or presupposed. Consequently, an enthymeme constructed on just the minor premise (and leaving out the major premise) would license the following rhetorical (not logical) inference: "because Socrates is a man, he is mortal." In the looser, rhetorical form, no mention of the major premise (all men are mortal) is required to reach a conclusion, and therefore the conclusion is not certain but rather only probable.

Aristotle discusses more than one kind of enthymeme, but the key point is that they are modeled on syllogisms, yet they license much less certain, "wilder" forms of inference. In semiotician and logician Charles Peirce's terminology, one might say that syllogisms are a framework for "deduction," while enthymemes license a much wider set of "abductions," or, in Peirce's more vernacular phrasing, they license what might otherwise be called good guesses, but guesses that could easily be wrong.

Aristotle explains the similarity between dialectical or logical demonstration and rhetorical demonstration, but he also enumerates a set of differences between them. Reading Aristotle's text on rhetoric, one might initially be convinced that very little separates dialectic from rhetoric, perhaps even that rhetoric is just a kind of dialectic. However, being more pragmatic than Plato, Aristotle enumerates a handful of criteria to distinguish them: (a) dialectic can be applied to all subjects, while rhetoric is especially useful for addressing public and practical matters; (b) dialectic is dialogical or conversational in nature, while rhetoric can take the form of uninterrupted speech; (c) dialectic is used for inquiries in fields of knowledge developed by experts or specialists, while rhetoric is primarily concerned with public opinion; (d) dialectic is an art applied without concern for an audience's intellectual limits, while rhetoric is practiced with audiences that might not be able to follow a long and complicated argument; (e) dialectic is designed to test the consistency of a set of statements, while rhetoric is intended to persuade an audience; and (f) rhetoric uses nonargumentative means of persuasion (e.g., slander, lies, emotional appeal), while dialectic does not.[27] Note that, according to Aristotle, very few formal characteristics of language distinguish dialectic from rhetoric. Instead, most of these criteria rely on a characterization of the aims of the speaker and the public addressed by the speaker.

Aristotle makes these distinctions between dialectic and rhetoric along lines still familiar to us today: think of the differences between an algebra teacher performing a proof at the whiteboard in front of her class and a political activist yelling into the television cameras at a march on the Capitol. We call both of these a "demonstration," but they are obviously very different.

Rhetoric departs sharply from dialectic especially with Aristotle's last criterion—nonargumentative means of persuasion. Laughter, tears, emotional cries, seduction, violence, threats, torture, bribery, lies, and flattery are all potential means of persuasion and therefore rhetorical in nature, but because they are not even loosely deductive in nature, in Aristotle's book, they do not count as enthymemes. Thus, beyond Aristotle's preferred enthymemes, rhetoric has a wild side that dialectic does not.

Ultimately, Aristotle's discourse on rhetoric is a moral ordering on forms of persuasion: the deductive logic of syllogisms is the best form of persuasion; less good, but still acceptable, are the enthymemes of rhetorical demonstration; and, finally, acknowledged but not condoned and judged to be less effective are the nonargumentative, nondemonstrable forms of persuasion. The latter we know from politics, theater, and painting; most generally, from the arts of imitation.

Aristotle distinguished three species of rhetoric: forensic,[28] epideictic,[29] and deliberative,[30] each associated with a specific time or tense and an area of practice. Forensic rhetoric is concerned with events of the past and is used to argue judicial courtroom cases. Epideictic rhetoric focuses on issues of the present for ceremonial occasions, such as state visits, births, deaths, marriages, festivals, and the Olympic Games. Deliberative rhetoric concerns support or opposition to potential future actions or policies and is used in legislative circumstances. Each of these modes of rhetorical address is, in any given instance, not exercised in exclusion from the two others but instead usually interlaced with them. So, for instance, in making arguments about the future, one uses deliberative persuasion but combined with forensic rhetoric—because the way to construct a case for future action is by citing what has been done in the past.

Epideictic rhetoric is that kind that promotes shared community values and is meant to be beyond or outside of controversy. Its subject is praise and blame. Practiced in, for instance, a funerary oration, it is usually a speech that celebrates and not one that censures (following the idiom "do not speak ill of the dead"). Yet, of course, it is not intrinsically beyond controversy.

Shakespearean Demonstration

Remember Marc Antony's speech after Caesar's death—according to William Shakespeare, *Julius Caesar*, act 3, scene 2[31]—in which Antony stirs up the crowd against Caesar's assassins (Brutus, Cassius, Casca) all the while, ironically, insisting that the assassins are honorable men:

> But yesterday the word of Caesar might
> Have stood against the world; now lies he there.
> And none so poor to do him reverence.
> O masters, if I were disposed to stir
> Your hearts and minds to mutiny and rage,
> I should do Brutus wrong, and Cassius wrong,
> Who, you all know, are honourable men.

Antony turns the crowd against Brutus and the others with a demonstration—a showing of Caesar's bloodstained cloak—narrating whose dagger made each bloody hole:

> Look, in this place ran Cassius' dagger through:
> See what a rent the envious Casca made:
> Through this the well-beloved Brutus stabb'd;
> And as he pluck'd his cursed steel away,
> Mark how the blood of Caesar follow'd it.

This excerpt from Shakespeare's play is an example of the epideictic species used simultaneously to praise dead Caesar and to tear down his assassins in a discourse that hinges on pointing and showing: a demonstration.

The ancient Greek prefix "epi-" can mean several prepositions, including "upon," "on," "over," "near," "at," "before," or "after." "Deictic" means "showing." Thus, "epideictic" can mean "on showing," or, in this case, "on showing Caesar's bloodied cloak." "Deictic" in ancient Greek has been translated into "capable of being demonstrated," since the root of "demonstrate" is "monstrāre," meaning "to show, to point out." In other words, epideictic rhetoric entails a demonstration, a showing, something that is pointed to.

In this way, that which is deictic is showable, demonstrable, and thus irrefutable, incontestable because we see it there, right before our eyes. While it may have forensic implications (e.g., the guilt of the assassins) and deliberative recommendations (e.g., the crowd's pursuit of the assassins), epideictic rhetoric is focused on the present, what is here and now before us and thus can be seen and pointed to. The deictic is inextricably visual—for instance, turning around Caesar's cloak—even if it is also a matter of language, like Marc Antony's speech.

It is easy to see that the contemporary form of the demo is also both visual and verbal. After all, Douglas Engelbart wrote, spoke, and showed (via video) in his 1968 "mother of all demos." The ancient form of demonstration was rooted in logical demonstration, ultimately drawing from the performance of proofs of geometry, where diagrams were an essential visual element and the mathematician's spoken and written words were the linguistic essential. Digging for these roots takes us to the same grounds we examined in chapter 5, where we considered the bifurcation of dialectic and logic and their respective descendants and derivatives. Certain kinds of operations have affinities with deduction but are barely related—even if we now frequently refer to the whole collection as "logic." However, there is another way, supplementary to that pursued in chapter 5, to understand what Aristotle likely drew from to define deductive demonstration. This alternative route takes us into a history of how deduction arose in ancient Greece prior to Aristotle to reveal what he likely thought of as the roots of deductive demonstration.

Demonstrations of Geometry as Models for Plato and Aristotle

At the beginning of his book *The Shaping of Deduction in Greek Mathematics: A Study in Cognitive History*, historian Reviel Netz states, "I will argue that the two main tools for the shaping of deduction were the diagram, on the one hand, and the mathematical language on the other hand. Diagrams—in the specific way they are used in Greek mathematics—are the Greek mathematical way of tapping human visual cognitive resources. Greek mathematical language is a way of tapping human linguistic resources…. But note that there is nothing universal about the precise shape of such cognitive methods. They are not neural; they are a historical construct."[32]

Netz provides us with a detailed understanding of what Plato (427–347 BCE) and Aristotle (384–322 BCE) took from the argumentation practices of early Greek mathematicians. He explores the cultural and material specificity of the invention of deductive demonstration as performed by a handful of mathematicians—such as Euclid (about 300 BCE)—engaged with the discovery of apodeictic assertions of geometry. "Apodeictic" means clearly established and beyond dispute because anything that is apodeictic is possible to demonstrate, to show. The epigraph to philosopher Bruno Latour's enthusiastic review of Netz's book is Netz's statement that "We may now say that the mathematical apodeixis is, partly, a development of the rhetorical epideixis."[33]

Netz writes the following about the language of geometry:

> A large Greek mathematical corpus—say, something like all the works in a given discipline— will have the following characteristics:
>
> - Around 100–200 words used repetitively, responsible for 95% or more of the corpus….
> - A similar number of formulae—structures of words—within which an even greater proportion of the text is written….
>
> These formulae are extremely repetitive.[34]

Thus, part of what makes for rigorous deduction is a very thin lexicon, an extreme economy of language: a couple of hundred words used repetitively.

As for the diagrams—forms of visual construction you are likely to be familiar with from high school geometry—Netz makes a startling statement: "There is a well-known distinction, offered by [the philosopher, who, as discussed in chapter 5, invented logic circuits, Charles] Peirce, between…types of signs. Some signs are indices, signifying by virtue of some deictic relation with their object [e.g., smoke's relation to fire]…. We have gradually acquired evidence that in some contexts the letters in Greek diagrams may be seen as indices…. The letters in the diagram are useful signposts. They do not stand for objects, they stand on them."[35] Netz's argument is that when the ancient Greek mathematicians were performing a deductive demonstration with a specific diagram, they were constructing a proof about that diagram and only that diagram! This is dramatically different from, for instance, Marc Antony's use of Caesar's cloak. Antony is using the cloak to represent Caesar and the brutal actions against him. The apodeictic demonstration of geometry, however, would allow no such thing: a demonstration performed with a diagram is only about that diagram; it is not about something that diagram might represent. This nonrepresentational use of signs is an extreme form of compartmentalization counter to abstraction, against generalization: render unto Caesar that which is Caesar's, but render unto geometry only what you can point at (in the lines and letters of the diagrams).

With this model of demonstration in mind, one can see that the ancient Greek masters of geometry would have thought it out of bounds to speculate on, for example, whether our space or outer space is Euclidean. According to Netz, "Proofs were done at an object-level, other questions being pushed aside. One went directly to diagrams, did the dirty work, and, when asked what the ontology behind it was, one mumbled something about the weather and went back to work."[36]

Netz claims that, despite the highly circumscribed nature of the original practice, Plato and then Aristotle and subsequent philosophers took the deductive demonstrations of geometry as their model for logical, dialectical argumentation: "The solid starting-point for Euclidean-style geometry is neither Euclid nor Autolycus, but Aristotle. His use of mathematics betrays an acquaintance with mathematics whose shape is only marginally different from that seen in Euclid; the marginal difference can, as a rule, be traced to the fact that Aristotle uses this mathematics for his own special purposes. The natural interpretation of this is that the mathematics Aristotle was acquainted with—and he was bound to be acquainted with most—was largely of the shape we know from Euclid."[37]

This "borrowing" from mathematics for the uses of philosophy was not, as it would be today, a borrowing from a famous field for one of lesser status. Netz's study shows that the reverse was the case. At the time of Plato, mathematics was almost unknown, an obscure field with only a handful of practitioners.[38] But Plato and his followers borrowed from mathematics because it offered a way to set a proposition outside matters of opinion, to put it beyond argumentation, to settle it without controversy.[39] As mentioned earlier, this was sustained through a highly circumscribed vocabulary; exclusive attention to the diagrams and nothing beyond the diagrams; and an extremely explicit and thus transparent discourse: the mathematicians showed all their work.[40] These, then, are the positive characteristics of what Aristotle took as a model of deductive demonstration, the means to establish true knowledge.

Aristotle's rhetorical, epideictic demonstration borrows from logical, dialectical demonstration that, in turn, borrows from the apodeictic, deductive proof methods of mathematics, specifically geometry: from apodeictic, to dialectic, to epideictic; respectively, the ideal, a model inspired by the ideal, and a method loosely based on the model.

Let us label this triplet "deictic" (apodeictic, dialectic, epideictic) since each of the moves is patterned on some form of demonstration. In the texts of Plato and Aristotle, we can discern an attempt to use a sparse and simple vocabulary to meet the demands of deductive, demonstrative rigor.[41] But what happened to the diagrams, the visual dimension of demonstration?

A written text *is* a visual artifact, as media theorist Marshall McLuhan reminds us: "Phonetic letters, the language and mythic form of Western culture, have the power of *translating* [my emphasis] or reducing all of our senses into visual and 'pictorial' or 'enclosed' space. More than anybody else, the mathematician is aware of the arbitrary and fictional character of this continuous, homogeneous visual space. Why? Because number, the language of science, is a fiction for *retranslating* [my emphasis] the Euclidean space fiction back into auditory and tactile space."[42] In the academic field of visual studies and in contemporary discussions of visual culture, we tend to forget that text is visual. McLuhan discussed how, prior to an age of literacy in ancient Greece, nothing was written down and everything that needed to be repeated was committed to memory and spoken. In an oral culture, one cannot point to or show one's words; in a literate culture, one can, because the words are visual when they are written.

We could consider specifics of the deductive demonstrations of geometry as they were translated into the texts of dialectics and logic, for example Aristotle's retention of single letters (e.g., X, Y, and Z) as variables to represent specific propositions in a logical statement. But even without careful scrutiny of these translations, it is still possible to see how practices of showing, of demonstration, persist in literate forms of deictic rhetoric. Among other things, the practices of academic citation, quotation, and theorization are evidence of this.[43]

Athenian Agonistics

To understand why Plato and his followers would want to borrow apodeictic methods, we need to have some insight into who and what they were up against: an old regime of poets and politicians and a new regime of lawyers and litigants.

As Eric Havelock argues in his book *A Preface to Plato*,[44] Plato was driven to distinguish a new form of education and government that moved beyond matters of opinion induced by a poeticized state of mind. Consequently, Plato was against traditional, oral-based forms of cultural memory, such as the recitation of Homeric poetry, because critical questions were not pursued at such performances. Thus, as briefly described at the beginning of chapter 5, on logic, the original form of dialectic was developed to interrupt such a performance, to ask the performer a question or request that something be repeated. Prior to widespread literacy in Greece, poetry was not just entertainment but also politics. The politicians were poets, because speaking in public required a memorable form and nothing in an oral culture was as memorable as words set out in rhyme and rhythm. In an oral culture, to be a politician who was not also a poet was to be forgotten.

Historian Walter Ong broadly characterizes this shift away from a regime of poet-politicians as a shift from orality to literacy, where written records replaced oral practices in culture and government.[45] But the Athenian move from poetry to prose was a gradual, challenging, and complicated process fought and facilitated by many, including Plato himself and Pericles (495–429 BCE), who fostered Athenian democracy in the "Golden Age" between the Persian and Peloponnesian wars.

The rise of democratic institutions introduced the political and economic conditions necessary for the emerging influence of Plato's rivals, the Sophists. Some of the Sophists were from Athens, but many arrived from elsewhere in Greece to provide an education in persuasive speaking to aspiring politicians. With new democratic institutions wherein decisions and leadership were no longer selected according to aristocratic authority, it became imperative not just for politicians but for all citizens to know how to speak persuasively. In the words of historian J. B. Bury, "The institutions of a Greek democratic city presupposed in the average citizen the faculty for speaking in public, and for anyone who was ambitious for a political career it was indispensable. If a man was hauled into a law court by his enemies and did not know how to speak, he was like an unarmed civilian attacked by soldiers."[46]

As the most influential leader in Athens during his lifetime, Pericles had multiple motivations for welcoming the Sophists, the virtuoso performers and teachers of persuasive speaking. His own rise to power was crucially dependent on his training as an orator.[47] His lover and companion, Aspasia of Miletus, was almost singular as a foreigner and a woman with a presence in Athenian public affairs and was known as a formidable speaker and a teacher of rhetoric.[48] Pericles and Aspasia mixed socially with the Sophists and at times were said to protect them politically.[49] Last, but probably not least, after introducing democratic reforms in Athens, Aspasia and Pericles himself were subject to litigious attacks by other citizens.[50]

Pericles was obviously exceptional among his fellow citizens and, in his patronage of the Sophists, was likely unique. But his case can be seen as an exemplar for why the Sophists' offer of education and skill in persuasive argument was so eagerly received by those Athenian citizens able to afford it: they needed to compete and win a position in an increasingly democratic Athens.

This spirit of competition—called "agonistics"—permeated all of society. This understanding of ancient Athens as a site of continuous competition has been pursued by philosophers Friedrich Nietzsche, Michel Foucault, Jean-François Lyotard, Gilles Deleuze, and others. Philosopher Daniel Smith has summarized this understanding:

> What the Greek cities invented…was the *agon* as a community of free men or citizens, who entered into agonistic relations of rivalry with other free men, exercising power and exerting claims over each other in a kind of generalized athleticism. In the Greek city, for example, a magistracy is an object of a claim, a function for which someone can pose a candidacy, whereas in an imperial State such functionaries were named by the emperor. This new and determinable type of human relation (agonistic) permeated the entire Greek assemblage; agonistic relations were promoted between cities (in war and the games), within cities (in the political Assembly and the legal magistratures), in family and individual relations (erotics, economics, dietetics, gymnastics), and even in the relation with oneself (for how could one claim to govern others if one could not govern oneself?).[51]

Painted like this, it is a picture of a free-for-all: any citizen can challenge any other citizen for anything, and the new democratic conditions provide new institutions, such as the court system, in which the resultant competitions can take place. To risk oversimplification, Plato thought these conditions were ridiculous. According to him, rule by the people, the *demos*, was susceptible to becoming rule by the mob. Instead, according to Plato, the wise, the philosophers, should be the rulers, because their thoughts are derived from true knowledge and are not dictated by mere popular opinion.

Plato set out his unlikely, utopian plan for government in *The Republic*, but, short a political revolution, Plato had a series of much more immediate arguments to make concerning specific competitions. Philosopher Hannah Arendt speculates that Plato was personally hurt by the death sentence assigned to his teacher Socrates.[52] In Socrates's trial, the opinion of the court was that he should be put to death, but—Plato asks—who were these citizens of the court who presumed to rule over the wisest of men, Socrates? According to Plato, these citizens were merely men of opinion, not men of knowledge, and were therefore unqualified, illegitimate claimants to the position of Socrates's jury. Accordingly, Gilles Deleuze wrote, "The one problem which recurs throughout Plato's philosophy is the problem of measuring rivals and selecting claimants."[53]

In principle, anyone in the public life of Pericles's ancient Athens could be a claimant for any number of positions or goods. In practice, of course, "anyone" meant male citizens of the age of majority, and to be a citizen required a certain amount of wealth. Moreover, after the legislation of Pericles, citizenship was only granted to those born in Athens of Athenian parents; that is, he instituted citizenship requirements of blood and soil. Consequently, Athenian "democracy" was limited to rich males of a specific parentage. Ironically, at least while this latter law was in place, it ruled out Pericles and Aspasia's own son, because Aspasia was a foreigner from Miletus.

Plato and the Simulacrum

But these limits intrinsic to Athenian suffrage were not enough for Plato. Even with these limits, Plato queried how the legitimacy of a claimant could be determined. What distinguishes a viable claimant? Plato pursues these questions in two dialogues: the *Phaedrus* and the *Statesman*. In a complementary dialogue, the *Sophist*, he pursues the converse question not of what distinguishes a viable claimant but rather what identifies the false rival.

In the latter dialogue, Plato determines that the Sophist is not just the worst of all claimants but an entirely false rival unfit and pernicious under any circumstances. In his judgment, Plato ranks the Sophist even below the poet and painter, who are both imitators but at least creators of copies, resemblances that have some affinities with what they are claimed to represent.

But what ranks below a bad copy? According to Plato, the canonical false rival is the Sophist who is a "simulacrum." Again, Daniel Smith can provide us with a succinct summary: "The essential Platonic distinction is thus more profound than the speculative distinction between model and copy, original and image, essence and appearance. The deeper, practical distinction moves between two kinds of claimants or " 'images,' or what Plato calls *eidolon*. 1. 'Copies' (*eikones*) are well-grounded claimants, authorized by their internal resemblance to the ideal model, authenticated by their close participation in the foundation. 2. 'Simulacra' (*phantasmata*) are like false claimants, built on a dissimilarity and implying an essential perversion or deviation from the Idea."[54] In Deleuze's words, "It is in this sense that Plato divides the domain of image-idols in two: on the one hand the iconic copies, on the other the phantastic simulacra."[55]

For Plato, the Sophists are simulacra, personae non gratae, ethically, educationally, politically, and philosophically without merit. In contemporary terms, Plato charged the Sophists with being relativists who did not believe in the truth and were determined to win at any cost; of pursuing their cause with irrational rather than rational forms of persuasion; of being profiteers or mercenaries willing to perform or teach for anyone who would pay; and of corruptly teaching their debased morals and methods to the young of Athens. This is what Plato made the name "simulacrum" mean.

Plato's mentor Socrates was charged with the same crime—impiety and corrupting the young. This is perhaps unsurprising, since many scholars have argued that Socrates was a Sophist and that the "Socratic method" was actually, more generally, the method of the Sophists.[56] Moreover, some scholars, such as Hannah Arendt, argue that—unlike Plato—Socrates saw no clear division between opinion (*doxa*) and truth. Accordingly, Socrates's aims differed from those Plato portrayed him as pursuing: "What Plato called *dialegesthai* [dialectic] Socrates called *maieutic*, the art of midwifery: he wanted to help others give birth to what they themselves thought anyhow, to find the truth in their *doxa*."[57] That Socrates was a Sophist and not a Platonist was perhaps clear to everyone except Plato.

In his reading of Plato's dialogue *Gorgias*, Bruno Latour retraces some of the same ground and draws parallels between Socrates and the Sophists, even as he distinguishes what he calls the "felicity conditions"[58] of dialectic versus those of rhetoric. In particular, for the definition of the latter, one must acknowledge that rhetoric is a kind of speech performed in front of large groups of people under rapidly changing conditions as political events unfold, with the aim of inspiring conviction to determine what to do next, what to do *now*, and not, as Plato would have it, with the aim of educating the crowd in some aspect of timeless knowledge.[59] In sum, the art of rhetoric is neither science nor mathematics. In Latour's words: "If Socrates had not, by mistake, tried to substitute one type of demonstration, geometry, for another, mass demonstration, *we would be able to honor the scientists without despising the politicians* [emphasis in the original]."[60] Latour wrote these lines for his book *Pandora's Hope: Essays on the Reality of Science Studies*. Despite the fact that he is commenting on ancient Greek philosophy, the topic of the book concerns contemporary frictions between scholars of science and technology studies (STS)—who are usually trained in the humanities and social sciences—and the scientists, engineers, and technologists, whom the STS scholars study. Latour's point is that STS scholars are frequently suspected of having no belief in reality and thus of playing the role of "Sophist" against Platonist scientists. He argues that this charge of "Sophist" is unwarranted, and he does two things to counter it. First, along with Deleuze and other philosophers, he "queers" the term "Sophist." He also simultaneously pulls apart Plato and the Platonist tendencies of those who make this charge against STS scholars. What is rhetorically remarkable is that Plato's slur—"Sophist!"—still packs a wallop so many years after Plato made it into a derogatory term.

What does it mean today to call someone a Sophist? I think the term carries the same condemnation, the same accusation, intended by Plato. Namely, a Sophist is considered a liar who makes things up to win the argument, regardless of truth and reality. But this can also be articulated in terms less morally freighted. A Sophist is, specifically and alternatively, one who is more engaged with poetics than with noetics. A Sophist engages argumentation in a manner closer to theater and the other arts of imitation and, consequently, further from, in spirit and execution, the methods of mathematics.

In other words, instead of following Plato and describing the Sophist as the antithesis of the legitimate claimant, we can describe the Sophist as one who is some relative distance from the mathematician who performs arguments in the form of the deductive demonstrations of geometry. Netz's history of the invention of deduction by ancient Greek mathematicians working on geometry and Plato's appropriation of deduction from mathematics for the purposes of philosophy make it clear that even Socrates was not performing the form of apodeictic argumentation that Plato idealized. Anyone other than geometers was arguing in a manner at least somewhat displaced from Plato's ideal form. Accordingly, sophistry, or the persuasive, public speech of rhetoric more generally, is a coupling of deductive demonstration with methods drawn from the arts. Thus, we are not following Plato, who wants rhetoric to be identical to dialectic. Instead, we are following Aristotle by plotting out the distance and differences between dialectic and rhetoric. Aristotle wrote, "It is … equally foolish to accept probable reasoning from a mathematician and to demand from a rhetorician scientific proofs."[61] The unease associated with the label of "Sophist" is proportional to the anxiety scientists feel as they move away from the ideal of deductive demonstration and further and further into the territory of theatrical performance and spectacle. Latour explains this anxiety: "What working scientists want to be sure of is they *do not make up*, with their own repertoire of actions, the new entities to which they have access."[62]

Deduction, to Induction, to Abduction

Even if the term "Sophist" is still a derogatory term, the ancient "simulacrum" today has a commended cognate: the "simulation." To follow this translation through the years, from simulacrum to simulation, we need to note that the ideal of deductive demonstration—in the seventeenth century, with the advent of empirical experimentation—served as the model for the creation of inductive demonstration. Many years later, inductive demonstrations were superseded by abductive demonstrations, in the form of computer simulations and "demos" that seamlessly fuse automatic inference with the arts of imitation.

This triplet of inference types (deduction, induction, abduction) is due to the philosopher Charles Sanders Peirce, as explained at the end of chapter 5, on logic. Historians of science who have found Peirce's terms useful include Ian Hacking, who, in his book on the history of probability, wrote:

> It is important to distinguish two broad classes of non-deductive reasoning. On the one hand there is inference and decision under uncertainty, and on the other there is "theorizing." C. S. Peirce marked such a distinction by calling the former induction and the latter abduction. Theorizing, or abduction, concerns the speculative creation of abstract theory to explain phenomena, together with the testing of such theories by their fit with old facts and their prediction of new discoveries.… Our confidence in theories does not seem amenable to any

probabilistic treatment. Inference and decision under uncertainty, in contrast, are specifically probabilistic [i.e., inductive].[63]

The transition from deduction to induction entailed the introduction of machines into argumentation, the reconceptualization of probability, and the reinvention of new forms of language intrinsically connected to the natural world. The transition from induction to abduction entailed the further enchantment of artificial languages, a movement away from numerical calculation, and a return to the arts of imitation. Abductive inference is tantamount to the rhetorical trope of synecdoche, a figure of speech in which the part is taken for the whole. Via synecdoche, one can say "boots on the ground" to refer to an army, or "sails on the bay" to refer to sailing ships. As with abduction, one is given fragments and asked to infer the whole.

Needless to say, the informed guessing of abduction is a far cry from the explicit, step-by-step reasoning of deduction. Concisely, the transition from deduction, to induction, to abduction can be spied through a quick examination of how the definitions of data and facts have changed. Geometry proofs start with "data"—originally, in Latin, "that which is given."[64] As such, data are beyond argumentation: they are given and not to be questioned. In contrast, laboratory science experiments—like those performed by Robert Boyle in the seventeenth century to turn the topic of alchemy into a modern science of chemistry—employed machines to produce facts. A "fact" in the original sense was not what was given but rather what was done ("fact" from the Latin *facere*, "to do"). As we saw in chapter 3, Francis Bacon urged the integration of the mechanical arts into the liberal arts to hasten their development, but this coupling of machines to demonstration broke what we have called the "Aristotelian barrier" separating different areas of knowledge. Consequently, this move from demonstration based on data to demonstration as the mechanical production of facts was strongly resisted, especially by those who were committed to the Aristotelian curricula taught by the liberal arts faculties of the time.

The Shaping of Induction

To make induction credible as a form of knowledge production, several things had to occur. First, there was a radical shift in the meaning of the term "probable." According to Hacking, in the early modern period, "The primary sense of the word *probabilitas* is not evidential support but support from respected people."[65] So, originally, a statement was probable if one could cite authority figures who subscribed to or supported that statement. Only later, after Galileo, did the probable become a notion of numerical likelihood: Hacking writes, "For Leibniz probability is what is determined by evidence and reason; for Galileo, probability has to do with approval."[66]

Next, commensurate with this shift in an understanding of "probable," we have the belief that empirical experiments can be a practice akin to deductive demonstration. Describing one of Galileo's experiments, philosopher of science Ian Hacking writes, "Here we have a very clear indication of the notion that experiments…can increase probability almost to demonstration.…Galileo longs for absolute demonstration. So did his chief contemporaries."[67] So, Galileo would have liked to use deductive demonstration to prove the soundness of his discoveries, but instead he went to the "lesser" method of empirical experimentation.

Why was experimentation considered inferior to deductive demonstration? One reason is tied to the status of the empirical experimenters of the time. Hacking tells us, "It is not to the 'high sciences' of astronomy, geometry, and mechanics that we must look. Instead it is those lowly empirics who had to dabble with opinion,"[68] explaining elsewhere, "In particular, medical science had no hope of being demonstrative; nor even had the 'natural magic' which is the precursor of chemistry. It is in the probable signs of the physicians and the alchemists that we shall find the evolving concepts that make our kind of probability possible."[69] In other words, medicine and alchemy were lowly practices compared to geometry and astronomy and other fields in which deductive demonstration was employed. The "high sciences" were matters of knowledge. The lowly practices were areas of opinion that had to employ empirical experimentation to find results that were, eventually, potentially probable, but never absolutely certain.

These two new concerns—the probable as numerically likely and demonstration by experimentation—were knitted together by a third radical shift, a shift in the understanding of signs. Philosopher Michel Foucault tells us that, "from the seventeenth century, signs were scrutinized to determine whether they could be linked to what they were said to signify."[70] Hacking elaborates on this with an example from astrology: "Can a man's future health be foretold by reading the stars? Within a certain regime of (non)rationality, this seems like a possibility. But as soon as we ask ourselves the question of how the sign is linked to its signifier, we find it not probable that the stars are connected to a man's state of health."[71]

Consequently, extending demonstration via experimentation required a new understanding of probability and of signs, or language more generally. Prior to the seventeenth century, language and nature were tangled together, and each was thought to resemble the other. Genesis 2:19 illustrates such an entanglement: God shows Adam the animals he has created, and Adam is immediately able to name them. Adam can "see" the name in the animal itself. This belief in an Adamic language connects speech and writing to the world, so practices like magical incantations did not seem unreasonable; saying the correct words would change the world.

Perhaps it is not a coincidence that at about the time when this belief in an enchanted, Adamic language was lost, Francis Bacon proposed the development of a "philosophical language" that would reestablish an essential relationship between language and the world. In Foucault's recounting of this new understanding of signs and language, "It is no longer the task of knowledge to dig out the ancient Word from the unknown places where it may be hidden; its job now is to fabricate a language, and to fabricate it well—so that, as an instrument of analysis and combination, it will really be the language of calculation."[72]

As argued in chapter 3, on work and machine languages, Bacon's proposal for a logical, philosophical language of this sort is the genealogical root of contemporary programming languages.[73]

This notion that nature was written in some natural or philosophical language was popularly circulated in the figure of the "Book of Nature," thought, by Christians, to be God's second book, after the holy scriptures.

In addition to the "Book of Nature," a second image of popular culture was crucial to the underwriting of experimental science, "God the watchmaker," in which the universe is seen to be a very complicated clocklike mechanism created by God. As explained by historian Steven Shapin, the clock metaphor prepared the ground for the credibility of demonstrations that incorporated machines: "Unless it was accepted that there was a basic similarity between the products of nature and those of human artifice, experimental manipulations with machines could not stand for how things were in nature, and the spread of the clock metaphor for nature, as well as the credibility of telescopic observations of the heavens, marks that acceptance."[74]

Boyle's Demonstrations

It is these four epistemological preconditions that prepare the way for inductive demonstrations: the probable as numerically likely, demonstration by experimentation, the Book of Nature, and God the watchmaker. Needless to say, the credibility of these four preconditions did not spread ubiquitously and immediately to everyone everywhere. Rather, we must look quite closely to see their intersection at very specific times and locations in the seventeenth century. Perhaps the most iconic of these locations is the Royal Society of London, where Robert Boyle's experiments with his air pump served as the canonical practice of this new form of demonstration.

Robert Boyle, inventor of the air pump, is probably one of the most studied figures in the history of science and is seen by many as the founder of experimental science, the one who invented a concrete method of implementing what Francis Bacon
had only imagined. Despite Boyle's current status, at the time he faced many material
obstacles (e.g., plugging the leaks in his pump) and strong opposition from other natural philosophers critical of his methods. For example, in their seminal book *Leviathan
and the Air-Pump: Hobbes, Boyle, and the Experimental Life*, Steven Shapin and Simon
Schaffer detail Thomas Hobbes's criticisms of Boyle.[75]

Hobbes, along with many others, was concerned that the kinds of facts mechanically produced by Boyle's inductive demonstrations could not be the foundation for
true knowledge. In other words, theirs were ontological concerns that could, at least
classically, only be resolved through dialectic deductive demonstration between small
groups of specialists.

However, Boyle's work was deployed not only in specialist debates of natural philosophy. The Royal Society also needed to use the air pump demonstrations as a form of
rhetoric to show the public and to inspire distinguished visitors to support their work:
"Boyle's air-pump together with Hooke's microscope constituted the show pieces of the
[Royal] Society; when distinguished visitors were to be entertained, the chief exhibits
were always experiments with the pump."[76] In the contemporary idiom, Boyle's air
pump was the Royal Society's most important "demo."

Of course, use of the air pump to persuade visitors of the value of the Royal Society
would have been empty rhetoric if the air pump was not simultaneously understood
to be a machine for the production of nonrhetorical, true knowledge. Used in front of
a group of specialists, fellows of the society, and knowledgeable visitors, Boyle's inductive demonstration was seen as a powerful and rigorous alternative to the classical
deductive demonstration. Consequently, when the Royal Society opened its doors to
demonstrate for the general public or distinguished aristocrats who were not specialists in natural philosophy, these inductive demonstrations were seen to be strongly
persuasive.

Even though the Royal Society membership understood the need to deploy Boyle's
air pump as a form of persuasive rhetoric, they were uneasy with how similar public
demonstrations seemed to be just another form of entertainment. Preparing for a visit
from King Charles II to the Royal Society, its cofounder, former president, and archi-
tect, Christopher Wren, wrote the following to Lord Brouncker:

> And if you have any notable experiment, that may appear to open new light into the principles
> of philosophy, nothing would better beseem the pretensions of the society; though possibly
> such would be too jejune for this purpose, in which there ought to be something of pomp.

On the other side, to produce knacks only, and things to raise wonder, such as Kircher, Schottus, and even jugglers abound with, will scarce become the gravity of the occasion. It must be something between both, luciferous in philosophy, and yet whose use and advantage is obvious without a lecture; and besides, that may surprise with some unexpected effect, and be commendable for the ingenuity of the contrivance.[77]

At the time, the king had already seen Boyle's air pump, so Wren is hoping to find something new but equally good for the king to see. He seeks something that shines light on contemporary issues of natural philosophy; a demonstration that can be understood without prefacing it with a long lecture; something that is not just a "knack," like juggling, with only entertainment value; and certainly not some spectacle like what might be shown by the then-famous German polymath Kircher, also known as the "Master of the Hundred Arts"!

Shapin and Schaffer's reference to "Kircher, Schottus, and even jugglers" is a reference to German Jesuit scholar Athanasius Kircher (1602–1680), then one of the most famous intellectuals in Europe, and his student and then assistant Gaspar Schottus (1608–1666), also a German Jesuit scientist. Kircher and Schottus emphasized the utility of spectacle in demonstration. Kircher had written, among other works, a book, *Ars Magna Lucis et Umbrae* (1646), showing images on a screen before the invention of the magic lantern by Dutch mathematician and scientist Christiaan Huygens (1629–1695) and others. He also designed a speaking statue and other mechanical inventions of wonder.[78]

Yet, not everyone at the Royal Society was against spectacle. Its first secretary, John Wilkins (whose plans for a universal characteristic, a philosophical language, we have already mentioned), seemed to have an affinity for it. He wrote a book, *Mathematical Magick* (1648), describing the construction of a number of mechanical devices and speculating on how a flying machine might be built. Wilkins devotes the latter part of his book to "Daedalus because he was one of the first and most famous amongst the Ancients for his skill in making Automata."[79] Nevertheless, despite Wilkins's enthusiasm for "magick," Wren, in his comments to Brouncker, wants to draw a line dividing the serious demonstrations of the Royal Society from what he sees to be the theatrical tricks, the sophistry, of philosophers like Kircher.

Historian Jan V. Golinski has pointed out this double role of experimental demonstration—as public spectacle and as serious science—in the workings of the Royal Society. According to Golinski, Robert Hooke (Boyle's colleague, who built the air pump for him) was the society's Curator of Experiments from 1662 to 1684 and from 1687 to 1688.[80] Golinski asserts, "[Public experiments] served to captivate spectators at meetings and encouraged attempts to extend the appeal of natural philosophy into society at large. But its use in these contexts also put at risk the public image of the natural philosopher, who became liable to be confused with a conjurer, showman, or wondermonger."[81]

So, Hooke was in the same bind as Plato: he had helped create a new form of demonstration for fellow philosophers, but as soon as the demonstration was performed for a larger public, it transformed into a kind of rhetoric, a form of persuasive performance whose affinities with theater and other arts were obvious.

The respective appellations of the three different types of demonstrations—deductive, inductive, and abductive—are indicative both of the kind of inference shown in the demonstration and of the kind of inference desired for the observer or participant in the demonstration. Thus, when Socrates performs his method, he reasons deductively but also takes his interlocutors and his audience through the same steps of deduction. What he hopes to show is the resolution to a copular question like, "What is justice?"

Analogously, when Boyle fires up his air pump and does an experiment witnessed by his colleagues of the Royal Society, he produces a set number of specific facts that he follows inductively to produce a more general truth; and, of course, he hopes his colleague-witnesses follow him in his inductive inference. The inductive demonstrations yielded equivalence relations that can now be phrased as algebraic equivalences. This is similar to Socrates's goal, but the copular verb "to be" is displaced by the algebraic equals sign, "=." For example, one set of Boyle's demonstrations yielded, inductively, the generalization we know today as Boyle's law: the pressure of a gas is inversely proportional to the volume when its temperature is constant; or, stated in algebraic terms, $PV = k$, where k is a constant.[82]

It has been claimed that Boyle's law was the first physical law to be expressed in the form of an algebraic equation describing the functional dependence of two variable quantities.[83] But, if you read Boyle's first publication on the topic, do not expect to find an equation. Moreover, even in prose form, Boyle's original formulation differs from how we phrase the law today. Because he was working specifically with air, he does not use the more general term "gas"; in addition to the term "pressure," Boyle also uses "spring"; and, instead of the term "volume," Boyle writes of the "density" and "dimension" of the air. Before showing the results of the experiment, Boyle states his hypothesis like this: "So here the same Air being brought to a degree of density about twice as great as that it had before, obtains a Spring twice as strong as formerly."[84] Immediately after stating his hypothesis, Boyle starts to describe his experimental demonstration.

To our modern eyes, Boyle's description might not seem like proper scientific prose. Right before the statement of the hypothesis, Boyle tells us that the experiment will require a glass tube of a certain construction. But then he begins the description of his experimental setup like this: "We were hindered from prosecuting the trial at that time by the casual breaking of the Tube." Thereafter, we are told how he did manage to get hold of some glass tubing but then how hard it was to bend the stuff, how they had to try bending it a couple of different ways, how they drilled a hole in the tube, but then it was the wrong size, blah, blah, blah, blah!

What is going awry with Boyle's prose, from the perspective of contemporary scientific publication, is that he is using far too many narrative resources and weaving into his story far too many details that are ultimately irrelevant to the results of the experiment. So, they broke the tube? Hmm. But what did they have for lunch? And, was he wearing his blue cravat on the day of the experiment?

What becomes clear is that Boyle is not just forging a new way to do natural philosophy using simple and complicated machines but that he is also inventing a new way to write about what he is doing. Furthermore, it is perfectly clear that he is borrowing from other contemporary prose forms that allow him to bring the reader virtually into his laboratory as a witness to the experimental demonstration. This borrowing becomes clear when he feels compelled, for example, to stick with a completely chronological account (and thus has to include what happened first: "we broke the tube!") or when he messes with the chronology and has to adapt narrative forms from other arts to fill in the gaps. For example, a few pages later, Boyle writes, "In the mean time (to return to our last mention'd Experiments)...."[85] Just as Plato's dialogues are written in a form that we recognize in theater and films today—dialogue between characters—Boyle borrows narrative forms not unlike what, perhaps, he found in the novels of his day.

What is not to be found in novels is the emerging characteristic form of the table, so well described by Michel Foucault in his book *The Order of Things*. Two pages after stating his hypothesis, Boyle presents a table of numbers. The first column displays measurements made, the last two are pressures (one the measured pressure, the other the calculated pressure), calculated according to the formula outlined in the hypothesis. There are very small differences between the figures in the same rows of the last two columns, indicating to the reader that the hypothesis was correct.

The last calculated column clearly shows that Boyle translated his prose—"the pressures and expansions are in reciprocal proportion"—into an equation of arithmetic something at least operationally akin to $PV = k$. My point is that he had to do the calculation with some notation not expressed in the published article.

Remember that, at the time, Isaac Newton was only starting to work on articulating a calculus and did not fully formulate many of the key ideas until a few years after Boyle's publication; that is, during the London plague years of 1665–1666. In addition, Leibniz, who also invented the calculus in parallel with Newton, did not even begin to study mathematics seriously until about ten years after Boyle's publication. So certainly there is some notion of "function" behind Boyle's thinking about his hypothesis, but it would be an anachronism to say Boyle used Leibniz's functions.

As discussed in chapter 3, on work and machine languages, functions (as defined by Leibniz) can be used to express a work language using terms of energy and, moreover, can be related to mechanical motion, temperature, and thermodynamics, more generally. In fact, Boyle's law was, years later, via Daniel Bernoulli (in the eighteenth century), James Prescott Joule (in the nineteenth century), and others, translated into the work language of functions by considering how the microscopic kinetic motion of air molecules is translated into, for instance, the macroscopically observable temperature of the air.

So, even though Boyle's original statements of his hypothesis and results were based on a philosophical language far cruder than Leibniz's functions, I think contemporary forms of calculus can be used to circumscribe the outer limits of the kinds of equivalence statements that inductive demonstration could yield. My wager is simply this: if one does not have the language to state a hypothesis, one certainly cannot design an experiment to inductively test the hypothesis. Ancillary to that thought is that in 1662 Boyle had, at best, some inchoate form of functions and calculus as a language in which to state his hypothesis, so thinking beyond the calculus would have been quite out of the question. Contemporary forms of induction are faced with analogous constraints.

Induction Today

Contemporary forms of induction are computational. The work language phrased in Leibniz's functions has been replaced with the work language that originates in Babbage's operations. More concisely, we can say that we now write equivalences as difference equations expressed in computer code and not as the differential equations of the calculus. Contemporary computational forms of induction are only called that in the technical literature of computer science and applied mathematics. In public, such as in journalists' accounts of "big data," computational forms of induction are called "machine learning." Machine learning comprises a number of techniques for inductively inferring "patterns" from large stores of data. How are these "patterns" expressed? As mentioned earlier, they are expressed as difference equations in computer code or, put more plainly, "patterns" are computer programs. Machine-learning algorithms are also computer programs that "learn patterns"; that is, machine-learning algorithms inductively construct computer programs to represent the "patterns" that they "find" in the data.

One could say that the founding document of contemporary machine learning was Ray Solomonoff's 1960 publication "A Preliminary Report on a General Theory of Inductive Inference."[86] Employing a theorem in Solomonoff's paper, Soviet mathematician Andrey Kolmogorov articulated a theory of complexity.[87] Stated concisely, the Kolmogorov complexity of a collection of data is the length of the shortest computer program that can generate the data as output. Inductive learning algorithms are designed to accept a collection of data and then search the space of computer programs to find the shortest one that is applicable. To imagine a "space of computer programs," recall the enumeration of rule sets discussed at the end of chapter 4, on algorithms.

In the worst case, the program that describes the data is tantamount to a listing of each item in the data set. This is the case when each piece of data, each measurement, is entirely independent of all the others. This can be understood as a metric of randomness. Now consider a case on the opposite end of this metric, in which the data can be described with a very concise function. For example, if the data comprises the points (0, 0), (1, 2), (2, 4), (26, 52), (50, 100), we can summarize the data with a simple equation of a line that passes through all of these points: $y = 2x$. One can imagine many cases that fall between these two ends of the complexity scale; for example, a case in which there are some regularities in the data, but once those regularities have been rendered as a set of equivalences stated in code, it turns out that the resultant computer program requires almost as many characters to write out as the original data.

Conceived according to Solomonoff and Kolmogorov, induction has become a set of data compression algorithms.[88] But note that the data being compressed today is not the data, the givens, of Euclid's deductive demonstrations. Data also differs from the matters of fact that were the aim of Boyle's inductive demonstrations. Today, data is imagined as neither given nor made but rather "captured" or "mined." In the popular press, data is akin to oil: it is said to be extracted, refined via machine learning, and then used to fuel both business and government.[89] In the popular press, data is also compared to money and capital: a new form of currency. As such, data today is neither something thought to be given nor is it like facts, conceptualized as made, as the result of something that was done. Yet, it is understood to be the aggregate result of what we, as individuals, leave as traces of our online activities watching videos, sending email, ordering books, transferring money, making and uploading for today's "maker culture" and DIY (do-it-yourself) enthusiasm. We all make data that is then captured and fed to the machine-learning algorithms.

In this newest form, the role Boyle cast for human witnesses to play in the production of facts is almost entirely effaced. The machines are still there, but the human witnesses have been mostly eliminated: machine-learning algorithms sometimes incorporate "supervision," but "supervised learning," even though it is a phrase current in the technical literature, is a misnomer. In these contexts, "supervision" means the kind of work we do for CAPTCHA[90] tasks we are asked to perform when logging into our online bank account; for example, select which of these photos has a street sign in it, type in the street address of the house in the photo, transcribe this badly digitized text, and so on.[91] The CAPTCHA tasks work to differentiate real people from "bots" (robot programs that perform a computer task automatically), which is why banks integrate them into their login protocols, but they are also used to help train, to "supervise," machine-learning algorithms aimed at identifying specific features in photos. Thus, our click traces from the CAPTCHAs are resold to companies working on machine-learning problems, but—I dare say—what we do when logging into our respective bank accounts can hardly be dignified by calling it "supervising" or "witnessing" an inductive demonstration. In these situations, we are performing, for free, a kind of "piece work" for the machine-learning algorithms and the corporations that own them.[92]

We also interact with machine-learning algorithms as consumers, when, for instance, Amazon or Netflix suggests which movie we should watch next; or, more subtly, when our Facebook newsfeed is mechanically curated; or when Google computes the ordering in our search results. On these sites, patterns of our past behavior have been detected, compared to the patterns of others, and used to order a list of the items on offer.

In some cases, our participation in these new forms of induction has been coerced: we have no choice whether to do the CAPTCHA task for our bank's login protocol. In other cases, our participation is accomplished through persuasive means: when we visit the website Google lists at the top of the list, when we buy the product Amazon suggests, or when we watch the video Netflix's algorithms offer as the best one for us, we have bought the "argument" calculated by the algorithm.

That these algorithms constitute a form of persuasion is easiest to see when they are used to help us make a decision. In these instances of decision support, one can see that even if, technically, machine-learning algorithms are data compression algorithms, their outputs need to be interpreted as social, economic, cultural, and political forces.

Imagine you are a Google executive trying to understand current trends in web searching. Google processes about 40,000 searches every second.[93] So, if you are a Google executive and want to have some notion of search trends over the course of the last hour, you will need a summary of 144 million searches. Let us say Google has developed some amazing machine-learning algorithm that can compress the data by a factor of ten thousand and still preserve its semantic sense. Well, then you only need to cipher out a pattern from 14,400 search queries. If each of these averages three or four words, then you have about eighty to ninety densely printed pages, a short "book," of text to work from. But you had better be quick! In an hour, the inductive machine-learning algorithm will have produced an entirely different book to summarize the next hour's search data.

With this example in mind, we can see the problem. Through automation by machine-learning algorithms, induction has survived the transition to a scale wildly larger than Boyle's laboratory. But even though induction has scaled, inductive demonstration has failed. While Boyle's demonstrations were able (in both face-to-face and written forms) to lead spectators through a process of induction by showing them the data and how it was produced, Google just has too much data to even attempt that.

From his data, Boyle induces a short, easy-to-understand statement, like $PV=k$. From the search data, the machine-learning algorithm induces eighty or ninety pages of statements. Boyle shows his work, step-by-step, and thereby demonstrates how he inductively arrived at his conclusions, but the Google executive is in a position analogous to that of a Google user: a huge mass of data has invisibly, via the machine-learning algorithm, been turned into a much smaller set. Neither the Google executive nor Google users like you and I are supposed to be able to follow the inductive inferences that led to the output result. Rather, both the executive and the consumer are left with only one thing to do: try to make sense of the data subset served to them and then select (or not) one or more items from that subset.

In Boyle's laboratory, the public were persuaded through a multistep argument and thus worked together with him and were properly collaborators. In contrast, when we are persuaded to accept something presented by Google, Amazon, or Netflix, we can only imagine how the inductive inference algorithm arrived at the choices with which we are presented. Our response is just, "Oh, yes, that looks like a good one!"

We are not collaborators, and even Google executives are not collaborators. We are corroborators, appreciators, or, as Peirce explains it, we are guessers because we are obliged to make up reasons of our own to explain why what we find on the screen is compelling: "Abduction is that kind of operation which suggests a statement in no wise contained in the data from which it sets out. There is a more familiar name for it than abduction; for it is neither more nor less than guessing."[94]

Inductive Inference Becomes Abductive Demonstration

Peirce elaborates on the process of abduction:

> A mass of facts is before us. We go through them. We examine them. We find them a confused snarl, an impenetrable jungle. We are unable to hold them in our minds. We endeavor to set them down upon paper; but they seem so multiplex intricate that we can neither satisfy

ourselves that what we have set down represents the facts, nor can we get any clear idea of what it is that we have set down. But suddenly, while we are poring over our digest of the facts and are endeavoring to set them into order, it occurs to us that if we were to assume something to be true that we do not know to be true, these facts would arrange themselves luminously. That is abduction.[95]

When induction is turned into a form of computation done by machines, demonstration becomes abductive, because the data and the processes by which it is assembled into a result are mostly unknown, if not completely inscrutable. Moreover, the conclusions we—the humans—reach may be inspired by some of the data but are not necessarily anchored in the data. Our conclusions can be fictions, fabulations, things we just make up. This new form of abduction is a form of production, a way of making things up, exactly—as Latour states—what makes scientists nervous but that is the primary form of work done by artists and interpreters of the arts alike.

Insightful diagnosis, playful interpretation, and creative invention are the operations demanded of a human faced with a screen full of data. Of course, these operations can also be given negative labels: wild guessing, distracted browsing, willful projection, *apophenia*, "seeing things" that are not there.[96]

Consider one of the founding documents of visual analytics, an emerging subfield in computer science that is an effort to employ information visualization techniques to vast databases. This document was drafted to articulate a research agenda for the new field, largely with funding from the United States Department of Homeland Security. This example of a research problem is taken from the executive summary of the report: "An urgent goal is to stop terrorist attacks before they occur. Analysts need the ability to piece together information buried in disparate data—including immigration records; patterns of travel; telephone calls; and names, affiliations, and locations of suspected terrorists—to enable them to spot an emerging attack before it can be executed."[97] Note that what is sought—"an emerging attack"—does not yet exist; it is not an attack. Visual analytics is thus characteristic of contemporary abductive demonstration, an effort to see something that does not exist in a mass of data too large for anyone to carefully examine.[98] Visual analytics is a practice of "seeing things": when examining the output of a data compression algorithm, humans try to see things that may or may not be there.

"To spot emerging trends" is a frequently declared desire in the literature of visual analytics, information visualization, data science, and other areas of research now being instituted in this age of "big data." What these new fields need to do is simultaneously encourage their practitioners to be creative, make things up, see things, but also exert discipline and rigor in these seeings and makings. These double demands are well known to most artists, but it is an ethical and moral imperative that they be pursued as rigorously in these new fields of data science and data visualization as they are in the arts. Clearly, if the US Department of Homeland Security is just "seeing things," it will be a nightmare, like the one depicted in the Hollywood movie *Minority Report*[99] (based on a story by Philip K. Dick), in which Tom Cruise plays an officer who leads a "precrime unit," arresting people for crimes they might commit in the future.[100]

That abductive demonstration can be misguided does not imply that previous forms of demonstration were clairvoyant. That we know how something is made (e.g., how Boyle deduced his law) does not imply that we know its meaning. As discussed, with Boyle's law, it took another century to understand it on a causal rather than just a correlative level; that is, an understanding of the kinetic motion of gas molecules had to wait until the nineteenth century.

Moreover, according to Peirce, abduction is already coupled to both deduction and induction, since neither can begin without a hypothesis. And where do hypotheses come from? They come from guessing, from abduction. Peirce writes, "Now, that the matter of no new truth can come from induction or from deduction, we have seen. It can only come from abduction; and abduction is, after all, nothing but guessing."[101] "Deduction proves that something must be; induction shows that something actually is operative; abduction merely suggests that something may be."[102]

Clearly, abduction has always had a role to play in demonstration, but now, with rising tides of data, abductive demonstration is overshadowing deductive and inductive forms of demonstration.

Technical Images

We are now shown pictures of data as forms of persuasion. In science, in journalism, and in industries like advertising, persuasion is accomplished by showing and looking at the data. But there is too much data, so what we see tends to be a still or moving image of some subset of the data: a visual representation of complicated calculations performed on the data. We have seen these images in the demos of Douglas Engelbart, Terry Winograd, and Nicholas Negroponte. We know these images as "info graphics" and data visualizations in the "data journalism" of online newspapers—bar graphs, pie charts, network diagrams, and overlays of figures on geographic maps (e.g., the projected red-and-blue maps of the United States calculated to guess the outcome of an upcoming election).[103] We see them in our doctor's office when the need arises for computationally mediated medical imagery, such as a positron emission tomography

(PET) scan.[104] They are deployed in public debates as graphical simulations, such as those used to argue that global climate change has arrived and is accelerating.[105] They are intrinsic to contemporary computer games and, as such, constitute a form of "procedural rhetoric."[106]

This new kind of image is computed from data. Philosopher Vilém Flusser calls this visual production a "technical image." Flusser distinguishes technical images from traditional images (e.g., photos taken with very simple cameras): "Ontologically, traditional images are abstractions of the first order insofar as they abstract from the concrete world while technical images are abstractions of the third order: They abstract from texts [e.g., computer programs] which abstract from traditional images which themselves abstract from the concrete world."[107]

According to Flusser, technical images are easily confused with traditional images. We forget about all of the calculation that went into, for instance, an animated film that looks "realistic." Because we forget that technical images are synthesized and not taken from direct observation, we tend to look at them as if they were windows onto the world and not as interpretations of the world. Flusser observes, "Consequently [we] do not criticize them as images, but as ways of looking at the world (to the extent that [we] criticize them at all)." Flusser concludes, "This lack of criticism of technical images is potentially dangerous."[108]

Both deductive and inductive demonstration admit objection, because we are shown each step as the argument is constructed. Abductive demonstration does not facilitate critique in any analogous fashion. Instead, we are presented with a statistical summary and/or a synthesized, technical image and/or a running simulation and told what the images mean. But how, in response, might one object? Without access to the whole data set and without access to the computer source code that computed the technical image, all one can say in objection is, "Oh, it doesn't look like that to me!" Eventually, we might collectively create a shared cultural competence about how to critique technical images, but right now objectors are left in the rhetorically weak position of pitting their subjective interpretation against the assertion of the technical image producers. We need a practice of visual literacy that is as acute for technical images as the literacies we now have for traditional images, as exercised in fields such as the visual arts, film, art history, graphic design, architecture, and other forms of art and design.

Of course, the technical images of abductive demonstration can be critiqued and countered, but doing so requires careful attention to the differences between different kinds of technical images. The technical images of video games differ from those of scientific visualization, computer simulations, and so forth. To illustrate this point with a very specific example, I want to return to an examination of black and white squares as a form of computation but in this chapter consider also black and white squares as one kind of abductive demonstration, as one of many forms of computational rhetoric.

The Technical Images of Abductive Demonstration

To critique a technical image, we need to examine how it is made—how it is computed. Knowing this, we then scrutinize the strength of the connections made between the production of the image and its presentation. In the example technical images that follow, we will examine how wild rhetorical claims made using the images are translated into assertions about the Church-Turing thesis and into detailed demonstrations of Turing completeness.

If a programming language or other formalism is said to be "Turing complete," a claim has been made that anything that can be computed using a universal Turing machine (UTM) can also be computed using the particular programming language. Claims of Turing completeness are usually substantiated by translating a UTM into the programming language in question.

These translations are either directly or indirectly contingent on the Chomsky hierarchy of formal languages, which places UTMs at the top of the hierarchy. Therefore, in the Chomsky hierarchy, Turing machines are seen as the most powerful form of computational machinery. For our present purposes, we do not need any more details about this, but in chapter 7, on grammar, we will do a close reading of the Chomsky hierarchy. In the conclusion to this book, in chapter 8, we will see that the Chomsky hierarchy can be questioned. But the omnipotence of Turing machines is considered to be true for the purposes of the kind of rhetorical demonstration we will be examining here.

Essentially, in the form of abductive demonstration we will examine, Turing completeness replaces Aristotle's enthymemes: we are meant to believe that the wildest of claims can be substantiated through a reference to a proof of Turing completeness. However, the rhetorical demonstration is not just the proof of Turing completeness but rather a set of technical images and a text that makes claims about the connections between the images and the proof.

A New Kind of Science

In 2002, physicist and computer scientist Stephen Wolfram[109] self-published a book with the title *A New Kind of Science*. We will be performing a detailed critique of both the text and the images of Wolfram's book, but first we need to pay attention to the rhetorical move Wolfram makes in titling his book in a way that calls to mind the giants of the seventeenth-century scientific revolution. Calling something a "new science" participates in a long tradition of hyperbolic rhetoric in natural philosophy. Historian Steven Shapin comments on this propensity of these seventeenth-century authors:

> Nothing so marked out the "new science" of the seventeenth century as its proponents' reiterated claims that it was new.... Text after text stipulated the novelty of its intellectual contents. In physics Galileo offered his *Discourses and Demonstrations concerning Two New Sciences*; in astronomy there was Kepler's *New Astronomy*; in chemistry and experimental mental philosophy Boyle published a long series of tracts called *New Experiments*; Pascal wrote about the vacuum in his *New Experiments about the Void*, as did Otto von Guericke in his *New Magdeburg Experiments on Empty Space*. Bacon's *New Organon* was labeled as a novel method meant to replace the traditional *Organon* (Aristotle's body of logical writings), and his *New Atlantis* was an innovative blueprint for the formal social organization of scientific and technical research.[110]

On the first page of his book, Wolfram attempts to justify the implicit claims of his title: "Three centuries ago science was transformed by the dramatic new idea that rules based on mathematic equations could be used to describe the natural world. My purpose in this book is to initiate another such transformation, and to introduce a new kind of science that is based on the much more general types of rules that can be embodied in simple computer programs."[111]

Many historians of science have pointed to the importance of empirical experimentation (like Boyle's inductive demonstration) as equally important to the invention of science, but, for Wolfram, the main issue is the formal language employed in science. He has, in Umberto Eco's phrase, resumed the ancient "search for the perfect language." Also, as we will soon see, Wolfram, for the purposes of his "new science," redefines "experiment" to mean repeatedly running a computer program and then looking at some of its outputs. That is to say, in Wolfram's hands, empirical experimentation is redefined from inductive demonstration into a form of abductive demonstration, with the main results being pictures for both scientists and a general public.

A rough schema of Wolfram's abductive demonstration is as follows. It is argued that complex systems of the natural and social worlds are difficult to model with "mathematical equations" (e.g., the calculus). Wolfram claims to have invented a formalism more powerful than the calculus. This formalism (specifically, matrices of black and white squares akin to the rule sets of arithmetic discussed in chapter 4) is Turing complete and therefore can be used to simulate anything. (Note here the conflation of Turing completeness with an inflated form of the Church-Turing thesis to argue that the formalism is "universal." This fallacy is discussed in chapter 2 of this book, and again in the book's conclusion in chapter 8.)

Further, Wolfram claims that, since the simulations constructed using this formalism produce visual output that looks like naturally occurring behaviors (of living creatures, human social dynamics, chemical reactions, physical mechanics, etc.), computer programs written in the invented formalism can be said to exhibit the same behaviors.

Finally, he makes a huge leap into the ideological commitment that materiality is of no consequence when he insists that behavior is behavior regardless of its materiality and life, the universe, and everything is just really big matrices of black and white squares or, in other words, a giant Turing machine.[112]

I hope that you understand that I do not think this is a watertight argument. I do think it is an interesting form of rhetoric, but this kind of abductive demonstration is fractured with gaps and full of holes. For instance, just because a formal language is not Turing complete does not mean it should be replaced with one that is. (In chapter 7, on grammar, we will visit some of the criteria employed to determine whether a Turing-complete language is indeed desirable.)

Next, even if a Turing-complete language is chosen, the black and white squares Wolfram prefers are not necessarily the best formal language to choose. Why not use C++ or Python?

Also, as I have already asserted, a proof of Turing completeness is not a knockdown argument that a language is universal in any sense beyond showing that it can be used to simulate any Turing machine. Furthermore, just because something looks like something else does not mean that it is something else. Even if I look a lot like my cousin, I am not my cousin.

The final objection I will mention is related to the penultimate: materiality is not immaterial. All that glitters is not gold.[113] Nevertheless, not just Wolfram but many theorists of complex systems, digital philosophers, data scientists, and information visualization experts perform arguments that follow the general schema outlined here.

Wolfram Beyond the Pale

Just as the ancient geometers (according to Netz) had their rules of correct demonstration (limited language and strict attention to the diagrams as indices, not representations), abductive demonstrators likewise have their own rules of the game. The community investment in these implicit rules surfaces abruptly when they are broken.

Wolfram breaks two of these presupposed rules when he goes on to say, "It has taken me the better part of twenty years to build the intellectual structure that is needed, but

I have been amazed by its results. For what I have found is that with the new kind of science I have developed it suddenly becomes possible to make progress on a remarkable range of fundamental issues that have never successfully been addressed by any of the existing sciences before."[114]

The first rule broken here, at the beginning of Wolfram's book, is common to the written conventions of most forms of science, engineering, and mathematics: "Do not write in the first person." The second rule has an equally large consensus: "Do not pretend to have invented everything yourself: cite the work of others."[115]

By breaking these unwritten rules, Wolfram drives his colleagues in science and mathematics around the bend. Cosma Shalizi is a faculty member at Carnegie Mellon University who vented his frustration with Wolfram right into the title of his review of *A New Kind of Science* (NKS): "A Rare Blend of Monster Raving Egomania and Utter Batshit Insanity."[116] Shalizi follows his incandescent title with a detailed and substantiated set of arguments against Wolfram, but you do not need to read more than the title to understand how inflammatory Wolfram's language can be.

No other reviews have titles as funny as Shalizi's, but many are equally harsh in substance. For example, *Scientific American* carried the following commentary:

> "The impact of *NKS* [*A New Kind of Science*] on all the areas of computer science and physics I'm familiar with has been basically zero," [Scott Aaronson, theoretical computer scientist at UT Austin] says. "As far as I can tell, the main impact is that people now sometimes use the adjective 'Wolframian' to describe breathtaking claims for the trivial or well-known." [Martin] Davis [Alonzo Church's former student and the author of *The Universal Computer: The Road from Leibniz to Turing*, cited in chapters 2 and 5 of this book] offers a sunnier take: "The book has a lot of beautiful pictures."[117]

One sin Wolfram shares with many of his colleagues—and which is therefore rarely mentioned—could be called "argumentation by appellation." Computer scientist Drew McDermott skewered a form of this bad habit peculiar to the subfield of artificial intelligence. McDermott calls this "artificial stupidity" and identified practices like naming a subroutine in a program "learn" and then circularly arguing that the program learns because it has a subroutine called "learn."[118]

Not wanting to facilitate stupidity in this book, I have refrained, until now, from telling you that Wolfram and others call their computational substrate of preference not "black and white squares" but "cellular automata." Cellular automata originated with John von Neumann's efforts in the 1940s to find a formal model of self-reproducing cellular organisms. Cellular automata have been studied ever since, with many interesting results invented by many people.[119] Wolfram makes his colleagues angry partly because he does not acknowledge the contributions of so many to this long-standing field and instead pretends to have invented it all himself.

Let me be clear: I do not object to the study of cellular automata. I object to facile arguments, made by Wolfram and others, that go like this: "Cellular automata are good models for biological, living cells because we named them 'cellular.'" In his book, Wolfram makes great use of this sort of "argumentation by appellation" not just for "cells" but also for "behaviors" (patterns on the screen are said to "behave" because he says that they behave), as well as for many other social, biological, and physical phenomena.

I point out the employment of these various nondemonstrative rhetorical strategies in Wolfram's text (namely, the use of first-person narration, the lack of citation, and argumentation by appellation) in order to more clearly distinguish these "tricks" from the core of abductive demonstration, a new form of persuasion shared by an ever increasing number of scientists, journalists, artists, and humanists.[120] Sheared of his idiosyncracies and his nondemonstrative hyperbolics, Wolfram's book provides an enlightening overview of how abductive demonstration is performed and inscribed. Wolfram links accepted forms of deductive and inductive demonstration with new forms of abductive—especially graphical—demonstration.

Statements and Rules as Images

As we examine Wolfram's demonstrations, we will pay close attention to how he ties his readers to his graphics. What are you supposed to be able to see in his diagrams and thus have demonstrated to you?

Wolfram's graphic design strategy is analogous to those we have already seen in the discussion of algorithms of arithmetic in chapter 4. However, while the cellular automata discussed there are two-dimensional, Wolfram's are one-dimensional. Remarkably, this simplified form can still constitute a Turing-complete formalism, and what is perhaps even more striking is that this simplification allows one to graphically represent the history of a computation as a single image rather than as a series of images.

Consider a text that is composed of many sentences, such as a book, or even a series of books, for example an encyclopedia. In principle, if one could find a long enough page—perhaps a scroll of paper hundreds of meters long—one could write all of the sentences of the text on one line; that is to say, one after the next, with none below the others on the page. Using ink and paper, this would be an eccentric way to print, but, for example, as a web page, this is easy to do. Wolfram calls this innovation

Figure 6.1
A single state of a one-dimensional cellular automaton.

Figure 6.2
An example rule.

"one-dimensional cellular automata" because all of the states, all of the statements, are inscribed on one line. So, a state—a series of statements—in Wolfram's graphics can look like a single row of black and white squares, as shown in figure 6.1.

The IF-THEN rules can be written in an equally parsimonious manner. The IF part of each rule takes the form of three squares, each of which is either black or white. The THEN part of each rule is one square that can be either white or black. Think of the IF part as a pattern that is matched against each square in the line of squares that constitutes the current state. When the IF part matches a portion of the current state, then the square in the middle of the pattern is recolored—rewritten—to the color of the square in the THEN part of the rule. Figure 6.2 provides an example of a rule with the IF part on the top and the THEN part underneath.

This rule might be narrated like this: if a white square is surrounded by two black squares, then the white square should be rewritten as a black square. Since each state of a computation is visualized as a long line of black and white squares, the history of a computation—the execution of a computer program—appears as multiple rows, a matrix, of black and white squares with the convention that the initial state of the computation (i.e., the state as it appears before the application of any of the rules) is positioned in the first row. The second row shows the state after each of the squares of the initial state has been rewritten according to the given rules, and so forth. Figure 6.3 gives an example.

This matrix of black and white squares—that appears to show a black triangle on a white background—represents the execution of a specific computer program for a dozen steps, starting with an initial state that contains only one black square. Wolfram calls this computer program rule 254. It is composed of the eight rules in figure 6.4.

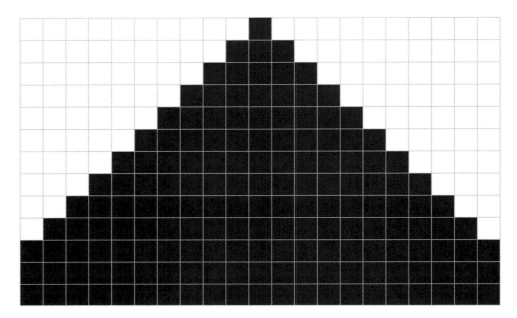

Figure 6.3
Execution of rule set 254.

Figure 6.4
The eight rules of rule set 254.

Notice that all of the rules except one result in a black square: for seven of the eight rules, an antecedent condition (the IF part) with one or more black squares results in a black square. Only when a white square is surrounded by white squares does it stay white after execution of the rule set. Succinctly, this set of eight rules could be stated like this: if a white square is surrounded by white squares, then keep it white; otherwise rewrite the color of the square to black.

Just as we did for the rules of arithmetic, we will again think of each set of rules as representing a binary number. Consider first the IF portions of the rules. Each rule can include three black or white squares in its IF portion (i.e., its antecedent). Note that there are a limited number of ways to color three black or white squares. Specifically, there are eight ways of doing this; that is, $2^3 = 8$. Instead of black and white

Figure 6.5
The THEN portions, the consequents, of rule set 254.

squares, let us just use 1s and 0s to enumerate the eight possibilities: 000, 001, 010, 011, 100, 101, 110, 111. These eight possibilities correspond to the numbers 0, 1, 2, 3, 4, 5, 6, 7 in binary notation.

Look again at rule set 254 as written in figure 6.4, the rule set that, given a single black square in the initial state, produces a figure that looks like a black pyramid in figure 6.3. Wolfram's convention is to list the antecedents of the rule sets in inverse order, from 7 to 0: 111, 110, 101, 100, 011, 010, 001, 000. He could just as well have listed them from 0 to 7, but the inverse order is what he chose, and that is now standard in the larger body of literature that has accrued around his work. So each of these rule sets has eight and only eight rules, and these rules are conventionally listed in order from 7 to 0, according to the antecedents of the rules (i.e., the IF portions of the rules).

Now let us consider the consequents, the THEN portions, of rule set 254 (see figure 6.5). Ignore the antecedents and just look at the consequents. Read as a binary number, this sequence of black and white squares is equivalent to 11111110, or, in decimal format, 254. Rule set 255 differs by one consequent from rule set 254. Rule set 255 has eight black squares for its consequents, 11111111. Rule set 253 also differs by one consequent from rule set 254. It has a penultimate white square and ends with a black square, 11111101. Analogously, rule set 0 has just a series of eight white squares for consequents: 00000000. Rule set 1 has one black square at the end: 00000001.

Since all of the rule sets have identical antecedents, the rule sets differ only according to their consequents, and since each rule set includes eight consequents, each represented as a black or white "bit," the total number of possible rules is equal to the total number of possible binary numbers one can represent with eight bits: $2^8 = 256$ (but, since numbering starts at 0, the final rule set has number 255, not 256).

Wolfram enumerates all possible rule sets in his black and white notion. He orders them according to the consequents of the rule sets from rule set 00000000 to rule set 11111111, from 0 to 255. If we consider each of these rule sets a potential computer programming language, their enumeration is remarkable because it is a list of all possible computer programs that can be articulated in Wolfram's notation for one-dimensional cellular automata.

Ordering the Images

When run starting with a single black square in the initial state, we know that rule set 254 produces a figure that looks like a black triangle. It is feasible to run all 256 rule sets with the same initial state of one black square. Wolfram calls this "one of the most elementary imaginable computer experiments: [he] took a sequence of simple programs and then systematically ran them to see how they behaved."[121] So, for Wolfram, running a set of computer programs constitutes a form of "experimental demonstration," and the execution trace of a program is "behavior."

I have replicated this "experiment" by writing JavaScript code to execute each of the 256 rule sets and display their respective outputs in a web page.[122] The results are shown in figures 6.6 and 6.7. The rule sets are listed left to right, top to bottom, with each result displayed with the rule set number shown just above the result. So, for instance, right above the penultimate figure, the one that looks like a black triangle, a "254" should be visible.

Examining figures 6.6 and 6.7 closely, one can note that there is another black triangle (222) that looks exactly like the one for rule set 254. There are also smaller black triangles (e.g., 206, 220, 252). One can see that there are other triangles that are not black but that have very simple repetitive patterns in them (e.g., 28, 50).[123]

Some rule sets yield even simpler results. Given a single black square in the initial state, rule sets such as 4 and 12 produce a single vertical line.[124] Rule sets such as 2 and 6 yield a simple diagonal line.[125]

There are rule sets that generate slightly more complex patterns, such as a vertical or a diagonal line on a striped background (27, 35, 43, 51, 59, etc.). Then there are the most boring rule sets, which just produce a completely white or completely black canvas, such as 0, 8, and 32.[126] Slightly less boring, perhaps, are those rule sets that produce just stripes, such as 7 and 19.[127]

Note also that a number of the rule sets, given an initial state with one black square, generate nested patterns. Rule sets 18, 22, 26, and 60 provide examples of this.[128]

Most of the rule sets mentioned so far are ones that Stephen Wolfram calls either "class 1" or "class 2." What are class 1 rules? Wolfram tells us that the execution of class 1 rules results in simple patterns given almost any initial state, be it simple (e.g., the initial states used here with one and only one black square and the rest white) or complicated (e.g., a random series of black and white squares).[129]

According to Wolfram, the execution of class 2 rules can result in many different patterns, "but all of them consist just of a certain set of simple structures that either remain the same forever or repeat every few steps."[130]

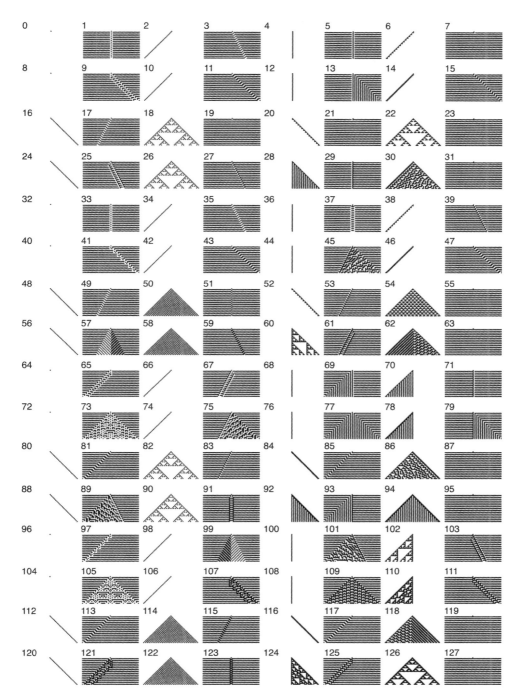

Figure 6.6
Execution traces of rule set 0 through rule set 127.

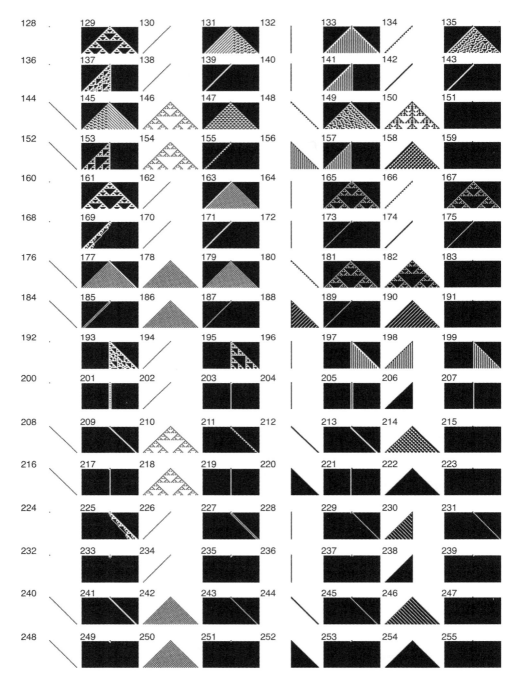

Figure 6.7
Execution traces of rule set 128 through rule set 255.

In Wolfram's class 3, the resulting patterns are said to be more complicated "and seem in many respects random, although triangles and other small-scale structures are essentially always at some level seen."[131]

Finally, "Class 4 involves a mixture of order and randomness: localized structures are produced which on their own are fairly simple, but these structures move around and interact with each other in very complicated ways."[132]

Wolfram insists that while class 1 rule sets generally yield the same pattern regardless of the initial state, the other classes are more sensitive to the initial state; that is, they yield different results given different initial states. Consequently, apparently, some of the rule sets that look like they are class 1 or class 2, as shown in the previous figures, are not. Some rule sets (including 22, 90, and 126) started with a single black square produce a simple, repetitive pattern, but started with a complicated initial state produce much more complicated patterns. For example, rule set 22, started with a single black square, produces the pattern in figure 6.8.

But rule set 22 started with an initial state that consists of a random series of black and white squares does not produce a simple, "class 2," repetitive pattern. See figure 6.9. Because of this, Wolfram states that rule set 22 is not in class 2 but rather in class 3.[133]

In his book, Wolfram repeatedly claims that one should be able to see the differences between the different classes just by looking. Yet, with some rule sets, we cannot see what we are meant to see when they are run with a simple initial state; for example, with rule set 22, we are told that we cannot see what is really there unless it is run with a more complicated initial state. So, as with prior forms of demonstration, without guidance, we, the untutored public, cannot see what is being demonstrated. This was also the case with Euclid's diagrams and likewise with Boyle's air pump. Demonstrations only show what they are intended to show if the public is willing to see the sites with a guide who narrates the tour and points out what to look at and when.

That Wolfram's visible "results" are not open for simple inspection becomes clear as soon as we look at execution traces of all 256 rule sets ourselves. Look again at the figures. Unassisted, can you see the four different classes Wolfram insists are there to be seen? Without Wolfram's narrative, I might very well have divided these images into two, three, or twenty classes. To my eye, Wolfram's four classes are not obvious. Wolfram pursues his argument with a new form of demonstration, in which we are told that we can "see for ourselves" the truth in the images. Yet, the images we are meant to look at, like the 256 images here, are "technical images,"[134] heavily mediated by calculation and thus not at all open to the naked eye.

Figure 6.8
Rule set 22 with one black square as input.

Figure 6.9
Rule set 22 with a random series of black and white squares as input.

To continue with Wolfram's narrative, we are told that even though classes 1, 2, and 3 can produce some interesting patterns, Wolfram is most interested in the fourth class. He states that rule sets 110, 124, 137, 193, and, possibly, 54 are class 4. Rule sets 110, 124, 137, and 193 are variants of each other. Wolfram asserts that we can see this by comparing their outputs (as shown in figure 6.10).

Wolfram writes, "A crucial feature of any class 4 system is that there must always be certain structures that can persist forever in it.... The existence of structures that move is a fundamental feature of class 4 systems.... It is these kinds of structures that make it possible for information to be communicated from one part of a class 4 system to another—and that ultimately allow the complex behaviors characteristic of class 4 to occur."[135]

Wolfram calls the patterns he sees in these execution traces "behaviors," as though a little square of black and white squares could behave in one way or another. This is an example of "argumentation by appellation." In the pictures showing results from rule sets 110, 124, 137, and 193, the small triangles that striate the page vertically are what Wolfram calls "structures that can persist forever." The diagonal lines are what Wolfram calls "structures that move." We will examine these "structures" more closely by looking at rule set 110.

Rule Set 110

The rules of rule set 110 are shown in figure 6.11. As discussed earlier, one can think of this as a computer program that, if started with some set of data encoded as a sequence of black and white squares in its initial state, processes that data and computes a series of potentially infinite results, each encoded as black and white squares in a series of states. Figure 6.12 includes an example where the initial state—the input data—is a large random binary number. It illustrates the computation after the rules of rule set 110 have been applied serially to 250 states after the initial state.

In figure 6.12, can you see what Wolfram calls "persistent structures" in the form of columns of triangles, and also "moving structures," in the form of diagonal lines made up of small black and white squares, with some diagonals "moving" to the left and others "moving" to the right? In the figure, there is a kind of "background pattern": little triangles over which the persistent and moving structures seem to be written. It turns out that we can make rule set 110 look like a class 2 system if we load up its initial state with the background pattern shown in figure 6.13—which is the fourteen-bit binary number 11111000100110 (decimal 15910) written repeatedly.

(a)

(b)

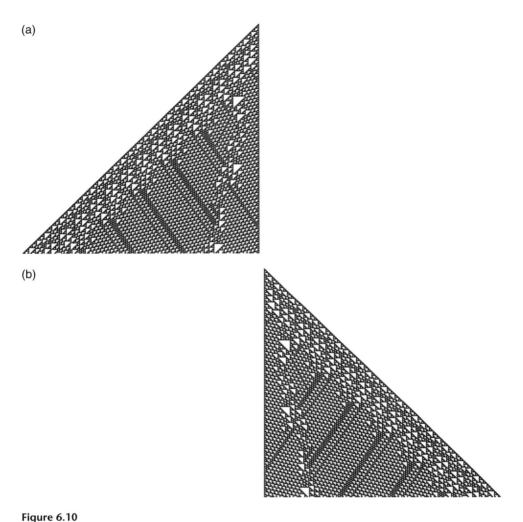

Figure 6.10
The execution traces with one input of (a) rule set 110, (b) rule set 124, (c) rule set 137, and (d)
rule set 193.

It took Wolfram and his colleagues years of work to find the background pattern
and the persistent and moving structures that could be written on top of it. They have
invented/discovered twenty-eight such structures for rule set 110.[136] They call structures that move "gliders," using the standard terminology developed originally for
John Conway's "Game of Life," a two-dimensional cellular automaton.[137]

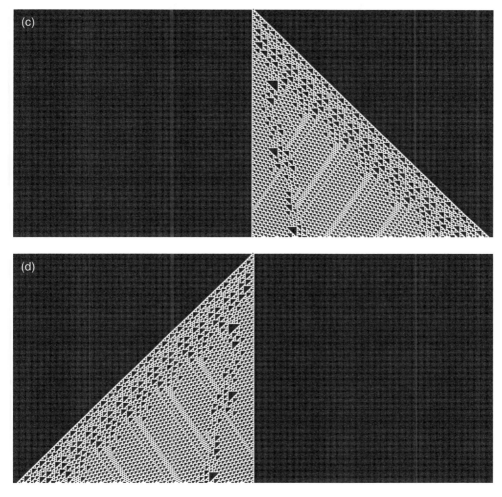

Figure 6.10
(continued)

Figure 6.11
Rule set 110.

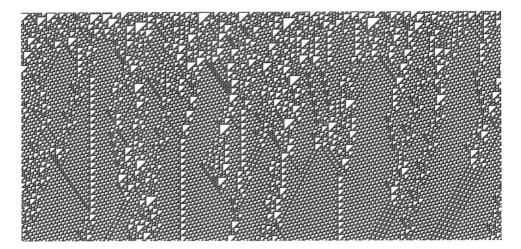

Figure 6.12
Rule set 110 with a random series of black and white squares as input.

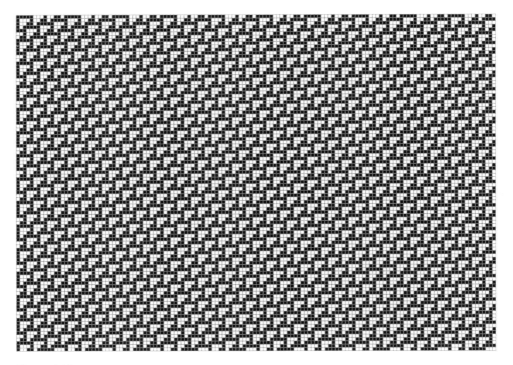

Figure 6.13
The background pattern for rule set 110.

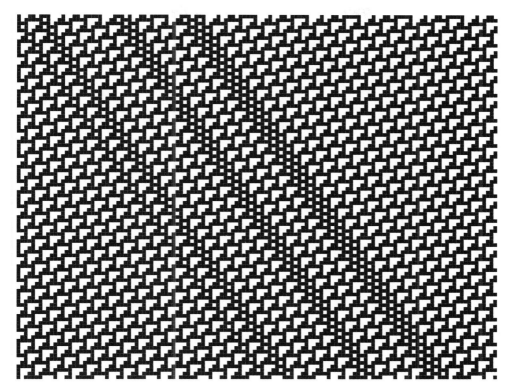

Figure 6.14
Gliders A1, A2, A3, and A4 move from left to right.

Some "gliders" move from left to right. Figure 6.14 shows examples of four such gliders. Let us call them A1, A2, A3, and A4 to distinguish them by their respective widths.

Other gliders move diagonally, in the opposite direction, from right to left, or do not move at all but rather continue "vertically" from state to state. Figure 6.15 illustrates three that, from left to right, we will call C (vertical), E (messy diagonal), and B1 (single-width diagonal).

All of these gliders are, of course, also just sequences of black and white squares or, alternatively, binary numbers: A1 = 100110; A2 = 111000100110; A3 = 111110001110100110; A4 = 111110001110111000100110; B1 = 11111000; C = 11111010011100110; E = 1100 00010011000100110.

We can set up these gliders so that they "collide" with one another. For example, for figure 6.16, an A2 glider was positioned on the left end of the initial state and a B1 glider was positioned on the right end of the initial state, with the background pattern

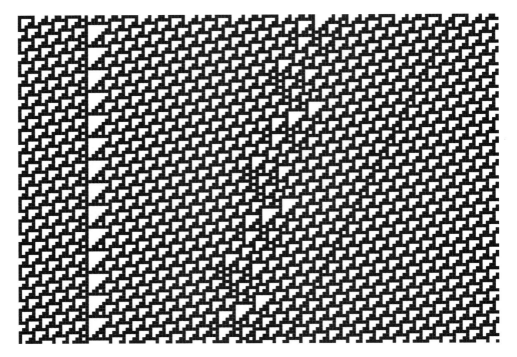

Figure 6.15
Glider C moves vertically. Gliders E and B1 move from right to left.

between them. At some point, they intersect, and after the "collision," the B1 glider disappears and the A2 glider becomes an A1 glider.

Seeing this, one can guess that a B1 glider will turn an A4 glider into an A3 glider and completely cancel out an A1 glider. So, if we call the background pattern Ø, we might write out these possible collisions using a notation of arithmetic like this: A4 + B1 = A3; A3 + B1 = A2; A2 + B1 = A1; A1 + B1 = Ø.

Since there are twenty-eight known gliders that can be written in the background pattern, there are a lot of different kinds of collisions that can be arranged that include not just gliders A1 and B1 but also C, E, and so forth. This set of possible collisions forms a complicated "arithmetic" that can be used to calculate.

We need to consider one more structure of rule set 110, which is known not as a "glider" but rather as a "glider gun" (again, the terminology comes from Conway's "Game of Life"), because it generates a series of A1 and B1 gliders. The glider gun is shown in figure 6.17.

For figure 6.17, the glider gun (in binary notation, 11111000101100011101110011 100011000100110) has been positioned in the middle of the initial state surrounded,

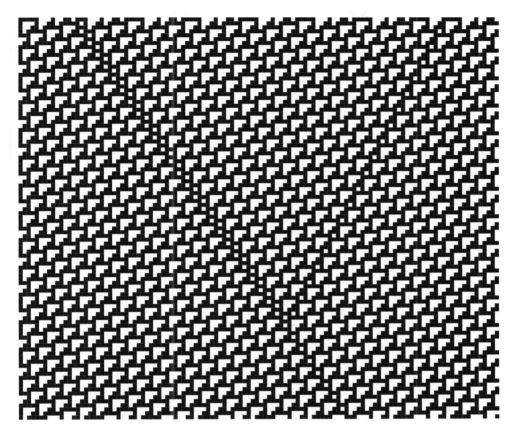

Figure 6.16
Gliders A2 and B1 collide.

on both sides, with multiple copies of the background. With each subsequent state computed, the glider gun floats to the left and, every few iterations, emits a B1 glider to the left and, less frequently, an A1 glider to the right.

What is wonderful, at least from a programmer's perspective, is that, knowing these "persistent" (e.g., C) and "moving" (e.g., A1 and B1) structures and their "arithmetic" of possible collisions, we can now write a computer program by encoding it as a series of gliders in the initial state. We saw one of the simplest such programs in the collision of A2 and B1, as shown in figure 6.16, where a new glider of type A1 was computed from the addition of an A2 and a B1 glider.

This insight allows us to see not only how rule set 110 might be understood as a computer program but also how the series of black and white squares that constitute the initial state can be written down to perform a computation, to—in other words—be

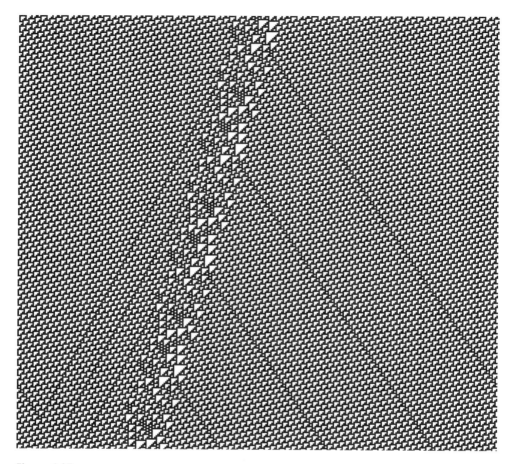

Figure 6.17
A glider gun for rule set 110.

a computer program. In this way, we can understand numbers or data as programs and programs as data. The binary numbers that encode A2 and B1, for instance, are not just numbers but also "moving structures" that can collide to create other numbers, other data, that may in turn collide with others. That data can be programs and programs can be data is one of the powerful insights of twentieth-century computing.

That rule set 110 can be understood as a programming language is counterintuitive to conventional computer science. In computer science, one usually designs a new programming language (or, for that matter, a new computer) by first considering what set of instructions will need to be supported and then by creating an interpreter (a computer program) that can execute these instructions. But if we consider rule set 110 as a programming language interpreter and the gliders (A1, B1, etc.) as instructions, we see how Wolfram has gone about things in a manner that is backward with respect to conventional computer science. First, he implemented a series of potential computer programming language interpreters (rule set 0 through rule set 255). Then he noticed that some of them supported more complicated structures (i.e., patterns) than others (those of class 4). Next, he and his staff spent years searching out the instructions—the moving and persistent structures—native to the class 4 rule set, especially rule set 110. Finally, he attempted to master the instruction set, the persistent and moving structures and their "arithmetic" of possible collisions, to determine how a series of instructions—a computer program—could be written to compute some result.

How many of Wolfram's 256 rule sets are programmable in the manner of rule set 110? How many support a sufficient number of persistent and moving structures to provide an "arithmetic" of possible collisions between gliders? According to Wolfram, rule sets of classes 1 and 2, when executed, seem to resolve too quickly into simple repetitive patterns. Rule sets of class 3 can produce many different structures or patterns, but they seem not to resolve but rather to dissolve into random configurations. Only rule sets of class 4 seem to provide the structures necessary to support programming.

Since it took Wolfram and his colleagues years to figure out how to program in rule set 110, it is perhaps obvious why Wolfram does not know for sure how many rule sets can be programmed. Perhaps because rule sets 110, 124, 137, and 193 appear to be visual variants of some sort, one might imagine that knowing how to program rule set 110 would make it easier to figure out how to program rule sets 124, 137, and 193.

For example, if we initialize rule set 193 with a sequence of rule set 110's background pattern, rule set 193—after about five states—produces a simple, repetitive pattern that looks like rule set 110's pattern but in a kind of "photographic negative" (i.e., the little triangles are black rather than white). Gliders A1, A2, and A4 work analogously but move from right to left rather than left to right. But in rule set 193, glider A3 does not work anything like it does when it is inserted in rule set 110's initial state. However, glider B1 also works, although—again—in the opposite direction, from left to right, even if it traces out a diagonal slope that is a little steeper than when it is used in rule set 110. So, it is possible, for example, to verify that $A1 + B1 = \varnothing$ in rule set 193, too.

With some detective work, one can further imagine that it might be possible to program rule sets 124, 137, and 197, too. But how one might program another, dissimilar, rule set, like 54, would certainly entail a much more involved investigation. Nevertheless, Wolfram figures that all class 4 rule sets can be programmed. He states his opinion thus: "I strongly suspect that it is true in general that any rule which shows overall class 4 behaviors will turn out—like rule 110—to be universal."[138]

By "universal," Wolfram means it is equivalent to a universal Turing machine. Thus Wolfram implies that all class 4 rule sets are Turing complete. Note that, on the one hand, what I have described is an abbreviation of Wolfram's full argument, since Wolfram's book is over 1,200 pages long. On the other hand, my description has been a recapitulation of Wolfram's argument in his style: each step of the argument couples written assertions with visual diagrams. Thus, we are led from Wolfram's "experiments" with 256 rule sets to the interpretation that these rule sets can be sorted into four "classes" through a detailed visual inspection of rule set 110 and then back "up" again to the larger generalization that all class 4 rule sets are "universal."

Notably absent from Wolfram's argument is the detailed deductive demonstration of what might appear to be the pivotal assertion; that is, he is missing a detailed proof that rule set 110 is equivalent to a universal Turing machine. One of Wolfram's one-time employees, Matthew Cook, did create such a detailed proof for rule set 110.[139] However, Cook's deductive demonstration was not published until after Wolfram's book was published.

In Wolfram's book, to make the claim for the universality of class 4 more generally and rule set 110 in particular, Wolfram does not use Cook's detailed proof but instead sticks to the relatively informal visual rhetoric I have used here. Nevertheless, Wolfram constructs his whole book around a very inflated form of the Church-Turing thesis. In his argument, one-dimensional cellular automata are not just able to simulate a universal Turing machine. No, indeed: Wolfram thinks of his formalism as equivalent to—or more powerful than—any and every psychological, social, economic, political, cultural, chemical, physical, metaphysical, artistic, and technological system.

Claims of Computational Equivalence

Wolfram describes this idea—his "Principle of Computational Equivalence"—in the introduction to his book, and concludes the book with an entire chapter devoted to it:[140]

> On the basis of many discoveries I have been led to a still more sweeping conclusion, sum-
> marized in what I call the Principle of Computational Equivalence: that whenever one sees
> behavior that is not obviously simple—in essentially any system—it can be thought of as cor-
> responding to a computation of equivalent sophistication. And this one very basic principle
> has a quite unprecedented array of implications for science and scientific thinking.... [F]rom
> the Principle of Computational Equivalence there also emerges a new kind of unity: for across
> a vast range of systems, from simple programs to brains to our whole universe, the principle
> implies that there is a basic equivalence that makes the same fundamental phenomena occur,

and allows the same basic scientific ideas and methods to be used. And it is this that is ulti-mately responsible for the great power of the new science that I describe in this book.[141]

Cook's apodeictic demonstration of the computational power of rule set 110 is criti-cally different from Wolfram's abductive demonstrations. That which is visible in an apodeictic demonstration can be contested, even refuted. In contrast, that which is visible in an abductive demonstration cannot be contested. For example, Wolfram's assertion that the 256 cellular automata fall into four classes can only be weakly cri-tiqued by saying, "Oh, I really can't see what you see in those pictures." Alternatively, one can see that my open-ended visual demonstration of how the gliders of rule set 110 can be combined into an "arithmetic" admits no direct refutation because it is a construction, a production, that only indicates how one might think about assem-bling a computer. In contrast, Cook's demonstration is a detailed transcoding of the gliders of rule set 110 into a universal Turing machine. In more common terms, Wol-fram is performing a demonstration of rhetoric, while Cook's work is a demonstration of logic.

Wolfram goes on to insist that his work on cellular automata has introduced, or will soon introduce, extraordinary advances in the fields of mathematics, physics, biology, social sciences (from economics to psychology), computer science, philosophy, art, and technology[142] and that, in order to do this, he has had to surpass all previous research in the fields of artificial intelligence, artificial life, catastrophe theory, chaos theory, complexity theory, computational complexity theory, cybernetics, dynamical systems theory, evolutionary theory, experimental mathematics, fractal geometry, general systems theory, nanotechnology, nonlinear dynamics, scientific computing, self-organization, and statistical mechanics.[143]

A New Kind of Rhetoric

Wolfram's claims of "computational equivalence" are suspect, maybe even, as his col-league Shalizi put it, "Raving Egomania and Utter Batshit Insanity." His claims are argued in a form of abductive demonstration that is quite unlike both deductive and inductive demonstration. This new kind of rhetoric assembles technical images in com-bination with an exposition of the computations done to create the images and, as dis-cussed, is not unique to Wolfram but shared by many in visual analytics, information visualization and data science, machine learning, new forms of data-driven journalism, and many other emerging fields.

Once we understand these practices as new kinds of rhetoric, we can develop the con-ceptual tools for countering the claims they make. These tools need to be adequate both for critiquing the images of abductive demonstration and for analyzing the claims made to connect the images to their underpinnings in computational theory and methods.

It is hard not to read Wolfram's claims of computational equivalence as inflated bragging, because in his book he employs so many forms of nondemonstrative prose, writing that falls well beyond the pale of this new form of rhetoric. More examples of this hyperbole are easy to find in his writing. For example, in a section titled "The personal story of the science in this book," Wolfram claims to have personally revolutionized all of the sciences, starting with work he did at age twelve:

> I can trace the beginning of my serious interest in the kinds of scientific issues discussed in this book rather accurately to the summer of 1972, when I was twelve years old.... [Then] around 1994 I began systematically investigating each of the various major traditional areas of science.... The typical issue was that there was some core problem that traditional methods or intuition had never successfully been able to address.... Yet over and over again I was excited to find that with my new kind of science I could suddenly begin to make progress—even on problems that in some cases had remained unanswered for centuries.[144]

This kind of egotism and hyperbole make it hard for his peers to see the affinities between his demonstrations and theirs, but, like Aristotle, I would like to insist that we throw the nondemonstrative forms of rhetoric to the side in order to better concentrate on the demonstrations—what is shown. And what is shown in Wolfram's text appears in the form of his remarkable graphical renderings of automata as black and white squares. Wolfram is employing a form of abductive demonstration that seems to be based on an older form of deductive demonstration (i.e., the sorts of proofs of Turing completeness practiced in theoretical computer science) but that is, at least in his case, largely decoupled from this narrower interpretation of universality in computation (i.e., a more modest understanding of the Church-Turing thesis).

Wolfram's "discovery" is not a new kind of science. Wolfram's contribution is a new kind of visual, public rhetoric—or at least his invention, his form of black-and-white diagrams, is a very persuasive contribution to this new kind of rhetoric. The proof of this is in the fact that his book was a bestseller, read—or at least purchased—by a public much larger than just physicists and computer scientists.[145] And, because it is a new kind of rhetoric, we can see that other developing forms of computer graphics (e.g., information visualization techniques of data science and machine learning) and other emerging genres of computational systems (e.g., computer games) are also rhetorical tropes or even entire sibling rhetorics based on analogous procedures of abductive demonstration. We need to be able to see how all of these, and Wolfram's book, are children of Engelbart's "mother of all demos."

7 Grammar

Schoolchildren learn that grammar is a set of rules that should be followed to speak and write correctly. Until the twentieth century, grammar was prescriptive. It was a political project of pedagogy for empire building and the foundation of educational standards for the emerging nation-state. Then, when it became a field of research—what we know today as linguistics—grammar became descriptive, too. Prescriptive grammar books for schools continue to be produced, but a new genre of grammar was born, aimed at describing how languages are spoken and written.

Linguists of the last century have made a massive effort to write down the rules of grammar that people *do* follow—in contrast with the rules of grammar that they *should* follow. When grammar was exclusively prescriptive, there was no mystery about who authored the rules or where they were to be found. They were to be found in grammar books authored by teachers of grammar. When grammar became descriptive, different answers to these questions had to be found. Where are the rules of a descriptive grammar? They must be in our brains, right? And who authored them? They must be inherent in our human makeup or learned via some form of induction by children surrounded by speakers of the language. At least those have been the working hypotheses for linguists.

Suddenly, with these new hypotheses about the authorship and location of rules, grammar became an object of research, something to be found "out there" or "inside us" and not simply in schoolbooks. Linguists characterized their work as a natural science and proposed that descriptive grammars were mechanisms running in our heads. Initially, the founders of modern linguistics, such as Ferdinand de Saussure (1857–1913), imagined these mechanisms to be mechanical devices. But by the 1930s and 1940s linguists had turned to contemporary work in mathematical logic to reframe the language mechanism of grammars as something we can call, anachronistically, software.

By the early 1960s, Noam Chomsky, his colleagues, and his students had securely tied the "devices" of descriptive grammar to computer programs and made the epistemologically audacious move of calling these grammars, devices, and computer programs theories of language. This represents a huge shift in intellectual culture. When a computer program, a piece of software, can be a theory, we have entered what I will call the "computational episteme." Theorizing in this episteme becomes coding, writing software.

While many still want to hang on to the idea that linguistics is a natural science, when theory becomes software, grammar becomes an art yet again. Why is that? Because now we ask whether the theory/software works, and getting something to work is what artists, designers, and artisans do. In this episteme, we employ theories to address questions of how something works. "Why" questions are largely pushed to the side. Consequently, we must also ask another set of questions, which are ultimately about ethics: For whom does the software/theory work? Under what circumstances? And at what cost?

The Order of Things and the Computational Episteme

In 1966, philosopher and historian Michel Foucault published a book, *The Order of Things*, in which he argued that there were vast differences, ruptures, between the ways in which language was understood in three time periods: from the early modern period to the end of the sixteenth century (the Renaissance); from the seventeenth century to the nineteenth century (the classical period); and from the nineteenth century until now (the modern period). In each of these periods, Foucault argues, one can find a distinctive set of ideas and approaches to language. He is especially concerned with how meaning is ascribed to language differently in these different periods: "In the sixteenth century, one asked oneself how it was possible to know that a sign did in fact designate what it signified; from the seventeenth century, one began to ask how a sign could be linked to what it signified. A question to which the Classical period was to reply by the analysis of representation; and to which modern thought was to reply by the analysis of meaning and signification."[1] "Epistemes" are what Foucault called this series of relations posited between language and meaning. He showed how even though one can see some continuities between the episteme of one period and that of another, the epistemes are fundamentally different from each other.[2]

Historians have repeatedly criticized Foucault for this periodization, because it is only descriptive of a small group of male, European intellectuals. But what is under scrutiny in *The Order of Things* is not the general knowledge of a grand public about language during certain periods of time. What Foucault actually does is give a close reading of a select number of scholarly texts about language (including those from rhetoric, logic, grammar, philology, literature, and linguistics). Instead of the term "episteme," it might have been more accurate to use a phrase (admittedly an awkward one) like "scholarly analysis of language."

However, even beyond the obvious generational, geographical, and gender diversity and differences of scholars then and now, it can be argued that Foucault was too hasty to couple "us" (of today) with the nineteenth-century moderns. I will argue that his "Renaissance," "Classical," and "modern" epistemes are inadequate and require the addition of a fourth that covers the time period from the beginning of the twentieth century until now. The fourth episteme is distinct from Foucault's modern episteme, because the fourth episteme is not primarily concerned with signification and meaning.

I will call this fourth episteme the "computational episteme" and emphasize that its primary approach to language pushes meaning to the margins. Essentially, within a "computational episteme," theories of language are devised to analyze it as if language itself was meaningless. While signification and meaning are central to the preceding epistemes named by Foucault, in many twentieth-century works of linguistics, literature, logic, and information, the idea that language forms can be studied in isolation from meaning is taken to be both possible and desired.

For example, Claude Shannon and Warren Weaver, in their book *A Mathematical Theory of Communication*, maintain that one of the tenets of their theory is that meaning plays no role in it: "The word information, in this theory, is used in a special sense that must not be confused with its ordinary usage. In particular, information must not be confused with meaning. In fact, two messages, one of which is heavily loaded with meaning and the other of which is pure nonsense, can be exactly equivalent, from the present viewpoint, as regards information."[3]

In this chapter, a genealogy of the computational episteme will be sketched, with special attention paid to the work of linguist Noam Chomsky because Chomskyan linguistics pushes meaning so forcefully to the margins, because it was so influential, and because it remains indirectly, but importantly, influential beyond its current status in the field of linguistics. We will be closely examining the connections Chomsky sees between his work and the seventeenth-century *Port-Royal Grammar*. Did Chomsky effectively translate the *Port-Royal Grammar* into software?

Chomsky's Crucible

Especially in the 1960s and 1970s, Chomsky's generative grammar became the crucible for linguistics, philosophy, literature, computer science, economics, sociology, political science,[4] and very many other fields. As a result, Chomsky's texts are some of the most cited of the twentieth century.[5] Until Chomsky's interventions of the 1950s, grammar was understood by many to be a relatively minor art of pedagogy. For example, in the United States, a common synonym for "elementary school" is "grammar school," since, as McLuhan explains in his dissertation, grammar persisted as a fundamental area of basic education even as its status as a field of knowledge and research fell. But Chomsky—along with the thousands of other academics recruited to his project—reinvigorated grammar and positioned it at the center of almost all areas of knowledge and research.

How was this done? It was accomplished primarily by rearticulating grammar by using information theory and computing. In an interview with the *New York Times*, Chomsky, in one statement, links grammar to computing and attempts to establish a direct connection to the seventeenth century, in the figures of Descartes and Galileo: "The emergence of language as a system of creative thought was sensed by Descartes and Galileo. But it was not really addressed till the mid-20th century because the tools weren't available to formulate it properly. You needed the modern theory of computability, which was developed by Alan Turing and other great mathematicians of the 1930s and '40s. I was lucky that I was becoming an undergraduate at just the time that all these great insights were emerging."[6]

In this statement, Chomsky modestly elides the fact that he himself contributed to the development of the modern theory of computability, and especially to the formal analysis of programming languages. So, to understand this resurrection of grammar in the mid-twentieth century, we need to examine Chomsky's technical contributions. But, as Chomsky reveals in the preceding quotation, he sees his work in a historical context.

Chomsky's first influential technical book was *Syntactic Structures*, published in 1957.[7] His historical claims for the genealogy of his grammar were published in 1966 in a book titled *Cartesian Linguistics*.[8] In the latter book, Chomsky declares that he can see the roots of his twentieth-century grammar in the works of seventeenth-century grammarians. In this chapter, we will consider the considerable technical changes Chomsky brought to the discipline of grammar and examine his historiography. We will ask whether Chomsky's grammar is a translation of the seventeenth-century *Port-Royal Grammar*, as he says it is. We will see that Chomsky's work was not so much a translation of seventeenth-century grammar as it was a radical break from it, and that this radical break has implications not just for linguistics but also for many areas of pedagogy, industry, and epistemology today.

A History of Grammar

To understand and evaluate Chomsky's historical claims, we need to consider what grammar was before Chomsky. For centuries, grammar was not a disinterested description of the structures of language but rather an explicitly *prescriptive*, political, and religious intervention prosecuted as pedagogy. Commentaries on the first grammars of vernacular European languages make the prescriptive program explicit. For example, in 1492, scholar Antonio de Nebrija presented his grammar of Castilian to Queen Isabella, to be used as a tool of empire, to tame the "outlandish tongues" of those her empire had conquered. In a letter to Isabella, he wrote,

> Recall the time when I presented you with a draft of this book earlier this year in Salamanca. At this time, you asked me what end such a grammar could possibly serve. Upon this, the Bishop of Avila interrupted to answer in my stead. What he said was this: "Soon Your Majesty will have placed her yoke upon many barbarians who speak outlandish tongues. By this, your victory, these people shall stand in a new need; the need for the laws the victor owes to the vanquished, and the need for the language we shall bring with us. My grammar shall serve to impart to them the Castilian tongue, as we have used grammar to teach Latin to our young."[9]

Vernacular grammars—of Castilian, French, and others—became essential works for the politics of empire and then, later, for the nation-state.[10] Latin grammar was an essential production of the Roman Empire and then the Roman Catholic Church. Later Christian missionaries of many denominations—eager to spread the word of God and to translate the Bible into languages throughout the world—produced grammars for a myriad of non-European languages.[11]

Following linguist Sylvain Auroux, we can understand grammar not just as a field of research and teaching but also as a process of empire and subjectification with two primary productions—dictionaries and written grammars—that are used to standardize languages and teach them. According to Auroux, this process, "grammatization," reaches its final state when one can learn a language purely through the consultation of its reference works: "The process of grammatization is never finished.... However, we can agree on what it means for a language to be grammatized. It is when one can speak it (or read it), in other words, to learn it (in a sufficiently restricted sense) using only the available language tools [e.g., printed grammars and dictionaries]."[12]

Auroux argues that to reach this stage in which a language is "grammatized," a language generally passes through ten milestones. If we call the language undergoing grammatization the "target language" and call the language that has already been grammatized the "source language," then we can state Auroux's ten milestones like this: (1) A written form of the target language is contrived using the alphabet and other written constructs of the source language; (2) expressions from the target are cited in a travel narrative written in the source language; (3) a partial gloss of a text of the source language is written in the target language; (4) a proper translation of an entire text from the source language is translated into the target language; (5) a grammar of the source language is translated into the target language (Auroux notes that this is a signal achievement because the target language thereby gains a translation of a set of "metalinguistic" terms that are used to describe all kinds of languages; e.g., words like "noun," "verb," "adjective," "subject," "object," "case," and "conjugation"); (6) a grammar of the source is adapted to serve as a grammar of the target language; (7) building on steps 5 and 6, a grammar of the target language is written using grammatical terms applicable to many languages (not just the source language); (8) lists of bi- or multilingual expressions are created, such as, for example, manuals of conversation or everyday interaction; (9) a bilingual dictionary is created for the target and the source languages; and (10) a monolingual dictionary is created for the target language.[13]

Auroux's milestones remind us that a grammar is a collaborative work of many people that results in not just a set of printed reference works but also the transformation or creation of institutions of education, publishing, and journalism. He reminds us that grammar is a social, cultural, economic, and political construct.

Auroux distinguishes the early modern works of grammar from the seventeenth- and eighteenth-century project of a general grammar: "Born after grammatization and reaching its apogee in the eighteenth century among the French encyclopedists, … general grammar was intended to be the science of the laws of language applicable to all languages."[14] The seventeenth- and eighteenth-century grammarians examined language and knowledge as woven together. Language in discourse was thought to express an order of knowledge.[15] General grammar was closely associated with the work done for Diderot and d'Alembert's *Encyclopédie*.[16]

A general grammar was linked to the search to find a philosophical language in which all knowledge could be stated. Since many thought this philosophical language was logic, a number of grammarians were also logicians attempting to integrate logic and grammar.[17] The philosopher Condillac was perhaps the most concise in his statement of this orientation that connected together—in a single art—language and knowledge, logic and grammar: "Every language is an analytic method, and every analytic method is a language. These two truths, as simple as new, have been proved; the first in my grammar; the second, in my logic. And we have been able to convince ourselves of the light which they spread over the art of speaking and the art of reasoning, which they reduce to one and the same art."[18]

Writing in the eighteenth century, Condillac was following an early modern train of thought that linked logic and grammar. In early modern Europe, most grammars were

Latin grammars; or, if they were not Latin grammars, they took Latin grammar as their model. Latin was then seen as a form of logic, a perfect and perfected language for all of the arts and sciences. Leonard Bloomfield (1887–1949), probably the most important American linguist in the era before Chomsky, wrote, "The medieval scholar saw in classical Latin the logically normal form of human speech. In more modern times this doctrine led to the writing of general grammars, which were to demonstrate that the structure of various languages, and especially of Latin, embodies universally valid canons of logic. The most famous of these treatises is the *Grammaire generale et raisonnée* of the Convent of Port-Royal, which appeared in 1660. This doctrine persisted into the nineteenth century.... It is still embodied in our school tradition, which seeks to apply logical standards to language."[19]

The *Port-Royal Grammar*

Bloomfield was commenting on the *Grammaire générale et raisonnée de Port-Royal*, written by Antoine Arnauld (1612–1694) and Claude Lancelot (1615–1695). The *Port-Royal Grammar* was a culmination and, in some sense, the summarization of a long-standing foreign language teaching project of the Convent of Port-Royal. In 1644, Lancelot had published a Latin grammar for beginners.[20] After that, he wrote similar works for Greek, Italian, and Spanish. One can understand Arnauld and Lancelot's general grammar as an attempt to articulate the affinities between these previous grammars.

Lancelot's grammars broke from traditional grammars because he distinguished between the teaching language and the language being taught. Previously, a Latin grammar would have been written in Latin: all of the rules and the examples would have been written in Latin. Essentially, one needed to already be a proficient reader of Latin if one was going to use one of these earlier grammars to learn Latin! Instead, Lancelot wrote the rules of Latin and explained the Latin examples in the native language of his students—namely, in French.[21]

While today we find it unsurprising that French-speaking Latin learners might have wanted to have the rules of Latin explained in French, Lancelot's teaching innovation opened a set of philosophical problems for grammarians of the time, who wondered: If Latin is not the logically normal form of human speech, then what is logic? As discussed in chapter 5 of this book, on logic, a questioner in the seventeenth century would likely have turned to Aristotle to answer a question like this. But the "logic" of grammar (e.g., the regularities observable in the conjugation of verbs) was not necessarily the same as the syllogisms of Aristotle.[22]

The *Port-Royal Logic*

Thus, a new grammar made a new logic necessary. In his introduction to the publication of a 1969 re-edition of Arnauld and Lancelot's general grammar,[23] Michel Foucault discusses the differences and interdependencies that arose between grammar and logic.[24] Logic was considered self-evident by the Port-Royal grammarians; it did not require explication. For them, logic was a direct expression of thought and meaning. Grammar, by contrast, *did* require explanation. To explain the form and content of a grammar, the Port-Royal grammarians needed recourse to a logic. This is resonant with the linguist Bloomfield's commentary about grammar and logic, already cited.

Two years after the *Grammar*, the Port-Royal priests produced a *Logic* (1662).[25] Foucault explains that, even though it was published first, the *Grammar* was actually constructed around the *Logic*, because the *Logic* defines a theory of the sign and its meaning, while the *Grammar* assumes such a theory of meaning.[26]

Grammarians' rules may be patterned on those of the logicians, but the classical grammarians' work starts where the logicians' ends. Even if we consider logic and grammar to be parts of a larger endeavor, there is a division of labor between the two. If logic shows us what thinking truly is, we should be able to see its workings in the words of one who speaks well: the meaning of such a discourse will be logical. But if the language of expression is not logic itself (e.g., if Latin is not the very definition of logic), then the work of the grammarian is to explain how the rules of a language as followed by the speaker connect it to logic. In other words, historically, logic provided a meaning for grammar. A speaker who violated a grammatical rule risked saying something meaningless.

For the Port-Royal grammarians, the rules of grammar are prescriptive—they are laws about how we ought to speak and write. Just like the laws of other human institutions, such as religion, politics, or society, the laws of grammar can be violated by people. Thus, for example, in their discussion of a grammatical rule, Lancelot and Arnauld examine the possibility of "sinning against" a rule.[27]

Compare Lancelot and Arnauld's discourse with discussions of $f = ma$ (force equals mass times acceleration), Isaac Newton's second law of motion, also formulated in the seventeenth century.[28] In such discussions about the second law of motion, we are unlikely to hear about how someone or something might "sin" against it. Newton's second law is not "telling" the abstract entities of force, mass, and acceleration what to do. It is describing *what* they do. The laws and thus the rules of physics are reasoned to be, by inductive demonstration, deterministic; the rules of language are not. For Lancelot and Arnauld, the rules of grammar are prescriptive, normative constructs that can be broken. However, as we will soon see, for most contemporary grammarians and linguists who followed them, grammatical rules *are* understood to be deterministic, because the rules are thought to be descriptive of what *does* take place, rather than prescriptive about what *should* take place.

The *Port-Royal Grammar* of the Twentieth Century

In the 1960s, the seventeenth-century *Port-Royal Grammar* was an obligatory passage point[29] for understanding grammar because of the intense scrutiny it received, especially in the respective works of Foucault and Chomsky.

Foucault highlights the pivotal role of Lancelot and Arnauld's *Grammar* in the formulation of the Classical episteme. At the center of the formulation of their *Grammar* are ideas and meaning—not syntax. As Foucault points out, in the Port-Royal grammar there is a "quasi-absence of syntax."[30] (The authors devote only one of twenty-six chapters to syntax.) In contrast, for instance, Chomskyan linguistics was initially devoted only to syntax.

Unsurprisingly, Foucault argues that seventeenth-century general grammar is very different from modern linguistics: "We find that new epistemological domain that the Classical age called 'general grammar.' It would be nonsense to see this purely and simply as the application of a logic to the theory of language. But it would be equally nonsensical to attempt to interpret it as a sort of pre-figuration of a linguistics."[31] In 1966, the same year that Foucault published *The Order of Things*, Noam Chomsky, probably the most prominent linguist then and today, published *Cartesian Linguistics*, in which he argues, contrary to Foucault, that the *Port-Royal Grammar* is not just a "pre-figuration" of contemporary linguistics but also effectively constitutes an early version of Chomsky's own linguistics, called transformational generative grammar: "In many respects, it seems to me quite accurate, then, to regard the theory of transformational generative grammar, as it is developing in current work, as essentially a modern and more explicit version of the Port-Royal theory."[32]

Chomsky versus Foucault

In 1971, at the invitation of Dutch philosopher Fons Elders, Michel Foucault and Noam Chomsky debated on Dutch television. The advertised topic of the debate was "human nature," but the substance of the debate hinged on their respective, and very different, understandings of language, grammar, science, and history.[33]

The convener and moderator of the debate, Fons Elders, very quickly brought the two men into sharp contrast by asking them to compare their respective understandings and relationships to the history of philosophical rationalism. Elders says, "You, Mr. Foucault are delimiting eighteenth-century rationalism. Whereas you, Mr. Chomsky, are combining eighteenth-century rationalism with notions like freedom and creativity."[34]

Chomsky responds first, saying, essentially, that even though he has declared his work to be "Cartesian," he feels free to cherry-pick[35] whatever he finds inspiring from Descartes and ignore the rest. He likens his approach to that of an "art lover" who is looking for inspiration, rather than the approach of a historian. He then goes on to insult Foucault's historical work—and the work of all historians—by indirectly calling Foucault an "antiquarian."[36] Chomsky continues by belittling his chosen seventeenth- and eighteenth-century references, insisting that they were all "groping towards" his own twentieth-century research project of transformational grammar, "possibly without even realizing what they were groping towards."[37]

Foucault ignores Chomsky's condescension and responds by telling him that if he wants philosophical rationalists who could credibly be cited to support his, Chomsky's, current point of view, he should be citing Pascal and Leibniz and "the whole Augustinian stream of Christian thought." Foucault tells Chomsky, "The grammar of Port-Royal, to which you [Chomsky] refer, is, I think, much more Augustinian than Cartesian."[38]

Chomsky as Historian

Foucault is hardly alone in implying that Chomsky is distorting history to serve his own purposes.[39] For example, in his withering critique of Chomsky, historian Hans Aarsleff argues that the *Port-Royal Grammar* owes more to John Locke via Condillac than to René Descartes's work. Aarsleff writes,

> I do not see that anything at all useful can be salvaged from Chomsky's version of the history of linguistics. That version is fundamentally false from beginning to end—because the scholarship is poor, because the texts have not been read, because the arguments have not been understood, because the secondary literature that might have been helpful has been left aside or unread, even when referred to.... Professor Chomsky has significantly set back the history of linguistics. Unless we reject his account, we will for a long while have no genuine history, but only a succession of enthusiastic variations on false themes.[40]

At the time, even some close to Chomsky's inner circle of colleagues and students were pointing out his historical inaccuracies and unscholarly citation of Descartes.[41] Historiographer of linguistics Marcus Tomalin summarizes the critiques like this: "Although (much to his annoyance) Chomsky's book [*Cartesian Linguistics*] has never really been taken seriously by linguistic historiographers, who tend to classify it as a work of ideological propaganda rather than as an objective historical assessment of the development of syntactic theory, it certainly seems to have inspired an interest in the task of situating TGG [Chomsky's transformational generative grammar] securely within the history of ideas."[42] Despite such criticism, Chomsky is tenacious—before, during, and after his debate with Foucault—in referring to his work as "Cartesian" and in citing the *Port-Royal Grammar* as a forerunner of his own work in grammar. To understand specifically why, one can cite from his book *Cartesian Linguistics* to focus on the parallels he finds so compelling.

In Chomsky's grammar, he makes a distinction between "surface structure" and the "deep structure" of a sentence. Chomsky finds this same distinction in the seventeenth-century work of Lancelot and Arnauld:

> Summarizing the Port-Royal theory in its major outlines, a sentence has an inner mental aspect (a deep structure that conveys its meaning) and an outer, physical aspect as a sound sequence....The deep structure consists of a system of propositions....The elementary propositions that constitute the deep structure are of the subject-predicate form, with simple subjects and predicates....To...produce a sentence from the deep structure that conveys the thought it expresses, it is necessary to apply rules of transformation that rearrange, replace, or delete items of the sentence.[43]

Furthermore—and crucially for the loose analogy he is drawing between his computationally based work and the pedagogically based work of Lancelot and Arnauld—Chomsky attributes to them the idea that the rules of a grammar are a "device," particularly a device with recursion:[44] "Notice that the theory of deep and surface structure as developed in the Port-Royal linguistic studies implicitly contains recursive devices and thus provides for infinite use of the finite means that it disposes, as any adequate theory of language must."[45]

Despite what Chomsky claims, no mention of "devices" is made in the text of the *Port-Royal Grammar*, so when Chomsky writes that it "implicitly contains recursive devices," one must conclude that he has a way to ferret out, without any textual evidence, what is implicitly in the *Grammar*.[46]

However, one of the authors of the *Port-Royal Grammar*, Antoine Arnauld, is usually understood to have been a Cartesian philosopher. If one wants to try to be more generous in one's reading of Chomsky's historical work, one might—with this information about Arnauld—then appreciate why Chomsky cites Descartes to entertain the idea that recursive devices or "instruments" are implicit in the *Grammar*. Chomsky writes, "Descartes had described human reason as "a universal instrument which can serve for all contingencies.""[47]

He continues, "In summary, one fundamental contribution of what we have been calling 'Cartesian linguistics' is the observation that human language...is...free to serve as an instrument of free thought and self-expression."[48]

This indirect connection between Descartes's usage of the term "instrument" and the Port-Royal grammarian Arnauld being considered a Cartesian provides us with a way to understand how Chomsky found implicit "devices" in the *Port-Royal Grammar* despite the fact that neither device nor its cognates appear in the text. It is important to Chomsky that one can see devices in the *Port-Royal Grammar*. Chomsky's anachronism concerning grammars as "recursive devices" is, as I will show later in this chapter, tied to what I think is singular and the most radical of Chomsky's interventions into linguistics: Chomsky redefines grammars to be recursive devices of software.

From Nineteenth-Century Brain Studies to Chomsky's Devices

While Chomsky, as a historian, provides us with little means to understand the history of his "recursive devices," we might find a more compelling genealogy in a series of logic machines. But, as Foucault suggested in his debate with Chomsky, this genealogy would decouple Chomsky's project from Descartes and tie it into a history that includes Pascal, Leibniz, and "the whole Augustinian stream of Christian thought." Logic machines or devices were discussed at the time the *Port-Royal Grammar* was published in the seventeenth century. For example, Leibniz theorized such a device in his dissertation (1666), following some ideas originally described by the Franciscan tertiary and Majorcan writer Ramon Llull (1232–1315).[49]

However, historians of linguistics argue that grammar machines (as distinct from logic machines) were not seriously considered until the twentieth century. Consequently, it is probably more likely that the precursors to Chomsky's devices can only be found three hundred years after the era in which Chomsky wants to find them.

So, what happened between the seventeenth century and the twentieth century that made grammar machines imaginable? In the nineteenth century, French physician, anatomist, and physical anthropologist Pierre Paul Broca (1824–1880) performed a series of experiments that provided anatomical proof of the localization of brain function. Specifically, he worked on a region of the frontal lobe (now called "Broca's area") localizing language function to the left hemisphere of the brain. Nineteenth-century linguists thus began to understand the "organ of speech" to be a specific area of the brain. According to linguist Roy Harris, a translator of linguist Ferdinand de Saussure and author of the book *The Language Machine*—which traces the intellectual origins of the idea that grammars are machines or devices—Saussure was the first to figure a language machine located in the human brain.[50] Thus, not until the early twentieth century did it become reasonable, via Broca and then Saussure, to imagine that the "language organ" was a grammar machine built into human brains.

Reading chapter 6, "The Language Mechanism," of Saussure's *Course in General Linguistics*,[51] one finds a sketch of Saussure's idea of a mechanism. He claims that it works like a (presumably mechanical) machine[52] "operating in our brains on the subconscious level,[53] governing a process of determination and choice not only of words and word orderings, but even phonetic elements."[54] Saussure points out that some choices in language are arbitrary and some are motivated: "A distinction could be drawn between lexicological languages, in which absence of motivation reaches a maximum, and grammatical languages, in which it falls to a minimum. This is not to imply that "lexical" and "arbitrary" are always synonymous, or "grammar" and "relative motivation" either. But they go together in principle,"[55] and, furthermore, "we must adopt the point of view demanded by the nature of linguistic structure itself, and study [the language] mechanism as a way of imposing a limitation upon what is arbitrary."[56]

Following Saussure, then, grammar is a mechanism in the brain that accounts for what is not arbitrary in language; it accounts for the regularities in language. This constitutes a radical change in the status of grammar.

According to Harris, prior to Saussure, grammar was a project of pedagogy and politics (of empire building and the foundation of educational standards for the emerging nation-state). Consequently, the rules of grammar of the nineteenth century and before were prescriptive instruction for students. Successful students could learn a standardized form of a language by learning rules of grammar. Grammarians engaged in this project of pedagogy—like the Port-Royal grammarians—could therefore imagine that one might "sin" against a prescriptive rule of grammar (as mentioned previously). But, after Saussure, grammar was understood to describe the workings of the brain. How could one "sin" against an anatomical description?

On the one hand, this poses a conundrum for the post-Saussurean grammarian or linguist who believes in the descriptive status of grammar rules: If rules describe a mechanism in the brain, then how can it be the case that people frequently make grammatical errors in their speech and writing?

On the other hand, as Harris points out, there was great strategic value in Saussure's remaking of grammar rules. By moving grammar rules into the brain and asserting that they are descriptive, Saussure disassociates linguistics from the business of teaching students prescriptive rules and also establishes linguistics as a natural science with its own autonomous object of study: "Thus, while proclaiming [language] to be a social reality, Saussurean linguistics attributes the constitution of this reality in the individual to automatic machinery over which no one, literate or illiterate, grammarian or ignoramus, has any control."[57]

Harris argues that Saussure's declaration that the rules of grammar are not prescriptive but instead descriptive of cognitive function was essential to the foundation of the modern field of linguistics as a science. When grammar was prescriptive—as it was for millennia—it was an art, an art of how things should be done with words. When grammar became descriptive, grammar was seen to be a science, a science of language, a part of linguistics.

We see now why Chomsky wants to tie his devices to very old texts. The devices are important because they establish the object of study for a science of linguistics. But to distinguish his particular linguistics from computer science, Chomsky must distinguish its object of study from computer hardware and software. One way to do that is to "find" the object of study in texts written centuries before the existence of computer hardware and software.

The Contradiction of Descriptive Grammar

Besides the notable lack of historical evidence to substantiate Chomsky's assertion that recursive devices already implicitly existed in the writings of the seventeenth century, there is another difficulty Chomsky—indeed all contemporary linguists—must examine in their chosen object of study. If one insists, as most contemporary linguists do, that the rules of grammar are descriptive and not prescriptive, then—as Harris points out—the cost of this declaration of description is the incorporation of a contradiction at the very center of contemporary linguistics.

Chomskyan linguistics expresses this contradiction by claiming (a) that the rules of grammar are descriptive of the speaker and thus dependent on the speaker and (b) that the rules of grammar are independent of the speaker: the rules of grammar are an autonomous machine that can be run independently of any speaker and can generate language. Thus, the rules of grammar do not just describe but also define—that is to say, prescribe—the form taken by language.[58]

This contradiction, as expressed by Chomsky and coauthor Morris Halle, appears like this: "We use the term 'grammar' with a systematic ambiguity. On the one hand, the term refers to the explicit theory constructed by the linguist and proposed as a description of the speaker's competence. On the other hand, we use the term to refer to this competence itself. The former usage is familiar; the latter, though perhaps less familiar, is equally appropriate."[59] The idea that a grammar can be not just a description of a competence but actually *be* that competence implies that the grammar could function by itself. Saussure needed Broca's work on the anatomy of the brain to credibly claim that there was a "language mechanism" in the brain. Analogously, Chomsky—as he mentions in his 2016 interview with the *New York Times,* cited earlier—needed the modern theory of computation to credibly claim that a grammar could autonomously define a competence. As we will see, Chomsky's proposal is tantamount to positing the rules of grammar as a form of software.

Chomsky's Grammars

So what, specifically, does a Chomskyan device look like? In an article published in 1964, "On the Notion 'Rule of Grammar,'" Chomsky describes in a precise manner what he means when he equates a grammar to a device: "By a grammar of the language L I will mean a device of some sort (that is, a set of rules) that provides, at least, a complete specification of an infinite set of grammatical sentences of L and their structural descriptions."[60]

So, a grammar is a device composed of a set of rules. But then, epistemologically, what is a grammar? It is, according to Chomsky, a theory: "A grammar, in the sense described above, is essentially a theory of the sentences of a language."[61]

Consequently, a grammar/theory is a set of rules that, in Chomsky's idiom, can look like the following.

Sentence $\rightarrow$ NounPhrase + VerbPhrase

NounPhrase $\rightarrow$ Article + Noun

VerbPhrase $\rightarrow$ Verb + NounPhrase

Article $\rightarrow$ the

Article $\rightarrow$ a

Noun $\rightarrow$ man

Noun $\rightarrow$ ball

Verb $\rightarrow$ hit

Verb $\rightarrow$ took

This example grammar is adapted from Chomsky's 1957 book *Syntactic Structures*[62] (a book he originally wrote for an undergraduate course at MIT).[63]

Each of the rules of the sort listed indicates that the symbol on the left-hand side is to be rewritten into the symbols on the right-hand side. Chomsky's arrow ($\rightarrow$) in transformational generative grammar recalls its use in mathematical logic of the early twentieth century, where it was used to mean logical implication. For example, David Hilbert and Paul Bernays used an arrow with this meaning: "The sign $\rightarrow$ between two statements means that the holding of the first entails the holding of the second, or in other words, that the first statement does not hold, without the second holding as well ('implication'). An implication A → B between two statements A and B is accordingly only wrong if A is true and B is false. In all other cases it is true."[64]

Hilbert and Bernays were commenting on Alfred North Whitehead and Bertrand Russell's magisterial work *Principia Mathematica* (1910–1913).[65] Instead of an arrow, Whitehead and Russell used ⊃ to indicate logical implication in their development of a theory of deduction;[66] for example, "p ⊃ q" denotes "p is true implies that q is true." Whitehead and Russell define implication as equivalent to a statement like this: NOT(p) OR q. In short, ⊃ is a logical operator composed from the "lower-level" operators OR and NOT. This disjunction "p ⊃ q" is true if p is false and q is either true or false; it is also true if p is true and q is true. Note that if we read p ⊃ q procedurally, the latter condition is of primary concern: "p ⊃ q" is read as "IF p THEN q."

While Chomsky's arrows are, in some ways, comparable to Hilbert's, his arrows do not denote logical implication—although, like the cellular automata rules we have seen in previous chapters, they can be read as IF-THEN rules. They are, in fact, more closely related to the rewrite rules developed in other works of mathematical logic. Linguist Geoffrey Pullum describes how Chomsky's rewrite rules are a direct outgrowth of earlier work by mathematical logician Emil Post to formalize logical proofs.[67] However, if we consult Post's 1943 paper,[68] we find that Post used neither Russell and Whitehead's symbol nor the arrow of Hilbert and Bernays. Instead, in his rewrite rules, Post simply uses the word "produce" instead of a → or a ⊃.[69] Consequently, today we can speak of these kinds of rewrite rules—Chomsky's as well as the rules of others—as "production rules."

As argued in chapter 3, a detailed articulation of operations—like this grammar— describes a division of labor. We can read Chomsky's grammar procedurally (instead of declaratively): to construct a Sentence, first construct a NounPhrase, then construct a VerbPhrase; to construct a NounPhrase, first pick an Article, then choose a Noun; and so on. Each grammar rule defines an operation that is defined in terms of sequences of other operations and, potentially, recursively, in terms of itself—thus introducing the possibility of repeating an operation over and over again. Thus, it is possible to talk about not just a division of labor but also a grammar of labor, a grammar of work.

The example grammar given earlier indicates that a Sentence is to be rewritten as a NounPhrase followed by a VerbPhrase. By convention, the symbols written in uppercase (e.g., Sentence) are called "nonterminals"; those in lowercase are called "terminals." Repeated application of the rewrite rules on the nonterminals eventually yields a sequence of terminals that can be read as a sentence; for example, "the man hit the ball." Such a repeated application of the rewrite rules is called a "derivation" of the

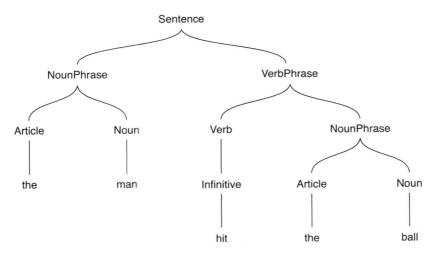

Figure 7.1
A derivation for the sentence "The man hit the ball."

sentence.[70] A derivation can be pictured as an inverted tree diagram like the one shown in figure 7.1.

The tree diagram in figure 7.1 shows us that the Sentence was rewritten as a Noun-Phrase and a VerbPhrase; the NounPhrase was rewritten as an Article and a Noun; the Article was rewritten as "the"; the Noun was rewritten as "man"; and so on. The same derivation can be represented as a bracketed string like this:

$[_{Sentence} [_{NounPhrase} [_{Article}$ the$]$ $[_{Noun}$ man$]]$ $[_{VerbPhrase} [_{Verb} [_{Infinitive}$ hit$]]$ $[_{NounPhrase} [_{Article}$ the$]$ $[_{Noun}$ ball$]]]]].$[71]

These rules make up what is called a phrase-structure grammar. In its original for-mulation (in the 1950s), along with the phrase-structure rules, Chomsky's grammar also included a set of transformational rules. Such rules were said to relate sentences together by transforming, for example, an active sentence into a passive sentence, a declarative into an interrogative, or an affirmative into a negative, among others.

Each transformational rule is composed of two parts: a structural analysis and a structural change. The analysis part of the rule is a pattern that is matched against the derivation of a sentence. That is to say, it is not matched against an unbracketed string of words like "the man hit the ball." Rather, it is matched against the inverted tree dia-gram of the sentence's derivation. The change part of the rule has two parts. The first part binds a series of variables—referred to as X_1, X_2, X_3, and so on—to specific termi-nals and nonterminals in the derivation tree. The second part specifies a rearrangement of the terminals and nonterminals as well as additions and deletions necessary to attain the related sentence. For example, Chomsky's active-to-passive transformational rule looks like this:

Structural analysis: NounPhrase—Verb—NounPhrase

Structural change: X_1—X_2—$X_3 \rightarrow X_3 + be + en$—$X_2$—$by + X_1$

This rule states that X_1 will be bound to the first NounPhrase, X_2 to the Verb, and X_3 to the second NounPhrase, and then asserts that they be put into reverse order with some additions (e.g., "be + en" denotes a past tense conjugation of the verb "to be") to formulate the passive form of the original sentence.[72] Thus, a sentence like "the man hit the ball" becomes, via this transformational rule, "the ball was hit by the man."

A transformational generative grammar is composed of two sets of rules: phrase-structure rules and transformational rules. Together, these sets of rules—or equations—define a grammar; and a grammar, according to Chomsky, is a "theory of the sentences of a language."

In addition to specific grammars, Chomsky proposes a general theory of grammar that is also composed of a set of rules or equations. His theory of grammar is therefore a theory of theories—a "metatheory" of the sort previously employed in the metamathematics of the nineteenth and twentieth centuries.

Simplicity, Complexity, and the Evaluation of Grammars

Of primary concern to Chomsky was the production of an evaluation procedure for grammars: given two grammars (i.e., two rule sets), an evaluation procedure should be able to determine which grammar is better.[73] The better grammar will be the one that can generate all of the sentences of the language but is simpler than the other. Chomsky elaborates on his criteria of "simplicity" in chapter 3 of his dissertation, "The Logical Structure of Linguistic Theory" (1955).[74] The title of Chomsky's dissertation implicitly cites an earlier work by logician Rudolf Carnap, *The Logical Structure of Language*.[75] As we will see, this citation of mathematical logic is fundamental to Chomsky's work. However, Chomsky's immediate concern with simplicity in his dissertation stems from the work of one of his graduate school professors, philosopher Nelson Goodman. Chomsky also cites Goodman's 1943 essay "On the Simplicity of Ideas"[76] in his 1951 master's thesis "The Morphophonemics of Modern Hebrew" (University of Pennsylvania).[77]

While Goodman's and then Chomsky's concerns with simplicity are specific to their respective areas of study, the notion that a theory should be as simple as possible is very old; see Franciscan friar William of Occam's (1287–1347) "razor": given two explanations of the same thing, choose the simpler one ("Entia non sunt multiplicanda praeter necessitatem"). For example, it would be perfectly correct to state Newton's second law like this: $f=ma+1-1$. So, why prefer $f=ma$? Because the latter is simpler. Analogously, Chomsky's example phrase-structure grammar given earlier would generate the same set of sentences if the first rule (Sentence $\rightarrow$ NounPhrase + VerbPhrase) was repeated three times in the grammar, but such a variation would include unnecessary redundancy.

Imagine a version of the phrase-structure grammar that generated all of the sentences but no derivations. It could be written like this:

Sentence $\rightarrow$ "the man hit the ball"

Sentence $\rightarrow$ "the man took the ball"

Sentence $\rightarrow$ "the ball hit the man"

etc.

Such a grammar would be simpler in some ways. But, of course, if it included all of the sentences generated by the other grammar, it would include many more rules: one rule per sentence. For Chomsky, such a grammar would be simpler but too simple, because it would generate sentences but no derivations for them. Without derivations, none of the transformational rules would apply, and without them, relations between active and passive, declarative and interrogative, and other sentences would also have to be enumerated explicitly; the grammar would explode in size and become much larger than Chomsky's example grammar. As will be discussed, Chomsky's grammars have an implicit size limit.

In his dissertation, Chomsky described a heuristic means of evaluating the simplicity of a grammar that involves three criteria:

> Putting it roughly, a grammar will meet these conditions [of simplicity] if, when the rules are given in a maximally condensed form, it is possible to arrange the resulting statements in a sequence in such a way that: (i) we can form all derivations by running through the sequence of rules from beginning to end;[78] (ii) no conversion X $\rightarrow$ Y will appear twice in the sequence (i.e., no rule need be repeated in several forms at various places in the grammar); (iii) each conditioning context is developed to exactly the extent relevant for the application of the rule in which it appears.[79]

Generally, the approach to defining simplicity outlined in Chomsky's dissertation is "metamathematics." In Chomsky's words, "Linguistic theory is…constructed in a meta-metalanguage to any natural language, and a metalanguage to the language in which the grammars are constructed."[80] In other words, the language to be analyzed by the grammarian is a "natural language" like English or French, the language the grammarian uses to phrase a theory of the natural language is a formal language that contains tokens like "NounPhrase" and "→," and the language the grammarian uses to articulate a theory of a theory, a theory of grammar, is also written in a formal language.

For metamathematicians, the formal language of the theory of theories is usually the same formal language as is used to formulate the theories. In Chomsky's case, then, a theory is a grammar, and a theory of grammar is essentially a grammar of grammars—a form of metamathematics. Outlined in his dissertation is a metamathematical approach to the problem of writing a grammar of grammars and thus providing a means of writing an evaluation procedure to determine whether one grammar is simpler than another.

Arithmetization and Chomsky's Grammars

Chomsky's metamathematics is a continuation of a very particular line of research: the arithmetization of logic and mathematics—as discussed in chapter 4, on algorithms—with precedents in the nineteenth century by mathematicians Karl Weierstrass (1815–1892), Richard Dedekind (1831–1916), Georg Cantor (1845–1918), and Giuseppe Peano (1858–1932). Much of this work was an exploration of the foundations of arithmetic and, ultimately, an effort to reduce numbers and arithmetic to a form of logic. This line of work continued into the twentieth century with Bertrand Russell (1872–1970) and Alfred North Whitehead (1861–1947) in their *Principia Mathematica* (published in three volumes, in 1910, 1912, and 1913, respectively), in which they sought to extend Gottlob Frege's (1848–1925) project and David Hilbert's (1862–1943) early work to reduce geometry to arithmetic (known as "Hilbert's Axioms," 1899)[81] and then Hilbert's famous address to the 1900 International Congress of Mathematicians in Paris, in which he posed twenty-three open questions to his colleagues. As discussed in chapter 2, on translation, Alan Turing's 1936 paper was a response to Hilbert's *Entscheidungsproblem* (decision problem).[82] This is the tradition of mathematical logic that Chomsky was referring to when he told the *New York Times* that in order to understand language as a system of creative thought, "You needed the modern theory of computability, which was developed by Alan Turing and other great mathematicians of the 1930s and '40s."

In 1927, David Hilbert wrote, "I should like to eliminate once and for all the questions regarding the foundations of mathematics, in the form in which they are now posed, by turning every mathematical proposition into a formula that can be concretely exhibited and strictly derived."[83] At the time, this aspiration to render everything—the means of mathematical inference, the objects of mathematical study, and their formal derivations—as a set of formulas to be analyzed logically still seemed remarkable. With Chomsky's project, it became clear that the objects, inferences, and derivations of linguistics could, analogously, be rendered as a set of formulas or, more plainly, a set of strings, bracketed and unbracketed. Thus, we can understand a natural language, such as English, as a set of strings, phrase-structure grammars, and transformational rules as another set of strings, and even derivations as (bracketed) strings.

This kind of formalization was novel in early twentieth-century mathematical logic (in the guise of arithmetization and, immediately before Kurt Gödel, in the formalism of Hilbert and his students, colleagues, and followers). Perhaps it is unsurprising, then, that linguists became interested in Hilbert's formalism, his metamathematics and proof theory. Linguistics historiographer Marcus Tomalin, in his book *Linguistics and the Formal Sciences: The Origins of Generative Grammar*, points out that the generation of linguists before Chomsky—including Leonard Bloomfield and Chomsky's dissertation adviser Zellig Harris—were engaged with metamathematics long before Chomsky wrote his dissertation:

> During the 1930s and 1940s...developments in the theory of logical syntax occurred, which were ultimately to have profound implications for linguistic research, and the starting point was usually Hilbert's proof theory, which seemed to imply that meaning-less syntactic manipulations could suffice to resolve a whole range of epistemological problems....Hilbert's work had influenced the Vienna Circle directly, and one of the most distinctive developments associated with Vienna-based research into the nature of logical systems in the 1930s was the shift of focus away from the structure of logic itself towards a concentration upon the structure of the language in which logical arguments are expressed. As mentioned previously, the most influential work of this type was due to Carnap [cited previously], whose *LSL* [*Logical Structure of Language*] appeared in 1934.[84]

Tomalin shows how Chomsky's work—although sometimes characterized as a "revolution"[85] in linguistics—was an outgrowth of a long-standing engagement between linguists and mathematical logicians, especially those influenced by Hilbert's project.[86]

Chomsky and the Computational Episteme

While Foucault's "Renaissance," "Classical," and "modern" epistemes may be applicable to at least some of the theories of linguists who followed Hilbert and preceded Chomsky, these epistemes are inadequate to describe a Chomskyan linguistics. A computational episteme is distinct from Foucault's modern episteme because the former is *not* primarily concerned with signification and meaning. Within a computational episteme, theories of language are devised to analyze language as if language form (its syntax) was independent of language meaning (its semantics).

As expressed by linguistics historians Geoffrey Huck and John Goldsmith, Chomskyan linguistics referred to the posited independence of syntax and semantics as the "autonomy hypothesis": "The idea that syntactic analysis could (in fact, must) be done without recourse to semantic terms, which has come to be known as the 'autonomy hypothesis,' has played a central role in all of Chomsky's work since his undergraduate days. It was also … a crucial component of the structuralist program of his [Chomsky's] teacher Zellig Harris."[87]

If the "autonomy hypothesis" is accepted, then grammatical analysis must proceed without reference to meaning. In Chomsky's words from 1977, "The study of meaning and reference and of the use of language should be excluded from the field of linguistics."[88] Chomsky's words largely follow those already expressed by, among others, Leonard Bloomfield and Zellig Harris. In 1931, Leonard Bloomfield pronounced, "Meanings cannot be defined in terms of our science and cannot enter into our definitions,"[89] and, according to linguistics historians Geoffrey Huck and John Goldsmith, "[Zellig] Harris's pronouncement in 1940 that 'the structures of language can be described only in terms of the formal, not the semantic differences of its units and their relations' … presaged the development of a distributional approach in which even difference of meanings has no place."[90]

Long before Chomsky, long before even Bloomfield, Hilbert's critics recognized and ridiculed formalism's decoupling of meaning from mathematics. Mathematician Henri Poincaré (1854–1912) sarcastically wrote, "Thus it will be readily understood that in order to demonstrate a theorem, it is not necessary or even useful to know what it means.… [W]e might imagine a machine where we should put in axioms at one end and take out theorems at the other, like that legendary machine in Chicago where pigs go in alive and come out transformed into hams and sausages. It is no more necessary for the mathematician than it is for these machines to know what he is doing."[91] Poincaré's comments sounded absurd in an era when no machines for proving theorems existed. Clearly, any machines used at the time in Chicago's slaughterhouses could not have proved a theorem, but computers can now be programmed to prove theorems, so Poincaré's remarks are dated and no longer elicit laughter.

We have seen in this book—especially in chapter 4, on algorithms, and in chapter 6, on rhetoric—that both computer programs and data can be encoded as black and white squares, as a series of bits, ones, and zeros. This idea to encode theorems, rules of inference, and derivations all as numbers or homogeneous formulas was an advanced technique in the metamathematics of the early and mid-twentieth century. Now it is commonplace, and we call it simply "digitization."

Once we have chosen some discrete format for digitization (e.g., Chomsky's choice of bracketed and unbracketed strings), methods as simple as counting and as complicated as machine "learning" can be computed automatically without reference to meaning. As we saw, for instance, in chapter 4, on algorithms, we can understand all possible procedures for doing arithmetic as cellular automata and can write a computer program to enumerate all such automata. Questions of meaning are left to the side. Clearly, even if Chomsky's work is perhaps one of the best examples of work done in a computational episteme, this mind-set—in which meaning is pushed to the margins—is active in many areas well beyond the reach of Chomskyan linguistics.

Meaning and Chomskyan Linguistics

While the "autonomy hypothesis" and the pronouncements of Bloomfield, Harris, and Chomsky effectively rule meaning to be beyond the bounds of linguistics, meaning has not been so easily avoided. It has been necessary for Chomsky and his colleagues to actively resist addressing meaning by positioning semantics as outside of but adjacent to their proper area of study: syntax. For example, Chomsky writes, "The requirement that this [Chomsky's] theory [of syntax] shall be a completely formal discipline is perfectly compatible with the desire to formulate it in such a way as to have suggestive and significant interconnections with a parallel semantic theory."[92]

These "interconnections" are related to what Chomsky called "kernel sentences" and the "deep structure" of sentences.[93] Kernel sentences are simple, active declaratives like "The man hit the ball." Transformational rules can be applied to turn the declarative into an interrogative ("Did the man hit the ball?"), the active into a passive ("The ball was hit by the man"), or to make more complicated sentences—for example, through the insertion of a prepositional phrase ("The man in the orange baseball cap hit the ball"). In his 1957 book *Syntactic Structures*, Chomsky expresses the hope that a theory of semantics could be based on an understanding of how phrase structure and transformational rules could be used to recover a kernel sentence from a derivation of a complicated sentence. The recovered kernel sentence—in conjunction with its derivation and the applied grammar rules—is considered the "deep structure" of a more complicated sentence. Thus, one might map out the connection between a more complicated question ("Did the man in the orange baseball cap hit the ball?") and its kernel sentence ("The man hit the ball"), potentially representing the answer to the question.

Yet Chomsky points out that the deep structure of a sentence is not, in general, equivalent to its semantics: "We can describe circumstances in which a 'qualificational' sentence such as 'everyone in the room knows at least two languages' may be true, while the corresponding passive 'at least two languages are known by everyone in the room' is false, under the normal interpretation of these sentences—e.g., if one person in the room knows only French and German, and another only Spanish and Italian. This indicates that not even the weakest semantic relation (factual equivalence) holds in general between active and passive."[94]

Nevertheless, Chomsky wants it both ways (both with and without semantics) and continues his discussion with the following statement: "These counter examples should not, however, blind us to the fact that there are striking correspondences between the structures and elements that are discovered in the formal grammatical analysis and specific semantic functions.... An investigation of the semantic function of level structure might be a reasonable step towards a theory of interconnections between syntax and semantics."[95]

Taken together, these comments might lead one to believe that Chomsky was suggesting that his investigation of syntax in isolation from semantics might be extended by considering syntactic deep structure as tantamount to a representation of meaning. As we saw earlier in this chapter, Chomsky reiterates this understanding almost ten years later when he attempts to find a precursor to his own work in the seventeenth-century *Port-Royal Grammar*, saying, "a sentence has an inner mental aspect (a deep structure that conveys its meaning)."[96] In the 1960s, however, a group of Chomsky's followers and colleagues pursued just such a project to connect Chomskyan deep structure with meaning—a project they called "Generative Semantics"—and were met with resistance and antagonism from Chomsky.[97]

Why would Chomsky have been so hostile to Generative Semantics when he seems to have advocated for just such an approach in his own writings? Clearly, the technical challenges of bridging deep structure and meaning are formidable, as Chomsky himself suggested in the comments cited earlier. Consider an example much simpler than Chomsky's. What happens if we add one more phrase-structure rule to the preceding grammar: "Noun → bottle"? Now it is possible for the grammar to generate an idiomatic phrase like "The man hit the bottle," meaning the man drank a lot of alcohol. Rendered in the passive, the idiom ("to hit the bottle") is lost: "The bottle was hit by the man." It is unclear how to encode idiomatic phrases into a Chomskyan transformational generative grammar in such a way that such phrases remain intact when transformational rules are applied to them.

Despite a myriad of technical difficulties, this does not seem to be Chomsky's principal objection to a project like Generative Semantics. Instead, his primary goal seems to be the establishment of formal theories of syntax as an autonomous discipline of research—autonomous from semantics in particular. In their history of Generative Semantics, Huck and Goldsmith reach the same conclusion—the dispute between the Generative Semanticists and Chomsky was not so much about technical difficulties as about the "autonomy hypothesis"; Chomsky came from a tradition and was determined to continue that tradition of defending formal syntactic analysis as an independent domain of study.[98]

Chomskyan Linguistics and Nondemonstrative Rhetoric

In his technical writings, Chomsky is rarely exclusively expository. Usually, he is writing to argue against other linguists or philosophers. In the chapter "Syntax and Semantics" in the book *Syntactic Structures*, he argues not only against a particular set of morphologists and experts in phonetics but also against any linguist who would question the independence of syntax from semantics. Chomsky frames the argument this way: "A great deal of effort has been expended in attempting to answer the question: 'How can you construct a grammar with no appeal to meaning?' The question itself, however, is wrongly put, since the implication that obviously one can construct a grammar with appeal to meaning is totally unsupported. One might with equal justification ask: 'How can you construct a grammar with no knowledge of the hair color of speakers?'"[99] In the pages that follow, some of Chomsky's specific debate partners emerge in the footnotes. But situated at the beginning of the chapter, this insulting comment seems to be aimed at all grammarians who have put meaning at the center of their work, including implicitly, of course, the Port-Royal grammarians, whom Chomsky later praises so effusively. Why does Chomsky, with this remark, ridicule the work of so many grammarians? This nondemonstrative rhetorical move is in keeping with his reputation as a formidable debate partner. He is simply trying to insult his colleagues.

That this is Chomsky's game plan becomes clear once we read what follows and see how Chomsky himself repeatedly appeals to meaning in the presentation of his own approach to grammar. For instance, look again at his example phrase-structure grammar. Why does he use English words as his terminal tokens, such as "hit," "man," and "ball"? Why not instead use words from a language we are unlikely to know—perhaps Norwegian—if he does not want to appeal to meaning in the construction of his own grammar?

Furthermore, as noted earlier, in his examples, Chomsky seems to have studiously avoided idioms like "The man hit the bottle" since they cannot be easily handled in transformational generative grammar. Another slight addition to his grammar would introduce slang, too. If we added one more production to allow "hit" to be a noun ("Noun → hit") as well as a verb, what could result? With that, the grammar would also cover the sentence "The man took a hit" and sentences that have no obvious meaning; for example, "The hit hit the hit." Clearly, in his presentation, Chomsky is avoiding examples that do not have an obvious, literal meaning.

Moreover, from a formalist perspective, there is no need to label the nonterminals in a grammar with meaningful names like "Noun" or "Verb" or even to use meaningful abbreviations like "N" and "V." Instead, numbered labels would more successfully avoid any appeal to meaning. One could rewrite the preceding grammar like this and still generate the same set of sentences: $X1 \rightarrow X2+X3$, $X2 \rightarrow X4+X5$, $X3 \rightarrow X6+X2$, $X4 \rightarrow$ the, $X4 \rightarrow a$, $X5 \rightarrow man$, $X5 \rightarrow ball$, $X6 \rightarrow hit$, $X6 \rightarrow took$. Why did Chomsky not write the grammar like this if he was trying to avoid any appeal to meaning?

Finally, we should underline the fact that Chomsky appeals to meaning even in his definition of grammar, cited earlier: "By grammar of the language L I [Chomsky] will *mean* [my emphasis] a device of some sort (that is, a set of rules) that provides, at least, a complete specification of an infinite set of grammatical sentences of L and their structural descriptions."[100] When Chomsky writes, in the sentence given earlier, "I will mean," he clearly appeals to meaning in the construction of his grammar. He also appeals to meaning in the construction of his grammar when he uses meaningful English words for the terminals and nonterminals of his grammar, when his examples are meaningful English sentences, and when he names his transformational rules with meaningful English phrases like "active to passive."

When Chomsky declares that one should not appeal to meaning in the construction of a grammar and then repeatedly does so himself, what is he trying to do? I think this would be confusing if we knew nothing about the "autonomy hypothesis" that Chomsky is already articulating in his dissertation: "Syntax and semantics are distinct fields of investigation. The subject of investigation will be syntactic structure, and we shall study it as an independent aspect of linguistic theory."[101]

Chomsky's interdiction of meaning appears to have nothing to do with his own approach to the study of language and a great deal to do with professional "empire building" within the field of linguistics. Insofar as, even today, syntax, semantics, and pragmatics are considered separate fields of investigation in linguistics and analytic philosophy, Chomsky was successful in securing a place at the table for syntax. His nondemonstrative rhetoric is a way to patrol the borders of his academic fiefdom.

Chomsky, Formalism, and Recursive Devices

Chomsky's interdiction of meaning is also indicative of his methodological orientation toward a Hilbertian formalism. We can also see an implicit nod to formalism in other parts of his definition of grammar. For example, if we reflect for a moment on Chomsky's, frequently repeated, appeal to the criterion that a grammar should specify an "infinite set" of sentences, we can see that this—like the interdiction of meaning—is a reference to the mathematician Cantor and others discussed earlier in this chapter who preceded and influenced David Hilbert and his offspring in linguistics.

No human language can have an infinite number of sentences. Nevertheless, imagine that if some language did include an infinite number of sentences, many would have to be billions, trillions, or even more words long. One might anticipate living for about eighty years or on the order of $80 \times 365 \times 24 \times 60 \times 60$ seconds—that is, more than two billion seconds, so a multibillion-word sentence could only occur if someone could sustain speech—in one continuous sentence, day and night—throughout their lifetime. Even then, anything longer than that—say a trillion-word sentence—would not be biologically possible.

Alternatively, imagine a language having a rich vocabulary with a million-word dictionary and a Proustian population that tends to speak sentences two hundred words in length. Even then, the total number of possible sentences would be on the order of one million to the power of two hundred, a very large number yet far short of infinite.

Even though Chomsky, throughout decades of work, repeatedly refers to the generation of an infinite number of sentences as a requirement for a grammar,[102] elsewhere he explains that, for him, there is a more compelling reason for grammars that incorporate a means of generating an infinite number of sentences. Chomsky writes, "In general, the assumption that languages are infinite is made in order to simplify the description of these languages. If a grammar does not have recursive devices…it will be prohibitively complex. If it does have recursive devices of some sort, it will produce infinitely many sentences."[103]

In sum, Chomsky needs to assume that languages are infinite so that "recursive devices" can appear in his grammars! Another way to phrase this is that Chomsky is determined to use his theoretical machinery regardless of whether it is applicable to his data. To a man with a hammer, everything looks like a nail. Chomsky's "hammer" is a kind of grammar tantamount to a piece of software. Let us call this "software-centered theory."

The notion of a "recursive device" plays a large role in Chomsky's theory of grammar, so let us examine an example. In principle, in English, it is possible to use an arbitrary number of adjectives before a noun. One can say "old man" but also "old old man," "wrinkled old man," "happy, well-dressed, brilliant, wrinkled old man," and so on. One way to express this in a grammar is with a recursive rule that references itself, like this grammar with two rules: "NounPhrase → Noun," "NounPhrase → Adjective + NounPhrase." The first of these two rules is the termination case indicating that no more adjectives are to be added. The second of these rules is the recursive case indicating that an adjective is to be added and then one of the two rules for NounPhrase is to be used again. We might write recursive rules for other structures as well, such as the construction of prepositional phrases that embed an undetermined number of other prepositional phrases; for example, "The man in the orange baseball cap with the San Francisco Giants logo on the brim (etc., etc.) hit the ball."

If one does not include a "recursive device" in the grammar, one is obliged to set a fixed limit on the number of times repetition might happen and then list each possibility separately in the grammar. For example, if we were to determine that three adjectives preceding a noun is sufficient to cover most English sentences, then we could replace the recursive case of the rule for noun phrase with these three rules:

NounPhrase → Adjective + Noun

NounPhrase → Adjective + Adjective + Noun

NounPhrase → Adjective + Adjective + Adjective + Noun.

Of course, in spoken and written language, there is a finite upper bound on the number of adjectives that are normally used. Using even ten adjectives to modify a noun phrase stands out as unusual or eccentric; for example, "He was a small, wrinkled, old, smelly, talkative, loud, skinny, strong, quick, lazy man." With a recursive rule, one can analyze and generate sentences with hundreds, thousands, millions, or billions of adjectives, but when would such a sentence actually occur in either print culture or everyday discourse?

So, if we were to decide that the outside limit of the number of adjectives preceding a noun can be only, say, twenty, then we could accommodate such noun phrases by adding twenty rules to the grammar. Chomsky's complaint against such a proposal—a grammar with twenty more rules—is that "this grammar will be so complex that it will be of little use or interest."[104]

What if, instead of a grammar with twenty more rules, we changed our notation a little bit so that we could write a grammar with one rule that contained more than twenty lines. It might look something like this:

NounPhrase → Noun

OR → Adjective + Noun

OR → Adjective + Adjective + Noun

etc.

I believe Chomsky would still object to this proposal. Chomsky's analysis of simplicity and complexity is subtler than just counting the number of rules in a grammar. His analysis includes an interpretation of the complexity of the metalanguage used to write the rules, an interpretation now known as the "Chomsky hierarchy."

The Chomsky Hierarchy

That counting the number of rules in a system could be a measure of its simplicity or complexity was proposed by Chomsky's graduate school professor Nelson Goodman but subsequently discarded by Chomsky. Instead, Chomsky tied simplicity to a very carefully articulated definition of a framework for measuring computational complexity, a definition introduced to every undergraduate in computer science under the rubric of the "Chomsky hierarchy,"[105] or sometimes (referencing his coauthor) the "Chomsky-Schützenberger hierarchy."[106]

Originally, Chomsky developed this hierarchy to argue that simpler devices, such as Markov processes, are too simple to describe human languages.[107] Later, as linguist E. Keith Brown points out in his overview of transformational generative grammar for *The Linguistics Encyclopedia*, in the late 1960s, linguists following Chomsky became concerned with the computational complexity of transformational rules: "Once the mathematical properties of this kind of rule were explored, it became clear that a grammar with transformations has the formal properties of a universal Turing machine: in other words, they are such a powerful tool that they can explain nothing except that language can be described in terms of some set of rules. An obvious effect of this unwelcome result was to see whether the power of the transformational component could be constrained."[108]

As discussed in chapter 2, on translation (and elsewhere in this book), any device with the formal properties of a universal Turing machine (UTM) is tantamount to a full-featured computer programming language. In other words, by the late 1960s, Chomskyan linguists were writing very complicated transformational rules. They were considered too complicated because they were written in a metalanguage that could allow an arbitrary symbol or sequence of symbols to be rewritten into any other sequence. To understand that this posed a problem, we need to further unpack Chomsky's thinking about the power and complexity of grammars and machines.

In the Chomsky hierarchy, grammars of the most powerful type are called "Type-0." Rules of Type-0 grammars can take the form $\alpha \rightarrow \beta$, where a Greek letter (like "α" or "β") conventionally denotes either a terminal symbol (usually written as a lowercase Roman letter; e.g., "a" or "b") or a nonterminal symbol (written as an uppercase Roman letter; e.g., "A" or "B").

Terminals constitute what will be the "leaves" of a derivation tree, so, typically, they are words like "ball," "man," or "hit." Nonterminals appear in the upper layers of a derivation and usually represent an abstraction of one or more terminals—for example, "Sentence," "NounPhrase," or "Verb."

If rules are of Type-0, allowing anything to be rewritten as anything else (nonterminals into nonterminals, nonterminals into terminals, but also terminals into nonterminals, and even terminals into other terminals), grammars can, in principle, generate absurdities; given the string "The man hit the ball," for example, a Type-0 grammar could generate a derivation relating it to the sentence "The last album of David Bowie was spectacular." This is because there are no restrictions on the grammar preventing, for instance, terminals being rewritten into other terminals. So, one could include a rule like this: "man → David Bowie." If transformational rules can be written to relate together such unlike sentences, the linguistic insight captured by such rules seems dubious—at least it did to the Chomskyans of the late 1960s. Consequently, a great amount of effort was expended to "climb down" the Chomsky hierarchy to simpler grammars, grammars with less computational complexity than a universal Turing machine.

Type-1 grammars have a more constrained form of rules than those of Type-0 grammars. Type-1 rules are of the form $\alpha A\beta \rightarrow \alpha B\beta$. Type-1 grammars are called "context sensitive" because nonterminals can only be rewritten into other nonterminals in specific contexts—here noted as "α" and "β."

Type-2 grammars are even less computationally complex. They allow nonterminals to be rewritten without consulting the context, but—unlike Type-0 rules—terminal symbols cannot be rewritten. Rules take the form of $A \rightarrow \alpha$, where, again, "α" can be either a terminal or a nonterminal symbol but where "A" stands exclusively for a nonterminal symbol. Type-2 grammars can also be referred to as "context-free grammars." Chomsky's example phrase-structure grammar, given earlier, is written as a Type-2, context-free grammar.

Finally, on the bottom rung of the Chomsky hierarchy are Type-3 grammars, also called "regular grammars." Rules can be of the forms $A \rightarrow \alpha$ or $A \rightarrow \alpha B$ or $A \rightarrow \varepsilon$, where "$\varepsilon$" denotes neither a terminal nor a nonterminal symbol but rather the empty string (i.e., a string containing nothing). Type-3 grammars are the simplest, the least computationally complex, and the least powerful.

To illustrate the Chomsky hierarchy, let us consider some examples. With a Type-3 grammar, it is possible to specify a "language" of bit strings with no particular order of appearance of the 1s and 0s: $S \rightarrow 0S$, $S \rightarrow 1S$, $S \rightarrow \varepsilon$. All possible bit strings can be generated with this grammar.

But what if we are only interested in a "language" that contains bit strings that start with an arbitrary number of 0s followed by the same number of 1s? To generate "sentences" like this and only like this—"01," "0011," "000111," and others—we need the power of a context-free grammar, a grammar of Type-2, a grammar more powerful than Type-3: $S \rightarrow 0S1$, $S \rightarrow \varepsilon$. Every time this grammar generates a 0, it also generates a

1, so there is no need for it to store the number of 0s it has generated before generating the 1s.

However, what if we want to generate strings like this: "010," "001100," "000111000"? That is, what if we want to generate only strings prefixed with an arbitrary number of 0s followed by the same number of 1s and terminated with a postfix of 0s equal in number to the 0s in the prefix? This is an example of a "language" that requires a grammar more powerful than a context-free grammar.

Try writing it as a context-free grammar and you will find that, after generating an arbitrary number of 0s (or an equal number of 0s and 1s)—let us call this number K—you will need to store K in order to determine how many 0s to include in the postfix of the string. You will also find that a Type-2, context-free grammar provides no facility for storing and retrieving a value.

Essentially, as one goes up the Chomsky hierarchy (from Type-3 up to Type-0), one gains more facility to store and retrieve information until one has, in Type-0 grammars, the facility to create variables, assign them values, and then retrieve the value of a variable whenever necessary. Looking at the example active-to-passive transformational rule shown earlier, one can see that rules of this form can be stated in a metalanguage that provides variables, that allows variables to be assigned values, and that allows the variables' respective values to be retrieved (and reordered).

In principle, a universal Turing machine has an infinite amount of memory or storage (for variables and values). Chomsky's accomplishment was to show that any universal Turing machine (UTM) could be translated into a Type-0 grammar; any linear-bounded automaton (LBA) could be translated into a Type-1 grammar; any pushdown automaton (PDA) could be translated into a Type-2 grammar; and any finite state automaton (FSA) could be translated into a Type-3 grammar.

Furthermore, there is an ordering on these machines and their corresponding grammars: anything that can be computed by an FSA can be computed by a PDA, but the converse is not true; that is, there are computations a PDA can perform that an FSA cannot. Our discussion of grammars and bit strings was an illustration of this. The ordering on these machines and grammars is an ordering of complexity and simplicity. A UTM is more powerful than, and more complex than, an LBA that is more complex than a PDA that is more complex than an FSA. The analogous ordering on grammars is this, from the most complex to the simplest: Type-0, Type-1, Type-2, Type-3.

Google research scientist and computational linguist Fernando Pereira has quipped, "The older I get, the further down the Chomsky hierarchy I go."[109] By this Pereira meant that early in his career he wrote grammars of Type-0 and then, as his work has progressed, he has written grammars with increasingly constrained and less powerful rule forms: grammars that are "simpler" because they are less computationally complex but that are more "complex" because they, necessarily, require many more rules—even if those rules are "simpler." This path "down" the Chomsky hierarchy has been, as the quotation from E. Keith Brown attests, the aspiration if not the practice of many linguists since the late 1960s.

Definite Clause Grammars

In 1980, Fernando Pereira and his colleague David H. D. Warren invented an ingenious notation (actually a "macro") for the Prolog programming language in order to write context-free grammars conveniently.[110] Recall from the section on logic programming in chapter 6 that Prolog predicates are a kind of inverted IF-THEN rule composed like this: THEN:- IF. To write "IF X is a man THEN X is mortal" in Prolog, one would write "mortal(X):- man(X)." A comma (",") in a Prolog predicate means AND, so "mortal(X):- man(x),not(god(X))" can be interpreted as "IF X is a man and X is NOT a god THEN X is mortal." Variables are written in uppercase in Prolog.

Pereira and Warren's Definite Clause Grammar (DCG) notation/macro allows one to write "sentence → noun_phrase,verb_phrase" and have it compiled automatically into a Prolog clause like this:

sentence(S):- append(NP,VP,S), noun_phrase(NP), verb_phrase(VP).

To understand the ingenuity of this, one needs to know that when the third argument of the Prolog append predicate is instantiated with a list and the first two arguments are left uninstantiated, the predicate will return all possible list pairs that, concatenated together, yield the given list. So, "append(List1,List2,[a,b,c])" will return multiple binding results for the variables List1 and List2:

List1 = [], List2 = [a,b,c]

List1 = [a], List2 = [b,c]

List1 = [a,b], List2 = [c]

List1 = [a,b,c], List2 = []

In Prolog, one can write the append predicate in two clauses:

append([],List,List).

append([First|Rest],List2,[First|List3]):- append(Rest,List2,List3).

The first clause can be read like this: appending the empty list (notated like this: []) to a list yields the list. The second clause is recursive: the result of appending one list, with the first element called First and with the remaining elements called Rest, to a second list,

List2, results in a list, which has First as its first element. The rest of the result is a list, List3, composed of the Rest of the first list appended to List2.

Consequently, in response to a query like "sentence([the,man,hit,the,ball])" the sentence predicate will attempt all possible partitions of the input list (e.g., [] and [the,man,hit,the,ball]; [the] and [man,hit,the,ball]; [the,man] and [hit,the,ball]; etc.) and try to match the first part with the predicate noun_phrase and the second with the predicate verb_phrase. If the matches are successful, the predicate sentence will return true.

Written like this, as a Prolog DCG, Chomsky's example phrase-structure grammar from *Syntactic Structures* will verify whether the input list is a grammatical sentence:[111]

sentence → noun_phrase, verb_phrase.

noun_phrase → article, noun.

verb_phrase → verb, noun_phrase.

article → [the].

article → [a].

noun → [man].

noun → [ball].

verb → [hit].

verb → [took].

To have the DCG verify a sentence and produce a derivation tree that labels each part of the sentence, we need to add parameters to each rule that are instantiated if the rule succeeds:[112]

sentence(sentence(NP,VP)) → noun_phrase(NP), verb_phrase(VP).

noun_phrase(noun_phrase(A,N)) → article(A), noun(N).

verb_phrase(verb_phrase(V,NP)) → verb(V), noun_phrase(NP).

article(article(the)) → [the].

article(article(a)) → [a].

noun(noun(man)) → [man].

noun(noun(ball)) → [ball].

verb(verb(hit)) → [hit].

verb(verb(took)) → [took].

With this version of the DCG, in response to a query like "sentence([the,man,hit,the, ball])" the sentence predicate will return a derivation that looks like this:

sentence(noun_phrase(article(the),noun(man)),
            verb_phrase(verb(hit),noun_phrase(article(the), noun(ball))))

If we want to include transformational rules, they can be written as Prolog predicates that take, as an input parameter, an instantiated derivation tree and produce as output, by instantiating a second parameter, a transformed derivation tree. For instance, here is a translation of Chomsky's active-to-passive transformational rule.[113]

active_to_passive(sentence(noun_phrase(A1,X1),
                          verb_phrase(verb(X2),
                                      noun_phrase(A2,X3))),
                  sentence(noun_phrase(A2,X3),
                          verb_phrase(auxilliary(Aux),
                                      verb(X2),
                                      prep_phrase(prep(by),
                                                  noun_phrase(A1,X1))))) :-
            conjugate_past_tense(X3,be,Aux).

In addition, we need a little more code to define the predicate conjugate_past_tense. Prolog is a full programming language and thus tantamount to a Type-0 grammar. We can see these powers employed in the use of variables (e.g., X1, X2, X3) in the transformational rule as well as the use of an extra predicate in the rule (conjugate_past_tense) that could employ an arbitrarily large computer program in its definition, although here the definition is trivial:

conjugate_past_tense(noun(N),Infinitive,PastTense) :-
            is_singular(N),
            singular_past_tense(Infinitive,PastTense).
conjugate_past_tense(noun(N),Infinitive,PastTense) :-
            is_plural(N),
            plural_past_tense(Infinitive,PastTense).
is_singular(ball).
is_singular(man).
is_plural(balls).
is_plural(men).
plural_past_tense(be,were).
singular_past_tense(be,was).

Using Pereira and Warren's DCG notation, it is straightforward to translate Chomsky's grammars into a computer program. Such translations, Chomsky's insistence that grammars are "devices," and his demonstrations that grammars can be translated into automata (UTM, LBA, PDA, FSA) together illustrate how Chomsky's grammars are machines tantamount to software. Moreover, Chomsky also wrote his theory of grammar (his theory of theories) in the same form. So, Chomsky is definitively in the genealogy of Hilbert's formalism, but he has taken it one step beyond what the mathematical logicians had done. Just as Turing found a way to translate the logical formalism of his machines into the material production of software and hardware, Chomsky translated the formalism of grammar rules into the same—a notation that is straightforward to translate into software.

Epistemologically, what is most striking about this is Chomsky's declaration that his grammars are theories. According to the *Oxford English Dictionary (OED)*, a theory is "the conceptual basis of a subject or area of study." Etymologically, "theory" derives from the ancient Greek word "θεωρια" connoting the act of viewing, contemplation, sight, and spectacle. The *OED* definition adds that "theory" is to be contrasted with "practice." This contrast is completely in keeping with Aristotle's tripartite division of human activity into material and technical production (*techne*); action that requires judgment, such as political and military action (*phronesis*); and theoretical knowledge (*episteme*). However, theories of the computational episteme—cast in Chomsky's mold—break the "Aristotelian barrier" (in the terms developed in chapter 3) because machines—specifically computer programs—are proposed as theories: Aristotle's *techne* and *episteme* are collapsed together.

Others of Chomsky's generation—cofounders of cognitive science, computer science, and artificial intelligence—also stated their theories in software, or in formalisms tantamount to software. Herbert Simon and Allen Newell put it like this in 1972: "A good information processing theory of a good human chess player can play good chess; a good theory of how humans create novels will create novels."[114]

Translation Today

Fast-forward to today and consider how grammars are written as software. Needless to say, they look almost nothing like the Prolog DCG shown here. Increasingly, linguistic software of this sort is being created using machine learning and, lately, using the techniques of so-called deep neural networks. Consider, for example, the "grammars" of Google's online machine translation system.[115] In 2016, Google completely rewrote it using some new techniques from machine learning.[116] The Google software engineers responsible for this published a series of papers on the overhaul, including one titled "Google's Multilingual Neural Machine Translation System: Enabling Zero-Shot Translation."[117]

In that paper, the Google researchers describe how they trained their machine-learning algorithm on hundreds of millions of sentence pairs like this English and French pair: ("To be, or not to be, that is the question" + "Être, ou ne pas être, c'est là question"). The amount of computation necessary for the machine learning was extraordinary: "Depending on the number of languages a full training can take up to 10M steps and 3 weeks to converge (on roughly 100 GPUs)."[118]

For those of us who are not machine-learning experts, it is striking that the quality of translations that are produced by the resulting system is not scored by humans but instead evaluated automatically by using a computer program.[119] Consequently, even if their neural network machine-learning algorithm can be properly called inductive (i.e., as described in chapter 6, on rhetoric and demonstration), the Google authors' demonstration is nevertheless abductive; first, because no human can follow what is being done step-by-step on a hundred GPUs (GPUs are computers) over the course of three weeks, and, second, because relative to the demonstration, no human ever sees more than the tiniest sliver of the translations done by the machine.

Symptomatic of this is that only about twenty example translations are presented in the text of the paper and all of them are translations of these four English sentences: (1) "Hello, how are you?" (2) "I wonder what they'll do next!" (3) "I must be getting somewhere near the centre of the earth." (4) "Here the other guinea-pig cheered, and was suppressed." This, it seems to me, is a curious choice of examples, but most pertinent to my assertion that the paper performs an abductive demonstration is the fact that only four source sentences are presented even though the data set would have allowed, in principle, hundreds of millions to be presented for inspection.

The visual diagrams of the article further underline its abductive character. The visualizations presented are colored network diagrams that look approximately like a plate of spaghetti with some colored marbles thrown in. The authors assert that the diagrams represent "74 triples of semantically identical cross-language phrases. That is, each triple contained phrases in English, Japanese and Korean with the same underlying meaning."[120] Despite the fact that there seems to be no obvious way to interpret these diagrams as meaning one thing or another, and despite the fact that the sample chosen (of 74 sentences) is, again, only a tiny sliver of the hundreds of millions of examples the authors used as data, the authors nevertheless conclude the following about their spaghetti-and-marbles diagrams: "Visual interpretation of the results shows that these models learn a form of interlingua representation for the multilingual model between all involved language pairs."[121]

Does Google's new translation software represent an interlingua or constitute a theory? Because it is so big, the software system itself could never be read by any one person in a lifetime. The technical papers describing it are structured as abductive demonstrations—demonstrations in which almost none of the steps taken to produce the software are shown (because there are so many steps) and in which almost none of the data analyzed is shared (because much of it was gathered by Google from its users and is not shared outside of the company). Consequently, and not only because the machine-learning algorithm requires hundreds of computers to run for weeks to achieve the claimed results, Google's results cannot be reproduced by anyone outside of Google. No one else has the necessary resources to reproduce the results. If Google's translation system is a theory, it is one derived from unreproducible results with data that cannot be shared and that has been rendered as a piece of software too big for anyone to read.

Deduction, Induction, Abduction

In 2011, Chomsky spoke at an event at the Massachusetts Institute of Technology called "Brains, Minds, and Machines," during which he commented on the epistemological status of these huge new statistically based computer programs, like Google's translation system.[122] Chomsky said, "It's true there's been a lot of work on trying to apply statistical models to various linguistic problems. I think there have been some successes, but a lot of failures. There is a notion of success…which I think is novel in the history of science. It interprets success as approximating unanalyzed data."

Peter Norvig, the director of research at Google, wrote a long response arguing that science and engineering develop together, in which he states, "Engineering success shows that something is working right and so is evidence (but not proof) of a scientifically successful model."[123] Norvig continues by insisting that these giant systems can be understood: "I agree that it can be difficult to make sense of a model containing billions of parameters. Certainly a human can't understand such a model by inspecting the values of each parameter individually. But one can gain insight by examining the properties of the model—where it succeeds and fails, how well it learns as a function of data, etc."[124]

Essentially, Chomsky argued that this is not science—and not a theory—because it tells us nothing about why language works the way it does. Norvig argued that indeed this is engineering, but engineering provides science with models that work and thus it explains how language works even if it does not explain why.

The Chomsky-Norvig disagreement seems inevitable. It seems inevitable that Chomsky—who narrates his own career in a lineage with Galileo and Descartes, maintains that there is no place for statistics in linguistics, and repeatedly denies the possibility of inductive learning[125]—would object to embracing the output of an inductive, statistical learning algorithm (a billion-parameter "equation") as a theory. Moreover, software with a billion parameters seems an anathema when scrutinized under the carefully considered and constructed criteria of Chomsky's hierarchy of formal languages. Chomsky is essentially replaying the role of a natural philosopher from the seventeenth century for whom deduction is the only acceptable form of demonstration.

In contrast, Norvig plays the role of the machine philosopher demonstrating results with a new form of induction. He makes it clear that he sees his own work as an outgrowth of a long line of scientific research (going back to Boyle) that employs statistics, probability, and inductive demonstration.

Such a disagreement between Chomsky and Norvig is inevitable, but to me it also seems, ultimately, inconsequential. When Chomsky and his generation declared that a theory should take the form of software, they changed the rules of what can be taken as knowledge. That Noam Chomsky, Herbert Simon, Allen Newell, and others wrote small pieces of software and that now the current generation—Peter Norvig and others—write huge pieces of software forged from big data seems more like a quantitative difference and not really a qualitative shift. Today's "paradigm," the contemporary "computational episteme," was launched by Chomsky and his generation, and we are still sailing that ship.

Theories of Arithmetic

Does big data make a big difference? Some would say that there is an enormous difference between computing then and computing now because now many big companies and nation-states have access to huge amounts of data. Surely, big data—especially for those rich in data, like Google—presents a new set of opportunities,[126] but does big data portend the end of theory, as journalist Chris Anderson proclaimed in a *Wired* editorial in June 2008 called "The End of Theory: The Data Deluge Makes the Scientific Method Obsolete."[127] Anderson proclaimed, "Today companies like Google, which have grown up in an era of massively abundant data, don't have to settle for wrong models. Indeed, they don't have to settle for models at all."[128] With this comment, Anderson misses the forest for the trees. The big story is not about the data. It is about the theories behind the machine-learning algorithms that comb through and find patterns in all that data. We have not reached the "end of theory." Instead, we need to recognize that computational theories are taking ridiculously simplistic forms.

In the title of the Google publication examined earlier, there is the phrase "Neural Machine Translation." This refers to a machine-learning technique for "neural networks," but note also that at this moment (in 2018) neural network (or "deep") machine learning is astoundingly popular and is regularly covered in nontechnical mass publications like *The Economist* and the *New York Times*.

What exactly *are* these "neural networks," also called "multilayer perceptrons"? Make no mistake, these things have almost nothing to do with neural science, despite the fact that neuroscientists have been interested in logic circuits and that mathematical logicians have been interested in neurons at least since the 1943 publication of Warren McCulloch and Walter Pitts's paper on the simulation of neural networks by logic circuits.[129]

To the untrained eye, it is hard to see how anyone could find the computational form of neural networks in any actual living biological system because, in its simplest form, it is just a weighted sum of inputs. The inputs are x_1 to x_d; the weights are w_1 to w_d; and the summation sign (Σ) indicates that each of the products of $w_j x_j$ should be added together:[130]

$$y = \sum_{j=1}^{d} w_j x_j + w_0$$

The preceding sum is now what a theory can look like. If you prefer it in code, here it is in JavaScript:

```
var y = 0; for (var j = 1; j <= d; j++) {y = y + (w[j] * x[j]) + w[0];}.
```

"Machine learning" happens when the weights in the sum are adjusted up or down. In short, the big news here is that even "learning" has become a form of arithmetic, and this form of arithmetic currently constitutes the conceptual framework for everything from computational linguistics to search engines and self-driving cars. Arithmetic is the new theory of everything.[131]

Incredibly, theories in the computational episteme are a form of arithmetic. But what is the justification for this? The justification is not that these theories give some grand insight into why the world is the way it is. No, the justification—the test—of a theory in this form is this: Does it work? If the translation is considered competent, if the chess playing is masterful, or if the self-driving car navigates within the law and without incident or accident, then the machine-learning theory is said to be good.

The big shift symptomatic of the computational episteme is the current understanding that theory and interpretation are now formulated in the pursuit of how-to knowledge and no longer in a search for answers to questions of why. Grammar made this shift under the ministrations of Dr. Chomsky when he reformulated it in a machine language easily translated into a running piece of software. Since then—as we have seen—many other areas of knowledge have undergone the same transformation, the same translation.

If we accept Norvig's criterion of success—"success shows that something is working right"—we have another set of questions to respond to. For whom is the software/theory working? Under what circumstances? At what cost to whom? These questions loop us back to the concerns of chapter 3, on work and machine languages. Whose work is being accomplished by software, and whose labor is being changed or eliminated? Thus, any theory in a computational episteme presupposes a politics of labor and automation.

8   Conclusion

When artist and new media theorist Lev Manovich published *The Language of New Media* almost twenty years ago, he introduced the term "software studies." Manovich wrote: "New media calls for a new stage in media theory.... To understand the logic of new media, we need to turn to computer science. It is there that we may expect to find the new terms, categories, and operations that characterize media that became programmable. *From media studies, we move to something that can be called 'software studies'—from media theory to software theory.*"[1] Manovich expands on this by outlining two ways we might "turn to computer science": "In new media lingo, to 'transcode' something is to translate it into another format. The computerization of culture gradually accomplishes similar transcoding in relation to all cultural categories and concepts. That is, cultural categories and concepts are substituted, on the level of meaning and/or language, by new ones that derive from the computer's ontology, epistemology, and pragmatics.... The principle of transcoding is one way to start thinking about software theory. Another way, which this book experiments with, is to use concepts from computer science as categories of new media theory."[2]

In this book, what Manovich calls "transcoding" I have called "translation." As I point out in chapter 2, in science and technology studies (STS), translation is a common methodology that is based on an even older tradition of the liberal arts and the humanities. In STS, the sociology of translation is more commonly referred to as actor-network theory (ANT). Methodologically, the challenge for this book has been to extend and amend actor-network theory so that it can be used to address the texts of software: the inscriptions of code and the technical papers of computer science.

As is probably clear from the distinction drawn by Manovich, the approach taken in this book (ANT) is the converse or complement of his approach. Rather than use concepts from computer science as categories of new media theory, I start with categories of the liberal and mechanical arts to trace their respective translations into concepts used in computer science and then examine how they are popularized, translated further, into other expressions and technologies that circulate in popular culture as forms of digital life.

As we have seen in this book, arithmetization has been an overwhelming force in the rewriting of ideas and institutions into software. When historians of science and mathematics use the word "arithmetization," they are usually referring to twentieth-century events following Kurt Gödel's work on the incompleteness of formal arithmetic.[3] Alternatively, as in the case of the phrase "arithmetization of analysis," what is being referred to is a search for the foundations of the calculus in the nineteenth century.[4] In this book, I have employed the term not only to connote these moments in the history of mathematics but also to point to the long-standing and continuing rise of arithmetic: the ongoing recasting of concepts as forms of arithmetic or calculation. This rise of arithmetic is historically entangled with what Descartes and Leibniz called a *mathesis universalis*, a dream of a universal science modeled on mathematics. In this book, arithmetization stands in for an urge to make everything into math—an urge that I have argued needs to be resisted.

Arithmetic—and, more generally, algebra, calculus, and other important topics in mathematics—has grown in importance for intellectual work and for industry (especially capitalism: from merchant, to industrial, and now financial).[5] With Boole we saw how logic could be translated into a simple form of arithmetic (as shown in chapter 5). Today, we see a similar translation inflicted on "learning." Machine "learning" has become metonymic for artificial intelligence and has been reduced to just the tuning of parameters in very big polynomials (as described at the end of chapter 7).[6] Other concepts of the liberal and mechanical arts that have been translated into technical concepts of computer science include algorithm, demonstration, grammar, language, machine, operation, process, rhetoric, and simulation.

I list algorithm at the beginning of this list not just because the list is ordered alphabetically but also because algorithm has been and arguably remains the key term of computer science. In this concluding chapter, we will consider the research and teaching agendas of computer science, which prioritize the algorithm, and contrast them with a possible agenda for software studies that instead privileges interaction and the pursuit of methods to invent and interrogate statements of assignment, connection, equivalence, and identity.

Inside the Algorithm

Computer Science as the Study of Algorithms

As mentioned in chapter 1, in 1967 Herbert Simon, Alan Perlis, and Allen Newell wrote a letter to the editor of the journal *Science* insisting that computer science is a science. In the letter, they reject the idea that computer science is limited to the study of algorithms,[7] but, as summarized by computer historian Paul Ceruzzi, "Computer science evolved in subsequent years to mean precisely what they [Simon, Perlis, and Newell] said it was not—the study of algorithms.... Six months after the appearance of the letter in *Science*, the ACM [Association for Computing Machinery] published Curriculum '68, a set of courses that the association felt would provide an intellectually defensible grounding in computer science for undergraduates. Curriculum '68 emphasized a mathematical and theoretical basis for computer science. The study of computer hardware was absent.... The ACM chose to emphasize algorithmic procedures, programming languages, and data structures."[8]

One might venture that the situation is different now, a half-century later, but consulting the ACM/IEEE *Computer Science Curricula 2013*, one still finds algorithms at the top of the list of eighteen different "knowledge areas" (see page 14): "Algorithms are fundamental to computer science and software engineering. The real-world performance of any software system depends on: (1) the algorithms chosen and (2) the suitability and efficiency of the various layers of implementation. Good algorithm design is therefore crucial for the performance of all software systems."[9]

Clearly, algorithms maintain their place at the forefront of computer science education. Because they occupy such a prominent role in the undergraduate curriculum, we can understand algorithms as "gatekeepers" into the major. If you cannot handle the mathematical and logical discourse of your introduction to algorithms course, you are unlikely to stick with computer science as your major course of study.

Algorithms are gatekeepers not just in the university curriculum, however; they fulfill the same role in industry. Questions about algorithms constitute the bulk of what interviewers ask prospective software developers at large tech firms like Microsoft, Amazon, Google, Apple, and Facebook. Here are the first few sentences of one of the top-selling books for aspiring software developers preparing for a job interview: "At most of the top tech companies (and many other companies), algorithm and coding problems form the largest component of the interview process. Think of these as problem-solving questions. The interviewer is looking to evaluate your ability to solve algorithmic problems you haven't seen before."[10]

Algorithms are an effort to translate software into mathematics. Ultimately, however, like all translations, they cannot be effected without loss, addition, or modification. This is especially challenging within computer science, where, as discussed in chapter 2, the ideal is lossless translation. As we saw in chapter 4, algorithms cover only a small slice of what we use computers for, so, empirically, algorithms are inadequate for the description and design of most systems. Computer science has been through many episodes in which the inadequacy of algorithms has been "proved" mathematically. (In the coming sections, we will look at two such episodes.) Nevertheless, despite their inadequacy, computer scientists cannot seem to move algorithms off the top of their agenda.[11] This inability has both practical and political implications.

Algorithms from the 1930s to the 1960s

As mentioned in chapter 4, Donald Knuth's formalization of the algorithm and his advocacy for it are two crucial reasons why algorithms were chosen as the fundamental unit of analysis for computer science.[12] But Knuth's definition was foreshadowed in the 1936 paper that Alan Turing wrote following M. H. A. Newman's course at Cambridge (which we mentioned in chapter 2). There, Turing focused on a very specific kind of machine, an automatic machine: "If at each stage the motion of a machine…is completely determined by the configuration, we shall call the machine an 'automatic machine.'…For some purposes we might use [choice] machines…whose motion is only partially determined by the configuration…. When such a machine reaches one of these ambiguous configurations, it cannot go on until some arbitrary choice has been made by an external operator…. In this paper I deal only with automatic machines."[13]

In chapter 5, on logic, I cited software historian Michael Mahoney's essay "Computer Science: The Search for a Mathematical Theory," in which he states that "A theory of computation appositive to the electronic digital stored program computer with random-access memory lay somewhere between the Turing machine and the switching circuit. Computer science arose out of the effort to fill that gap."[14] Mahoney follows this search from Turing's machines, to von Neumann and others' theory of automata, and on through the Chomsky-Schützenberger hierarchy of formal languages (discussed in chapter 7, on grammar).

Continuing this search leads us to see how Turing's machines appear in the guise of algorithms in Donald Knuth's series *The Art of Computer Programming*. According to Knuth, algorithms have inputs and outputs and have "finiteness"—that is, they terminate in a finite amount of time. In other words, algorithms are machines that accept data, calculate, and then finish by rendering an output. They do not require what Turing calls "external operators," so they are tantamount to Turing's "automatic machines."

Why Algorithms?

Already in the nineteenth century, in Babbage's writings (which we examined in chapters 3 and 4), one can see a desire to build automatic machines in order to put people out of the loop for three reasons: to eliminate errors, to speed things up, and to spare humans the need to perform low-level labor. With these economies in mind, one can understand why it was (and still is) compelling to try to design automatic machines—machines that can be given some input and can return some output without human intervention.

Yet even though automatic machines would seem to be a way to eliminate human error, as discussed in chapter 4, human error is not in fact eliminated but rather only displaced by them. If the automatic machine is designed incorrectly, if the wrong machine is chosen for the job, if mistakes are made in the choice of input, or if the output is misread, human error makes its mark—even with automatic machines.

So, despite the fact that Turing's machines and Knuth's algorithms are, by definition, not interactive, they nevertheless need to interface with human subjects in multiple ways to be of any use. In other words, automatic machines and algorithms are axiomatically well defined but metaphorically like animals without habitats—they might be able to stay alive in an isolated cell at the zoo, but not without a lot of resources, both human and material.

When Software Looks Like Math

Despite the fact that algorithms are modeled as mathematical functions (with inputs and outputs), mathematical functions (as developed from Leibniz on) are inadequate for representing the operations of software. Operations are not all functions, so software is not mathematics. Alternatively, more precisely, only some software can be rendered as mathematics—the software that implements algorithms!

Functional programming is the programming paradigm that is most associated with efforts to overcome the gap that lies between the functions of mathematics and the operations of computing. Functional programming is rooted in the lambda-calculus of Alonzo Church (discussed in chapter 2)[15] because the first functional programming language, Lisp, was described as an implementation of the lambda-calculus.[16]

A quick comparison of algebraic notation and the lambda-calculus can illustrate why figuring software as mathematics might seem to be a reasonable simile. Consider, for example, the first of the three classical laws of thought, the law of identity, which is rendered in algebra as $x=x$; or, stated as a function, $f(x)=x$. Rendering this law in Church's lambda-calculus is almost as easy; we write $\lambda x.x$. In this expression, the λ denotes that what follows is the definition of a function, the x before the point is an argument for the function, and the x after the point is the body of the function, a description of the calculation to be performed by the function and of the output.

So, given an input of 2, $\lambda x.x$ returns the output of 2. In the notation of the lambda-calculus, the application of the function to an input is written like this: $(\lambda x.x)y$. When the input is specifically 2, it is written like this: $(\lambda x.x)2$.

How does this work? The workings of the lambda-calculus are explained in terms of substitution—also known as "beta reduction." When a function is evaluated, the value of the argument (i.e., the input) is substituted into the body of the function wherever the argument of the function appears in the body. The substitution is written using a slash and square brackets, $(\lambda x.x)y = [y/x]x$, where y/x indicates that wherever x appears in the body, it will be replaced with the value y, and the x that follows the square brackets is the full text of the body of the identity function.

Just for practice, let us reiterate this notation. Consider another function. The successor function, given an integer, returns the next integer: $\lambda x.x+1$. If the successor function is given the input 1, its output will be 2; given 2, it returns 3; given 3, it returns 4; and so forth. In the notation just introduced, one would write the last calculation like this: $(\lambda x.x+1)3 = [3/x]x+1 = 4$.

The Church-Turing Thesis, Again

As discussed in chapter 2, Turing demonstrated the equivalence between his automatic machines—now called Turing machines—and Alonzo Church's lambda-calculus. Church's student Stephen Kleene coined the phrase the "Church-Turing thesis" to refer to this equivalence. Also in chapter 2, we examined how the Church-Turing thesis has been popularized and expanded to the fantastical idea that Turing's 1936 paper shows that machines of any sort—whether or not they have been rendered as a Turing machine or in the lambda-calculus—can be simulated by a Turing machine. But neither Turing nor Church proved that *all* machines could be rendered in their formalisms. What can be written in their formalisms is any procedure that meets the definition of an algorithm. Nevertheless, this hyperbolic popularization of the Church-Turing thesis is repeated again and again—even today.

Computer scientist Edward Lee has written a technically precise but easily accessible refutation of this popularization of the Church-Turing thesis. Lee writes, "Turing and Church considered only machines that operate on digital data, and only machines that compute algorithmically, via a step-by-step process. We routinely build machines that satisfy neither of these properties, such as my dishwasher."[17] This quotation is from the beginning of Lee's discussion. In the rest, he leads us through some of the technical literature of computer science that refutes the notion that a universal Turing machine (UTM) is more than just a programmable Turing machine. Imagine if a UTM were really universal: we could download an app on our smartphones to wash dishes, function as a bicycle, or mow the lawn!

But what about self-driving cars? What about robots? Can't a robot be designed to wash the dishes? Probably. But the point is that while such a robot would likely incorporate many algorithms that could be modeled as functions, the design of the whole thing—all of the interacting parts of the software systems of such a robot—cannot be modeled as a mathematical function.

Outside the Algorithm

Beyond Algorithms: Case 1, Milner's Calculus for Concurrent Systems

To understand the gap that lies between mathematical functions and most software, we can read the works of Robin Milner, who extended the lambda-calculus to try to bridge this gap. In his Turing Award lecture, "Elements of Interaction,"[18] Milner explains why the lambda-calculus needed to be extended: "For the much smaller world of sequential computation, a common semantic framework is founded on the central notion of a mathematical function and is formally expressed in a functional calculus—of which Alonzo Church's λ-calculus is the famous prototype. Functions are an essential ingredient of the air we breathe, so to speak, when we discuss the semantics of sequential programming. But for concurrent programming and interactive systems in general, we have nothing comparable."[19] Milner called his extension to the lambda-calculus a Calculus for Concurrent Systems (CCS).

Milner continues his comparison like this: "In the λ-calculus, all computation comes down to just one thing, called *reduction*—the act of passing an argument to a function; we may call this the *atom of behavior* of the λ-calculus. In just the same way, an *interaction*— the passage of a single datum between processes—is the atom of behavior in CCS."[20]

Robots incorporate multiple concurrent processes, as does any other system that includes software and interacts with the world—even interfaces as simple as keyboards that asynchronously capture our keystrokes as we type. The lambda-calculus (and therefore algorithms and Turing's automatic machines) are inadequate for modeling such concurrent systems, because they exclude, by definition, any form of interaction.

Turing machines are automatic machines that have input and output but do not stop to interact with a user, an "external operator." Functions of the lambda-calculus work by substituting variables and reducing the body of the function without stopping to interact. These formalisms are imagined to work instantaneously. For example, substituting the value of y into the variable x is supposed to be "atomic" in the sense that interrupting substitution *in medias res* is not addressed in the notation: $(\lambda x.x)y = [y/x]x$, but what if, in the midst of the substitution, something changes the value of y?

Milner illustrates this possibility with three simple programs, each of which includes one or two assignment statements. Recall from chapter 2 that an assignment statement in an ALGOL-like language can be written like this: $y := 1$, meaning that after the assignment statement has executed, the variable y contains the value 1. Here are Milner's three example programs:

P1: $y := 1; y := y + 1;$

P2: $y := 2;$

P3: $y := 3.$

P1 and P2, if run without any interference, both give the variable y the value 2. In P1, it takes two assignment statements to accomplish this: first y gets the value 1, and then it gets the value $1 + 1$ or 2. So, in a functional notation, P1 and P2 are equivalent, because they both assign the variable y the value 2.

However, if we run either P1 or P2 concurrently with P3, P1 and P2 will not be equivalent. Assume that assignment statements take about the same amount of time to execute; that is, to move the value into the memory location designated by the variable. Then, run concurrently, P2 and P3 will result in y having the value of either 2 or 3 (depending on which assignment statement finishes last). By comparison, when P1 and P3 are executed concurrently, y will be 2, 3, or 4—again depending on which assignment statement finishes last.

Let us use the notation Q | R to mean that the programs Q and R are executed concurrently—in parallel—and let us denote the possible results of execution as a set in which the elements are the possible value(s) of the variable y: P1 = {2}, P2 = {2}, P1 | P3 = {2, 3}, and P2 | P3 = {2, 3, 4}.

The point of Milner's example is that even though P1 = P2, when run concurrently with P3, they are different. Specifically, if we use sets to denote the range of the "functions," P1 and P2 cease to be the same when they are combined with a third "function."

Milner's little example poses a big problem for any effort to model software as a Turing machine, as an algorithm, or as a function of the lambda-calculus, because the composition of mathematical functions is not supposed to change the definitions of the functions being composed. Yet, composing functions with the | operator is quite unlike composing functions by using addition, subtraction, multiplication, or division.

Imagine what arithmetic would be like if $1 + 1 = 2$, 3, or 4, depending on whether and when other operations of arithmetic are under way!

Why is this a big problem for mathematicians? The short answer is simply that computer programs are not mathematical functions, or at least not simply mathematical functions. The longer answer is that in actual systems that connect with other systems and that are used by people, timing and interaction are crucial, and Turing, as noted, ruled out interaction right from the start by limiting his formalism to automatic machines akin to mathematical functions and subsequently known as algorithms.

Beyond Algorithms: Case 2, Wegner's Interaction Machines

In 1997, Peter Wegner made this case to his fellow computer scientists in an article for the *Communications of the ACM* titled "Why Interaction Is More Powerful than Algorithms."[21] Wegner first critiques Turing machines (and thereby also algorithms): "A Turing machine is a closed, non-interactive system, shutting out the external world while it computes."[22] He then introduces a construct he calls "interaction machines" and demonstrates how Turing machines cannot capture the behavior of interaction machines, thus showing how interaction machines are more powerful than algorithms and Turing machines.

The simplest interaction machine in Wegner's paper is an "identity machine," which never terminates and just reflects back, as output, whatever is input. A video camera that both records and simultaneously plays back its recording in a preview window is a good example of such an identity machine. By being constantly coupled to the world external to the machine (via a constantly changing video stream), the construction of the machine exceeds the functionality of a Turing machine, which requires a fixed input and computes a single output.

Arguments of the type presented by Wegner frequently cite, directly or indirectly, the Chomsky hierarchy (discussed in chapter 7). The hierarchy is arranged around the idea that some machines are simpler than others, so it is imagined to be impossible to translate a more complicated machine into a type of machine that is lower down in the Chomsky hierarchy. Recall that universal Turing machines (UTMs, or Type-0 grammars) are at the top of Chomsky's hierarchy, and finite state automata (FSAs, or Type-3 grammars) are at the bottom. Conventional pedagogy in computer science education teaches us that UTMs are the most powerful of all, but Wegner is essentially arguing—as is Milner—that machines that interact with the world external to the machine are more powerful than UTMs.[23]

The Mathematical Worldview versus the Interactive Worldview

As a college student studying computer science, one would likely encounter, in an introductory course on the theory of computation, the notion that UTMs are the most powerful model of computation. But in courses of the computer science curriculum that focus on systems—on operating systems, interface design, software engineering, and so on—the Chomsky hierarchy is frequently ignored because in systems courses one must regularly design and implement interaction machines, choice machines, that cannot be specified as mathematical functions or algorithms. For example, building an interface that includes a button requires coding what will happen when a user clicks the mouse. Interfaces, operating systems—in fact, all kinds of software systems—are designed to deal with interruptions and interactions.

Wegner's point, that interaction machines are more powerful than algorithms, is common knowledge to most software practitioners. Nevertheless, Turing machines and algorithms maintain their place at the core of computer science education. Wegner calls this the "mathematical worldview" and contrasts it with the "interactive world-view," in which one can understand that not all software systems are algorithms or Turing machines.[24]

It is the mathematical worldview that underpins the claims of Stephen Wolfram and others (as examined in chapter 6)—the view that continues to value the Chomsky hierarchy and place Turing machines at the top of it. Wolfram and others argue that certain sets of rules (like those of rule set 110) are capable of simulating any Turing machine and are thus Turing complete. Once Turing completeness is established, the arguments proceed on the presupposition that a UTM is the most powerful machine of all possible machines and thus capable of reproducing the behavior of any and all other processes—ergo their Turing-complete formalism (e.g., one-dimensional cellular automata) is a universal (and therefore perfect) language, and the dynamics of everything in the universe is tantamount to the execution of the formalism.

Given the work done by Wegner, Milner, and others showing the limits of Turing machines, Wolfram's demonstrations of what he calls "Computational Equivalence," which pivot on Turing completeness, are hyperbole. Remember that if Wolfram's automata are only as powerful as a UTM, he cannot even render Professor Lee's dishwasher in his formalism!

The puzzle is not whether Wolfram is correct. He is not. Rather, as explored in chapter 6, the question is, why is he considered convincing in the first place? And for whom is his rhetoric of abductive demonstration, which pivots on the assumed omnipotence of Turing machines, considered a winning style of argumentation?

We face an analogous puzzle with Chomsky and his followers. Why is his hierarchy of automata and grammars considered so important that it is taught to all undergraduate students in computer science? And why did so many specialists in so many different fields find his transformational generative grammar so compelling? Perhaps more to the point, why was it compelling to refigure the art of grammar—which was, at its zenith, no less than the art of interpretation—as a matter of calculation? For this work, Chomsky became one of the most cited authors of the twentieth century.

The mathematical worldview continues to win the day in computer science—and now in many other areas of research that take computer science to be foundational. But, in Michael Mahoney's words, "If computers and programs were 'inherently mathematical objects,' the mathematics of the computers and programs of real practical concern had so far proven elusive. Although programming languages borrowed the trappings of mathematical symbolism, they did not translate readily into the mathematical structures that captured the behavior of greatest concern to computing.... For that reason, computer science remains an amalgam of mathematical theory, engineering practice, and craft skill."[25]

The Agenda of Computer Science

As a step toward understanding how the mathematical worldview can be hegemonic even if it is not omnipotent in computing, we can turn to Mahoney's notion of an "agenda":

> In tracing the emergence of a discipline, it is useful to think in terms of its agenda, that is, what practitioners of the discipline agree ought to be done, a consensus concerning the problems of the field, their order of importance or priority, the means for solving them, and perhaps most importantly, what constitute solutions.... Conflicts within a discipline often come down to disagreements over the agenda.... Irresolvable conflict may lead to new disciplines in the form of separate agendas.... As the shared Latin root indicates, agendas are about action: what is to be done?[26]

So even if we see computing as an amalgam of mathematical theory, engineering practice, and craft skill, as Mahoney does, looking at the ACM/IEEE *Computer Science Curricula 2013* we can see that mathematics, under the label of algorithms, remains at the top of the agenda.

How might things be otherwise? What would a reordering look like with arts and crafts at the top? Many software developers already see themselves as being rooted in the arts and crafts. Notice, for instance, how many hits you get if you search for books with titles like "X Recipes" or "X Cookbook," where X is the name of a programming language such as JavaScript or Python. One can see that it is standard practice to replace algorithms with the much more expansive construct of recipes, a construct that traces the art and the craft of software right back to the studios and workshops of the artists and artisans of the eighteenth century, as discussed in chapter 3. When algorithms are displaced by a serious engagement with recipes and cookbooks, we have moved out of computer science and software engineering and into the software arts.[27]

Surely software could be designed and produced under conditions in which algorithms are present but are not the central conceptual construct, but what costs would be encumbered by whom if we moved away from a worldview in which software is seen primarily as mathematics? And who would pay? To paraphrase Donna Haraway, we might ask, what counts as knowledge, for whom, and at what cost?[28]

Algorithms Borrow Prestige from Mathematics

Computer science would likely lose prestige if it moved algorithms off the top of its agenda. As argued by computer historians Paul Ceruzzi and Nathan Ensmenger, "In his compelling interweaving of history and mathematics, Knuth not only defined for computer science an intellectual lineage worthy of the most basic and fundamental of sciences but also skillfully distanced electronic computing from its origins in mechanical computation and electrical engineering."[29] Privileging algorithms on its agenda, computer science distances itself both from its arts and crafts origins and from its less prestigious cousins in engineering. As we saw in chapters 6 and 7, figures like Wolfram and Chomsky attempt to position themselves as direct descendants of Descartes and Galileo. This lineage to the history of mathematics and physics is a source of social capital that can be borrowed from by fields that figure themselves as mathematical.

Algorithms Are Easy to Test

Even if algorithms are not of primary importance in the design and implementation of systems, they are easy to test. This is partly self-reinforcing. If the ACM/IEEE *Computer Science Curricula* feature algorithms, then those who have training in computer science have a lot of experience with algorithm tests. So, when it comes time to devise another examination or set of interview questions in academia or industry, the easiest thing to do is to create another test about algorithms.

This testing regime is also part of a much longer tradition: exams about algorithms closely resemble math tests of the kind that were instituted at the start of computer science—before fixed curricula were in place. Computer historian Nathan Ensmenger writes about these tests from the 1950s and 1960s:

> Despite the growing consensus within the industry…that mathematical training was irrelevant to the performance of most commercial programming tasks, popular aptitude tests such as IBM PAT [Programmer Aptitude Test of 1959] still emphasized mathematical ability.…[T]he kinds of questions that could be easily tested using multiple-choice aptitude tests and mass-administered personality profiles necessarily focused on mathematical trivia, logic puzzles,

and word games. The test format simply did not allow for any more nuanced, meaningful, or context-specific problem solving. And in the 1950s and 1960s at least, such questions did privilege the typical male educational experience.[30]

One might imagine that this would be easy enough to fix, but it has not yet been fixed. As discussed earlier, the typical coding interview for a high-tech company still demands that the applicant design and code algorithms—in essence reproducing, in industry, the mathematical worldview of academic computer science. It seems clear, from both historical work[31] and contemporary studies,[32] that even if these tests about algorithms are not selecting for the crucial skill of software design, they are a factor that filters for gender.

Interaction, Identity, and Software Studies

Looping Back to the First Work of Software Studies

Manovich coined the phrase "software studies" in 2001, but Philip Agre's 1997 book *Computation and Human Experience*[33] is generally acknowledged as the first work of software studies *avant la lettre*. In his preface, Agre contrasts his work with what computer historians do—especially a book by historian Paul N. Edwards[34]—by positioning his own work within computer science, specifically within artificial intelligence (AI): "While I applaud this kind of [historical] work, I have headed in an entirely different direction. This book is not only an internalist account of research in AI; it is actually a work of AI—an intervention within the field that contests many of its basic ideas while remaining fundamentally sympathetic to computational modeling as a way of knowing."[35]

While Agre's book was not published until 1997, much of the technical work it is based on was done while he was a doctoral student at the MIT Artificial Intelligence Laboratory. In 1987, the year before he finished his dissertation,[36] Agre coauthored a highly cited paper on a system, Pengi, that was based on a theory of activity novel for AI.[37] In 1995, he co-edited a double issue of the journal *Artificial Intelligence* on those technical topics, specifically computational research on interaction and agency.[38] Consequently, it is hardly a surprise that he claims that his book is a contribution to computer science and not a work of history.

He elaborates by suggesting that there is nevertheless a difference between what he does and what other computer scientists do: "What is needed, I will argue, is a critical technical practice—a technical practice for which critical reflection upon the practice is part of the practice itself."[39] Agre claims that he is not just a critic but also a reformer of the field of AI: "Even though I was convinced that the field was misguided and stuck, it took tremendous effort and good fortune to understand how and why. Along the way I spent several years attempting to reform the field by providing it with the critical methods it needed—a critical technical practice."[40]

Actually, if we read the authors Agre acknowledges in his book, in his dissertation, and in his published articles, we can see that some of the symptoms had already been diagnosed, starting with philosopher Hubert Dreyfus (a longtime critic of AI and a specialist in the philosophy of Martin Heidegger) and then with his students and colleagues, especially Lucy Suchman. Agre writes: "In order to find words for my new-found intuitions, I began studying several nontechnical fields. Most importantly, I sought out those people who claimed to be able to explain what is wrong with AI, including Hubert Dreyfus and Lucy Suchman. They, in turn, got me started reading [Martin] Heidegger's *Being and Time* (1961 [1927]) and [Harold] Garfinkel's *Studies in Ethnomethodology* (1984 [1967])."[41]

Suchman's diagnosis of the problem revolves around a construct of AI research called a "plan" and the AI computer programs called "planners."[42] Her book *Plans and Situated Actions: The Problem of Human-Machine Communication* was published a year before Agre's dissertation. She distinguishes two alternative views of action:

> The first, adopted by most researchers in artificial intelligence, locates the organization and significance of human action in underlying plans.... [T]his view of purposeful action is the basis for traditional philosophies of rational action and for much of the behavioral sciences.... On the planning view, plans are prerequisite to and prescribe action, at every level of detail.... The alternative view...is that...[t]he coherence of action is tied in essential ways not to individual predispositions or conventional rules but to local interactions contingent on the actor's particular circumstances.[43]

AI planning techniques were (and still are) employed in many areas, especially in robotics, but began with Herbert Simon and Allen Newell's efforts to program computers to construct logic proofs and solve puzzles.[44] Plans, as they were conceived of at the time, were computer programs, but specifically algorithms with definite inputs and outputs: computer programs that do not interact with the surrounding environment.

This plans-as-algorithms viewpoint was dominant for many years. For example, years later, in 1996, Simon was still skeptical about the importance of interactions and interfaces for studying machines and organisms: "Given an airplane, or given a bird, we can analyze them...without reference to the interface between what I have called the inner and outer environments."[45]

Ignoring interactions with the surrounding environment could be represented as a coherent approach to analysis, but it gave rise to a set of empirical problems when computer scientists tried to construct practical applications. For example, Rodney Brooks was a professor at MIT when Agre was getting his degree. Attempting to build robots that could navigate inside a house turned out to be incredibly difficult using a plan-as-algorithm construct. To move from one place to another, the robot would have to survey the environment, plan out each step, and then execute the plan as a program. But these plans/programs were easily foiled. What if, on the way through the living room, someone placed a chair in front of the robot? The robot would be stuck and would have to stop and reformulate its plan. In the quotation where Agre is talking about the field being "stuck," he is obviously thinking about some very concrete examples. Brooks developed an (inter)actionist approach to robots and launched a company, iRobot, in 1990; by 2002, the company was manufacturing a robot to take on the task of vacuuming the house—a robot one can now buy under the brand of "Roomba."

On the Agenda of Software Studies

Agre and others' intervention into artificial intelligence can be compared to what was done by Wegner and Milner. By introducing interaction into a subfield dominated by a type of algorithm, they were able to displace the algorithm and reform the research agenda of their respective subfield of computer science: Agre and others displaced the plan as algorithm and reformed planning and robotics; Wegner displaced the Turing machine and reformed studies of automata; and Milner displaced the lambda-calculus and reformed the analysis of distributed systems.

Collectively, these and other interventions and developments have had an influence on the agenda of the entire field of computer science. We see this in the increasing importance of systems, not just algorithms, in computer science curricula, and we see it in the popularity and importance of interaction in academic and industrial settings. The large fields of human-computer interaction (HCI), computer-supported cooperative work (CSCW), and game design are just three sites where interactions, not algorithms, are the focus of design and research. Researchers in these areas frequently have training beyond computer science, especially in design and the social sciences.[46]

In *The Language of New Media*, Manovich names interactivity as one of the defining characteristics of new media and goes so far as to state that "in relation to computer-based media, the concept of interactivity is a tautology."[47] Michael Murtaugh, in his entry "Interaction" for *Software Studies: A Lexicon*, reiterates Manovich's claim, traces a history of interactive computing to the kind of systems J. C. R. Licklider championed in the early 1960s, and points out the power of Wegner's interaction machines in comparison to Turing machines.[48] More recently, in an article titled "Feral Computing: From Ubiquitous Calculation to Wild Interactions," Matthew Fuller and Sónia Matos again discuss Wegner's interaction machines in the context of ubiquitous computing and produce a genealogy of work in interaction that ties it to the feedback loops of first- and second-generation cybernetics.[49]

These authors, taken together, could be interpreted as an advocacy group to move interaction (as an issue both for interface and also system design) to the top of the agenda for computer science. But if we see all of these essays as advocacy for interaction, we need to be wary that we risk an overlap that is a lowest common denominator, a definition of interaction that is hardly interesting, let alone compelling. For example, Milner's definition of "interaction," as cited earlier, is simply "the passage of a single datum between processes"—at best a pale ghost of the rich model of interaction Suchman takes as her focus, namely human-to-human conversational interaction. Milner and Suchman seem to be speaking about two very different things even when they both use the term "interaction."

As stated in the introduction to this book, the software arts is a new name for the pursuit of software-based methods to invent and interrogate statements of assignment, connection, equivalence, and identity. We saw the simplest of these methods in chapter 2, in a discussion of assignment statements (e.g., $y := 1$). From this perspective, despite the fact that he is examining only very simple interactions, Milner's discussion is very interesting because he calls into question this simplest of methods for assigning equivalence. In his calculus, Milner articulates a new means of assigning values to variables—in fact, he also rethinks the very definitions of values and variables. In other words, at the core of computational theory is an investigation into reference, assignment, equivalence, and identity.

Nevertheless, even if Milner's definition was revolutionary for theoretical computer science, it is hardly recognizable as interaction in any elaborated history of interaction that might be found in centuries of work from philosophy and social science or the arts.[50] How much more compelling might it be if we were to study questions of assignment, equivalence, and identity in conditions of interaction much richer than Milner's "passage of a single datum between processes"?[51]

Instead of following Manovich's lead "to use concepts from computer science as categories of new media theory," software studies should be actively finding ways to go beyond computer science, to fix computer science's omissions and mistakes, and to construct its own research agenda. Interaction, assignment, equivalence, and identity could be at or near the top of that agenda.

How might one start? Consider what was, for decades, regarded as the founding essay of artificial intelligence, also by Alan Turing. The essay is composed around a game of identity and conversational interaction, the "imitation game." In his 1950 essay, Turing proposes a Wittgensteinian language game,[52] the "imitation game," to replace the question "Can machines think?" Turing's imitation game includes a proposal to program a computer to play the role of a man attempting to imitate a woman (an intriguing proposal concerning the reproduction and representation of gender difference). Note how his game resonates with the very old philosophical discussion—going back to at least the writings of Plato—about imitation, copies, and simulation, discussed in chapter 6.

Turing describes the imitation game like this:

> It is played with three people, a man, a woman, and an interrogator who may be of either sex. The interrogator stays in a room apart from the other two. The object of the game for the interrogator is to determine which of the other two is the man and which is the woman.... It is [the man's] object in the game to try and cause [the interrogator] to make the wrong identification.... The object of the game for [the woman] is to help the interrogator.... We now ask the question, "What will happen when a machine takes the part of [the man] in this game?" Will the interrogator decide wrongly as often when the game is played like this as he does when the game is played between a man and a woman? These questions replace our original [question], "Can machines think?"[53]

This essay was frequently cited until the 1990s, and a large number of artificial intelligence projects were developed in the 1960s and 1970s to address the challenges Turing raised in his 1950 paper.[54] But now it is almost never mentioned in the technical literature of artificial intelligence. Strangely, even when it was cited, Turing's imitation game was usually renamed the "Turing Test" and renarrated to exclude any mention of gender difference. This "Turing Test" was said to be a comparison between the performance of a computer program and a human of unspecified gender. Over time, AI researchers decoupled their research agenda from even this misreading of Turing's essay, and in 1994 it was publicly repudiated by two prominent AI researchers, Patrick Hayes and Kenneth Ford, in an invited keynote address at one of the most important conferences in AI, in an essay titled "Turing Test Considered Harmful."[55] Today AI has collapsed into a discourse about a set of algorithms (e.g., contemporary machine learning) and no longer seriously addresses the issues of identity and interaction, the aesthetics or politics of doubling, simulacra, gender stereotypes, and the uncanny raised by Turing's original thoughts on the subject.[56]

When Hayes and Ford denied the usefulness of Turing's game for AI research, they saw it as theoretically dubious and practically useless: "From a practical perspective, why would anyone want to build machines that could pass the Turing Test? As many have observed, there is no shortage of humans, and we already have well-proven ways of making more of them. Human cognition, even high-quality human cognition, is not in short supply. What extra functionality would such a machine provide, even if we could build it?"[57] Today, when we have these kinds of computational conversational agents, or bots, battling it out with people in video games and on Wikipedia, Twitter, and Facebook, the lost innocence of Hayes and Ford is both heart-rending and laughably naive. When bots on Facebook and Twitter play illegally in electoral politics all over the world, we are unnervingly schooled in the "extra functionality" such a machine provides. Detecting what is a bot and what is not may be a crucial question for the future of democracy. What if software studies were to take up Turing's essay, the founding vision that was discarded by AI researchers? Along with the translation of dialectic, rhetoric, grammar, and the many software arts, let us put questions of identity, equivalence, assignment, and interaction on the research agenda for software studies and for democracy.

Notes

All the code for the book can be found at the website http://softwarearts.info.

Chapter 1

1. C. P. Snow, *The Two Cultures and the Scientific Revolution,* The Rede Lecture, *1959* (New York: Cambridge University Press, 1959).

2. Historian Steven Shapin begins his book on the topic with this witticism: "There was no such thing as the Scientific Revolution, and this is a book about it." See Steven Shapin, *The Scientific Revolution* (Chicago: University of Chicago Press, 1996), 1.

3. Software Arts was also a company, founded in 1979 by Dan Bricklin and Bob Frankston to develop VisiCalc, the first spreadsheet program for personal computers. Software Arts was bought by Lotus Development in 1985; Lotus was acquired by IBM in 1995.

4. Specialists in philology (the study of ancient texts and languages) will insist that by tracing artificial languages back only to the seventeenth century (e.g., the proposal of Francis Bacon) I am underestimating their actual age by centuries. For example, Frits Staal, in a history of artificial languages, describes an early grammar of Sanskrit by Pāṇini (fourth century BCE) as an artificial language. See Frits Staal, "Artificial Languages across Sciences and Civilizations," *Journal of Indian Philosophy* 34 (2006). Pāṇini's grammar arguably has computational powers equivalent to today's software. See John Kadvany, "Pāṇini's Grammar and Modern Computation," *History and Philosophy of Logic* 37, no. 4 (2016). On the other end of the scale, there are computer historians who argue that software was not considered a language until about the mid-1950s. See David Nofre, Mark Priestley, and Gerard Alberts, "When Technology Became Language: The Origins of the Linguistic Conception of Computer Programming, 1950–1960," *Technology and Culture* 55, no. 1 (2014). Historiographically, this book diverges from both the philologists and the computer historians because my aim is not to pinpoint the exact origins of programming languages. My argument is against neither the philologists nor the computer historians. It is an argument against the idea that computing is exclusively a discipline of science, engineering, and mathematics. My point is that computing is principally a language art, and my aim is to emphasize the confluence of the language arts and the mechanical arts.

5. Bob Cringely, dir., *Triumph of the Nerds*, Season 1, episode 3, "Great Artists Steal," 1996, 26:41–26:58.

6. Cited in Jonah Lehrer, "Steve Jobs: 'Technology Alone Is Not Enough,'" *New Yorker*, October 7, 2011, http://www.newyorker.com/news/news-desk/steve-jobs-technology-alone-is-not-enough.

7. In a 1990s interview discussing the first Macintosh, Jobs was asked why he had the signatures of the team who had created the Macintosh embossed into the interior of the computer's casing. He said, "Because the people who worked on it consider themselves, and I certainly consider them, artists. These are the people that under different circumstances would be painters and poets but, because of that time that we live in, this new medium has appeared in which to express oneself to one's fellow species. And, that's a medium of computing." This clip from the interview was included in a film directed by Alex Gibney, *Steve Jobs: The Man in the Machine* (2015), 28:22–28:51.

8. Recent newspaper stories document the fading interest in the humanities and liberal arts; see, for example, Tamar Lewin, "As Interest Fades in the Humanities, Colleges Worry," *New York Times*, October 30, 2013.

9. "The competencies that liberal arts majors emphasize—writing, synthesis, problem solving—are sought after by employers.…The long-held belief by parents and students that liberal arts graduates are unemployable ignores the reality of the modern economy, where jobs require a mix of skills not easily packaged in a college major," said George Anders, author of the book *You Can Do Anything: The Surprising Power of a "Useless" Liberal Arts Education* (Boston: Little, Brown and Company, 2017). This quotation is from a larger article on the lifetime earnings of many different college majors. See Jeffrey Selingo, "Six Myths about Choosing a College Major," *New York Times*, November 3, 2017.

10. Chad Wellmon, *Organizing Enlightenment: Information Overload and the Modern Research University* (Baltimore: Johns Hopkins University Press, 2015).

11. "Insanely great" was a phrase Jobs frequently used; see Steven Levy, *Insanely Great: The Life and Times of Macintosh, the Computer That Changed Everything* (New York: Penguin Books, 2000).

12. Apple, "Inclusion Inspires Innovation," https://www.apple.com/diversity/.

13. Harold Abelson, Gerald Jay Sussman, and Julie Sussman, *Structure and Interpretation of Computer Programs*, MIT Electrical Engineering and Computer Science Series (Cambridge, MA: MIT Press; New York: McGraw-Hill, 1985), https://mitpress.mit.edu/sicp/. In the 1980s and 1990s, at the height of its popularity, the book was one of the most widely adopted introductory texts throughout the world. Now it is out of print—although available on the web—and much less frequently used. I speculate that the loss of *SICP* (the acronym of the book, which was frequently used when its popularity was high) from the computer science curriculum has exacerbated the "arterial sclerosis" of computer science and that a less diverse student body circulates through computer science departments because most computer science faculty insist on a position in science and engineering far away from the arts and humanities.

14. Edsger Dijkstra, "The Humble Programmer," *Communications of the ACM* 15, no. 10 (1972): 14.

15. Donald Ervin Knuth, *Literate Programming*, CSLI Lecture Notes (Stanford, CA: Center for the Study of Language and Information, [1984] 1991), 99.

16. P. Naur and B. Randell, eds., *Software Engineering: Report on a Conference Sponsored by the NATO Science Committee, Garmisch, Germany, 7th to 11th October 1968* (Brussels: Scientific Affairs Division, NATO, 1969), 13, republished with the report on the second conference (of 1969) in P. Naur, B. Randell, and J. N. Buxton, eds., *Software Engineering: Concepts and Techniques, Proceedings of the NATO Conferences* (New York: Petrocelli/Charter Publishers, Inc., 1976), http://homepages.cs.ncl.ac.uk/brian.randell/NATO/.

17. Michael Mahoney, "Finding a History for Software Engineering," *IEEE Annals of the History of Computing* 26, no. 1 (2004).

18. For another rigorous and critical reading of these foundational documents of software engineering, see Frederica Frabetti, *Software Theory: A Cultural and Philosophical Study*, Media Philosophy (London: Rowman and Littlefield International, 2014).

19. Naur, Randell, and Buxton, *Software Engineering*, 15.

20. Mahoney, "Finding a History for Software Engineering," 8.

21. Allen Newell, Alan J. Perlis, and Herbert A. Simon, "What Is Computer Science?," *Science* 157, no. 3795 (1967). In 1968, one of the authors of this letter, Alan Perlis, was a prominent participant at the Software Engineering Conference. A specific line of the 1967 letter to *Science* perhaps foreshadows his participation. In the letter, the others name and respond to six objections to the idea that computer science is a science. The sixth objection is that computers belong to engineering, not science. Their response is: "They belong to both, like electricity (physics and electrical engineering) or plants (botany and agriculture)."

22. John R. Rice and Saul Rosen, "History of the Computer Sciences Department of Purdue University," in *Studies in Computer Science: In Honor of Samuel D. Conte, R. Demillo and J. Rice*, ed. Richard DeMillo and John Rice (Dordrecht, Netherlands: Kluwer Academic/Plenum Press, 1994). Apparently, some nonacademic institutions did have computer science departments before Purdue and Carnegie Tech. For example, according to the description of the Clifford Shaw archive at the Smithsonian Institution, the RAND Corporation already had a computer science department in the 1950s. Allen Newell and Herbert Simon worked with Clifford Shaw at the RAND Corporation in the 1950s. See Anonymous, "John Clifford Shaw Papers, 1933–1993: Overview of the Collection," Archives Center, National Museum of American History, Smithsonian Institution, http://amhistory.si.edu/archives/AC0580.html.

23. Alan Perlis subsequently moved from Carnegie Mellon University to Yale University.

24. Allen Newell and Herbert A. Simon, "Computer Science as Empirical Inquiry: Symbols and Search," *Communications of the ACM* 19, no. 3 (1976).

25. Newell and Simon, "Computer Science as Empirical Inquiry," 14.

26. Jeannette M. Wing, "A Vision for the 21st Century: Computational Thinking," *Communications of the ACM* 49, no. 3 (2006). The lead sentence of Wing's text states, "Computational

thinking: It represents a universally applicable attitude and skill set everyone, not just computer scientists, would be eager to learn and use." Note the emphasis on "universally applicable."

27. A search for "computational thinking" in NSF's database of active and expired awards shows that hundreds of grants have been awarded to research and teach computational thinking. See http://nsf.gov/awardsearch/simpleSearchResult?queryText=computational+thinking&ActiveAwards=true&ExpiredAwards=true.

28. The code.org website contains information about its donors, which include Google, Microsoft, Verizon, AT&T, Facebook, and many other corporations and individual corporate leaders. See https://code.org/about/donors.

29. Computer science educator Yasmin Kafai suggests that we consider "computational participation" as a more appropriate framework instead of "computational thinking," for exactly this reason. See Yasmin B. Kafai and Quinn Burke, *Connected Code: Why Children Need to Learn Programming*, John D. and Catherine T. Macarthur Foundation Series on Digital Media and Learning (Cambridge, MA: MIT Press, 2014).

30. Bruno Latour, *The Pasteurization of France* (Cambridge, MA: Harvard University Press, 1988), 186.

31. See Stuart Zweben, "Computing Degree and Enrollment Trends: Undergraduate Enrollment Grows for Sixth Straight Year and Ph.D. Production Reaches an All-Time High," http://www.cra.org/uploads/documents/resources/taulbee/CRA_Taulbee_CS_Degrees_and_Enrollment_2012-13.pdf.

32. See Tracy Camp, "Women in Computer Sciences: Reversing the Trend," *Syllabus* 2 (August 2001).

33. The exclusion of women from computer science has been a problem from the start of computing and is not just a development of the last few decades. As Nathan Ensmenger compellingly narrates in his book *The Computer Boys Take Over*, computer programming started in the 1940s as almost exclusively women's work and then, in the 1950s and 1960s, through a series of biased hiring practices rampant throughout the computer industry, programming became a male-dominated profession. See Nathan L. Ensmenger, *The Computer Boys Take Over: Computers, Programmers, and the Politics of Technical Expertise* (Cambridge, MA: MIT Press, 2012), 78.

34. For example, see J. P. Mangalindan, "How Tech Companies Compare in Employee Diversity," *Fortune,* http://fortune.com/2014/08/29/how-tech-companies-compare-in-employee-diversity/.

35. This is an issue followed in, among other publications, the *New York Times*. See Mike Isaac, "Behind Silicon Valley's Self-Critical Tone on Diversity, a Lack of Progress," *New York Times*, June 28, 2015.

36. Peter Denning, "The Science in Computer Science," *Communications of the ACM* 56, no. 5 (2013).

37. π can be calculated with a procedural translation of the following mathematical statement:

$$\sum_{k=0}^{\infty} \frac{1}{16^k}\left(\frac{4}{8k+1} - \frac{2}{8k+4} - \frac{1}{8k+5} - \frac{1}{8k+6}\right).$$

For a description of the invention of this statement, see David H. Bailey, Peter B. Borwein, and Simon H. Plouffe, "On the Rapid Computation of Various Polylogarithmic Constants," *Mathematics of Computation* 66, no. 218 (April 1997): 903–913. Thanks to Nachum Dershowitz for pointing me to this remarkable area of research.

38. See the definition of the binary128 or "quadruple precision" format in IEEE, "754-2008—IEEE Standard for Floating-Point Arithmetic," 2008, http://ieeexplore.ieee.org/document/4610935/.

39. See especially the work of Turing Award winner William Morton Kahan (http://amturing .acm.org/award_winners/kahan_1023746.cfm) and his efforts to establish the IEEE Standard 754 floating point standard, the most common representation today for real numbers on computers, as narrated by sociologist of science Donald MacKenzie in Donald MacKenzie, "Negotiating Arithmetic, Constructing Proof: The Sociology of Mathematics and Information Technology," *Social Studies of Science* 23, no. 1 (1993). To those unfamiliar with the area, it may be surprising to learn how errors of arithmetic are built into computer hardware because of various constraints of engineering and industrial imperatives. It was a very contentious and long (eight years) road to the standardization of arithmetical operations in computer hardware.

40. In the preface to volume 1 of his multivolume work *The Art of Computer Programming*, Donald Knuth writes the following: "The subject of these books might be called 'nonnumerical analysis.' Although computers have traditionally been associated with the solution of numerical problems such as the calculation of the roots of an equation, numerical interpolation and integration, etc., topics like this are not treated here except in passing.…Numbers occur in such [nonnumerical analysis] problems only by coincidence, and the computer's decision-making capabilities are being used rather than its ability to do arithmetic." See Donald Ervin Knuth, *The Art of Computer Programming*, vol. 1-4A (Boston: Addison-Wesley, 2011), 2.

41. Perlis wrote, "I personally feel that the ability to analyze and construct processes is a very important ability, one which the student has to acquire sooner or later. I believe that he does acquire it in a rather diluted way during four years of an engineering or science program. I consider it also important to a liberal arts program." Alan Perlis, "The Computer in the University," in M. Greenberger, ed., *Management and the Computer of the Future* (Cambridge, MA: MIT Press, 1962), 210.

42. Michael Mateas, "Procedural Literacy: Educating the New Media Practitioner," *On the Horizon: Special Issue on Games in Education* 13, no. 2 (2005).

43. Ian Bogost, *Persuasive Games: The Expressive Power of Videogames* (Cambridge, MA: MIT Press, 2007), 246.

44. J. W. Backus, F. L. Bauer, J. Green, C. Katz, J. McCarthy, P. Naur, A. J. Perlis, H. Rutishauser, K. Samuelson, B. Vauquois, J. H. Wegstein, A. van Wijngaarden, and M. Woodger, "Revised Report on the Algorithmic Language ALGOL 60," *Communications of the ACM* 6, no. 1 (1963).

45. Gerald Jay Sussman and Guy Lewis Steele, Jr., "Scheme: An Interpreter for Extended Lambda Calculus (AIM-349)" (MIT AI Lab Memo, December 1975).

46. Casey Reas and Ben Fry, *Processing: A Programming Handbook for Visual Designers and Artists*, 2nd ed. (Cambridge, MA: MIT Press, 2014).

47. Alan C. Kay, "The Early History of Smalltalk," *ACM SIGPLAN Notices* 28, no. 3 (1993).

48. See https://scratch.mit.edu/info/credits.

49. Seymour Papert, *Mindstorms: Children, Computers, and Powerful Ideas* (New York: Basic Books, 1980).

50. Papert, *Mindstorms*.

51. Miriam Joseph, *The Trivium: The Liberal Arts of Logic, Grammar and Rhetoric* (Philadelphia: Paul Dry Books, 2002), 3–4.

52. McLuhan's dissertation was submitted to Cambridge University in 1943 but went unpublished until 2006.

53. Arthur Francis Leach, *Educational Charters and Documents, 598 to 1909* (Cambridge: Cambridge University Press, 1911), as cited in Marshall McLuhan and W. Terrence Gordon, *The Classical Trivium: The Place of Thomas Nashe in the Learning of His Time* (Corte Madera, CA: Gingko Press, 2006), 6.

54. Early modern artists and designers, such as Leon Battista Alberti, Leonardo da Vinci, and Giorgio Vasari, argued for the inclusion of architecture, painting, and sculpture in the liberal arts.

55. Henry Seidel Canby, *Alma Mater: The Gothic Age of the American College* (Farrar and Rinehart, 1936).

56. Alexandra Oleson and John Voss, *The Organization of Knowledge in Modern America, 1860–1920* (Baltimore: Johns Hopkins University Press, 1979).

57. U.S. Code, Title 7, Chapter 13, Subchapter I, § 304.

58. Janice Radway, "Research Universities, Periodical Publication, and the Circulation of Professional Expertise: On the Significance of Middlebrow Authority," *Critical Inquiry* 31, no. 1 (2004).

59. Radway, "Research Universities, Periodical Publication, and the Circulation of Professional Expertise."

60. Richard C. Atkinson and William A. Blanpied, "Research Universities: Core of the US Science and Technology System," *Technology in Society* 30 (2008).

61. In 1872, philosopher Friedrich Nietzsche delivered a set of lectures in Basel, Switzerland, arguing against similar developments (i.e., similar to the American situation) in the Prussian educational system. Nietzsche argued against the institutional expansion of education (making it available to a larger population) and against increased specialization. See Friedrich Wilhelm Nietzsche and Damion Searls, *Anti-education: On the Future of Our Educational Institutions* (New York: New York Review Books Classics, 2016).

62. Anne Burdick, Johanna Drucker, Peter Lunenfeld, Todd Presner, and Jeffrey Schnapp, *Digital_ Humanities* (Cambridge, MA: MIT Press, 2012), 5–6.

63. Richard Conniff, "How Science Came to Yale," *Yale Alumni Magazine*, March–April 2015.

64. Sheldon Pollock, "Future Philology? The Fate of a Soft Science in a Hard World," *Critical Inquiry* 35 (2009).

65. Barbara Cassin, Emily Apter, Jacques Lezra, and Michael Wood, *Dictionary of Untranslatables: A Philosophical Lexicon*, ed. Barbara Cassin (Princeton, NJ: Princeton University Press, 2014), 1147.

66. "[Pamela Long's] book has focused on the thesis that artisans influenced the methodology of the new sciences that developed from the mid-sixteenth century. Marxist scholars such as [Boris] Hessen, [Franz] Borkenau, [Henryk] Grossman, and [Edgar] Zilsel, as well as non-Marxists such as Robert Merton, argued that artisans, or modes of production, or machines used by artisans exerted such influence." See Pamela O. Long, *Artisan/Practitioners and the Rise of the New Sciences, 1400–1600* (Corvallis: Oregon State University Press, 2011), 127.

67. Claude Elwood Shannon and Warren Weaver, *The Mathematical Theory of Communication* (Urbana: University of Illinois Press, 1949), 31.

68. See Shannon and Weaver, *The Mathematical Theory of Communication*, 8.

69. Plato, extracts from the *Sophist*, secs. 267b, 267e, 268c, 268d. See Plato, Edith Hamilton, Huntington Cairns, and Lane Cooper, "Sophist," in *The Collected Dialogues of Plato, Including the Letters* (New York: Bollingen Foundation, distributed by Pantheon Books, 1963).

70. Gilles Deleuze and Rosalind Krauss (translator), "Plato and the Simulacrum," *October* 27 (Winter 1983).

71. Warren Weaver, "Translation," in *Machine Translation of Languages*, ed. W. N. Locke and D. A. Booth (Cambridge, MA: MIT Press, 1955).

72. At the time, one skeptic was Jerome Wiesner, later President John F. Kennedy's science adviser, president of the Massachusetts Institute of Technology, and then cofounder of the MIT Media Laboratory.

73. Warren Weaver's influence can be partly explained by the fact that he was approving major grants for the Rockefeller Foundation. Weaver was director of the Division of Natural Sciences at the Rockefeller Foundation from 1932 through 1955.

74. https://translate.google.com/.

75. Michel Serres, *Hermès III, La Traduction* (Paris: Éditions de Minuit, 1974).

76. The foundational texts of ANT were reprinted in Madeleine Akrich, Michel Callon, and Bruno Latour, *Sociologie de la traduction: Textes fondateurs* (Paris: École des mines de Paris, 2006).

77. Bruno Latour, "On Recalling ANT," in *Actor Network Theory and After*, ed. John Law and John Hassard (Oxford: Blackwell, 1998), 15–16.

78. Bruno Latour, *An Inquiry into Modes of Existence: An Anthropology of the Moderns* (Cambridge, MA: Harvard University Press, 2013).

79. Michael S. Mahoney, "The History of Computing in the History of Technology," *Annals of the History of Computing* 10 (1988).

80. Edwards, *The Closed World*, x.

81. "What may count as nature for late industrial people? What forms does love of nature take in particular historical contexts? For whom and at what cost?" See Donna Jeanne Haraway, *Primate Visions: Gender, Race, and Nature in the World of Modern Science* (New York: Routledge, 1989), 1.

82. Latour, *The Pasteurization of France*, 157–158.

83. Algirdas Julien Greimas, *On Meaning: Selected Writings in Semiotic Theory* (Minneapolis: University of Minnesota Press, 1987).

84. Harold Garfinkel, *Studies in Ethnomethodology* (Englewood Cliffs, NJ: Prentice-Hall, 1967).

85. Bruno Latour, *Science in Action: How to Follow Scientists and Engineers through Society* (Cambridge, MA: Harvard University Press, 1987).

86. Ada Lovelace, "Sketch of the Analytical Engine Invented by Charles Babbage [by LF Menabrea, Translated and Appended with Additional Notes, by Augusta Ada, Countess of Lovelace]," in *Scientific Memoirs, Selected from the Transactions of Foreign Academies of Science and Learned Societies*, vol. 3 (London: Richard and John Taylor, 1843).

87. Sterne writes, "This is not to say I simply want to replace a grand narrative of ever-increasing fidelity with a grand narrative of ever-increasing compression. I am merely proposing compression as one possible basis for inquiry into the history of communication technology—in the same sense that *representation* has served." See Jonathan Sterne, *MP3: The Meaning of a Format* (Durham, NC: Duke University Press, 2012), Kindle locs. 4967–4969.

88. Ray J. Solomonoff, *A Preliminary Report on a General Theory of Inductive Inference*," Report V-131 (Cambridge, MA: Zator Corporation, 1960).

89. Noam Chomsky, *Language and Responsibility* (New York: New Press, 1977), 139.

Chapter 2

1. Pedro Almodóvar, *The Skin I Live In* (Madrid: El Deseo Producciones, 2011).

2. Mary Shelley, *Frankenstein; or, the Modern Prometheus* (London: Lackington, Hughes, Harding, Mavor and Jones, 1818).

3. Sigmund Freud, "The Uncanny (1919)," in *The Standard Edition of the Complete Psychological Works of Sigmund Freud*, vol. 17, *An Infantile Neurosis and Other Works (1917–1919)* (London: Hogarth and Institute of Psycho-Analysis, 1950).

4. Sigmund Freud, "Fetishism (1927)," in *The Standard Edition of the Complete Psychological Works of Sigmund Freud*, vol. 5, *Miscellaneous Papers, 1888–1938* (London: Hogarth and Institute of Psycho-Analysis, 1950).

5. Laurie Anderson, *Big Science* (Burbank, CA: Warner Brothers, 1982).

6. In chapter 5, in a discussion of logic programming, a different symmetrical, almost commutative sort of assignment by unification will be presented.

7. John Palfrey and Urs Gasser, *Born Digital: Understanding the First Generation of Digital Natives* (New York: Basic Books, 2008).

8. Nicolas G. Carr, *The Shallows: What the Internet Is Doing to Our Brains* (New York: W. W. Norton, 2010).

9. Slavoj Žižek, *Enjoy Your Symptom! Jacques Lacan in Hollywood and Out* (New York: Routledge, 2007).

10. Michel Callon and Bruno Latour, "Unscrewing the Big Leviathan; or How Actors Macrostructure Reality, and How Sociologists Help Them to Do So," in *Advances in Social Theory and Methodology*, ed. K. Knorr and A. Cicourel (London: Routledge and Kegan Paul, 1981), 293.

11. Jan Golinski, "Precision Instruments and the Demonstrative Order of Proof in Lavoisier's Chemistry," *Osiris* 9 (1994).

12. For a philosophically and historically rigorous recounting of how water came to be seen as first an element, then a compound, then HO, and then, finally, H_2O, see Hasok Chang, *Is Water H_2O? Evidence, Pluralism and Realism*, Boston Studies in the Philosophy of Science 293 (Dordrecht: Springer, 2012).

13. Madeleine Akrich, Michel Callon, and Bruno Latour, *Sociologie de la traduction: Textes fondateurs* (Paris: École des mines de Paris, 2006).

14. Claus Pias, "Technologies of Simulation," History and Theory of New Media Lecture Series (University of California, Berkeley, October 15, 2015).

15. Mark Priestley, *A Science of Operations: Machines, Logic and the Invention of Programming* (New York: Springer, 2010).

16. Martin Davis, *The Universal Computer: The Road from Leibniz to Turing* (New York: W. W. Norton, 2000).

17. Many of us trace our academic "genealogy" back to Leibniz. For example, if one asks, Who was my PhD adviser?, Who was my adviser's adviser?, Who was my adviser's adviser's adviser?, and so on, eventually, after quite a few "generations," one finds Leibniz at the root. In my case, one finds Gottfried Leibniz's biological father, Friedrich Leibniz, at the root. Friedrich Leibniz was the adviser of Gottfried Leibniz's dissertation adviser, Jakob Thomasius. My derivation is as follows: Warren Sack (MIT, 2000), Kenneth Haase (MIT, 1990), Marvin Minsky (Princeton, 1954), Albert Tucker (Princeton, 1932), Solomon Lefschetz (Clark, 1911), William Story (Leipzig, 1875), Carl Gottfried Neumann (Königsberg, 1856), Friedrich Julius Richelot (Königsberg, 1831), Carl

Gustav Jacob Jacobi (Humboldt, 1825), Enno Heeren Dirksen (Göttingen, 1820), Johann Tobias Mayer (Göttingen, 1773), Abraham Gotthelf Kästner (Leipzig, 1739), Christian August Hausen (Halle-Wittenberg, 1713), Johann Christoph Wichmannshausen (Leipzig, 1685), Otto Mencke (Leipzig, 1665), Jakob Thomasius (Leipzig, 1643), Friedrich Leibniz (Leipzig, 1622). According to the *Mathematics Genealogy Project* (http://genealogy.math.ndsu.nodak.edu/id.php?id=143630), Friedrich Leibniz had only one doctoral student, Jakob Thomasius (Leipzig, 1643), but over 121,000 academic "descendants." Gottfried Leibniz (Leipzig, 1666) wrote his dissertation under his father's student, Jakob Thomasius. Nevertheless, philosopher Alain Badiou spurs us to imagine other origins. "No one is obliged to be a Leibnizian, even if we must recognise in this philosophy the archetype of one of the three great orientations in thought, the constructivist or nominalist orientation (the other two being the transcendent and the generic)." See Alain Badiou, *Number and Numbers* (Cambridge: Polity Press, 2008), 27.

18. Norbert Wiener, *Cybernetics: Or Control and Communication in the Animal and the Machine* (Cambridge, MA: MIT Press, 1948).

19. Louis Couturat, *Logique de Leibniz, d'après des documents inédits* (Paris: Félix Alcan, 1901), 116.

20. Howard Gardner, *The Mind's New Science: A History of the Cognitive Revolution* (New York: Basic Books, 1985).

21. Jean François Lyotard, *The Postmodern Condition: A Report on Knowledge, Theory and History of Literature* (Minneapolis: University of Minnesota Press, 1984), 4.

22. Hannah Arendt, *The Human Condition* (Chicago: University of Chicago Press, 1958).

23. Antonio Gramsci, Quintin Hoare, and Geoffrey Nowell-Smith, *Selections from the Prison Notebooks of Antonio Gramsci* (New York: International Publishers, 1972), 326, as cited in Stuart Hall, "The Rediscovery of 'Ideology': Return of the Repressed in Media Studies," in *Culture, Society, and the Media*, ed. Michael Gurevitch, Tony Bennett, James Curran, and Janet Woollacott (New York: Routledge, 1982), 73.

24. For a contemporary, technical, highly cited version of these flawed conceptualizations of how ideas move and change, see David Easley and Jon Kleinberg, *Networks, Crowds, and Markets: Reasoning about a Highly Connected World* (Cambridge: Cambridge University Press, 2010).

25. For an ambivalent discussion of the merits of the metaphor of "spreadable media," see Henry Jenkins, Sam Ford, and Joshua Green, *Spreadable Media: Creating Value and Meaning in a Networked Culture* (New York: New York University Press, 2013).

26. Richard Dawkins, *The Selfish Gene* (Oxford: Oxford University Press, 1976).

27. Mass communications research arguably starts with Harold Lasswell's work on propaganda in World War I. See Harold D. Lasswell, *Propaganda Technique in the World War* (New York: Peter Smith, 1927).

28. Lazarsfeld characterized his own research program as "administrative" and contrasted it with "critical" research, especially that of the Frankfurt School (with which he had collaborated). He discusses the limits and complementarity of administrative and critical research programs

in Paul Lazarsfeld, "Remarks on Administrative and Critical Research," *Studies in Philosophy and Social Science* 9 (1947): 2–16. Lazarsfeld's research collaborator at Columbia University, sociologist Robert K. Merton, in addition to being one of the founders of the study of media and communication, was one of the founders of the fields of contemporary history of science and science and technology studies (STS). Merton's son is well-known economist Robert C. Merton.

29. There are some exceptions, such as the dissertation work of my former student Nicolas Ducheneaut. See Nicolas Ducheneaut, "Socialization in an Open Source Software Community: A Sociotechnical Analysis," *Computer Supported Cooperative Work* 14, no. 4 (2005); Warren Sack, Françoise Detienne, Nicolas Ducheneaut, Jean-Marie Burkhardt, Dilan Mahendran, and Flore Barcellini, "A Methodological Framework for Socio-cognitive Analyses of Collaborative Design of Open Source Software," *Computer Supported Cooperative Work* 15, nos. 2–3 (2006).

30. See, for example, these two excellent ethnographies of open source software developers: Christopher M. Kelty, *Two Bits: The Cultural Significance of Free Software* (Durham, NC: Duke University Press, 2008); Gabriella Coleman, *Coding Freedom: The Ethics and Aesthetics of Hacking* (Princeton, NJ: Princeton University Press, 2012).

31. "Nous ne connaissons les choses que par les systèmes de transformation des ensembles qui les comprennent. Au minimum, ces systèmes sont quatre. La deduction, dans l'aire logico-mathématique. L'induction, dans le champ experimental. La production, dans les domains de practique. La traductions dans l'espace des textes. Il n'est pas complètement obscure qu'ils répètent le meme mot. Qu'il n'y ait de philosophie que de la duction—au préfixe, variable et nécessaire, près—on peut passer sa vie à tenter d'éclairer cet état de choses." See Michel Serres, *Hermès III, La Traduction* (Paris: Éditions de Minuit, 1974), 9.

32. Reviel Netz, *The Shaping of Deduction in Greek Mathematics: A Study in Cognitive History* (Cambridge: Cambridge University Press, 1999).

33. "Irreductions" was published as an appendix to a larger work. See Bruno Latour, *The Pasteurization of France* (Cambridge, MA: Harvard University Press, 1988), 176.

34. Bruno Latour, *Science in Action: How to Follow Scientists and Engineers through Society* (Cambridge, MA: Harvard University Press, 1987).

35. Latour, *Science in Action*, 15.

36. David Hilbert and Wilhelm Ackermann, *Grundzüge der Theoretischen Logik* (Berlin: Springer, 1928), 73, 77, as cited by Charles Petzold, *The Annotated Turing: A Guided Tour through Alan Turing's Historic Paper on Computability and the Turing Machine* (Indianapolis, IN: Wiley, 2008), 260.

37. Andrew Hodges, *Alan Turing: The Enigma: The Book That Inspired the Film "The Imitation Game,"* updated edition (Princeton, NJ: Princeton University Press, 2014), 116–117.

38. The origin of this type of equation is attributed to Diophantus, a man who lived in ancient Alexandria. Hilbert's original tenth problem was eventually solved in 1970 through the work of Martin Davis, Yuri Matiyasevich, Hilary Putnam, and Julia Robinson. See the last endnote of chapter 7, on grammar, for a description of the remarkable results of this work.

39. It appears, for instance, in logician Alonzo Church's 1936 paper but did not really gain widespread currency until the 1960s, according to Charles Petzold, *The Annotated Turing*, 42.

40. Alan Turing, "On Computable Numbers, with an Application to the Entscheidungs Problem," paper presented at the Proceedings of the London Mathematical Society, 1936, published in *Proceedings of the London Mathematical Society,* 2nd ser., 42, no. 1 (1937).

41. David Alan Grier, *When Computers Were Human* (Princeton, NJ: Princeton University Press, 2005).

42. Turing, "On Computable Numbers."

43. Alonzo Church, "An Unsolvable Problem of Elementary Number Theory," *American Journal of Mathematics* 58, no. 2 (1936).

44. Alan M. Turing, "Computability and Λ-Definability," *Journal of Symbolic Logic* 2, no. 4 (1937).

45. Alonzo Church, "Reviewed Work: On Computable Numbers, with an Application to the Entscheidungsproblem. A. M. Turing," *Journal of Symbolic Logic* 2, no. 1 (1937).

46. Ludwig Wittgenstein, *Remarks on the Philosophy of Psychology*, vol. 1 (Oxford: Blackwell, 1980), 1096, as cited in Wilfried Sieg, "Calculations by Man and Machine: Conceptual Analysis," in *Reflections on the Foundations of Mathematics: Essays in Honor of Solomon Feferman*, ed. Wilfried Sieg, Richard Sommer, and Carolyn Talcott (Natick, MA: A. K. Peters/CRC Press, 2002), 391. We find this same quotation from Wittgenstein repeated to the same effect in, among other places, the entry for the "Church-Turing Thesis" in the *Stanford Encyclopedia of Philosophy*. See B. Jack Copeland, "Church-Turing Thesis," in *Stanford Encyclopedia of Philosophy*, ed. Edward N. Zalta (Stanford, CA: Stanford University Press, 2002).

47. Robin O. Gandy, "The Confluence of Ideas in 1936," in *The Universal Turing Machine: A Half-Century Survey*, ed. R. Herken (New York: Oxford University Press, 1988), 86.

48. Robert I. Soare, "Computability and Recursion," *Bulletin of Symbolic Logic* 2, no. 3 (1996), as cited in Nachum Dershowitz and Yuri Gurevich, "A Natural Axiomatization of Computability and Proof of Church's Thesis," *Bulletin of Symbolic Logic* 14, no. 3 (2008).

49. Gandy, "The Confluence of Ideas in 1936," 81.

50. See Umberto Eco, *The Search for the Perfect Language*, The Making of Europe (Oxford: Blackwell, 1995). Eco's history of this project starts with the biblical myth of the language of Eden understandable to all before the rise of the Tower of Babel. He includes Dante's proposal for a universal vernacular in place of Latin; the Catalan Franciscan tertiary Ramon Llull's combinatorial system of letters and symbols designed to explore metaphysical connections; the Kabbalistic search for hidden messages in sacred Hebrew texts; the Rosicrucians' symbolic writing in seventeenth-century Germany; and French Enlightenment thinkers' invention of philosophical languages organized around fundamental categories of knowledge.

51. See Antoine-Louis-Claude Destutt de Tracy, "Tome I—Chapitre 11: Réflexions sur ce qui précède, et sur la manière dont Condillac a analysé la pensée," in *Éléments d'idéologie* (Paris: P. Didot l'aîné, 1800–1815).

52. Terry Eagleton lists many of these definitions of ideology:

(a) the process of production of meanings, signs and values in social life;

(b) a body of ideas characteristic of a particular social group or class;

(c) ideas which help to legitimate a dominant political power;

(d) false ideas which help to legitimate a dominant political power;

(e) systematically distorted communication;

(f) that which offers a position for a subject;

(g) forms of thought motivated by social interests;

(h) identity thinking;

(i) socially necessary illusion;

(j) the conjuncture of discourse and power;

(k) the medium in which conscious social actors make sense of their world;

(l) action-oriented sets of beliefs;

(m) the confusion of linguistic and phenomenal reality;

(n) semiotic closure;

(o) the indispensable medium in which individuals live out their relations to a social structure;

(p) the process whereby social life is converted to a natural reality.

See Terry Eagleton, *Ideology: An Introduction* (London: Verso, 1991), 1–2.

53. Fredric Jameson, *The Political Unconscious: Narrative as a Socially Symbolic Act* (Ithaca, NY: Cornell University Press, 1981).

54. One can draw the square as it appears in the following figure.

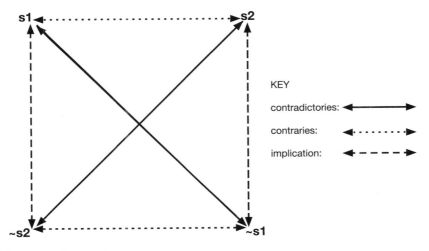

Semiotic square of oppositions.

Jameson writes,

> The enumeration of the advantages of the square can begin at once with the observation that it is a decisive enlargement on the older structural notion of the binary opposition: s1 versus s2 is clearly just a binary opposition, or in the language of philosophical logic a "contrary," that is, a strong opposition (white versus black, male versus female), but one that the square now reveals to encompass far more than two available positions. It immediately implies, for example, the two supplementary slots of what logic calls a "contradictory," where ~s1 and ~s2 are the simple negatives of the two dominant terms, but include far more than either: thus "non-white" includes more than "black," "non-male" more than "female." Meanwhile, the two compound or "synthetic" positions of S and ~S offer still greater conceptual enlargements, S standing as a complex or utopian term, in which the opposition of "white" and "black" might be transcended (mestizo, for example), whereas ~S stands as the neutral term, in which all of the privations and negations are assembled ("colorless," for example). Finally, the transversal axes map the place of tensions distinct from the principal or binary one, while the synthesis hypothetically proposed by uniting the two sides of the square ("white" plus "non-black") designates alternative conceptual combinations. The entire mechanism then is capable of generating at least ten conceivable positions out of a rudimentary binary opposition.… [I]t constitutes a virtual map of conceptual [semiotic] closure, or better still, of the closure of ideology itself, that is, as a mechanism, which, while seeming to generate a rich variety of possible concepts and positions, remains in fact locked into some initial *aporia*…that it cannot transform from the inside by its own means.

See Fredric Jameson, "Foreword," *On Meaning: Selected Writings in Semiotic Theory / Algirdas Julien Greimas*, trans. Paul J. Perron and Frank H. Collins (Minneapolis: University of Minnesota Press, 1987), xiii–xv.

55. In the history of this disagreement post-Turing (specifically after Turing's 1950 paper launching an area now known as "artificial intelligence," a paper to be discussed in the conclusion of this book), those who hold the latter position often do so voicing skepticism over artificial intelligence researchers' goal of writing software that "thinks" or has "consciousness" like a human. See especially philosopher John Searle's "Chinese room argument" in John R. Searle, "Minds, Brains and Programs," *Behavioral and Brain Sciences* 3 (1980).

56. Gandy, "The Confluence of Ideas in 1936," 82.

57. Alan M. Turing, "Intelligent Machinery, National Physical Laboratory Report (1948)," in *Machine Intelligence*, vol. 5, ed. B. Meltzer and D. Michie (Edinburgh: Edinburgh University Press), 9, cited in Copeland, "Church-Turing Thesis."

58. A. M. Turing, "Proposal for Development in the Mathematics Division of an Automatic Computing Engine (ACE)," in *A.M. Turing's ACE Report of 1946 and Other Papers*, ed. B. E. Carpenter and R. W. Doran (Cambridge, MA: MIT Press, 1986), 38–39. Also cited in Turing, "Intelligent Machinery."

59. Gandy, "The Confluence of Ideas in 1936," 83.

60. G. W. Leibniz, "Machina arithmetica in qua non additio tantum et subtractio set et multiplicato nullo, divisio vero paene nullo animi labore peragantur" (1685), English trans. M. Kormes, in *A Source Book in Mathematics*, ed. D. E. Smith (New York: McGraw-Hill, 1929), 173–181, cited in Martin Davis, *The Universal Computer: The Road from Leibniz to Turing* (New York: W. W. Norton, 2000), 8.

61. Vannevar Bush, "As We May Think," *The Atlantic*, July 1945, https://www.theatlantic.com /magazine/archive/1945/07/as-we-may-think/303881/.

62. In his biography of Alan Turing, Andrew Hodges notes that, at the time, there was an upper-class enthusiasm for mathematics and science (shared by Turing's family and Cambridge University colleagues) but a disdain for "lower-class" engineering work with machines and devices, a disdain that Turing ignored to develop one of the first working computers; for example, Hodges writes, "It was particularly remarkable in England, where there existed no tradition of high status academic engineering, as there was in France and Germany and (as with Vannevar Bush) in the United States." See Andrew Hodges, *Alan Turing: The Enigma: The Book That Inspired the Film "The Imitation Game,"* updated edition (Princeton, NJ: Princeton University Press, 2014), 199.

63. Turing, "Intelligent Machinery," 7.

64. S. C. Kleene, *Mathematical Logic* (New York: Wiley, 1967), 232.

65. Note that some would say that Turing used the term "mechanical" as a technical term, as a term of art that is not to be understood in its common or conventional sense but rather as a highly specialized term proper only to the publication forums of mathematics and logic. For an example of this argument, see Copeland, "Church-Turing Thesis." My understanding is that if one uses technical terms in a popularization of one's technical work, one inevitably uses the technical term with an audience that does not understand the term in its technically circumscribed form. Instead, the term is understood as part of the common vernacular regardless of the intentions of the speaker. To expect otherwise is as silly as I would be to write this footnote in Norwegian expecting all its readers to understand it in the way a Norwegian would. *Ikke sant?*

66. This is section 6 of Turing, "On Computable Numbers." The definition of the universal machine is continued in section 7. For an in-depth explanation of these sections and the rest of Turing's paper, see Petzold, *The Annotated Turing*, especially "Chapter 9: The Universal Machine."

67. Priestley, *A Science of Operations*, 1.

68. The way these limits are frequently introduced in the undergraduate computer science curriculum is through an analysis of the "halting problem," said to have been introduced in Turing, "On Computable Numbers." However, as Petzold (*The Annotated Turing*, 329) points out, the author of the "halting problem" was not Turing but rather Martin Davis (another of Alonzo Church's former doctoral students, Princeton, 1950), as articulated in his renowned text *Computability and Unsolvability*. See Martin Davis, *Computability and Unsolvability* (New York: McGraw-Hill, 1958; New York: Dover, 1982), 70.

69. See Copeland, "Church-Turing Thesis," for a scathing critique of the wild interpretations of the Church-Turing thesis that have been popularized with the literature of philosophy of mind, cognitive science, and artificial intelligence; for example, "A myth seems to have arisen concerning Turing's paper of 1936, namely that he there gave a treatment of the limits of mechanism and established a fundamental result to the effect that the universal Turing machine can simulate

the behaviour of any machine. The myth has passed into the philosophy of mind, generally to pernicious effect."

70. Stephen Hilgartner, "The Dominant View of Popularization: Conceptual Problems, Political Uses," *Social Studies of Science* 20, no. 3 (1990).

71. Warren McCulloch, "Mysterium Iniquitatis of Sinful Man Aspiring into the Place of God," *Scientific Monthly* 80, no. 1 (1955), 35–39, as cited in Petzold, *The Annotated Turing*, 335.

Chapter 3

1. Francis Bacon, *Novum Organum or True Suggestions for the Interpretation of Nature* (New York: P. F. Collier and Son, [1620] 1902), sec. 124.

2. Evelyn Fox Keller, *Reflections on Gender and Science* (New Haven, CT: Yale University Press, 1995), 33–42.

3. The year of the publication of the *Novum Organum*, 1620, also seems to be the year that Bacon's wife, Alice Barnham, met her lover, John Underhill, whom she married less than two weeks after Bacon's death, in April 1626.

4. Francis Bacon, "Aphorisms—Book II on the Interpretation of Nature, or the Reign of Man," in *Novum Organum*, sec. 31.

5. Jean Le Rond d'Alembert, *Preliminary Discourse to the Encyclopedia of Diderot,* trans. Richard N. Schwab (Chicago: University of Chicago Press, [1751] 1995), 123.

6. d'Alembert, *Preliminary Discourse to the Encyclopedia of Diderot*, 122

7. d'Alembert, *Preliminary Discourse to the Encyclopedia of Diderot*, 123.

8. Pamela O. Long, *Openness, Secrecy, Authorship: Technical Arts and the Culture of Knowledge from Antiquity to the Renaissance* (Baltimore: Johns Hopkins University Press, 2001), Kindle locs. 61–63.

9. Bernard Stiegler, *Technics and Time*, vol. 1, *The Fault of Epimetheus* (Stanford, CA: Stanford University Press, 1998), 3–4.

10. Charles Babbage, *On the Economy of Machinery and Manufactures* (Amazon Digital Services, [1832] 2011), https://www.amazon.com/dp/B004TS7610/ref=dp-kindle-redirect?_encoding=UTF8 &btkr=1.

11. Babbage, *On the Economy of Machinery and Manufactures*, preface.

12. Babbage, *On the Economy of Machinery and Manufactures*, preface.

13. Writing about Deleuze, philosopher John Rajchman described it thus:

> Deleuze was a philosopher who thought that philosophies are singular creations. Each philosopher creates a philosophy, indefinite enough for there to be others. The idea of philosophy is thus not fixed—there is no

one method, no one way of doing it. Rather each philosophy invents a distinctive *agon* with its own *dramatis personae*: in each we find what Deleuze comes to call an "image of thought," even if the image is not always obvious....Each of the "personae" through which a philosophy dramatizes its ideas suggests a manner in which philosophy is oriented and the kind of struggle in which it is involved....Plato invents the *persona* of Socrates and his *agon* with the Sophists; Kant instead invents a Judge watching over the bounds of reason; Leibniz casts himself rather as a defense attorney for God in a world that seems to have abandoned him, ever adducing new principles, while Spinoza, in giving up even such a God, creates instead the *persona* of an Innocent, a "sort of child-player against whom one can do nothing." In each case we have different ways the contest or "game" of philosophy is [played].

See John Rajchman, *The Deleuze Connections* (Cambridge, MA: MIT Press, 2000), 32, 42.

14. In chapter 19 of *On the Economy of Machinery and Manufactures*, Babbage goes further than just urging attention to the mechanical arts and arguing that the division of labor of the mechanical arts applies also to the liberal arts. The title of chapter 19 is "On the Division of Mental Labor." In other words, physical labor and mental labor are both seen by Babbage to be equally amenable to division. Babbage attributes this insight to M. Prony.

15. Babbage continues like this: "It is not a bad definition of man to describe him as a tool-making animal. His earlier contrivances to support uncivilized life, were tools of the simplest and rudest construction. His latest achievements in the substitution of machinery, not merely for the skill of the human hand, but for the relief of the human intellect, are founded on the use of tools of a still higher order." See Charles Babbage, "Calculating Machines, Chapter XIII, the Exposition of 1851," in *Charles Babbage: On the Principles and Development of the Calculator and Other Seminal Writings by Charles Babbage and Others,* ed. Philip Morrison and Emily Morrison, eds. (Mineola, NY: Dover, 1961), 322.

16. Johan Huizinga, *Homo Ludens: A Study of the Play-Element in Culture* (Boston: Routledge & Keegan Paul, 1949).

17. Hannah Arendt, *The Human Condition* (Chicago: University of Chicago Press, 1958), 80 (footnote).

18. Hannah Arendt speculated that "The very reason for the elevation of labor in the modern age was its 'productivity,' and the seemingly blasphemous notion of Marx that labor (and not God) created man or that labor (and not reason) distinguished man from the other animals was only the most radical and consistent formulation of something upon which the whole modern age was agreed." See Arendt, *The Human Condition*, 85–86.

19. See Benjamin Franklin, *Poor Richard's Almanack* (Philadelphia: B. Franklin, 1735).

20. Max Weber, *The Protestant Ethic and the Spirit of Capitalism* (New York: Routledge, [1930] 1992).

21. Charles-Augustin de Coulomb wrote,

Nous venons de voir que l'effet d'une machine avoir toujours pour mesure un poids élevé, multiplié par la hauteur à laquelle il est élevé. A présent, pour pouvoir comparer l'effet avec la fatigue que les hommes éprouvent en produisant cet effet, il faut déterminer la fatigue qui répond à un certain degré d'action....Daniel Bernoulli, qui a discuté cette question, en ayant égard à la plus grande partie de ses elements, dit que la fatigue des hommes est toujours proportionnelle à leur quantité d'action; en sorte qu'en n'outre-passant pas leurs forces naturelles, l'on peut faire varier à volunté la vîtesse, la pression, et le temps, et que, pour vu que le produit de ses quantités soit une quantité constant, il en résultera toujours pour l'homme un meme degré de fatigue.… [L]a quantité qui exprime le maximum d'action relativement à la fatigue doit être l'objet principal des recherches qui vont suivre.

Charles-Augustin de Coulomb, "Résultat de Plusieur Expériences destinées à determiner la quantité d'action que les hommes peuvent fournir pour leur travail journalier, suivant les différentes manières don't ils emploient leur forces," *Théorie des Machines Simples, en Ayant Égard au Frottement de leurs Parties et à la Roideur des Cordages* (Paris: Bachelier, 1821), 256–257.

22. One foot-pound is defined to be equal to 1.355818 joules.

23. Note that kg means kilogram; m means meter; s means second; N means newton; Pa means pascal (a unit of pressure defined as one newton per square meter); W means watt (a unit of power defined as one joule per second); C means coulomb (a unit of electrical charge defined as a constant current of one ampere in one second, or approximately 6.241×10^{18} electrons); and V means volt (a unit of electric potential difference and electromotive force defined as the electric potential between two points of a conducting wire when an electric current of one ampere dissipates one watt of power between those points).

24. Claude E. Shannon, "A Mathematical Theory of Communication," *Bell System Technical Journal* 27 (July and October 1948).

25. My proposal here, to distinguish information from computation by distinguishing the language of labor (i.e., the mathematical formulation of mechanics) from the language of skilled work (i.e., the computational formulation of operations and processes), is a response to a query posed by Arendt:

> It is surprising at first glance, however, that the modern age—with its reversal of all traditions, the traditional rank of action and contemplation no less than the traditional hierarchy within the *vita activa* itself, with its glorification of labor as the source of all values and its elevation of the *animal laborans* to the position traditionally held by the *animal rationale*—should not have brought forth a single theory in which *animal laborans* and *homo faber*, "the labour of our body and the work of our hands," are clearly distinguished. Instead, we find first the distinction between productive and unproductive labor, then somewhat later the differentiation between skilled and unskilled work, and, finally, outranking both because seemingly of more elementary significance, the division of all activities into manual and intellectual labor.

See Arendt, *The Human Condition*, 85.

26. I introduce this particular example to allow readers of philosopher Ludwig Wittgenstein to compare it to the work language he discusses at the beginning of his *Philosophical Investigations*: "Let us imagine a language for which the description given by Augustine is right. The language is meant to serve for the communication between a builder A and an assistant B. A is building with building-stones: there are blocks, pillars, slabs and beams. B has to pass the stones, and in that order in which A needs them. For this purpose they use a language consisting of the words 'block', 'pillar', 'slab', 'beam'. A calls them out;—B brings the stone which he has learnt to bring at such-and-such a call.—Conceive that as a complete primitive language." See Ludwig Wittgenstein, *Philosophical Investigations* (New York: Macmillan, 1953), sec. 1.2.

27. Herbert A. Simon and Allen Newell, "Heuristic Problem Solving: The Next Advance in Operations Research," *Operations Research* 6, no. 1 (January–February, 1958): 1–10. Note that this quip was published in an article with "operations research" in its title and in a journal called *Operations Research*. I will return to the importance of "operations" for this second work and machine language. In a journal article published shortly before his death, Simon provides a short sketch of such a history that starts with Adam Smith and Voltaire (1694–1778), the French philosopher and contributor to Diderot and d'Alembert's *Encyclopédie*. See Herbert A. Simon, "Bounded Rationality in Social Science: Today and Tomorrow," *Mind and Society* 1, no. 1 (2000).

28. Now there is also a flourishing area of the social sciences—especially within sociolinguistics, sociology, and anthropology—devoted to detailed analyses of the language of work. The Work Practice and Technology Laboratory directed by Lucy Suchman at Xerox PARC in the 1980s was seminal in this area. The Association for Computing Machinery (ACM) Conference on Computer-Supported Cooperative Work (CSCW) is a venue where research of this kind is presented from the many sociologists, linguists, and anthropologists who now play a prominent role in information technology research in large corporations. The relevance of this area of the social sciences to the design of computer hardware and software is well represented within the field of CSCW and is highlighted by stars such as anthropologist Genevieve Bell, who was until recently vice president and fellow at Intel.

29. These biographical details are taken from Antoine Picon, *French Architects and Engineers in the Age of Enlightenment* (Cambridge: Cambridge University Press, 1992), 346–349.

30. Jean-Rudolphe Perronet, *Explication de la Façon dont on Réduit le Fil de Laiton à Différentes Grosseurs dans la Ville de Laigle* (Manuscript 2384), ed. École Nationale des Ponts et Chaussées (Paris: Archives of the École Nationale des Ponts et Chaussées, 1739); Jean-Rudolphe Perronet, *Description de la Façon dont on Fait les Épingles à Laigle en Normandie* (Manuscript 2385), ed. École Nationale des Ponts et Chaussées (Paris: Archives of the École Nationale des Ponts et Chaussées, 1740).

31. Historian Jean-Louis Peaucelle points out that even though Perronet wrote his two treatises on the manufacture of pins by 1740, Perronet's contribution to the *Encyclopédie* was the second version of the entry "Épinglier." The first version of the entry was written by Alexandre "Delaire" Deleyre, who was sent by Diderot to investigate the manufacture of pins in Laigle in 1755. In a subsequent edition (1765), Perronet's text was published in place of Delaire's. In 1783, the entry on pins edited together the Delaire and the Perronet articles. Adam Smith's book *The Wealth of Nations* was published in 1776, yet, apparently, the version of the *Encyclopédie* that inspired him included Delaire's entry, not Perronet's. See Jean-Louis Peaucelle, "La division du travail: Adam Smith et les éncyclopedistes observant la fabrication des épingles en Normandie," *Gérer et Comprendre, Annales des mines,* No. 57 (September): 35–51.

32. Antoine Picon, "Gestes ouvriers, opérations et processus techniques: La vision du travail des encyclopédistes," *Recherches sur Diderot et sur l'Encyclopédie, Société Diderot* 13 (1992): 143–144.

33. Alexandre Deleyre, "Épingle," in *Encyclopédie, ou dictionnaire raisonné des sciences, des arts et des métiers, etc.*, ed. Denis Diderot and Jean Le Rond d'Alembert, University of Chicago Artfl

Encyclopédie Project (Chicago: University of Chicago, [1755] Autumn 2017), https://artflsrv03
.uchicago.edu/philologic4/encyclopedie1117/navigate/5/2993/.

34. As noted, historian of science Pamela Long points out that how-to manuals and recipes from
many of the mechanical arts have a very long history. But historian Sean Takats argues that by
the middle of the eighteenth century in France, cooks especially had made considerable progress
in theorizing their own profession and authoring an increasing number of books. Takats writes,
"What had transpired in the decades before 1740 for cooking to stray from the purely mechanical
to the intellectual? The transformation of *la cuisine* from place and action to knowledge resulted
from a passionate campaign conducted by cooks to theorize their work." See Sean Takats, *The
Expert Cook in Enlightenment France*, Johns Hopkins University Studies in Historical and Political Science (Baltimore: Johns Hopkins University Press, 2011), Kindle locs. 1910–1912. By the
1740s, some cooks had become well-known authors. Consider, for instance, the publication by
cook François Menon, *La Cuisinière Bourgeoise* (1746), which was reprinted in many subsequent
editions and became the best-selling cookbook of the century. That the writing style employed
in these increasingly popular cookbooks might have influenced Diderot and his collaborators
seems more likely than not. Takats demonstrates the connection by citing Diderot: "Writing in
the *Encyclopédie*, Diderot agreed: 'insofar as our cuisine is concerned, it cannot be disputed that
it is an important branch of chemistry.' The *Encyclopédie*'s article on chemistry included a discussion of cooking, noting that 'Panificium [breadmaking] is certainly in the domain of chemistry:
cooking is a type of domestic chemistry.' The argument that cooking had entered the world of
science convinced booksellers to categorize the latest cookbooks under headings such as 'Arts and
Sciences. Medicine. Chemistry' and 'Pharmacopeia, Chemistry, and Alchemy.'" See Takats, *The
Expert Cook in Enlightenment France*, Kindle locs. 2586–2591.

35. Armand Mattelart, *The Information Society: An Introduction* (London: Sage, 2003), 18.

36. As cited in David Alan Grier, *When Computers Were Human* (Princeton, NJ: Princeton University Press, 2005), 36. The original article by Prony is Gaspard-Clair-François-Marie Riche de Prony,
"Notice sur les grandes tables logarithmiques et trigonométriques, adaptées au nouveau système
métrique décimal, lue à la séance publique du 7 juin 1824" (paper presented at the Recueil des
discours lus dans la séance publique de l'Académie Royale des Sciences, Paris, 1824).

37. As described for instance by Allan Bromley, the failure to build the Analytical Engine was partly
the result of a falling out between Babbage and engineer Joseph Clement, who had worked with
Babbage for years on his previous invention, the Difference Engine. See Allan Bromley, "Difference and Analytical Engines," in *Computing before Computers*, ed. William Aspray (Ames: Iowa
State University Press, 1990), 66–67.

38. Mark Priestley, *A Science of Operations: Machines, Logic and the Invention of Programming* (New
York: Springer, 2010), Kindle locs. 1019–1022.

39. See Charles Babbage, "On a Method for Expressing by Signs the Action of Machinery," in
*Charles Babbage: On the Principles and Development of the Calculator and Other Seminal Writings
by Charles Babbage and Others,* ed. Philip Morrison and Emily Morrison (Mineola, NY: Dover,

1961), 346–356. See also Charles Babbage, "Laws of Mechanical Notation," in Morrison and Morrison, eds., *Charles Babbage*, 357–362. Babbage's graphical notation is displayed and analyzed in a November 7, 2011 *New York Times* article at https://archive.nytimes.com/www.nytimes.com/interactive/2011/11/07/science/before-its-time-machine.html. The original image is archived at the Science Museum Archive/Science and Society Picture Library. Used by permission.

40. Ada Lovelace, "Sketch of the Analytical Engine Invented by Charles Babbage [by LF Menabrea, translated and appended with additional notes, by Augusta Ada, Countess of Lovelace]," in *Scientific Memoirs, Selected from the Transactions of Foreign Academies of Science and Learned Societies*, vol. 3 (London: Richard and John Taylor, 1843), 693, as cited in Priestley, *A Science of Operations*, Kindle locs. 1328–1330. Clearly, this is a key citation in Priestley's book, since Lovelace's phrase "a science of operations" is the title of his book.

41. In the history of science, one can find efforts to reconceptualize areas in terms of operations where, previously and institutionally, Leibniz's calculus and functions reigned. Notable is the philosophy of physics—"operationalism"—proposed by Percy Bridgman. See Percy Williams Bridgman, "Operational Analysis," *Philosophy of Science* 5 (1938), as discussed in Hasok Chang, "Operationalism," in *The Stanford Encyclopedia of Philosophy*, ed. Edward N. Zalta (Stanford, CA: Stanford University Press, 2009).

42. Picon, "Gestes ouvriers, opérations et processus techniques."

43. Roland Barthes, "Les planches de l'Encyclopédie de Diderot et d'Alembert," in *Nouveaux Essais Critiques* (Paris: Seuil, 1972), 99.

44. Herman Goldstine and John von Neumann, *Planning and Coding for an Electronic Instrument* (Princeton, NJ: Institute for Advanced Study, 1947), 2.

45. The development of the flow diagram is traced in Joseph Dumit, "Circuits in the Brain and How They Got There," in *Plasticity and Pathology: On the Formation of the Neural Subject*, ed. David Bates and Nima Bassiri (New York: Fordham University Press, 2016).

46. See John Bender and Michael Marrinan, *The Culture of the Diagram* (Stanford, CA: Stanford University Press, 2010), for a fascinating discussion on the presence and absence of people in the plates of the *Encyclopédie*, especially those plates that concern the mechanical arts and the workshops of the artisans, such as the pinmaker workshop.

47. https://developer.microsoft.com/en-us/windows/kinect.

48. https://developer.apple.com/library/ios/documentation/EventHandling/Conceptual/EventHandlingiPhoneOS/motion_event_basics/motion_event_basics.html.

49. Philip Agre, "Surveillance and Capture: Two Models of Privacy," *The Information Society* 10 (1994).

50. Specialists in the history and sociology of work are keenly aware of the simplistic understandings propagated by many influential but underinformed accounts of the "division of labor." For example, rereading the texts of Delaire and Perronet written for the *Encyclopédie*, historian

Jean-Louis Peaucelle critiques Adam Smith's misunderstandings. In the texts from the *Encyclopédie* attention is paid to the fact that craftsmen performing different operations in a pin-producing workshop were paid different salaries: the more experienced, the more skilled, and those engaged in the more dangerous tasks received higher salaries. According to Peaucelle, the men who put the point on the pin were paid the most and were engaged in a terribly dirty job since the mill that was used threw steel dust into the air. These salary differentials were an important factor in the division of labor. Furthermore, Peaucelle argues that the division of labor in these workshops was not a consequence of the introduction of machines into the workshop—as Smith seems to have thought—but rather the inverse was the case. Examining the evidence from the firsthand accounts of Delaire and Perronet, the introduction of machines seems to have been the consequence of already existing divisions of the labor in the workshop. See Peaucelle, "La division du travail: Adam Smith et les éncyclopedistes observant la fabrication des épingles en Normandie," *Gérer et Comprendre, Annales des mines*, no. 57 (September): 35–51.

Chapter 4

1. Donald Ervin Knuth, *The Art of Computer Programming*, vol. 1, *Fundamental Algorithms* (Reading, MA: Addison-Wesley, 1968), 27–29.

2. Tarleton Gillespie, "Algorithm," in *Digital Keywords: A Vocabulary of Information Society and Culture*, ed. Benjamin Peters (Princeton, NJ: Princeton University Press, 2016).

3. Antoinette Rouvroy and Thomas Berns, "Gouvernementalité algorithmique et perspectives d'émancipation: Le disparate comme condition d'individuation par la relation? Politique des algorithmes. Les métriques du web," *Réseaux* 31, no. 177 (2013); David M. Berry, *Critical Theory and the Digital* (New York: Bloomsbury, 2014); Tarleton Gillespie, Pablo J. Boczkowski, and Kirsten A. Foot, *Media Technologies: Essays on Communication, Materiality, and Society* (Cambridge, MA: MIT Press, 2014); Louise Amoore and Volha Piotukh, *Algorithmic Life: Calculative Devices in the Age of Big Data* (London: Routledge, 2016). Bernhard Rieder's article on the PageRank algorithm of Google is a rare and welcome exception in this literature. It is actually an analysis of an algorithm. See Bernhard Rieder, "What Is in Pagerank? A Historical and Conceptual Investigation of a Recursive Status Index," *Computational Culture: A Journal of Software Studies*, no. 3 (September 28, 2012), http://computationalculture.net/what_is_in_pagerank/.

4. Donald Ervin Knuth, "Section 1.3: MIX," in *The Art of Computer Programming*, vol. 1.

5. Donald Ervin Knuth, *The Art of Computer Programming*, fasc. 1, *MMIX* (Reading, MA: Addison-Wesley, 1999).

6. Knuth wrote:

> Algorithms are concepts which have existence apart from any programming language.… I believe algorithms were present long before Turing et al. formulated them, just as the concept of the number "two" was in existence long before the writers of first grade textbooks and other mathematical logicians gave it a certain precise definition.… A computational method comprises a set Q (finite or infinite) of "states," containing a subset X of "inputs" and a subset Y of "outputs"; and a function F from Q into itself. (These quantities are

usually also restricted to be finitely definable, in some sense that corresponds to what human beings can comprehend.)…In this way we can divorce abstract algorithms from particular programs that represent them.

See Donald Ervin Knuth, "Algorithm and Program; Information and Data," *Communications of the ACM* 9, no. 9 (1966): 654. Note also that from 1960, the journal in which he published this statement, *Communications of the ACM (CACM)*, published algorithms in ALGOL, a then-new programming language. In practice, therefore, and in contradiction to Knuth's explicit declaration (but in concert with his own writing practice), the editors of the *CACM* tied the definition of algorithms to a specific programming language, namely ALGOL.

7. Alonzo Church, "An Unsolvable Problem of Elementary Number Theory," *American Journal of Mathematics* 58, no. 2 (1936): 356. Note that one does not need to chain Church and Knuth together to get this circularity. Church defines algorithms in terms of effective methods and defines effective methods in terms of algorithms all by himself, on page 356. Specifically, after the sentence quoted, he continues like this: "Conversely it is true, under the same definition of effective calculability, that every function, an algorithm for the calculation of the values of which exists, is effectively calculable."

8. As noted in chapter 2 and expanded on by computational theorists and historians Nachum Dershowitz and Yuri Gurevich, it might be better to cite Turing here rather than Church, but my point is that the history of the theory of computing does not necessarily help Knuth clarify his position, and he does not help himself by picking a term as loaded as "effective" from this history. See Nachum Dershowitz and Yuri Gurevich, "A Natural Axiomatization of Computability and Proof of Church's Thesis," *Bulletin of Symbolic Logic* 14, no. 3 (2008).

9. See David Alan Grier, *When Computers Were Human* (Princeton, NJ: Princeton University Press, 2005).

10. Neither was algorithm a word or concept in ancient Babylonia. Historian of science and technology Michael Mahoney commented on the likely anachronisms of scientists writing history: "When scientists study history, they often use their modern tools to determine what past work was 'really about'; for example, the Babylonian mathematicians were 'really' writing algorithms. But that's precisely what was not 'really' happening. What was really happening was what was possible, indeed imaginable, in the intellectual environment of the time; what was really happening was what the linguistic and conceptual framework then would allow. The framework of Babylonian mathematics had no place for a metamathematical notion such as algorithm." See Michael S. Mahoney, *Histories of Computing* (Cambridge, MA: Harvard University Press, 2011), 39.

11. "algorithm, n." *OED Online,* June 2018. Oxford University Press, http://www.oed.com.oca.ucsc.edu/view/Entry/4959?redirectedFrom=algorithm.

12. Pamela O. Long, *Openness, Secrecy, Authorship: Technical Arts and the Culture of Knowledge from Antiquity to the Renaissance* (Baltimore: Johns Hopkins University Press, 2001), Kindle locs. 212–213.

13. Knuth, *The Art of Computer Programming*, vol. 1, 29.

14. Bernard Chazelle, "The Algorithm: Idiom of Modern Science," https://www.cs.princeton.edu /~chazelle/pubs/algorithm.html.

15. Sean Takats, *The Expert Cook in Enlightenment France*, Johns Hopkins University Studies in Historical and Political Science (Baltimore: Johns Hopkins University Press, 2011).

16. Hayden White, *Metahistory: The Historical Imagination in Nineteenth-Century Europe* (Baltimore: Johns Hopkins University Press, 1973).

17. Plato, "The Republic, Book VII," in *The Complete Works of Plato* [Annotated], trans. Benjamin Jowett (Latus ePublishing). Kindle.

18. Note that some medical doctors still consider the ability to do arithmetic to be intrinsic to normal adults:

> A few days into his tour of duty at the 86th Combat Support Hospital in Baghdad, Colonel Geoffrey Ling, a U.S. Army neurologist, noticed something unusual. Soldiers who had sustained severe head injuries in blasts from improvised explosive devices (IEDs) appeared to be in much worse shape than he would have expected given his experience with patients who had suffered seemingly similar injuries in car accidents and assaults…. "Their [brain] scans were stone-cold normal, and when you talked to them, they seemed fine," says Ling…. "But, when I started testing them, like asking them to do addition, they were clearly not normal."

See Emily Singer, "Brain Trauma in Iraq," *Technology Review* (May–June 2008): 53, https://www .technologyreview.com/s/409938/brain-trauma-in-iraq/.

19. As classicist Eric Havelock explains it, arithmetic as practiced by a philosopher was a profoundly defamiliarizing form of thought, radically interruptive of poetic thought characteristic of everyday life in a preliterate, oral culture:

> When Plato…proceeds to construct the outline of the actual curriculum of his Academy, he too faces the same problem of awakening the prisoners in the cave from their long illusion. The first subject on the curriculum proposed for this purpose is arithmetic. This takes the place of the Socratic interrupting question. Why arithmetic, if not because it is a primary example of a mental act which is not one of recollection and repetition, but of problem-solving? To establish a numerical relationship is to achieve a small leap of the mind…. This cannot be a mimetic process; it involves not identification with a series or list of phenomena, but the very reverse. One has to achieve personal separation from the series in order to look at it objectively and measure it.

See Eric Alfred Havelock, *Preface to Plato* (Cambridge, MA: Belknap Press / Harvard University Press, 1963), Kindle loc. 210.

20. Rigorous pursuit of this question would require us to differentiate the ancient Greek *arithmétiké* (number) from *logistiké* (calculation). Allan Bloom, in his translation of Plato's *Republic*, points out that "In Greek mathematics the study of numbers and their attributes (arithmétiké) is distinguished from that of calculation (logistiké), which involves operations with numbers (addition, subtraction, etc.)." See Plato, *The Republic*, trans. Allan Bloom (New York: Basic Books, 1982). Historian Bruce Kimball, commenting on Bloom's translation, wrote, "Both [arithmétiké and logistiké] are subsequently subsumed under 'arithmetic' in the liberal arts tradition." See Bruce Kimball, *The Liberal Arts Tradition: A Documentary History* (New York: University Press of America,

2010), 29. Note that the sections of *The Republic* cited here are translations done by Benjamin Jowett in the nineteenth century. Jowett uses the term "arithmetic." In contrast, in his twentieth-century translation, Allan Bloom uses—instead of "arithmetic"—the terms "calculation" and "number." Philosopher of mathematics Howard Stern argues that the convergence of number and calculation does not really take place until the twentieth century, when, in the unintended consequences of David Hilbert's research program, calculation overwhelmed number: "The final irony of this story, and the collapse of Hilbert's dream of establishing the consistency of the logic of the logos by means restricted to *logistiké*, lies in the discovery by Gödel, Post, Church, and Turing that there is a general theory of *logistiké*, and that this theory is nonconstructive; in particular, that neither the notion of consistency nor that of provability (in general) is effective; and further that all sufficiently rich consistent systems…are incomplete." See Howard Stern, "Logos, Logic, and Logistiké: Some Philosophical Remarks on 19th C. Transformation of Mathematics," in *History and Philosophy of Mathematics*, vol. 11, ed. William Aspray and Philip Kitchner (Minneapolis: University of Minnesota Press, 1988).

21. Donald Ervin Knuth, *The Art of Computer Programming*, vol. 2, *Seminumerical Algorithms*, 2nd ed. (Reading, MA: Addison-Wesley, 1981), 180. Contemporary scholarship on ancient Mesopotamian mathematics concurs with Knuth that the Babylonians had more than one number system, but the characteristics he assigns to each are not precisely correct, according to historian of mathematics Carlos Gonçalves of the University of São Paulo (personal communication). More recent scholarship on the archaeological evidence of cuneiform tablets attempts to identify the educational program used to train scribes in ancient Mesopotamia of the second millennium before the Common Era. Historian Christine Proust finds that the system in which the scribes were trained was a floating-point, radix-sixty system—a sexagesimal system. We still see it today in measurements of time, geometrical angles, and geographic coordinates of latitude and longitude. The scribes' system was designed to facilitate the operations of multiplication and division, but, ironically, the floating-point representation meant addition could be difficult and large quantities were not easily encoded. Proust writes that "the positional sexagesimal numbers of paleobabylonian mathematics are basically instruments intended for calculation and not for the representation of quantities." See Christine Proust, "Du calcul flottant en Mésopotamie," *Société des Mathematique de France (SMF) / Gazette des Mathématiciens*, no. 138 (October 2013): 45. On page 32, she humorously interrogates this weakness of "higher mathematics" compared to the "lower mathematics" of merchants and shepherds: "'But how did they count sheep?,' I am often asked. The answer is that sheep are never counted with the positional [floating point] numbers…to add sheep is beyond the elementary mathematics taught at the scribe schools [!!]."

22. Frank Swetz, *Capitalism and Arithmetic: The New Math of the Fifteenth Century* (Chicago: Open Court, 1989), 30.

23. In a history of Indian artificial languages and mathematics, Frits Staal describes a different development in arithmetic from Mesopotamia. According to Staal, "Indian grocers and other merchants combined the use of place value (already known to the Babylonians) with the Indian numerals including the zero." In contrast, "Indian mathematicians used cumbrous expressions derived from linguistics.…Was it to add the prestige of the science of language to the humdrum

activity of mathematical calculation?" See Frits Staal, "Artificial Languages across Sciences and Civilizations," *Journal of Indian Philosophy* 34 (2006): 130–131. Thus, in India too, the grocers used one kind of arithmetic and the philosophers another.

24. "In universities where practical arithmetic was taught in conjunction with theoretical arithmetic, the fees for studying theoretical arithmetic were often twice the amount charged for practical work, demonstrating the perceived discrepancy between the value[s] of the two subjects. If a student in the early Renaissance wished to learn commercial mathematics, he usually did not go to the university, but sought out a reckoning master, a man skilled in the arts of commercial computation, with whom to study." See Swetz, *Capitalism and Arithmetic*, 15.

25. Swetz, *Capitalism and Arithmetic*, 27–28.

26. Keith Devlin writes:

> Traders recorded their numerical data using Roman numerals and performed calculations either by a fairly elaborate and widely used fingers procedure or with a mechanical abacus. That state of affairs started to change soon after 1202, the year a young Italian man, Leonardo of Pisa—the man whom a historian many centuries later would dub "Fibonacci"—completed the first general purpose arithmetic book in the West, *Liber abbaci*, that explained the "new" methods in terms understandable to ordinary people (tradesmen and businessmen as well as schoolchildren). While other lineages can be traced, Leonardo's influence, through *Liber abbaci*, was by far the most significant and shaped the development of modern western Europe.

See Keith Devlin, *The Man of Numbers: Fibonacci's Arithmetic Revolution* (New York: Bloomsbury, 2011), Kindle locs. 39–45.

27. Karl Menninger, *Number Words and Number Symbols* (Cambridge, MA: MIT Press, 1969), 435, as cited in Swetz, *Capitalism and Arithmetic*, 17.

28. Charles Petzold argues that our contemporary usage of the term dates only from the 1960s, presumably owing much to Donald Knuth's usage of the phrase and widely read description of the techniques of the "analysis of algorithms." See Charles Petzold, *The Annotated Turing: A Guided Tour through Alan Turing's Historic Paper on Computability and the Turing Machine* (Indianapolis, IN: Wiley, 2008), 42. Petzold's observation is discussed in chapter 2 of this book.

29. See V. A. Uspenskii, "Arithmetization," in *Encyclopedia of Mathematics*, ed. Ulf Rehmann (Dordrecht: Kluwer Academic, 2002).

30. George Boole, *George Boole's Collected Logical Works, Volume II: The Laws Of Thought (1854)* (Chicago: Open Court, 1940). Boole's book title is a reference to Aristotle and the classical tradition that followed from Aristotle's work.

31. Boole, *The Laws of Thought*, 35.

32. This is a simplification of Boole's accomplishment. There is, of course, a whole body of specialist literature on the philosophy and history of Boole's work that can provide a more accurate rendering than I do here. See, for example, Juan Luis Gastaldi, "Une archéologie de la logique du sens: Arithmétique et contenu dans le processus de mathématisation de la logique au XIXe siècle" (PhD thesis, Université de Bordeaux 3, 2014).

33. Ludwig Wittgenstein, *Wittgenstein's Lectures on the Foundations of Mathematics, Cambridge, 1939* (Chicago: University of Chicago Press, 1976), 203.

34. Wittgenstein, *Lectures on the Foundations of Mathematics*.

35. Wittgenstein, *Lectures on the Foundations of Mathematics*, 230–231.

36. Wittgenstein, *Lectures on the Foundations of Mathematics*, 97.

37. Cf. David Hilbert's discussion: "We assume that we have the capacity to name things by signs, that we can recognize them again. With these signs we can then carry out operations that are analogous to those of arithmetic and that obey analogous laws." Cited in Wilfried Sieg, "Hilbert's Programs: 1917–1922," *Bulletin of Symbolic Logic* 5, no. 1 (1999).

38. As cited in Grier, *When Computers Were Human*, 15.

39. As cited in Grier, *When Computers Were Human*, 16.

40. Grier, *When Computers Were Human*, 20.

41. As cited in Grier, *When Computers Were Human*, 23. Grier, in turn, attributes it to a 1993 journal article by Curtis Wilson, saying further that a 1995 text by Wilson gives a fairly complete account and assessment of the controversy. See Curtis Wilson, "Clairaut's Calculation of Halley's Comet," *Journal of the History of Astronomy* 24 (1993); Curtis Wilson, "Appendix: Clairaut's Calculation of the Comet's Return," in *The General History of Astronomy*, ed. Rene Taton and Curtis Wilson (Cambridge: Cambridge University Press, 1995).

42. In 1939, Turing was working on a mechanical calculating machine. His contemporaries were surprised since in prewar England mathematics was considered "high-level" work and mechanical engineering "low-level" labor. From the perspective of one of Turing's contemporaries, Kenneth Harrison, "he well knew from conversations with Alan [Turing] that a pure mathematician worked in a symbolic world and not with things. The machine seemed to be a contradiction. It was particularly remarkable in England, where there existed no tradition of high-status academic engineering, as there was in France and Germany and (as with Vannevar Bush) in the United States. Such a foray into the practical world was liable to be met with patronising jokes within the academic world." See Andrew Hodges, *Alan Turing: The Enigma: The Book That Inspired the Film "The Imitation Game*, rev. ed. (Princeton, NJ: Princeton University Press, 2014), 199.

43. Morrison, Philip and Emily Morrison, eds. *Charles Babbage: On the Principles and Development of the Calculator and Other Seminal Writings by Charles Babbage and Others* (Mineola, NY: Dover, 1961), xiv.

44. Charles Babbage, "On the Application of Machinery to the Purpose of Calculating and Printing Mathematical Tables," in Morrison and Emily Morrison, eds., *Charles Babbage*, 298.

45. Luigi Federico Menabrea, "Sketch of the Analytical Engine Invented by Charles Babbage. With Notes upon the Memoir by the Translator, Ada Augusta, Countess of Lovelace," in Morrison and Emily Morrison, eds., *Charles Babbage*, 243–244.

46. Mahoney, *Histories of Computing*.

47. Federica Frabetti, *Software Theory: A Cultural and Philosophical Study*, Media Philosophy (London: Rowman and Littlefield International, 2014), 70.

48. Bernard Stiegler, *Technics and Time*, vol. 1, *The Fault of Epimetheus* (Stanford, CA: Stanford University Press, 1998).

49. Frabetti, *Software Theory*, Kindle loc. 4134.

50. Frabetti, *Software Theory*, Kindle loc. 320.

51. Historian David Bates provides a short overview of how errors were theorized in early artificial intelligence, especially in the work of Alan Turing and Herbert Simon. He contextualizes Turing and Simon in longer philosophical genealogies including Martin Heidegger and René Descartes. See David W. Bates, "Automatisation et erreur," in *La vérité du numérique: Recherche et enseignement supérieur à l'ère des technologies numériques*, ed. Bernard Stiegler (Paris, France: FYP editions, 2018), 29–40. Previous work by Bates traces the concept of error in Enlightenment thought. See David W. Bates, *Enlightenment Aberrations: Error and Revolution in France* (Ithaca, NY: Cornell University Press, 2002).

52. Sigmund Freud, *Jokes and Their Relation to the Unconscious*, trans. James Strachey, The Standard Edition (New York: W. W. Norton, [1905] 1960), 14, 18.

53. Marvin Minsky, Turing Award winner and cofounder of the field of artificial intelligence, noted that Freud's processes could be interpreted as computational processes or computer programs. See Marvin Minsky, "Jokes and Their Relation to the Cognitive Unconscious," *Cognitive Constraints on Communication*, ed. Lucia Vaina and Jaako Hintikka (Boston: Reidel, 1981). See also Marvin Minsky, *Society of Mind* (New York: Simon and Schuster, 1986).

54. See Freudian psychoanalyst Jacques Lacan on condensation and displacement as compared to metonymy and metaphor, for example in Elizabeth A. Grosz, *Jacques Lacan: A Feminist Introduction* (New York: Routledge, 1990).

55. John Seely Brown and Kurt VanLehn, "Repair Theory: A Generative Theory of Bugs in Procedural Skills," *Cognitive Science* 4, no. 4 (1980): 379.

56. See Kurt VanLehn, "Learning One Subprocedure per Lesson," *Artificial Intelligence*, no. 31 (1987).

57. This particular formulation of the rules of arithmetic is mine, but physicist and computer scientist Stephen Wolfram refers to this kind of notation as a "mobile automaton" because, at any given moment, a single column of squares is rewritten according to the rules of the automaton and then, in the next moment, the adjacent column of cells is rewritten using the same rules. In short, at any given moment, only one column of squares is "in focus," and the others are not taken into consideration in the application of the rules. As execution of the automaton proceeds, each of the columns is considered in turn. In a conventional "nonmobile" automaton, all of the squares are rewritten, in parallel, by the rules of the automaton. See Stephen Wolfram, *A New Kind of Science* (Champaign, IL: Wolfram Media, 2002), 71.

58. One can watch the rules match the columns of the sum at http://softwarearts.info/Automata/Arithmetic/. The code for this web page is written in four files of JavaScript and HTML. (1) rules.js contains a set of rules for addition and another set for subtraction. Both rule sets are written using 1s and 0s rather than with black and white squares. However, the rules are exactly analogous to the rules presented here in black and white. (2) automaton.js is an interpreter for rules written in this format (i.e., written as binary, mobile automata). Given a rule set like the one for addition and a starting state like $87 + 56 = ?$, it runs the rules on each column, from right to left, until it hits the left-hand edge. (3) display.js transforms the rules, the start state, and the execution of the rules into an animated web page by translating everything into moving and static black and white squares coded as HTML. Finally, (4) index.html links the three other files together and specifies the start state, the rule set to be used, the execution rate (i.e., how fast one wants to see the rules matched against the columns of the sum), and the size of the display (i.e., the size of the squares to be displayed).

59. VanLehn, "Learning One Subprocedure per Lesson."

60. Spike Jonze, dir., *Her* (Los Angeles: Annapurna Pictures, 2013).

61. Stuart J. Russell and Peter Norvig, *Artificial Intelligence: A Modern Approach*, 3rd ed. (Upper Saddle River, NJ: Prentice Hall, 2010), 694.

62. See, for example, Chris Anderson, "The End of Theory: The Data Deluge Makes the Scientific Method Obsolete," *Wired*, June 2008.

63. Machine-learning specialists Daphne Koller (a professor at Stanford) and Andrew Ng (a former professor at Stanford) cofounded Coursera, one of the largest MOOC sites.

64. Brown and VanLehn, "Repair Theory," 379.

65. Applying the insights of semiotician and mathematician Brian Rotman, one could say that Brown and VanLehn's theory is an illustration of how the body has been taken out of mathematics. See Brian Rotman, *Ad Infinitum … The Ghost in Turing's Machine: Taking God Out of Mathematics and Putting the Body Back In* (Stanford, CA: Stanford University Press, 1993).

66. "Were a language ever completely 'grammatical' it would be a perfect engine of conceptual expression. Unfortunately, or luckily, no language is tyrannically consistent. All grammars leak." See Edward Sapir, *Language: An Introduction to the Study of Speech* (New York: Harcourt, Brace, 1921), 39.

Chapter 5

1. See, for example, Herman H. Goldstine, *The Computer—from Pascal to Von Neumann* (Princeton, NJ: Princeton University Press, 1980).

2. See, for example, Wolfe Mays and D. G. Prinz, "A Relay Machine for the Demonstration of Symbolic Logic," *Nature* 165 (February 4, 1950), 197.

3. Published in 1929, Presburger's arithmetic was a first-order theory of the natural numbers containing addition but no multiplication. Mojżesz Presburger, "Ueber die Vollstaendigkeit eines

gewissen Systems der Arithmetik ganzer Zahlen, in welchem die Addition als einzige Operation hervortritt," *Comptes Rendus du I congrés de Mathématiciens des Pays Slaves* (Warsaw, Poland: n.p., 1929), 92–101. Presberger wrote a procedure that would allow one to determine if a statement, written in his arithmetic is true. In 1954, Martin Davis programmed Presburger's procedure for a Johnniac computer at the Princeton Institute for Advanced Study. This was probably the first software written to perform logical deductions, but Davis did not publish a paper about his software until later. See Martin Davis, "The Early History of Automated Deduction," in *Handbook of Automated Reasoning,* ed. Alan Robinson and Andrei Voronkov (Amsterdam: Elsevier, 2001).
The first such software that was reported in a publication was probably Allen Newell and Herbert Simon's "Logic Theorist." Martin Gardner writes,

> Is it possible to build a logic machine or program a digital computer to solve logic problems in areas where there either is no decision procedure, or the procedure is so complex and time-consuming that it is beyond the speed and capacity of present machines? The answer is certainly yes. A strenuous effort is now under way to develop a complex information-processing system (called by its inventors the "logic-theory machine") capable of searching for proofs of logic theorems in a manner closely analogous to the way a human logician searches for such proofs, namely, by trial and error, intuition, and sheer luck....The system is designed for digital computers, and satisfactory empirical tests of it were made in 1956 with the Rand Corporation's computer Johnniac.

See Martin Gardner, *Logic Machines and Diagrams* (New York: McGraw-Hill, 1958), 143.

4. Eric Alfred Havelock, *Preface to Plato* (Cambridge, MA: Belknap Press / Harvard University Press, 1963), Kindle locs. 2637–2638.

5. According to the *Encyclopedia of Philosophy*, "The term 'dialectic' originates from the Greek expression for the art of conversation." See "Dialectic," in *Encyclopedia of Philosophy*, vol. 2, ed. Paul Edwards (New York: Macmillan and Free Press, 1967).

6. See philosopher and historian Michel Foucault's description of the "Cartesian moment" in Michel Foucault, *The Hermeneutics of the Subject: Lectures at the Collège de France, 1981–1982* (New York: Palgrave-Macmillan, 2005).

7. In Plato's dialogues, Socrates repeatedly asserts, during his dialectical interventions, that he knows nothing.

8. Herodotus, *The History*, trans. David Grene (Chicago: University of Chicago Press, 2010), I.55.

9. Walter J. Ong, *Orality and Literacy: The Technologizing of the Word* (New York: Routledge, 2002), 172.

10. Arthur Schopenhauer, *The Art of Controversy, and Other Posthumous Papers* (London: Allen and Unwin, 1921).

11. Marshall McLuhan and W. Terrence Gordon, *The Classical Trivium: The Place of Thomas Nashe in the Learning of His Time* (Corte Madera, CA: Gingko Press, 2006), 47.

12. Léon Robin, *Greek Thought and the Origins of the Scientific Spirit* (London: Routledge, [1928] 1996), 92, as cited in McLuhan and Gordon, *The Classical Trivium*, 39–40.

13. Aristotle, *Physica*, W. D. Ross, ed. (Oxford: Clarendon Press,1950), 6.9.239b14–18.

14. Vincent Ardourel, "A Discrete Solution for the Paradox of Achilles and the Tortoise," *Synthese* 192 (2015).

15. See Ardourel's explanation of "discrete variational mechanics," the computational technique he employs to "solve" the paradox: "DM [discrete variational mechanics] is nowadays mainly developed by computer scientists in order to make accurate and stable numerical computations possible." See Ardourel, "A Discrete Solution for the Paradox of Achilles and the Tortoise," 2852.

16. Philosopher W. V. Quine thought that Zeno's paradox was not a paradox, because it could be easily solved by calculation:

> Some of the ancient paradoxes of Zeno belong under the head of falsidical [i.e., not veridical] paradoxes. Take the one about Achilles and the tortoise. Generalized beyond these two fictitious characters, what the paradox purports to establish is the absurd proposition that so long as a runner keeps running, however slowly, another runner can never overtake him. The argument is that each time the pursuer reaches a spot where the pursued has been, the pursued has moved a bit beyond. When we try to make this argument more explicit, the fallacy that emerges is the mistaken notion that any infinite succession of intervals of time has to add up to all eternity. Actually when an infinite succession of intervals of time is so chosen that the succeeding intervals become shorter and shorter, the whole succession may take either a finite or infinite time. It is a question of a convergent series.

See W. V. Quine, *The Ways of Paradox and Other Essays*, revised and enlarged ed. (Cambridge, MA: Harvard University Press, 1976), 3–4. Quine's "solution" relies on a discovery of the calculus that an infinite geometric series can converge. Yet, for many, including for instance philosopher Henri Bergson, this is not a solution unless you believe that time is infinitely divisible. The objection can be rendered as a question: How can someone do an infinite number of actions (e.g., moving halfway there, then halfway again, etc.) in a finite amount of time? Bergson's resolution was to refute this presupposition and assert that time, for human thought and action, is an indivisible whole. See Henri Bergson, *Creative Evolution*, trans. A. Mitchell (New York: Holt, Rinehart and Winston, 1911), 308. In other words, Quine thinks Zeno's paradox is not a paradox, because it can be translated into a simple calculation, while, in contrast, a Bergsonian position would call Quine's calculation ridiculous because it presupposes an absurd model of time, one that is not applicable in the realms of human thought and human action. Bergson and Albert Einstein had a famous debate about time in 1922. This debate was reenacted and reimagined by philosophers Bruno Latour and Elie During, artist Olafur Eliasson, and historian Jimena Canales at the Centre Pompidou in 2010. See Bruno Latour, "Some Experiments in Art and Politics," *E-Flux Journal* 23 (March 2011); Elie During, *Bergson et Einstein: La querelle du temps* (Paris: Presses Universitaires de France, 2011); Jimena Canales, *The Physicist and the Philosopher: Einstein, Bergson and the Debate That Changed Our Understanding of Time* (Princeton, NJ: Princeton University Press, 2015).

17. Foucault writes,

> So, throughout Antiquity (in the Pythagoreans, Plato, the Stoics, Cynics, Epicureans, and Neo-Platonists), the philosophical theme (how to have access to the truth?) and the question of spirituality (what transformations in the being of the subject are necessary for access to the truth?) were never separate.…Now, leaping over several centuries, we can say that we enter the modern age … when it is assumed that what gives access to the truth, the condition for the subject's access to the truth, is knowledge (*connaissance*) and knowledge

alone. It seems to me that what I have called the "Cartesian moment" takes on its position and meaning at this point, without in any way my wanting to say that it is a question of Descartes, that he was its inventor or that he was the first to do this. I think the modern age of the history of truth begins when knowledge itself and knowledge alone gives access to the truth. That is to say, it is when the philosopher (or the scientist, or simply someone who seeks the truth) can recognize the truth and have access to it in himself and solely through his activity of knowing, without anything else being demanded of him and without him having to change or alter his being as subject.... [T]here are the internal conditions of the act of knowledge and of the rules it must obey to have access to the truth: formal conditions, objective conditions, formal rules of method.

See Foucault, *The Hermeneutics of the Subject*, 17–18.

18. Feminist epistemologists show how Foucault's "Cartesian moment" marks a form of male privilege. In feminist epistemology and standpoint theory, the main question of epistemology—What can be known?—has been expanded to a question of two parts, the second being, What can be known by whom? For an elaboration see, for example, Sandra G. Harding, *Whose Science? Whose Knowledge?: Thinking from Women's Lives* (Ithaca, NY: Cornell University Press, 1991). For example, are there forms of women's knowledge that differ from men's knowledge? Furthermore, are women allowed, licensed, or considered to be capable of understanding what is taken to be men's knowledge, and vice versa? Contemporary work in science studies provides us with plenty of empirical evidence to document the contemporary currency of gender biases in the fields of science and technology. See, for example, Evelyn Fox Keller, *Reflections on Gender and Science* (New Haven, CT: Yale University Press, 1995).

19. Chris Anderson, "The End of Theory: The Data Deluge Makes the Scientific Method Obsolete," *Wired*, June 2008.

20. The gender gap in computer science and Silicon Valley—documented in chapter 1—graphically illustrates a contemporary betrayal of the Cartesian promise that anyone and everyone can be knowledgeable. The employment statistics of large Internet firms cited in chapter 1 are one way of documenting this betrayal. Another way is simply to track contemporary discourse, such as the telling comments made by Lawrence Summers: "Harvard President Lawrence H. Summers has triggered criticism by telling an economics conference Friday that the under-representation of female scientists at elite universities may stem in part from 'innate' differences between men and women, although two Harvard professors who heard the speech said the remarks have been taken out of context in an ensuing national media frenzy."

See Daniel J. Hemel, "Summers' Comments on Women and Science Draw Ire: Remarks at Private Conference Stir Criticism, Media Frenzy," *The Harvard Crimson*, January 14, 2005.

21. See Anonymous, "Logique," *Encyclopédie, ou dictionnaire raisonné des sciences, des arts et des métiers, etc.*, eds. Denis Diderot and Jean le Rond d'Alembert (University of Chicago: ARTFL Encyclopédie Project (Autumn 2017 Edition)), Robert Morrissey and Glenn Roe (eds), 9:637–9:641, http://encyclopedie.uchicago.edu/.

22. Arguably, although Bacon did introduce a method he called "induction," his method was unlike what we would call induction today. The version of induction introduced by Scottish philosopher David Hume (1711–1776) has displaced Bacon's:

It is often said that [Francis Bacon] wrote the first modern treatment of induction, but here we must be careful. He certainly never advocated induction by simple enumeration—in which one lists a bunch of A with property B and concludes that all A are B. Bacon has no use for such reasoning. As he says in Section 105 of his *Novum Organum* "The induction that proceeds by simple enumeration is puerile." Bacon wanted to get beyond the data of sense by constructing abstract models of the world. He calls that induction. He believes sound theories will be suggested to the scientist only if he makes a grand catalogue of phenomena, but Bacon does not aim at inference under uncertainty. He aims at the construction of novel and deep theories that will explain the inchoate data of sense. The word "induction" is confusing, for Bacon called such theorizing induction. After Hume many people came to reserve the word for something different.

See Ian Hacking, *The Emergence of Probability: A Philosophical Study of Early Ideas about Probability, Induction and Statistical Inference*, Cambridge Series on Statistical and Probabilistic Mathematics (Cambridge: Cambridge University Press, 1975), 76.

23. "Logique," in Diderot and d'Alembert, *Encyclopédie*, 9:641.

24. "Logique," in Diderot and d'Alembert, *Encyclopédie*, 9:637–9:638.

25. "Logique," in Diderot and d'Alembert, *Encyclopédie*, 9:638.

26. McLuhan and Gordon, *The Classical Trivium*, 42.

27. David Cram, "Rhetoric and Music in the Early Modern Period," in *The Making of the Humanities*, vol. 1, ed. Rens Bod, Jaap Maat, and Thijs Weststeijn (Amsterdam: Amsterdam University Press, 2004), 264.

28. Jaap Maat, *Philosophical Languages in the Seventeenth Century: Dalgarno, Wilkins, Leibniz* (Boston: Kluwer Academic, 2004).

29. Umberto Eco, *The Search for the Perfect Language*, The Making of Europe (Cambridge, MA: Blackwell, 1995).

30. Martin Davis, *The Universal Computer: The Road from Leibniz to Turing* (New York: W. W. Norton, 2000).

31. For a listing and description of Peano's axioms, see, for example, the Wolfram site, http://mathworld.wolfram.com/PeanosAxioms.html.

32. David Hilbert, "On the Foundations of Logic and Arithmetic," *The Monist* 15, no. 3 (1905): 340.

33. Philosopher Alain Badiou has described Peano's project like this:

Peano is inscribed in the twentieth century's general movement of thought—forged, in fact, at the end of the nineteenth century—whose characteristic gesture is the destitution of Platonism, in the guise of that which had always been its bastion: mathematics, and especially the Idea of number.... We see here, as if in the pangs of its birth, the real origin of what [French philosopher Jean-François] Lyotard calls the "linguistic turn" in Western philosophy, and what I call the reign of the great modern sophistry: if it is true that mathematics, the highest expression of pure thought, in the final analysis consists of nothing but syntactical apparatuses, grammars of signs, then *a fortiori* all thought falls under the constitutive rule of language.

See Alain Badiou, *Number and Numbers* (Cambridge: Polity Press, 2008), 48.

34. Badiou, *Number and Numbers*, 27.

35. Gottfried Wilhelm Leibniz, "The Art of Discovery," in *Leibniz: Selections*, ed. Philip P. Wiener (New York: Charles Scribner's Sons, [1685] 1951), 51.

36. Martin Davis explains that Leibniz's efforts to reduce argumentation to calculation were at least partially motivated by his diplomatic dream of reuniting the various branches of the Christian church to overcome religious differences and the violence then rampant in Europe and especially in what is now Germany. See Davis, *The Universal Computer*, 14.

37. Claude Elwood Shannon, "A Symbolic Analysis of Relay and Switching Circuits" (MS thesis, Electrical Engineering, Massachusetts Institute of Technology, 1940 [finished in 1937]).

38. According to Gordon Moore, "We won't have the rate of progress that we've had over the last few decades. I think that's inevitable with any technology; it eventually saturates out. I guess I see Moore's law dying here in the next decade or so, but that's not surprising." See Rachel Courtland, "Gordon Moore, the Man Whose Name Means Progress: The Visionary Engineer Reflects on 50 Years of Moore's Law," Interview, *IEEE Spectrum*, March 30, 2015, https://spectrum .ieee.org/computing/hardware/gordon-moore-the-man-whose-name-means-progress.

39. Charles S. Peirce, "Letter, Peirce to A. Marquand," in *Writings of Charles S. Peirce: A Chronological Edition*, vol. 5 *(1884–1886)*, ed. Christian J. W. Kloesel, Nathan Househ, Marc Simon, André De Tienne, Ursula Niklas, Aleta Houser, Cathy L. Clark, and Max H. Fisch (Bloomington: Indiana University Press, [1886] 1993). The image of the letter is courtesy of the Manuscripts Division, Department of Rare Books and Special Collections, Princeton University Library. See "Letter from Charles Peirce to Allan Marquand, December 30, 1886," C0269, Allan Marquand Papers, Box 17, Folder 29.

40. Allan Marquand, "A New Logic Machine," *Proceedings of the American Academy of Arts and Sciences* 21 (1885): 303.

41. Gardner, *Logic Machines and Diagrams*.

42. For a visual history of these machines, see the book produced by the office of designers Ray and Charles Eames. See Glen Fleck, Office of Charles and Ray Eames, and International Business Machines Corporation, *A Computer Perspective: Background to the Computer Age* (Cambridge, MA: Harvard University Press, 1990).

43. According to Gardner,

> As we have seen, Allan Marquand, in about 1885, saw the value of operating his logic machine electrically and even drew a circuit pattern for it, but there is no evidence that this version of his device was ever actually constructed. As far as I have been able to discover, the first man actually to build an electrical logic machine was Benjamin Burack, of the department of psychology, Roosevelt College, Chicago. His article [Benjamin Burack, "An Electrical Logic Machine," *Science* 109 (June 17, 1949): 610] was the first published description of the device, although the machine was built and demonstrated as early as 1936.

See Gardner, *Logic Machines and Diagrams*, 125.

44. Claude E. Shannon, "A Symbolic Analysis of Relay and Switching Circuits," *Transactions of the AIEE* 57 (1938).

45. According to Shannon,

> Any circuit is represented by a set of equations, the terms of the equations representing the various relays and switches of the circuit. A calculus is developed for manipulating these equations by simple mathematical processes, most of which are similar to ordinary algebraic algorithms. This calculus is shown to be exactly analogous to the Calculus of Propositions used in the study of logic. For the synthesis problem the desired characteristics are first written as a system of equations, and the equations are then manipulated into the form representing the simplest circuit. The circuit may then be immediately drawn from the equations.

See Shannon, "A Symbolic Analysis of Relay and Switching Circuits" (thesis), 2.

46. Ludwig Wittgenstein, *Tractatus Logico-Philosophicus*, trans. Frank P. Ramsey (London: Kegan Paul, 1922), Proposition 5.101. Truth tables also appeared one year earlier in Emil Post, "Introduction to a General Theory of Elementary Propositions," *American Journal of Mathematics* 43, no. 3 (1921): 167, although it appears likely that Peirce had already invented truth tables by 1885. See Irving H. Anellis, "Peirce's Truth-Functional Analysis and the Origin of the Truth Table," *History and Philosophy of Logic* 33 (2012).

47. Wittgenstein writes,

> Suppose the scheme of implication were somehow represented by electric wires…. Say a galvanometer needle points to nought if the wiring is correct: if it is not, there is some deflection.—If you counted to see whether the wiring was correct, your opinion would be confirmed by what happens on the galvanometer. The result gives us an added check: we agree, and the needle did what we expected…. What I want to say is that there is no galvanometer needle here. The whole point of the simile is that it is a bad one.

See Ludwig Wittgenstein, *Remarks on the Foundations of Mathematics* (Cambridge, MA: MIT Press, 1978), 259.

48. See Pitirim A. Sorokin and Robert K. Merton, "Social Time: A Methodological and Functional Analysis," *American Journal of Sociology* 42, no. 5 (March 1937): 615–629. See also Edward M. Reingold and Nachum Dershowitz, *Calendrical Calculations, The Ultimate Edition*, 4th Edition, Kindle Edition (Cambridge: Cambridge University Press, 2018).

49. Michael S. Mahoney, *Histories of Computing* (Cambridge, MA: Harvard University Press, 2011), 133.

50. Harold Abelson, Gerald Jay Sussman, and Julie Sussman, *Structure and Interpretation of Computer Programs*, 2nd ed., MIT Electrical Engineering and Computer Science Series (Cambridge, MA: MIT Press; New York: McGraw-Hill, 1996).

51. Abelson, Sussman, and Sussman, *Structure and Interpretation of Computer Programs*, 489.

52. The website for the book is at http://softwarearts.info. The original code in Scheme is in section 3.3.4 of Abelson, Sussman, and Sussman, *Structure and Interpretation of Computer Programs*.

53. We will see in chapter 7, on grammar, that by their choice of a metalinguistic approach to language design, Abelson, Sussman, and Sussman owe a substantial debt to formal language theory of both mathematical logic and linguistics such as Chomskyan linguistics.

54. Cordell Green, "Application of Theorem Proving to Problem Solving," in *International Joint Conference on Artificial Intelligence*, ed. Donald E. Walker and Lewis M. Norton (New York: Gordon and Breach, 1969), 236.

55. A. Colmerauer and P. Roussel, "The Birth of Prolog," *ACM SIGPLAN Notices* 28, no. 3 (1993): 37.

56. R. A. Kowalski, "The Early Years of Logic Programming," *Communications of the ACM* 31, no. 1 (1988): 38.

57. R. A. Kowalski, "History of Logic Programming," in *History of Logic*, vol. 9, *Logic and Computation*, ed. D. Gabbay, J. Siekmann, and J. Woods (Amsterdam: Elsevier, 2014), 523.

58. R. A. Kowalski, "Algorithm = Logic + Control," *Communications of the ACM* 22, no. 7 (1979).

59. According to Kowalski, "Predicate logic is a high-level, human-oriented language for describing problems and problem-solving methods to computers. In this paper, we are concerned not with the use of predicate logic as a programming language in its own right, but with its use as a tool for the analysis of algorithms." See Kowalski, "Algorithm = Logic + Control," 424.

60. José Ferreirós, "The Road to Modern Logic—an Interpretation," *Bulletin of Symbolic Logic* 7, no. 4 (December 2001): 448.

61. Ferreirós, "The Road to Modern Logic," 454.

62. Ferreirós dates this invention quite precisely to 1928: "The first really modern treatise of formal logic is not *Principia Mathematica* [by Russell and Whitehead], but Hilbert & Ackermann's *Grundzüge der Theoretischen Logik* [the book Turing cites in his 1936 paper]. The book is noteworthy because here one can find, for the first time in a treatise on logic, a study of FOL [first-order logic] as a separate system (under the name of 'restricted functional calculus'), posing the question of its metatheoretical properties, e.g., completeness. But FOL appears only as an interesting subsystem, and the work culminates by presenting the so-called 'extended functional calculus,' a peculiar version of the theory of types." See Ferreirós, "The Road to Modern Logic," 445–446. Other historians of logic describe contemporary predicate logic as the outcome of two independent derivations, one by Frege, the other by Peirce. According to Eric M. Hammer, "Peirce's work in logic included a number of major contributions, including…[d]evelopment of first-order logic independently of Frege." See Eric M. Hammer, "Semantics for Existential Graphs," *Journal of Philosophical Logic* 27, no. 5 (October 1998): 489.

63. Sun-Joo Shin and Eric Hammer, "Peirce's Deductive Logic," in *The Stanford Encyclopedia of Philosophy*, ed. Edward N. Zalta (Stanford, CA: Stanford University Press, 2014), https://plato .stanford.edu/entries/peirce-logic/.

64. All of the Prolog code for this chapter can be found on the book website: http://softwarearts .info.

65. Ivan Bratko, in the best introduction to Prolog programming, explains procedural meaning by contrasting it with declarative meaning:

> In our examples so far it has always been possible to understand the results of the program without exactly knowing how the system actually found the results. It therefore makes sense to distinguish between two levels of meaning of Prolog programs; namely, the declarative meaning and the procedural meaning. The declarative meaning is concerned only with the relations defined by the program. The declarative meaning thus determines what will be the output of the program. On the other hand, the procedural meaning also determines how this output is obtained; that is, how the relations are actually evaluated by the Prolog system.

See Ivan Bratko, *Prolog Programming for Artificial Intelligence*, 2nd ed. (New York: Addison-Wesley, 1990), 25.

66. If the query is posed without any unbound variables, then it can potentially succeed, confirming, for example, that "socrates" is "mortal." The query "?- mortal(socrates)." returns "true."

67. This series of examples is also an indirect commentary on the long history of logic, combinatorics, and Christian theology that begins in the thirteenth century with philosopher and Franciscan tertiary Ramon Llull. See Martin Gardner's chapter, "The *Ars Magna* of Ramon Llull," in Martin Gardner, *Logic Machines and Diagrams* (New York: McGraw-Hill, 1958), 1–27.

68. A. Bondarenko, P. M. Dung, R. A. Kowalski, and F. Toni, "An Abstract Argumentation-Theoretic Approach to Default Reasoning," *Journal of Artificial Intelligence Research* 93, nos. 1–2 (1997), as cited in Kowalski, "History of Logic Programming," 539.

69. Phan Minh Dung, "On the Acceptability of Arguments and Its Fundamental Role in Nonmonotonic Reasoning, Logic Programming and N-Person Games," *Artificial Intelligence* 77 (1995): 324.

70. Dung, "Acceptability of Arguments."

71. Bertrand Russell, *The Principles of Mathematics*, vol. 1 (Cambridge: Cambridge University Press, 1903), 5.

72. Wittgenstein, *Remarks on the Foundations of Mathematics*, 271.

73. Wittgenstein, *Remarks on the Foundations of Mathematics*, 260.

74. Colmerauer and Roussel, "The Birth of Prolog."

75. S. Muggleton, "Inductive Logic Programming," *New Generation Computing* 8, no. 4 (1991).

76. A. C. Kakas, R. A. Kowalski, and F. Toni, "Abductive Logic Programming," *Journal of Logic and Computation* 2, no. 6 (1993).

77. Eugene Charniak and Drew McDermott, *Introduction to Artificial Intelligence* (New York: Addison-Wesley, 1985).

78. K. Eshghi, "Abductive Planning with Event Calculus," in *Fifth International Conference and Symposium on Logic Programming*, ed. Robert Kowalski and Kenneth Bowen, Seattle, August 15–19 (Cambridge, MA: MIT Press, 1988).

79. For an overview, see Marc Denecker and Antonis Kakas, "Abduction in Logic Programming," in *Computational Logic (Kowalski Festschrift)*, ed. A. C. Kakas and F. Sadri, Lecture Notes in Artificial Intelligence 2407 (Berlin: Springer-Verlag, 2002).

80. The notion of a "programming paradigm" is in reference to historian Thomas Kuhn's work but was introduced into computer science by Turing Award winner Robert Floyd. See Robert W. Floyd, "The Paradigms of Programming: 1978 Turing Award Lecture," *Communications of the ACM* 22, no. 8 (1979).

Chapter 6

1. Association for Computing Machinery / Institute of Electrical and Electronics Engineers (ACM/IEEE).

2. Douglas C. Engelbart and William K. English, "A Research Center for Augmenting Human Intellect" (paper presented at the AFIPS '68 Proceedings of the Fall Joint Computer Conference, part I, San Francisco, CA, December 9–11, 1968).

3. About a year later, Engelbart's research group at SRI hosted the second site (after UCLA) of the ARPANET, the direct predecessor of the Internet. William Stewart writes, "Douglas Engelbart's NLS system at the Stanford Research Institute (SRI), running an SDS-940 computer with the Genie operating system … connected at about 10:30 P.M. on October 29th, 1969.… [T]he connection was established over a 50 kbps line provided by the AT&T telephone company." See William Stewart, "ARPANET—the First Internet," http://www.livinginternet.com/i/ii_arpanet.htm.

4. One hour and forty minutes of Engelbart's demo can be screened online. See, for example, https://www.youtube.com/watch?v=yJDv-zdhzMY.

5. After Engelbart left SRI, members of his research group, the Augmentation Research Center (ARC), dispersed to continue their work elsewhere, most notably at Xerox Palo Alto Research Center (Xerox PARC), where Bill English (co-inventor of the computer mouse along with Engelbart), several ARC alumni, and others, such as Turing Award winner Alan Kay (who had attended Engelbart's demo as a recent PhD graduate from the University of Utah), recreated and expanded on the ARC work. As the story goes, later, on a visit to Xerox PARC, a young Steve Jobs saw this vision of the future of the interface and then recreated and distributed it through Apple Computer, ultimately in the form of a Macintosh computer.

6. Steven Levy, *Insanely Great: The Life and Times of Macintosh, the Computer That Changed Everything* (New York: Penguin Books, 2000), 42.

7. For the history of the connections between the computer industry and the counterculture, see especially the work of science studies scholar Fred Turner, who writes:

> Individual members of [Engelbart's research group] maintained substantial connections to various elements of the counterculture. In the late 1960s, Engelbart and others experimented with LSD and visited several communes; in 1972 they attended sessions of Werner Erhard's Erhard Seminar Training (EST) movement. As Engelbart later recalled, he was "very empathetic to the counterculture's notions of community and how that could help with creativity, rationality and how a group works together."

See Fred Turner, *From Counterculture to Cyberculture: Stewart Brand, the Whole Earth Network, and the Rise of Digital Utopianism* (Chicago: University of Chicago Press, 2006), 109.

8. *Oxford English Dictionary*, entry 2.a. for "demo":

2. orig. U.S. a. An item of merchandise (esp. a car or other vehicle) which can be tested by prospective buyers; esp. one which is then sold at a reduced price; a demonstration model. [Examples] 1935 La Crosse (Wisconsin) Tribune & Leader Press 29 Sept. 15/4 (advt.) Used car specials 1935 Olds Six demo. 1949 N.Y. Times 23 Jan. v. 6 (advt.) Sensational values…New Cars & Demos included.

9. At the time, the director of the ARPA Information Processing Techniques Office was Internet pioneer Robert Taylor. See John Markoff, *What the Dormouse Said: How the Sixties Counterculture Shaped the Personal Computer Industry* (New York: Penguin, 2005), 240.

10. Interestingly, while Engelbart's vision was never forgotten, his pioneering role was forgotten for decades. However, starting in the 1990s, well before the end of his life in 2013, he was again recognized as the visionary he was with a series of symposia and prestigious awards, including the National Medal of Technology, conferred by President Bill Clinton in 2000.

11. Stewart Brand's biography/chronology as posted to the website of the Long Now Foundation: http://sb.longnow.org/SB_homepage/Bio.html.

12. Turner explained the aims of Brand and USCO like this: "The members of USCO created art intended to transform the audience's consciousness. They also drew on many diverse electronic technologies to achieve their effects. Strobe lights, light projectors, tape decks, stereo speakers, slide sorters—for USCO, the products of technocratic industry served as handy tools for transforming their viewers' collective mind-set. So did psychedelic drugs. Marijuana and peyote and, later, LSD, offered members of USCO, including Brand, a chance to engage in a mystical experience of togetherness." See Turner, *From Counterculture to Cyberculture*, 49.

13. Stewart Brand, "Chapter 1: Demo or Die," in *The Media Lab: Inventing the Future at MIT* (New York: Viking, 1987), 4–5.

14. I was a graduate student and then a research scientist at the MIT Media Lab for most of the decade of the 1990s.

15. Eight minutes of Terry Winograd's famous SHRDLU demo is available online at https://www.youtube.com/watch?v=bo4RvYJYOzI.

16. It was also considered a seminal work in the field of cognitive psychology. Its main academic journal devoted an entire issue to Winograd's dissertation. See Terry Winograd, "Understanding Natural Language," *Cognitive Psychology* 3, no. 1 (January 1972).

17. Arthur L. Norberg, ed., *An Interview with Terry Allen Winograd* (Minneapolis: Charles Babbage Institute, Center for the History of Information Processing, University of Minnesota, December 11, 1991), https://conservancy.umn.edu/handle/11299/107717.

18. Norbert Wiener, "Some Moral and Technical Consequences of Automation," *Science* 131, no. 3410 (May 6, 1960): 1355–1358.

19. Alan M. Turing, "Computing Machinery and Intelligence," *Mind* 49 (1950).

20. Philosopher Hannah Arendt distinguishes rhetoric from dialectic like this: "The chief distinction between persuasion and dialectic is that the former always addresses a multitude (*peithein ta pléthé*) whereas dialectic is possible only as a dialogue between two. Socrates' mistake was to address his judges in the form of dialectic, which is why he could not persuade them." See Hannah Arendt, "Philosophy and Politics," *Social Research: An International Quarterly* 57, no. 1 (Spring 1990): 79.

21. Bruno Latour writes:

> About what do they talk so irreverently? *Cookery* [my emphasis to highlight the connection to cookbooks and recipes] first, and then the skills of the greatest playwrights, the greatest sculptors, the greatest musicians, the greatest architects, the greatest orators, the greatest statesmen, the greatest tragedians. All of these people are dumped because they don't know what they know in the didactic fashion that Professor Socrates wants to impose on the people of Athens.…[T]hese were the only means by which the *demos* could accomplish this most extraordinary feat: to represent itself publicly to the public, to render visible what it is and what it wants. All the centuries of art and literature, all the public spaces, the temples, the Acropolis, the agora—Socrates is denigrating one by one…Socrates appeals to reason and reflection—but then all the arts, all the sites, all the occasions where this reflexivity takes the very specific form of the whole dealing with the whole, are deemed illegitimate.…No wonder Socrates was called the numbfish! What he paralyzes with his electric sting is the very life, the Body Politic [of Athens].

See Bruno Latour, *Pandora's Hope: Essays on the Reality of Science Studies* (Cambridge, MA: Harvard University Press, 1999), 244–245.

22. In a text frequently cited in discussions of aesthetics, Pliny the Elder (23–79 CE) recounts a competition between artists in which Zeuxis painted a bunch of grapes so realistic that birds flew to the canvas to eat them, but Parrhasios painted an image of a curtain on a wall and tricked his rivals into trying to open the curtain. Parrhasios won the competition for tricking trained artists and not just birds. See Pliny, *Natural History: A Selection* (London: Penguin, 1991), 323–342.

23. Note that the term "simulacra" is used in French translations of Plato's term "phantasmata," but in English translations of, for instance, the *Sophist*, one is more likely to find a phrase like "phantastic likenesses." My use of "simulacrum" thus follows the contemporary French philosophical discourse on the topic and the ways the French discussion has been imported via translation into English. See, for example, Gilles Deleuze (trans. Rosalind Krauss), "Plato and the Simulacrum," *October* 27 (Winter 1983).

24. Nietzsche's legacy is difficult to reconstruct:

> Nietzsche never wrote a systematic treatise on the sophists and instead discussed them in a rather fragmentary manner in a variety of texts over a period of almost two decades. Further, with the exception of three quite brief passages—in *Human, All-Too-Human* 221, *Dawn* 168, and the "Ancients," *Twilight of the Idols* 2—Nietzsche did not publish any of his remarks about the sophists, confining his discussions to his 1872–1873 lecture notes in the history of Greek rhetoric ("Description of Ancient Rhetoric" and "The History of Greek Eloquence"), the 1872 essay "Homer's Contest," and several passages collected posthumously in *The Will To Power*.

See Scott Consigny, "Nietzsche's Reading of the Sophists," *Rhetoric Review* 13, no. 1 (Autumn 1994).

25. Philosopher and anthropologist of finance Fabian Muniesa has called this effort the philosophical problem of the simulacrum. See Fabian Muniesa, *The Provoked Economy: Economic Reality and the Performative Turn* (New York: Routledge, 2014), 20. Muniesa insists, however, that this

is more than a problem for philosophy, that understanding or misunderstanding "simulacra" as real or not real has implications for how the financial markets work. For example, Muniesa cites Ellen Hertz, "Stock Markets as 'Simulacra': Observation That Participates," *Tsantsa* 5 (2000). Hertz argues that the "simulacra" of financial markets are the "speculators" who are said not to be adding real economic value and are in contrast to "investors," who do add value even if "investors" and "speculators" are objectively doing the same thing: buying and selling financial instruments on the market. The only way they can be distinguished is according to their private motivations, not their public actions.

26. Aristotle, *Rhetoric*, trans. W. Rhys Roberts (New York: Modern Library, 1954), I.1.

27. See section 3 of Christof Rapp, "Aristotle's Rhetoric," in *The Stanford Encyclopedia of Philosophy*, ed. Edward N. Zalta (Stanford, CA: Stanford University Press, Spring 2010), https://plato .stanford.edu/entries/aristotle-rhetoric/.

28. Aristotle, *Rhetoric*, I.10–14.

29. Aristotle, *Rhetoric*, I.9.

30. Aristotle, *Rhetoric*, I.4–8.

31. William Shakespeare, *Julius Caesar*, 1623, http://shakespeare.mit.edu/julius_caesar/index.html.

32. Reviel Netz, *The Shaping of Deduction in Greek Mathematics: A Study in Cognitive History* (Cambridge: Cambridge University Press, 1999), 6–7.

33. Netz, *The Shaping of Deduction in Greek Mathematics*, 293, as cited in Bruno Latour, "The Netz-Works of Greek Deductions," *Social Studies of Science* 38, no. 3 (2008).

34. Netz, *The Shaping of Deduction in Greek Mathematics*, 161.

35. Netz, *The Shaping of Deduction in Greek Mathematics*, 47.

36. Netz, *The Shaping of Deduction in Greek Mathematics*, 57.

37. In the following sentence, Netz continues, saying, "This implies that by, say, c. 360 B.C., much of Greek mathematics was articulated in the Euclidean style." See Netz, *The Shaping of Deduction in Greek Mathematics*, 275.

38. Netz states, "We cannot be far mistaken in assuming that, on average, no more than one or two Greek mathematicians were born each year. Probably the average was even lower." See Netz, *The Shaping of Deduction in Greek Mathematics*, 283.

39. According to legend, Plato had the following inscribed above the door to his Academy: let no one ignorant of geometry come under my roof. This is the declaration paraphrased by computer scientist Seymour Papert in a quotation I included in the introduction to this book.

40. Netz writes, "How is necessity sustained by proofs? … As a rule, the necessity of assertions is either self-evident (as in starting-points) or dependent on nothing beyond the immediate background. Rarely, an immediate post-factum justification is required, made briefly so as not to yield a hiatus; sometimes a recycling is made, but this is done only once or twice in a

given proof and such recyclings are made at relatively short distances. Finally, the structure of derivation is fully explicit. Immediate inspection is possible; this, and no meta-mathematical consideration, is the key to necessity." See Netz, *The Shaping of Deduction in Greek Mathematics*, 214–215.

41. Netz points out that although Aristotle is relatively easy to follow on this point, Plato is not:

> Plato's works suggest that mathematicians already had a certain terminology—Plato does this by allowing his mathematical passages to be filled with what looks like jargon. This jargon is often different from the Euclidean one, but there is no reason to suppose Plato is trying to use the correct jargon. Otherwise, Plato is strangely reticent about such aspects of mathematical practice as, for instance, the use of letters in diagrams. In general, his use of mathematics is done at a considerable distance from it, and does not allow us to see clearly what was the shape of the mathematics he knew.

See Netz, *The Shaping of Deduction in Greek Mathematics*, 276.

42. Marshall McLuhan, *The Gutenberg Galaxy: The Making of Typographic Man* (Toronto: University of Toronto Press, 1962), 177.

43. The visual metaphors of Plato's philosophy offer another way to see how the visual persists in a mostly verbal and written practice of dialectic. Havelock writes, "One can say that repeatedly, in striving for a language which shall describe that new level of mental activity which we style abstract, he [Plato] tends to relapse into metaphors of vision….The crucial example is his [Plato's] use of the Greek word for 'view' or 'contemplation' (*theoria*), which to be sure has properly and happily transmuted itself into our word 'theory,' signifying a wholly abstract level of discourse, but which in Plato continually suggests the 'contemplation' of realities which once achieved are there to be seen." See Eric Alfred Havelock, *Preface to Plato* (Cambridge, MA: Belknap Press / Harvard University Press, 1963), Kindle locs. 3399–3403.

44. Havelock, *Preface to Plato*.

45. Walter J. Ong, *Orality and Literacy: The Technologizing of the Word* (New York: Routledge, 2002).

46. John Bagnell Bury, *A History of Greece to the Death of Alexander the Great* (London: MacMillan, 1900), 241. Bury originally published this text in 1900 but still, in the fall of 1981, my first term at Yale College, I was required to purchase a later edition of Bury's book as a primary text for Professor Donald Kagan's "Introduction to Ancient Greek History." Professor Kagan's lectures for his course are available online as part of the Open Yale courses project at http://oyc.yale.edu/classics/clcv-205, but, in the current course offering, I note that Professor Kagan no longer uses the Bury textbook. See http://oyc.yale.edu/classics/clcv-205#syllabus.

47. See Pericles's famous funeral oration as recorded in book 2 of Thucydides's *History of the Peloponnesian War*. See Thucydides, *The Peloponnesian War* (New York: E. P. Dutton, 1910).

48. In Plato's dialogue *Menexenus*, Socrates mentions Aspasia as Pericles's rhetoric teacher as well as his own:

> Socrates: I have an excellent mistress in the art of rhetoric—she who has made so many good speakers, and one who was the best among all the Hellenes—Pericles, the son of Xanthippus.
> Menexenus: And who is she? I suppose that you mean Aspasia.

See Plato, *The Complete Works of Plato* [Annotated], trans. Benjamin Jowett (Latus ePublishing), Kindle locs. 18619–18621.

49. G. B. Kerferd, *The Sophistic Movement* (Cambridge: Cambridge University Press, 1981), 18.

50. See Plutarch, *Pericles*, chap. 32, in Plutarch, *Plutarch's Lives*, trans. Bernadotte Perrin (Cambridge, MA: Harvard University Press, 1916).

51. Daniel Smith, "Essay 1: The Concept of the Simulacrum: Deleuze and the Overturning of Platonism," in *Essays on Deleuze* (Edinburgh: Edinburgh University Press, 2012), 5. Does this characterization of political, social, economic, and personal life sound familiar? Philosopher McKenzie Wark contends that this is also the state of the world today: "Welcome to gamespace. Gamespace is where and how we live today. It is everywhere and nowhere: the main chance, the best shot, the big leagues, the only game in town." See McKenzie Wark, *Gamer Theory* (Cambridge, MA: Harvard University Press, 2007).

52. Arendt, "Philosophy and Politics."

53. Gilles Deleuze, *Difference and Repetition* (New York: Columbia University Press, 1994), 60.

54. Gilles Deleuze, *The Logic of Sense*, trans. Mark Lester and Charles Stivale (New York: Columbia University Press, 1990), 296, as cited in Smith, "The Concept of the Simulacrum," 11.

55. Deleuze writes:

> How are we to explain the fact that of the three great texts on division—the *Phaedrus*, the *Statesman*, and the *Sophist*, the method of division is paradoxically employed not to evaluate just claimants but, rather, to hunt down the false claimant as such, to define the being (or rather the nonbeing) of the simulacrum. The sophist himself is the simulacral being, the satyr or centaur, the Proteus who intrudes and insinuates himself everywhere. Construed thus, however, the ending of the *Sophist* may well contain the most extraordinary adventure of Platonism. Plato, by dint of inquiring in the direction of the simulacrum, discovers, in the flash of an instant as he leans over its abyss, that the simulacrum is not simply a false copy, but that it calls into question the very notions of the copy…and of the model. The final definition of the sophist leads us to the point where we can no longer distinguish him from Socrates himself: the ironist operating in private by elliptical arguments.

See Deleuze, "Plato and the Simulacrum."

56. According to Kerferd, "The Socratic method, to the extent that it may have originated with Socrates, nonetheless originated from within the sophistic movement, if only because Socrates himself was a part of that movement." See Kerferd, *The Sophistic Movement*, 34.

57. Arendt, "Philosophy and Politics," 81.

58. Latour borrows this notion of "felicity conditions" from speech act theory. See J. L. Austin, *How to Do Things with Words,* The William James Lectures (Cambridge, MA: Harvard University Press, 1962). See also John R. Searle, *Speech Acts: An Essay in the Philosophy of Language* (London: Cambridge University Press, 1969). In recent work, Latour intimately connects different felicity conditions to different modes of existence. See Bruno Latour, *An Inquiry into Modes of Existence: An Anthropology of the Moderns* (Cambridge, MA: Harvard University Press, 2013).

59. Bruno Latour, *Pandora's Hope: Essays on the Reality of Science Studies* (Cambridge, MA: Harvard University Press, 1999), 237, 241–242.

60. Latour, *Pandora's Hope*, 252.

61. Aristotle, *The Nicomachean Ethics,* W. D. Ross, J. L. Ackrill, and J. O. Urmson, eds. (New York: Oxford University Press, 1998), bk. I.3.

62. Latour, *Pandora's Hope*, 259.

63. Ian Hacking, *The Emergence of Probability: A Philosophical Study of Early Ideas about Probability, Induction and Statistical Inference*, Cambridge Series on Statistical and Probabilistic Mathematics (Cambridge: Cambridge University Press, 1975), 75.

64. Daniel Rosenberg writes:

> The semantic function of data is specifically rhetorical.…The word "data" comes to English from Latin. It is the plural of the Latin word *datum*, which itself is the neuter past participle of the verb *dare*, to give. A "datum" in English, then, is something given in an argument, something taken for granted. This is in contrast to "fact," which derives from the neuter past participle of the Latin verb *facere*, to do, whence we have the English word "fact," for that which was done, occurred, or exists. The etymology of "data" also contrasts with that of "evidence," from the Latin verb *vidére*, to see. There are important distinctions here: facts are ontological, evidence is epistemological, data is rhetorical.

See Daniel Rosenberg, "Data before the Fact," in *"Raw Data" Is an Oxymoron*, ed. Lisa Gitelman (Cambridge, MA: MIT Press, 2013), 18.

65. Hacking, *The Emergence of Probability*, 22–23.

66. Hacking, *The Emergence of Probability*, 26.

67. Hacking, *The Emergence of Probability*, 26–27.

68. Hacking, *The Emergence of Probability*, 28.

69. Hacking, *The Emergence of Probability*, 24.

70. Michel Foucault, *The Order of Things: An Archaeology of the Human Sciences* (New York: Routledge, 2002), Kindle locs. 1277–1279.

71. According to Hacking, "Each thing has a signature and the physician must master the signatures. Signatures are ultimately derived from the sentences in the stars, but a bountiful God has made them legible on earth." See Hacking, *The Emergence of Probability*, 42.

72. Foucault, *The Order of Things*, Kindle locs. 1717–1724.

73. The story of philosophical languages is told in Umberto Eco, *The Search for the Perfect Language*, The Making of Europe (Cambridge, MA: Blackwell, 1995). The specific moment of this story evoked in the Foucault quotation earlier is elaborated in Hacking, *The Emergence of Probability*, 81: "In the Renaissance there were signs, real signs, written by God on nature. People spoke with signs, but so did the world around us. The testimony of man and of nature was one. Then the sign became divided into "natural" and "arbitrary." Hence the desperate plunge into "real

characteristic" which would conjoin, if only in constant conjunction, what the atheist Hobbes had put asunder. But just as there was required a theory of the conventional side of signs, so there was needed a theory of their natural side, which is internal evidence and probability."

74. Steven Shapin, *The Scientific Revolution* (Chicago: University of Chicago Press, 1996), Kindle locs. 954–956.

75. Steven Shapin and Simon Schaffer, *Leviathan and the Air-Pump: Hobbes, Boyle, and the Experimental Life: With a New Introduction by the Authors* (Princeton, NJ: Princeton University Press, 2011).

76. Marie Boas Hall, *Boyle and Seventeenth-Century Chemistry* (Cambridge: Cambridge University Press, 1958), 185, as cited in Shapin and Schaffer, *Leviathan and the Air-Pump*, 30.

77. Christopher Wren, 30 July/9 August 1663, in Thomas Birch, *The History of the Royal Society of London for the Improving of Natural Knowledge, from Its First Rise*, 4 vols. (London: Royal Society, 1756–1757), 1: 288, as cited in Shapin and Schaffer, *Leviathan and the Air-Pump*, 31.

78. See Mark Waddell, *Jesuit Science and the End of Nature's Secrets* (Burlington, VT: Ashgate, 2015), 142–143. Waddell argues that English squeamishness about spectacle and public display was rooted not in a lingering Platonism but, in part, by the anti-Catholicism of the time.

79. John Wilkins, "Foreword," in *Mathematical Magick* (Oxford: Rick Baldwin, 1648).

80. Jan V. Golinski, "A Noble Spectacle: Phosphorus and the Public Cultures of Science in the Early Royal Society," *Isis: A Journal of the History of Science* 80 (1989): 16.

81. Golinski, "A Noble Spectacle," 24.

82. Boyle's experiments that led to this were done not with his air pump but rather with a specially constructed J-shaped tube filled with mercury (like the air pump, also built by Robert Hooke). See Shapin and Schaffer, *Leviathan and the Air-Pump*, 168. See also Charles Webster, "The Discovery of Boyle's Law, and the Concept of the Elasticity of Air in the Seventeenth Century," *Archive for History of Exact Sciences* 2 (1965).

83. Robert Curley, *Scientists and Inventors of the Renaissance* (Encyclopedia Britannica and Rosen Publishing, 2012), 95.

84. Robert Boyle, "Chapter V: Two New Experiments Touching the Measure of the Force of the Spring of Air Compress'd and Dilated," in *A Defence of the Doctrine Touching the Spring and Weight of the Air* (London: Thomas Robinson, 1662), 59.

85. Boyle, "Two New Experiments Touching the Measure of the Force of the Spring of Air Compress'd and Dilated," 67.

86. Ray Solomonoff, *A Preliminary Report on a General Theory of Inductive Inference*, Report V-131 (Cambridge, MA: Zator Corporation, February 4, 1960). This work was elaborated in Ray Solomonoff, "A Formal Theory of Inductive Inference Part I," *Information and Control* 7, no. 1 (March 1964), and Ray Solomonoff, "A Formal Theory of Inductive Inference Part II," *Information and Control* 7, no. 2 (June 1964).

87. Andrey Kolmogorov, "On Tables of Random Numbers," *Sankhyā Series A* 25 (1963).

88. Media scholar Jonathan Sterne suggests that we consider "the histories of communication and representation in terms of compression." That a kind of guessing, of abduction, can now be translated into an algorithm of data compression seems to illustrate Sterne's point. However, Sterne argues that this new primacy of compression should compel us to turn our attention away from media and toward an investigation of data formats. See Jonathan Sterne, *MP3: The Meaning of a Format* (Durham, NC: Duke University Press, 2012), Kindle locs. 267–268. Instead, I argue that this translation, which rewrites a form of reasoning into an algorithm, should give us pause and compel us to mind the gap and consider what has been lost when such a radical reduction has been executed on what we might previously have considered a form of human thought. In other words, let us resist equating thinking and learning with data compression.

89. See, for example, Jonathan Vanian, "Why Data Is the New Oil," *Fortune*, July 11, 2016, http://fortune.com/2016/07/11/data-oil-brainstorm-tech/.

90. CAPTCHA is an acronym for Completely Automated Public Turing test to tell Computers and Humans Apart. The "Turing Test" will be discussed in the conclusion to this book.

91. Luis von Ahn, Manuel Blum, Nicholas J. Hopper, and John Langford, "CAPTCHA: Using Hard AI Problems for Security" (paper presented at EUROCRYPT 2003: International Conference on the Theory and Applications of Cryptographic Techniques, May 2003).

92. Tiziana Terranova, "Free Labor: Producing Culture for the Digital Economy," *Social Text, 63* 18, no. 2 (Summer 2000).

93. http://www.internetlivestats.com/google-search-statistics/.

94. Charles S. Peirce, "The Proper Treatment of Hypotheses: A Preliminary Chapter, toward an Examination of Hume's Argument against Miracles, in Its Logic and in Its History (MS 692)," in *Historical Perspectives on Peirce's Logic of Science: A History of Science*, ed. Carolyn Eisele (New York: Mouton De Gruyter, [1901] 1985).

95. Charles S. Peirce, "A Deleted Passage," in *Pragmatism as a Principle and Method of Right Thinking: The 1903 Harvard "Lectures on Pragmatism,"* ed. Patricia Ann Turisi (Albany: State University of New York Press, [1903] 1997).

96. Hito Steyerl, "A Sea of Data: Apophenia and Pattern (Mis-)Recognition," *E-Flux Journal* 72 (April 2016), https://www.e-flux.com/journal/72/60480/a-sea-of-data-apophenia-and-pattern-mis-recognition/.

97. James J. Thomas and Kristin A. Cook, "Executive Summary," in *Illuminating the Path: The Research and Development Agenda for Visual Analytics*, ed. James J.Thomson and Kristin A. Cook (National Visualization and Analytics Center and IEEE, 2005), 2.

98. Perusal of the technical literature of visual analytics reveals the occasional use of the term "abduction" to describe the type of inferencing the computational tools are built to facilitate; for example, the research project at the University of North Carolina, Charlotte, on abductive

intelligence (see http://srvac.uncc.edu/research/stab-story-abduction-proactive-intelligence). See also the description of abduction in S. J. Attfield, S. J., S. K. Hara, and B. L. William Wong, "Sensemaking in Visual Analytics: Processes and Challenges," *International Symposium on Visual Analytics Science and Technology*, ed. J. Kohlhammer and D. Keim (Salt Lake City, UT: IEEE, 2010).

99. Steven Spielberg, dir., *Minority Report* (2002). 20th Century Fox.

100. "Predictive policing" is the name of the current, very real, and increasingly popular executive power exercised by intelligence agencies, the military, and the police at many scales of government—from towns and cities to nation-states and international military interventions.

101. Charles S. Peirce, "On the Logic of Drawing History from Ancient Documents, Especially from Testimonies," in *Collected Papers of Charles Sanders Peirce*, vols. 7–8, ed. Arthur W. Burks (Cambridge, MA: Harvard University Press, [1901] 1958), 219.

102. Charles S. Peirce, "Harvard Lectures on Pragmatism," in *Collected Papers of Charles Sanders Peirce*, vols. 1–6, ed. Charles Hartshorne and Paul Weiss (Cambridge, MA: Harvard University Press, [1901] 1931–1935), 171–172.

103. "Classic" books explaining this genre include Edward R. Tufte, *The Visual Display of Quantitative Information* (Cheshire, CT: Graphics Press, 2001), and Stuart K. Card, Jock Mackinlay, and Ben Shneiderman, *Readings in Information Visualization: Using Vision to Think* (San Francisco: Morgan Kaufmann, 1999).

104. Joseph Dumit, *Picturing Personhood: Brain Scans and Biomedical Identity* (Princeton, NJ: Princeton University Press, 2004).

105. Paul N. Edwards, *A Vast Machine: Computer Models, Climate Data, and the Politics of Global Warming* (Cambridge, MA: MIT Press, 2010).

106. Ian Bogost, *Persuasive Games: The Expressive Power of Videogames* (Cambridge, MA: MIT Press, 2007).

107. Vilém Flusser, *Towards a Philosophy of Photography* (London: Reaktion Books, 2000), 14.

108. Flusser, *Towards a Philosophy of Photography*, 15.

109. Stephen Wolfram earned a PhD from the California Institute of Technology at age 20 and won a MacArthur "Genius" Award in 1981 at the age of 21. See https://www.macfound.org/fellows /93/. After that, Wolfram made his fortune creating the Mathematica software system, and Steve Jobs became one of the first supporters of the software when he bundled it with the computers made by NeXT Corporation.

110. Shapin, *The Scientific Revolution*, Kindle locs. 659–664.

111. Stephen Wolfram, *A New Kind of Science* (Champaign, IL: Wolfram Media, 2002), 1.

112. In the satirical fictional writings of Douglas Adams, the computer Deep Thought takes 7.5 million years to calculate the answer to life, the universe, and everything. It determines that the

answer is 42. See Douglas Adams, *Life, the Universe and Everything*, vol. 3 of *The Hitchhiker's Guide to the Galaxy* (London: Pan Macmillian, [1982] 2009).

113. See William Shakespeare, *Merchant of Venice*, 1600, http://shakespeare.mit.edu/merchant /full.html.

114. Wolfram, *A New Kind of Science*, 1.

115. Wolfram also breaks a third rule here and throughout the book, but it is not a rule peculiar to science and mathematics. Rather, it is a more or less ubiquitous rule of social decorum: "Do not insist that you are smart, even if you are."

116. http://bactra.org/reviews/wolfram/.

117. J. R. Minkel, "A New Kind of Science Author Pays Brainy Undergrad $25,000 for Identifying Simplest Computer: But Will It Jumpstart Stephen Wolfram's Scientific Revolution?," *Scientific American*, October 25, 2007, https://www.scientificamerican.com/article/simplest-computer-new -kind-science/.

118. Drew McDermott, "Artificial Intelligence Meets Natural Stupidity," in *Mind Design: Philosophy, Psychology, Artificial Intelligence*, ed. John Haugeland (Cambridge, MA: MIT Press, 1981), 5–18.

119. See, for example, Palash Sarkar, "A Brief History of Cellular Automata," *ACM Computing Surveys* 32, no. 1 (March 2000): 80–107.

120. For example, Lev Manovich's "cultural analytics," Richard Rogers's "digital methods," Franco Moretti's "distant reading," and Duncan Watt's "computational social science." See Lev Manovich, "Instagram and Contemporary Image" (manovich.net, 2016); Richard Rogers, *Digital Methods* (Cambridge, MA: MIT Press, 2013); Franco Moretti, *Distant Reading* (London: Verso, 2013); Duncan Watts, "Computational Social Science: Exciting Progress and Future Directions," *The Bridge on Frontiers of Engineering (National Academy of Engineering)* 43, no. 4 (December 20, 2013), https://www.nae.edu/19582/Bridge/106112/106118.aspx. See also the journal *Big Data and Society* at http://journals.sagepub.com/home/bds and especially Rob Kitchin, "Big Data, New Epistemologies and Paradigm Shifts," *Big Data and Society* 1, no. 1 (April–June 2014): 1–12

121. Wolfram, *A New Kind of Science*, 2.

122. The JavaScript code can be run or downloaded at the book's website: http://softwarearts .info.

123. For very simple, repetitive patterns, see also the results for rule sets 58, 69, 70, 77, 78, 79, 92, 93, 94, 109, 114, 118, 122, 133, 141, 147, 156, 157, 158, 163, 177, 178, 179, 186, 188, 190, 197, 198, 199, 214, 230, 242, 246, and 250.

124. The following rule sets also produce a single vertical line: 36, 44, 68, 76, 100, 108, 132, 140, 164, 172, 196, 204, 228, and 236.

125. Given a single black square, the following rule sets also yield some sort of simple diagonal line: 10, 14, 16, 20, 24, 34, 38, 42, 46, 48, 52, 56, 66, 74, 80, 84, 88, 98, 106, 112, 116, 120, 130, 134, 138, 139, 142, 143, 144, 148, 152, 155, 162, 166, 170, 171, 173, 174, 175, 176, 180, 184, 185,

187, 189, 194, 202, 208, 209, 211, 212, 213, 216, 226, 227, 229, 231, 234, 240, 241, 243, 244, 245, and 248.

126. The least interesting patterns produced include those of rule sets 40, 64, 72, 128, 136, 151, 159, 160, 168, 183, 191, 192, 200, 215, 223, 224, 232, 233, 235, 237, 239, 247, 249, 251, 253, and, of course, 255.

127. Stripes are also generated by rule sets 21, 23, 31, 55, 63, 87, 95, 119, and 127.

128. The following rule sets also produce nested patterns: 82, 90, 102, 105, 126, 129, 146, 150, 153, 154, 161, 165, 167, 181, 182, 195, 210, and 218.

129. Wolfram, *A New Kind of Science*, 231.

130. Wolfram, *A New Kind of Science*, 232.

131. Wolfram, *A New Kind of Science*, 235.

132. Wolfram, *A New Kind of Science*.

133. Wolfram, *A New Kind of Science*, 262.

134. Flusser, *Towards a Philosophy of Photography*.

135. Wolfram, *A New Kind of Science*, 281.

136. Matthew Cook, "Universality in Elementary Cellular Automata," *Complex Systems* 15 (2004): 13.

137. Elwyn R. Berlekamp, John Horton Conway, and Richard K. Guy, *Winning Ways for Your Mathematical Plays*, 2nd ed., 4 vols. (Natick, MA: A. K. Peters, 2001), 931.

138. Wolfram, *A New Kind of Science*, 691.

139. Cook, "Universality in Elementary Cellular Automata," 1–40. For his proof, the necessary components of a known Turing-complete computational system are articulated in the formalism of the cellular automaton and the pieces are assembled into a fully functioning simulation of the known system. Cook first assembles a tag system (see Emil Post's work cited in chapter 7, on grammar) known to be Turing complete. His paper describes a multistep construction in which tag systems are built using a simpler construction, cyclic tag systems, which are in turn built with the even simpler operations of the gliders of rule set 110.

140. Wolfram, *A New Kind of Science*, 715–848.

141. Wolfram, *A New Kind of Science*, 5–7.

142. Wolfram, *A New Kind of Science*, 7–11.

143. Wolfram, *A New Kind of Science*, 12–16.

144. Wolfram, *A New Kind of Science*, 21–22.

145. Judith Rosen writes, "In its first week on sale, the 1,179-page book, which retails for $44.95, hit #1 on Amazon.com. Within a month, it reached #16 on the *New York Times* extended bestseller

list, though it was unclear whether the book would be able to sustain its momentum.... Three more printings and 150,000 additional copies later, the answer is 'yes.'" See Judith Rosen, "Weighing Wolfram's 'New Kind of Science,'" *Publishers Weekly* 250, no. 2 (January 13, 2003), https://www.publishersweekly.com/pw/print/20030113/40516-weighing-wolfram-s-new-kind-of-science.html.

Chapter 7

1. Michel Foucault, *The Order of Things: An Archaeology of the Human Sciences* (New York: Routledge, 2002), Kindle locs. 1277–1284.

2. What Foucault called "epistemes" is similar to what historian Thomas Kuhn called "paradigms." In Kuhn's vocabulary, paradigms are "incommensurable." See Thomas S. Kuhn, *The Structure of Scientific Revolutions* (Chicago: University of Chicago Press, 1970).

3. Claude Elwood Shannon and Warren Weaver, *The Mathematical Theory of Communication* (Urbana: University of Illinois Press, 1949), 8.

4. For example, the 2009 winner of the Nobel Memorial Prize in Economic Sciences, Elinor Ostrom, coauthored a grammar of institutions. See Sue E. S. Crawford and Elinor Ostrom, "A Grammar of Institutions," *American Political Science Review* 89, no. 3 (September 1995).

5. "The top ten cited sources during the period [1972–1992] were: Marx, Lenin, Shakespeare, Aristotle, the Bible, Plato, Freud, Chomsky, Hegel and Cicero." See "Chomsky Is Citation Champ," *MIT Tech Talk*, April 15, 1992, http://news.mit.edu/1992/citation-0415.

6. Sam Tanenhaus, "Noam Chomsky and the Bicycle Theory," *New York Times*, October 31, 2016.

7. Noam Chomsky, *Syntactic Structures* (The Hague: Mouton, 1957).

8. Noam Chomsky, *Cartesian Linguistics: A Chapter in the History of Rationalist Thought* (New York: Harper and Row, 1966).

9. As cited in Ivan Illich and Barry Sanders, *ABC: The Alphabetization of the Popular Mind* (San Francisco: North Point Press, 1988), 68.

10. Benedict R. O'G. Anderson, *Imagined Communities: Reflections on the Origin and Spread of Nationalism* (London: Verso, 2006).

11. This work continues in institutions such as SIL International, which describes itself as follows: "SIL International is a faith-based nonprofit organization committed to serving language communities worldwide as they build capacity for sustainable language development. SIL does this primarily through research, translation, training and materials development.... Founded in 1934, SIL (originally known as the Summer Institute of Linguistics, Inc.) has grown from a small summer linguistics training program with two students to a staff of over 5,000, coming from over 84 countries. Currently SIL works alongside speakers of more than 1,600 languages in over 85 countries." See https://www.sil.org/about.

12. Sylvain Auroux, *La revolution technologique de la grammatisation* (Liège: Pierre Mardaga, 1994), 121.

13. Auroux, *La revolution technologique de la grammatisation*, 122.

14. Auroux, *La revolution technologique de la grammatisation*, 138.

15. Michel Foucault explained the project like this:

> General grammar is not at all the same as comparative grammar: the comparisons it makes between different languages are not its object; they are merely employed as a method. This is because its generality does not consist in the discovery of peculiarly grammatical laws, common to all linguistic domains, which could then be used to display the structure of any possible language in an ideal and constricting unity; if it is indeed general, then it is so to the extent that it attempts to make visible, below the level of grammatical rules, but at the same level as their foundation, the representative function of discourse—whether it be the vertical function, which designates what is represented, or the horizontal function, which links what is represented to the same mode as thought.

See Foucault, *The Order of Things*, Kindle locs. 2293–2299.

16. Foucault writes, "Hence, too, the project of creating an encyclopaedia 'of the sciences and arts,' which would not follow the connecting links of knowledge itself but would be accommodated in the form of the language, within the space opened up in words themselves." See Foucault, *The Order of Things*, Kindle locs. 2230–2231.

17. Foucault writes, "Destutt de Tracy [the inventor of the field of 'ideology' as discussed in chapter 2] once observed that the best treatises on logic, in the eighteenth century, were written by grammarians: this is because the prescriptions of grammar at that time were of an analytic and not an aesthetic order." See Foucault, *The Order of Things*, Kindle locs. 2213–2214.

18. Condillac writes, "Toute langue est une méthode analytique, et toute méthode analytique est une langue. Ces deux vérités, aussi simples que neuves, ont été démontrées; la première dans ma grammaire; la seconde, dans ma logique; et on a pu se convaincre de la lumière qu'elles répandent sur l'art de parler et sur l'art de raisonner, qu'elles réduisent à un seul et même art." See Condillac, *La Langue des Calculs* (Paris: Sandoz et Fischbacher, [1780] 1877).

19. L. Bloomfield, *Language* (New York: Holt, 1933), 6–7, as cited in Robin Lakoff, "Review of 'Grammaire générale et raisonnée' by C. Lancelot, A. Arnauld and Herbert H. Brekle," *Language* 45, no. 2, pt. 1 (June 1969): 343.

20. C. Lancelot, *Nouvelle méthode pour apprendre facilement la langue latine* (Paris: A. Vitré, 1644).

21. Michel Foucault, "Introduction," in *Grammaire générale et raisonnée*, ed. A. Arnauld and C. Lancelot (Paris: Republications Paulet, 1969), reproduced in Michel Foucault, "Introduction," in *Dits et Écrits: 1954–1988* (Paris: Gallimard, 2001), 762.

22. Commenting on the *Port-Royal Grammar* and the work that followed, the *Port-Royal Logic*, linguist Noam Chomsky wrote, "[The analysis of verbs] plays a role in the theory of reasoning developed later on in the Logic. It is used to develop what is in effect a partial theory of relations, permitting the theory of the syllogism to be extended to arguments to which it would otherwise not apply." See Chomsky, *Cartesian Linguistics*, 44.

23. The *Port-Royal Grammar* continued to be an important reference work well into the nineteenth century, as evidenced by its history of publication and republication:

See Jacques Bourquin, "Port-Royal Grammar," in *The Linguistics Encyclopedia*, ed. Kirsten Malmk-jaer (New York: Routledge, 1991).

> After its first publication in Paris in 1660, it was published again with successive additions in 1664, 1676, 1679, and 1709. In 1754, the French grammarian Duclos added to the text of 1676 "Remarks" that were regularly reprinted in later editions (1768, 1783 etc.). Moreover, the 1803 edition is preceded by an "Essay on the origin and progress of the French language" by Petitot. In the editions of 1830 (Delalain, Paris) and 1845 (Loquin, Paris), the Logic or the Art of Thinking by Arnauld and Nicole (1662) is published together with the grammar. The grammar also represents volume 41 of the *Works of Antoine Arnauld gent* (Paris, 1780). More recently, H. E. Brekle has published a critical edition (Stuttgart, 1966); the edition of 1845 has been reprinted with an historical introduction by A. Bailly (Slatkine, Geneva, 1968) and the 1830 edition with an introduction by M. Foucault (Paulet, Paris, 1969).

For the purposes of this chapter, I have referenced the 1803 edition available at the Bibliothèque nationale de France's website, http://gallica.bnf.fr: Claude Lancelot and Antoine Arnauld, *Grammaire Génerale et Raisonnée de Port-Royale, précédée d'un essai sur l'origine et les progès de la langue française (par M. Petitot)* (Paris: Chez Perlet, 1803).

24. Foucault writes:

> With logic we reflect on what nature makes us do…. [Logic] shows what is really thought and, therefore, what is true thought. Logic is the art of self-clarifying thinking and its articulation in words…. Grammar is more complex because the rules which constitute the art of speaking are not justified solely by their clarity and by making one conscious of that clarity. Grammatical rules need to be justified; and their justification needs to be demonstrated. This is the reason why, between grammar as the art of speaking and grammar as a discipline containing the foundations of this art, the relation is not purely and simply a relation of reflection: it is one of explanation. The foundations of the rules need to be examined. In grammar, as soon as I speak clearly, I speak according to the rules. But if I want to know why my language necessarily obeys these rules, it makes me return to the principles on which they are based.

See Foucault, "Introduction," in *Dits et Écrits*, 768–769.

25. Antoine Arnauld, Pierre Nicole, Claude Lancelot, and Petrus Le Mangnier, *La logique, ou, L'art de penser: Contenant, outre les règles communes, plusieurs observations nouvelles, propres à former le jugement* (Paris: Chez Jean Guignart, Chez Charles Saureux, 1662).

26. Foucault, "Introduction," in *Dits et Écrits*, 770.

27. "If one understood it, one would never sin against this rule." See Lancelot and Arnauld, *Grammaire Génerale et Raisonnée de Port-Royale*, 321.

28. Isaac Newton, *Philosophiæ Naturalis Principia Mathematica* [Mathematical Principles of Natural Philosophy] (London: Jussu Societatis Regiæ ac Typis Joseph Streater, 1687).

29. The concept of an "obligatory passage point" was developed by Michel Callon as a key issue in actor-network theory. See Michel Callon, "Elements of a Sociology of Translation: Domestication of the Scallops and the Fishermen of St Brieuc Bay," in *Power, Action and Belief: A New Sociology of Knowledge?*, ed. John Law (London: Routledge, 1986), 196–233.

30. Foucault, "Introduction," in *Dits et Écrits*, 774.

31. Foucault, *The Order of Things*, Kindle locs. 2127–2129.

32. Chomsky, *Cartesian Linguistics*, 38–39.

33. Recordings of the debate can be found online. See, for example, http://aphelis.net/chomsky
-foucault-debate-complete-video-recording/. The transcript of the debate was first published in Fons
Elders, *Reflexive Water: The Basic Concerns of Mankind* (London: Souvenir Press, 1974), 135–197. It
later appeared in Arnold I. Davidson, *Foucault and His Interlocutors* (Chicago: University of Chicago
Press, 1997), 107–145, and John Rajchman, *The Chomsky-Foucault Debate on Human Nature* (New
York: New Press, 2006), 1–67. The transcript can also be found online. See, for example, https://
chomsky.info/1971xxxx/.

34. Rajchman, *The Chomsky-Foucault Debate*, 9–10.

35. In the field of history, the fault of what I am calling "cherry picking" is frequently referred
to as "Whiggishness," an indirect citation of Herbert Butterfield, *The Whig Interpretation of History*
(New York: W. W. Norton, 1931).

36. One of Foucault's main references, philosopher Friedrich Nietzsche, points out why "antiquarian" is a pejorative term. See Friedrich Wilhelm Nietzsche, "On the Uses and Disadvantages
of History for Life," in *Nietzsche: Untimely Meditations*, ed. Daniel Breazeale and R. J. Hollingdale
(Cambridge: Cambridge University Press, 1997), 57–124. Not just Nietzscheans but also many
other contemporary historians would use the term "antiquarian" to describe someone overly
concerned with trivial facts and unconcerned with coherent argumentation and the bigger
picture.

37. Chomsky explains:

> Chomsky: Well, first I should say that I approach classical rationalism not really as a historian of science or
> a historian of philosophy, but from the rather different point of view of someone who has a certain range of
> scientific notions and is interested in seeing how at an earlier stage people may have been groping towards
> these notions, possibly without even realizing what they were groping towards.
>
> So one might say that I'm looking at history not as an antiquarian, who is interested in finding out and
> giving a precisely accurate account of what the thinking of the seventeenth century was—I don't mean to
> demean that activity, it's just not mine—but rather from the point of view of, let's say, an art lover, who
> wants to look at the seventeenth century to find in it things that are of particular value, and that obtain part
> of their value in part because of the perspective with which he approaches them.
>
> And I think that, without objecting to the other approach, my approach is legitimate; that is, I think it is
> perfectly possible to go back to earlier stages of scientific thinking on the basis of our present understanding,
> and to perceive how great thinkers were, within the limitations of their time, groping towards concepts and
> ideas and insights that they themselves could not be clearly aware of.

See Rajchman, *The Chomsky-Foucault Debate*, 10–11.

38. Rajchman, *The Chomsky-Foucault Debate*, 14.

39. Outside of linguistics, other scholars have pointed out that Chomsky's historical "Whiggishness" goes beyond his reading of Descartes. For instance, Chomsky extensively cites nineteenth-
century German philosopher, diplomat, and linguist Wilhelm von Humboldt (1767–1835).
Software studies scholar David Golumbia writes the following about Chomsky's use of Humboldt:

> One reason Chomsky reaches out to Humboldt's anti-authoritarian writings is because Humboldt has come
> down to us in a much less savory form that Chomsky does not discuss. Humboldt was the most famous
> advocate of the view that the races and the languages they spoke were part of an historic progression, so
> that some cultures and peoples were seen to be primitive forms. Much of Humboldt's work was devoted to

developing typologies of human groups, according to which Indo-European languages in particular represented a true advancement from the languages spoken by others around the world. Whether we call this Hegelianism or Romanticism or outright racism, it forms a critical part of the background of Humboldt's entirety of views, and it is curious that Chomsky leaves this out while stressing the connection of Humboldt's ethics with his linguistic views.

See David Golumbia, *The Cultural Logic of Computation* (Cambridge, MA: Harvard University Press, 2009), Kindle locs. 708–712.

40. Hans Aarsleff, "The History of Linguistics and Professor Chomsky," in *From Locke to Saussure* (Minneapolis: University of Minnesota Press, 1982), 116–117.

41. See, for example, Robin Lakoff's detailed review of a reedition of the *Port-Royal Grammar* and Chomsky's use of it in his book *Cartesian Linguistics*. Lakoff insists that the *Port-Royal Grammar* and Chomsky's twentieth-century grammar project are not so much indebted to Descartes as to a continuation of the work of Sanctius, a Spanish scholar who taught at the University of Salamanca in the sixteenth century. See Lakoff, "Review of 'Grammaire générale et raisonnée.'"

42. Marcus Tomalin, *Linguistics and the Formal Sciences: The Origins of Generative Grammar*, Cambridge Studies in Linguistics (Cambridge: Cambridge University Press, 2006), Kindle locs. 145–147.

43. Chomsky, *Cartesian Linguistics*, 40. As we will see later in this chapter, despite the assertion here that his "deep structure" is the meaning of a sentence, Chomsky does not think the deep structure of a sentence is equivalent to its meaning.

44. Recursion is a common idiom in contemporary computer programming, frequently used instead of an iterative loop. For example, in JavaScript, one can define the Fibonacci series (1, 1, 2, 3, 5, 8, 13, etc.) recursively like this:

function fibonacci (n) {if (n <= 1) {return(1);} else {return(fibonacci(n-1) + fibonacci(n-2));}}.

45. Chomsky, *Cartesian Linguistics*, 41. Lancelot and Arnauld discuss not devices but reason as the means by which finite means can be used to create an infinite production. They wrote: "One of the greatest proofs of reason…is the use we make of it to signify our thoughts, and this marvelous invention of composing from twenty-five or thirty sounds an infinite variety of words." See Lancelot and Arnauld, *Grammaire Génerale et Raisonnée de Port-Royale*, 270.

46. It is difficult to see why Chomsky attributes to Lancelot and Arnauld even implicit ideas about "devices." I have spent some time searching the 1803 edition (available online through the French Bibliothèque Nationale Gallica service: http://gallica.bnf.fr/) for any term that might be a cognate for "device." In French, one might render this term as "dispositif," "appareil," "machine," or possibly "engin," but none of these words appear in the *Port-Royal Grammar*. One might possibly translate "device" as "organe," and this is the only term present in the text. There are ten occurrences of "organe" in the almost 500 pages of the *Port-Royal Grammar*. Some of those occurrences are anatomical in nature—for example, the mouth is referred to as an organ on page 249. The reference to "organe" most pertinent to Chomsky's claim is on page 18, where speech is metaphorically described as an organ: "Now no one can doubt that man does not receive the organ of speech." Yet Lancelot and Arnauld's discussion of the "organ of speech" spans no more than a page and is not revisited later in the text.

47. Chomsky, *Cartesian Linguistics*, 15.

48. Chomsky, *Cartesian Linguistics*, 29. "Instrument" appears only once in the text of the *Port-Royal Grammar* (in a Latin phrase and thus as the word "instrumentum"). See page 454 of the edition accessible on the Gallica service website. See also Descartes's statement that "reason is a universal instrument" in René Descartes, *A Discourse on the Method: Of Correctly Conducting One's Reason and Seeking Truth in the Sciences*, trans. Ian Maclean, Oxford World's Classics (Oxford: Oxford University Press, 2006), 47. One should note that Descartes made this statement while arguing that machines "would never be able to use words or other signs by composing them as we do to declare our thoughts to others." See Descartes, *A Discourse on the Method*, 46.

49. Martin Gardner, *Logic Machines and Diagrams* (New York: McGraw-Hill, 1958), 25, fn. 1.

50. Roy Harris, *The Language Machine* (London: Duckworth, 1987), 111.

51. Ferdinand de Saussure, *Course in General Linguistics*, trans. Roy Harris (Chicago: Open Court, [1916] 1986).

52. Saussure, *Course in General Linguistics*, Kindle locs. 2739–2740.

53. Saussure, *Course in General Linguistics*, Kindle loc. 2747.

54. Saussure, *Course in General Linguistics*, Kindle loc. 2772.

55. Saussure, *Course in General Linguistics*, Kindle locs. 2829–2831.

56. Saussure, *Course in General Linguistics*, Kindle locs. 2823–2824.

57. Harris, *The Language Machine*, 111.

58. This is exactly the contradiction inherent in any "law" of the natural sciences, such as Newton's second law. Such a law is said to describe natural phenomena. But laws of a legal order are prescriptive, not descriptive. Clearly, it is possible to break laws of the latter sort by committing a criminal act. But what sort of criminal can break Newton's second law? Mathematician and scientist Giuseppe Longo has a long-term project under way to explore this homonym "law" as applied to the natural sciences compared to its use in legal systems: "The notion of the physical law, which has dominated all references to 'the laws of nature' for at least four centuries, is profoundly impregnated with religious metaphysics and juridical references which have not only shaped it, but given it legitimacy." See Giuseppe Longo, "Laws of God, Men and Nature," https://www.iea-nantes.fr/en/chercheurs/longo-giuseppe_275.

59. Noam Chomsky and Morris Halle, *The Sound Pattern of English* (Cambridge, MA: MIT Press, 1968), 135.

60. Noam Chomsky, "On the Notion 'Rule of Grammar,'" in *The Structure of Language: Readings in the Philosophy of Language*, ed. Jerry A. Fodor, Jerrold J. Katz, and W. V. Quine (Englewood Cliffs, NJ: Prentice-Hall, 1964), 119–120.

61. Chomsky, "On the Notion 'Rule of Grammar,'" 120.

62. My adaptation is of the grammar listed on page 46 of Chomsky's *Syntactic Structures*. For a longer discussion of this example grammar, see E. Keith Brown, "Transformational-Generative Grammar," in *The Linguistics Encyclopedia*, ed. Kirsten Malmkjaer (New York: Routledge, 1991).

63. Chomsky writes, "You know what *Syntactic Structures* was. It was course notes for an undergraduate course at MIT. Van Schooneveld showed up here once and took a look at some of my course notes from the undergraduate course I was teaching and said I ought to publish it. Since it had not been published anywhere, I said, why not, and that is what *Syntactic Structures* was." See Noam Chomsky, *The Generative Enterprise Revisited: Discussions with Riny Huybregts, Henk Van Riemsdijk, Naoki Fukui and Mihoko Zushi* (Berlin: De Gruyter Mouton, 2004), 89–90.

64. David Hilbert and Paul Bernays, *Foundations of Mathematics*, vol. 1, Bernays Project Text no. 12, trans. Ian Mueller (Pittsburgh: Carnegie Mellon University, [1934] 2003).

65. Alfred North Whitehead and Bertrand Russell, *Principia Mathematica*, 3 vols. (Cambridge: Cambridge University Press, 1910–1913).

66. The definition of implication is on page 94 of the second edition. See Alfred North Whitehead and Bertrand Russell, *Principia Mathematica*, vol. 1, 2nd ed. (Cambridge: Cambridge University Press, 1925), 94, nos. *1–*5.

67. Geoffrey K. Pullum, "On the Mathematical Foundations of Syntactic Structures," *Journal of Logic, Language and Information* 20 (2011).

68. Emil Post, "Formal Reductions of the General Combinatorial Decision Problem," *American Journal of Mathematics* 65, no. 2 (1943).

69. More recently, John Kadvany has shown that Emil Post's production rules had been anticipated in a fourth-century BC Sanskrit grammar formulated by Pāṇini: "This technique for controlling formal derivations was rediscovered by Emil Post in the 1920s and later shown by him to be capable of representing universal computation. The same implicit computational strength of Pāṇini's formalism follows as a consequence." Needless to say, Pāṇini's "notation" for production rules differed markedly from those of Chomsky, Post, and all of the other more recent mathematical logicians. Just how Pāṇini did "write" production rules is one of the main findings of Kadvany's article. See John Kadvany, "Pāṇini's Grammar and Modern Computation," *History and Philosophy of Logic* 37, no. 4 (2016).

70. "Derivation" is another term appropriated from mathematical logic. There it means the steps followed to produce a logical proof.

71. Noam Chomsky and Marcel Schützenberger, "The Algebraic Theory of Context Free Languages," in *Computer Programming and Formal Systems*, ed. P. Braffort and D. Hirschberg (Amsterdam: North-Holland, 1963), 119.

72. This is an adaptation of rule 12 in Chomsky, *Syntactic Structures*, 112.

73. Chomsky, *Syntactic Structures*, 51.

74. A digitized version of the entire dissertation can be found online at http://alpha-leonis.lids .mit.edu/wordpress/wp-content/uploads/2014/07/chomsky_LSLT55.pdf. The dissertation was

published twenty years later as a book but with several omissions. See Noam Chomsky, *The Logical Structure of Linguistic Theory* (New York: Plenum Press, 1975).

75. Rudolf Carnap, *The Logical Structure of Language* (New York: Routledge, 1937).

76. Republished in Nelson Goodman, *Fact, Fiction and Forecast* (London: University of London, 1954).

77. As noted in Tomalin, *Linguistics and the Formal Sciences*, Kindle loc. 1647.

78. Note that this condition implies that the rules are to be read procedurally (first do this, then do this, then do this, etc.) rather than declaratively—otherwise the order of the rules would make no difference.

79. Chomsky, *The Logical Structure of Linguistic Theory*, 125, as cited in Tomalin, *Linguistics and the Formal Sciences*, Kindle locs. 1758–1762.

80. Chomsky, *The Logical Structure of Linguistic Theory*, 77.

81. David Hilbert, *The Foundations of Geometry*, 2nd ed. (Chicago: Open Court, [1899] 1980).

82. David Hilbert and Wilhelm Ackermann, *Principles of Mathematical Logic* [Grundzüge der Theoretischen Logik], trans. Lewis M. Hammond, George G. Leckie, and F. Steinhardt (New York: Chelsea, [1928] 1950).

83. Hilbert and Bernays, *Foundations of Mathematics*, 464, as cited in Tomalin, *Linguistics and the Formal Sciences*, Kindle locs. 635–637.

84. Tomalin, *Linguistics and the Formal Sciences*, Kindle locs. 1313–1317.

85. In a chapter titled "The Chomskyan Revolution," writer and linguist Randy Allen Harris commented that "[Chomsky] demolished effortlessly, enfeebling the arguments and dumbfounding the arguers. He is said, in short, to have rescued linguistics from a long dark night of confusion, to have pulled back the curtain Bloomfield mistakenly drew over the mind; to have finally—and we could see this one coming for some time—made linguistics a science.... Like all good myths, these ones are true, and, of course, false." See Randy Allen Harris, *The Linguistics War* (Oxford: Oxford University Press, 1995), 51–52.

86. For a simultaneously laudatory and critical review of Tomalin's book, see B. C. Scholz and G. K. Pullum, "Tracking the Origins of Transformational Generative Grammar," *Journal of Linguistics* 43 (2007). Scholz and Pullum summarize the book and their review like this: "[Tomalin] locates the intellectual roots of TGG [transformational generative grammar] in the methods developed by 19th- and 20th-century mathematics and logic for exhibiting the conceptual structure of theories and constructing rigorous proofs of theorems.... Tomalin argues persuasively that the two-level approach to theorising now associated with early TGG (grammars as theories of languages, plus a metatheory about the form of grammars) was a specialised adaptation to linguistics of techniques developed for doing metatheoretical work on mathematics and logic, which were also adopted and applied in the philosophy of science."

87. Geoffrey J. Huck and John A. Goldsmith, *Ideology and Linguistic Theory: Noam Chomsky and the Deep Structure Debates* (London: Routledge, 1995), 13.

88. Noam Chomsky, *Language and Responsibility* (New York: New Press, 1977), 139.

89. Leonard Bloomfield, "Review of 'Was Ist Ein Satz?' by Johan Ries," *Language* 7 (1931), as cited in Huck and Goldsmith, *Ideology and Linguistic Theory*, 8.

90. Zellig Harris, "Review of Louis H. Gray, 'Foundations of Language,'" *Language* 16 (1940), as cited in Huck and Goldsmith, *Ideology and Linguistic Theory*, 10.

91. Henri Poincaré, *Science and Method* (New York: Dover, 1952), as cited in Martin Davis, *The Universal Computer: The Road from Leibniz to Turing* (New York: W. W. Norton, 2000), 93.

92. Chomsky, *Syntactic Structures*, 103.

93. According to Chomsky, "In order to understand a sentence it is necessary to know the kernel sentences from which it originates…and the phrase structure of these elementary components, as well as the transformational history of development of the given sentence from these kernel sentences." See Chomsky, *Syntactic Structures*, 92.

94. Chomsky, *Syntactic Structures*, 100–101.

95. Chomsky, *Syntactic Structures*, 102.

96. Chomsky, *Cartesian Linguistics*, 40.

97. Historians of linguistics have woven the story of the rise and fall of Generative Semantics from multiple insider perspectives. See Huck and Goldsmith, *Ideology and Linguistic Theory*.

98. Huck and Goldsmith write:

> Concerning the autonomy of syntax, all of the Generative Semanticists were willing to give it up if necessary, that is, to take it as a refutable auxiliary hypothesis. It appears to us that this shift towards a mediationalist commitment, and the concomitant restructuring and reranking of the core propositions of Chomsky's research program, more than a disagreement over the content or validity of the testable hypotheses that were proposed, [were what] the disputes of the 1960s and 1970s were primarily about. The issues that were actually debated, we suggest, were no more than proxies for these more fundamental and less technical disagreements.

See Huck and Goldsmith, *Ideology and Linguistic Theory*, 19.

99. Chomsky, *Syntactic Structures*, 93.

100. Chomsky, "On the Notion 'Rule of Grammar,'" 119–120.

101. Chomsky, *The Logical Structure of Linguistic Theory*, 57, as cited in Huck and Goldsmith, *Ideology and Linguistic Theory*, 12.

102. According to Chomsky, "One requirement that a grammar must certainly meet is that it be finite. Hence the grammar cannot simply be a list of all morpheme (or word) sequences, since there are infinitely many of these." See Chomsky, *Syntactic Structures*, 18.

103. Chomsky, *Syntactic Structures*, 23–24.

104. Chomsky, *Syntactic Structures*, 23.

105. Chomsky and Schützenberger, "The Algebraic Theory of Context Free Languages."

106. Computational complexity is measured according to a chosen model of computation. The Chomsky hierarchy is an ordering on models of computation and provides a framework that contextualizes the measurement of the computational complexity of any specific algorithm. Turing machines have, frequently, been the model chosen. The Chomsky hierarchy can be invoked to justify why Turing machines (or some other model) should be the basis for a measurement of complexity.

107. As Chomsky explains:

> In fact, *Syntactic Structures* is a very misleading book. What is misleading about it is the role that the discussion of automata plays in it, which, I think, has misled a lot of people. There is a natural progression there from finite automata to context-free grammars to transformational grammars, but it is a very misleading progression. In *The Logical Structure of Linguistic Theory* [*LSLT*] there is no talk about finite automata or weak generative capacity at all. In fact that discussion was put into *Syntactic Structures* because of the MIT-context. When I came to MIT in 1955 after finishing *LSLT*, I discovered that people really were euphoric, if that is the right word, about Markov processes. There was a tremendously strong feeling about this among engineers and psychologists and other prestigious types. Markov processes are an even narrower class (probabilistic features aside) than finite automata; they are K-order systems where you go back at most K symbols to determine, probabilistically, the next output. That was the special case that was being considered. The notion of finite discrete source seemed to offer a break-through. It was felt that these were going to be the fundamental concepts for the study of language and mind. And it was only for this reason that I ever started working on their formal properties. In *Syntactic Structures* this becomes a more or less central topic, because of the local MIT context—the notes were for MIT students—but it was really a very peripheral one.

See Chomsky, *The Generative Enterprise Revisited*, 89–90.

108. Brown, "Transformational-Generative Grammar," 491.

109. See fn. 15 in Peter Norvig, "On Chomsky and the Two Cultures of Statistical Learning," http://norvig.com/chomsky.html.

110. Fernando C. N. Pereira and David H. D. Warren, "Definite Clause Grammars for Language Analysis—a Survey of the Formalism and a Comparison with Augmented Transition Networks," *Artificial Intelligence* 13 (1980).

111. A Prolog implementation of this grammar can be found at the book website: http://softwarearts.info.

112. A Prolog implementation of this grammar can be found at the book website: http://softwarearts.info.

113. A Prolog implementation of this rule can be found at the book website: http://softwarearts.info.

114. Allen Newell and Herbert A. Simon, *Human Problem Solving* (Englewood Cliffs, NJ: Prentice-Hall, 1972), 11, cited in Philip Mirowski, *Machine Dreams: Economics Becomes a Cyborg Science* (Cambridge: Cambridge University Press, 2002), 464–465.

115. Online at http://translate.google.com.

116. See the following blog post and the technical articles listed at the end of it: https://research .googleblog.com/2016/09/a-neural-network-for-machine.html.

117. Melvin Johnson, Mike Schuster, Quoc V. Le, Maxim Krikun, Yonghui Wu, Zhifeng Chen, Nikhil Thorat, Fernanda Viégas, Martin Wattenberg, Greg Corrado, Macduff Hughes, and Jeffrey Dean, "Google's Multilingual Neural Machine Translation System: Enabling Zero-Shot Translation," *Transactions of the Association for Computational Linguistics* 5 (2017), 339–352. A preprint of this journal article can be found online. See Melvin Johnson, Mike Schuster, Quoc V. Le, Maxim Krikun, Yonghui Wu, Zhifeng Chen, Nikhil Thorat, Fernanda Viégas, Martin Wattenberg, Greg Corrado, Macduff Hughes, and Jeffrey Dean, "Google's Multilingual Neural Machine Translation System: Enabling Zero-Shot Translation," https://arxiv.org/abs/1611.04558. I will sometimes be citing the preprint because it contains some details omitted in the journal publication.

118. Johnson et al., "Google's Multilingual Neural Machine Translation System" (preprint), 4.

119. Johnson et al. explain, "We evaluate our models using the standard BLEU score metric.... [W]e report tokenized BLEU scores as computed by the multi-bleu.pl script, which can be downloaded from the public implementation of Moses [http://www.statmt.org/moses/]." See Johnson et al., "Google's Multilingual Neural Machine Translation System," 342. Note that BLEU scoring is a standard automated measure of machine translation and, in the technical language of information retrieval, is a modified form of "precision." BLEU scoring matches machine-translated sentences against human-authored translations of the same sentences, but the human-authored translations may have been completed years earlier, and the quality of a machine translation is scored by running a script (multi-bleu.pl) and not by having humans read the output from the system. Thus, the reported quality of translation achieved by a system is only in a very indirect manner related to whether a bilingual human might judge the machine translations to be of good quality.

120. Johnson et al., "Google's Multilingual Neural Machine Translation System," 347.

121. Johnson et al., "Google's Multilingual Neural Machine Translation System," 350.

122. Chomsky's comments can be found at http://languagelog.ldc.upenn.edu/myl/PinkerChom skyMIT.html. Also, Chomsky continued his conversation on this topic with a journalist from *The Atlantic* magazine. See Yarden Katz, "Noam Chomsky on Where Artificial Intelligence Went Wrong: An Extended Conversation with the Legendary Linguist," *The Atlantic*, November 1, 2012, https://www.theatlantic.com/technology/archive/2012/11/noam-chomsky-on-where-artificial -intelligence-went-wrong/261637/.

123. Norvig, "On Chomsky and the Two Cultures of Statistical Learning."

124. Norvig, "On Chomsky and the Two Cultures of Statistical Learning."

125. According to Huck and Goldsmith, "Chomsky has said that he was convinced from his days as a student of Goodman's that there is no inductive learning (Chomsky, *LSLT*, pp. 33 & 51)." See Huck and Goldsmith, *Ideology and Linguistic Theory*, 24.

126. Alon Halevy, Peter Norvig, and Fernando Pereira, "The Unreasonable Effectiveness of Data," *IEEE Intelligent Systems* 24, no. 2 (March 2009). The abstract for their paper reads as follows: "Problems that involve interacting with humans, such as natural language understanding, have not proven to be solvable by concise, neat formulas like F=ma. Instead, the best approach appears to be to embrace the complexity of the domain and address it by harnessing the power of data: if other humans engage in the tasks and generate large amounts of unlabeled, noisy data, new algorithms can be used to build high-quality models from the data." Note how the authors directly compare their models with Newton's second law.

127. Chris Anderson, "The End of Theory: The Data Deluge Makes the Scientific Method Obsolete," *Wired*, June 2008.

128. Anderson, "The End of Theory."

129. Warren S. McCulloch and Walter Pitts, "A Logical Calculus of the Ideas Immanent in Nervous Activity," *Bulletin of Mathematical Biophysics* 5 (1943). In this book, the McCulloch and Pitts article was briefly discussed at the end of chapter 2.

130. For a fuller description, see any of a myriad of textbooks on machine learning; for example, Ethem Alpaydin, *Introduction to Machine Learning*, Adaptive Computation and Machine Learning Series (Cambridge, MA: MIT Press, 2004), Kindle loc. 271.

131. This observation brings us back to Hilbert's "decision problem" discussed in chapter 2, on translation. As mentioned in an earlier footnote, Hilbert's first articulation of the decision problem posed in the context of Diophantine equations was not solved by Turing in 1936, but only much later (1970) by Martin Davis, Yuri Matiyasevich, Hilary Putnam, and Julia Robinson. Work on Hilbert's problem resulted in the discovery of an astounding set of connections between computability theory and number theory. In an interview published in 2008, Martin Davis informally states what was originally his conjecture and later one of the results in an interview: "anything that can be done by an algorithmic process could also be defined by a specific Diophantine equation." Allyn Jackson, "Interview with Martin Davis," *Notices of the American Mathematical Society* 55, no. 5 (May 2008): 564. In a 2016 article, Yuri Matiyasevich explains in more concrete terms what this means: "My paper [Yuri Matiyasevich, "Existential Arithmetization of Diophantine Equations," *Annals of Pure and Applied Logic* 157, nos. 2–3 (2009): 225–233] presents a unifying technique allowing one to eliminate bounded universal quantifiers and simulate by means of exponential Diophantine equations Turing machines, register machines, and partial recursive functions in the same 'algebraic' style." Yuri Matiyasevich, "Chapter 2: Martin Davis and Hilbert's Tenth Problem," in *Martin Davis on Computability, Computational Logic, and Mathematical Foundations*, ed. E.G. Omodeo and A. Policriti, Outstanding Contributions to Logic 10 (Springer: Switzerland, 2016), 43. In other words, any algorithm can be translated into a set of polynomials!

Chapter 8

1. Lev Manovich, *The Language of New Media* (Cambridge, MA: MIT Press, 2001), 48. Emphasis in original.

2. Manovich, *The Language of New Media*, 47–48.

3. See V. A. Uspenskii, "Arithmetization," in *Encyclopedia of Mathematics*, ed. Ulf Rehmann (Dordrecht: Kluwer Academic, 2002).

4. V. A. Uspenskii, "Arithmetization of Analysis," in Rehmann, *Encyclopedia of Mathematics*.

5. See also William Deringer, *Calculated Values: Finance, Politics, and the Quantitative Age* (Cambridge, MA: Harvard University Press, 2018).

6. Software studies scholar Adrian MacKenzie puts it like this:

> The importance of lines and flat surfaces can hardly be underestimated in machine learning. Finding lines of best fit underpins many of the machine learners that attract more attention (neural nets, support vector machines, random forests). Linear regression with its pursuit of the straight line or plane projects the basic alignments of vector space. It renders all differences as distances and directions of movement. Drawing lines or flat surfaces at various angles and directions is perhaps the main way in which the volume of data is traversed and a relation between input and output, between predictors and prediction, consolidated as a loci or a data strain loci or a data strain.

See Adrian Mackenzie, *Machine Learners* (Cambridge, MA: MIT Press, 2017), 63.

7. Allen Newell, Alan J. Perlis, and Herbert A. Simon, "What Is Computer Science?," *Science* 157, no. 3795 (1967).

8. Paul Ceruzzi, *A History of Modern Computing*, 2nd ed. (Cambridge, MA: MIT Press, 2003), 102–103.

9. The Joint Task Force on Computing Curricula of the Association for Computing Machinery (ACM) and the IEEE Computer Society, *Computer Science Curricula 2013: Curriculum Guidelines for Undergraduate Degree Programs in Computer Science*, December 20 (New York: ACM), 55.

10. Gayle Laakmann McDowell, *Cracking the Coding Interview: 189 Programming Questions and Solutions*, 6th ed. (Palo Alto, CA: CareerCup, 2015).

11. For an elaboration of the notion of an agenda for the discipline of computing, see Michael S. Mahoney, *Histories of Computing* (Cambridge, MA: Harvard University Press, 2011), 130.

12. Computer historian Nathan Ensmenger comments on the influence of Knuth, saying, "As Paul Ceruzzi has convincingly demonstrated, by the beginning of the 1970s Knuth and his colleagues had successfully established the algorithm as the fundamental unit of analysis of computer science." See Nathan L. Ensmenger, *The Computer Boys Take Over: Computers, Programmers, and the Politics of Technical Expertise* (Cambridge, MA: MIT Press, 2012), 131.

13. Alan M. Turing, "On Computable Numbers, with an Application to the Entscheidungsproblem," *Proceedings of the London Mathematical Society*, 2nd ser., 42, no. 1 (January 1, 1937): 232.

14. Mahoney, *Histories of Computing*, 133.

15. For a clear and concise introduction to Church's lambda-calculus, see Raúl Rojas, *A Tutorial Introduction to the Lambda Calculus* (Berlin: Freie Universitat Berlin, 1997–1998), https://www.inf.fu-berlin.de/lehre/WS03/alpi/lambda.pdf.

16. John McCarthy. "Recursive Functions of Symbolic Expressions and Their Computation by Machine, Part I," *Communications of the ACM* 3, no. 4 (April 1960_: 184–195.

17. Edward Ashford Lee, *Plato and the Nerd: The Creative Partnership of Humans and Technology* (Cambridge, MA: MIT Press, 2017), 145.

18. Robin Milner, "Elements of Interaction," *Communications of the ACM* 36, no. 1 (January 1993).

19. Milner, "Elements of Interaction," 78.

20. Milner, "Elements of Interaction," 83.

21. Peter Wegner, "Why Interaction Is More Powerful than Algorithms," *Communications of the ACM* 40, no. 5 (May 1997).

22. Wegner, "Why Interaction Is More Powerful than Algorithms," 82.

23. See especially Dina Goldin and Peter Wegner, "The Interactive Nature of Computing: Refuting the Strong Church-Turing Thesis," *Minds and Machines* 18, no. 1 (March 2008).

24. Goldin and Wegner, "The Interactive Nature of Computing," 20.

25. Mahoney, *Histories of Computing*, 146.

26. Mahoney, *Histories of Computing*, 130.

27. Besides cookbooks, one might also consider other crafts, such as weaving. Philosopher and cultural theorist Sadie Plant has explored the relations between the craft of weaving and computing. See Sadie Plant, *Zeroes + Ones: Digital Women + the New Technoculture* (New York: Doubleday, 1997). More recently, Stephen Monteiro has demonstrated the historical connections between weaving, textiles, and the construction of computer hardware. See Stephen Monteiro, *The Fabric of Interface: Mobile Media, Design, and Gender* (Cambridge, MA: MIT Press, 2017).

28. Donna Jeanne Haraway, *Primate Visions: Gender, Race, and Nature in the World of Modern Science* (New York: Routledge, 1989), 1.

29. Ensmenger, *The Computer Boys Take Over*, 131.

30. Ensmenger, *The Computer Boys Take Over*, 78.

31. Janet Abbate, *Recoding Gender: Women's Changing Participation in Computing*, History of Computing (Cambridge, MA: MIT Press, 2012).

32. Software engineer Tracy Chou and others (especially the group called "Project Include") have crowdsourced up-to-the-minute diversity statistics at many companies in Silicon Valley. As of March 29, 2018, the spreadsheet records a total of 19,053 software engineers, of whom 3,778 (i.e., about 20 percent) are women. See Chou's article, "Where Are the Numbers?," https://medium.com/@triketora/where-are-the-numbers-cb997a57252. The GitHub repository that contains data on many high-tech firms is at https://github.com/triketora/women-in-software-eng. A Google spreadsheet that lists the data in a more readable format is at https://docs.google.com/spreadsheets/d/1BxbEifUr1z6HwY2_IcExQwUpKPRZY3FZ4x4ZFzZU-5E/edit#gid=0.

33. Philip Agre, *Computation and Human Experience*, Learning in Doing (New York: Cambridge University Press, 1997).

34. Paul N. Edwards, *The Closed World: Computers and the Politics of Discourse in Cold War America*, Inside Technology (Cambridge, MA: MIT Press, 1996).

35. Agre, *Computation and Human Experience*, xiv.

36. Philip Agre, "The Dynamic Structure of Everyday Life," Technical Report 1085 (PhD diss., Massachusetts Institute of Technology, Artificial Intelligence Laboratory, October 12, 1988).

37. Philip E. Agre and David Chapman, "Pengi: An Implementation of a Theory of Activity," in *AAAI-87: Proceedings of the Sixth National Conference on Artificial Intelligence, Seattle, WA, July 13–17, 1987,* ed. Kenneth Forbus and Howard Shrobe (Cambridge, MA: MIT Press, 1987), 268–272

38. See Philip Agre, "Computational Research on Interaction and Agency," *Artificial Intelligence* 72 (1995).

39. Agre, *Computation and Human Experience*, xii.

40. Philip Agre, "Toward a Critical Technical Practice: Lessons Learned in Trying to Reform AI," in *Bridging the Great Divide: Social Science, Technical Systems, and Cooperative Work*, ed. Geof Bowker, Les Gasser, Leigh Star, and Bill Turner (Hillsdale, NJ: Erlbaum, 1997).

41. Agre, "Toward a Critical Technical Practice."

42. For a more contemporary view on the topics of plans and planning, see Malik Ghallab, Dana S. Nau, and Paolo Traverso, *Automated Planning Theory and Practice* (Amsterdam: Elsevier/ Morgan Kaufmann, 2004).

43. Lucy Suchman, *Plans and Situated Actions: The Problem of Human-Machine Communication* (Cambridge: Cambridge University Press, 1987), 27–28.

44. Allen Newell and Herbert A. Simon, *Human Problem Solving* (Englewood Cliffs, NJ: Prentice-Hall, 1972), cited in Philip Mirowski, *Machine Dreams: Economics Becomes a Cyborg Science* (Cambridge: Cambridge University Press, 2002), 464–465. Agre interviewed Newell shortly before Newell's death. With Agre the skeptic and Newell the co-inventor and a supporter of the plans-are-programs/algorithms view, it is an interesting exchange. See Philip Agre, "Interview with Allen Newell," *Artificial Intelligence* 59 (1993).

45. Herbert A. Simon, *The Sciences of the Artificial*, 3rd ed. (Cambridge, MA: MIT Press, 1996).

46. See, for example, Natasha Singer, "Intel's Sharp-Eyed Social Scientist," *New York Times*, February 15, 2014.

47. Manovich, *The Language of New Media*, 55.

48. Michael Murtaugh, "Interaction," in *Software Studies: A Lexicon*, ed. Matthew Fuller (Cambridge, MA: MIT Press, 2008).

49. Matthew Fuller and Sónia Matos, "Feral Computing: From Ubiquitous Calculation to Wild Interactions," in *How to Be a Geek: Essays on the Culture of Software* (Cambridge: Polity Press, 2017).

50. See Céline Bonicco-Donat, *Une archeology de l'interaction: De David Hume à Erving Goffman* (Paris: Vrin, 2016).

51. Samuel Bianchini and Erik Verhagen, eds., *Practicable: From Participation to Interaction in Contemporary Art,* Leonardo Book Series (Cambridge, MA: MIT Press, 2016).

52. Turing's essay has been intensely discussed for decades, but few of these discussions link Turing's method of rephrasing the question "Can machines think?" as a (language) game to the methodology that Wittgenstein used more generally to reanalyze the so-called problems of philosophy as language games. Two sorts of evidence make this link between Turing's thinking and Wittgenstein's plausible. There are a sparse number of texts arguing exactly this. See, for instance, Otto Neumaier, "A Wittgensteinian View of Artificial Intelligence," *Artificial Intelligence: The Case Against,* ed. Rainer Born (London: Croom-Helm, 1987), 132–173. But most interestingly, there are some of Wittgenstein's own writings that seem to foreshadow by almost twenty years the approach Turing takes:

> This objection is expressed in the question: "Could a machine think?" I shall talk about this at a later point, and now only refer you to an analogous question: "Can a machine have a toothache?" You will certainly be inclined to say "A machine can't have toothache." All I will do now is to draw your attention to the use you have made of the word "can" and ask you: "Did you mean to say that all our past experience has shown that a machine never had a toothache?" The impossibility of which you speak is a logical one. The question is: What is the relation between thinking (or toothache) and the subject which thinks, has toothache, etc.?

See Ludwig Wittgenstein, *The Blue and Brown Books: Preliminary Studies for the "Philosophical Investigations"* (New York: Harper Torchbooks, 1958), 16. This publication comprises notes taken during Wittgenstein's lectures from the academic years of 1933–1934 and 1934–1935.

53. Alan M. Turing, "Computing Machinery and Intelligence," *Mind* 49 (1950): 433–434.

54. For example, Joseph Weizenbaum, *Computer Power and Human Reason: From Judgment to Calculation* (New York: W. H. Freeman, 1976).

55. Patrick Hayes and Kenneth Ford, "Turing Test Considered Harmful," *Fourteenth International Joint Conference on Artificial Intelligence,.* vol. 1, ed. Chris S. Mellish (San Mateo, CA: Morgan Kaufmann), 972–977. August 20–25, 1995, Montreal. Their title is a riff on the title of a pivotal document in the fight to frame computer science as a kind of mathematics: Edsger Dijkstra, "Go to Statement Considered Harmful," *Communications of the ACM* 11, no. 3 (1968).

56. I have considered this oversight in several writings over the last couple of decades, including Joseph Dumit, "Artificial Participation: An Interview with Warren Sack," in *Zeroing in on the Year 2000: The Final Edition,* ed. George E. Marcus, Late Editions 8 (Chicago: University of Chicago Press, 2000); Warren Sack, "Artificial Intelligence," in *The Encyclopedia of Aesthetics,* vol. 1, ed. Michael Kelly (New York: Oxford University Press, 1998); and starting with Warren Sack, "Replaying Turing's Imitation Game," paper presented at Console-ing Passions: Television, Video and Feminism (Madison, WI, April 25–28, 1996).

57. Hayes and Ford, "Turing Test Considered Harmful," 974.

Bibliography

Aarsleff, Hans. 1982. "The History of Linguistics and Professor Chomsky." In *From Locke to Saussure*, 101–119. Minneapolis: University of Minnesota Press.

Abbate, Janet. 2012. *Recoding Gender: Women's Changing Participation in Computing*. History of Computing. Cambridge, MA: MIT Press.

Abelson, Harold, Gerald Jay Sussman, and Julie Sussman. 1996. *Structure and Interpretation of Computer Programs.*2nd ed. MIT Electrical Engineering and Computer Science Series. Cambridge, MA: MIT Press; New York: McGraw-Hill.

Adams, Douglas. (1982) 2009. *Life, the Universe and Everything*, Vol. 3 of *The Hitchhiker's Guide to the Galaxy*. London: Pan Macmillian.

Agre, Philip. 1988. "The Dynamic Structure of Everyday Life." Technical Report 1085. PhD diss., Massachusetts Institute of Technology, Artificial Intelligence Laboratory.

Agre, Philip. 1993. "Interview with Allen Newell." *Artificial Intelligence* 59:415–449.

Agre, Philip. 1994. "Surveillance and Capture: Two Models of Privacy." *The Information Society* 10:101–127.

Agre, Philip. 1995. "Computational Research on Interaction and Agency." *Artificial Intelligence* 72:1–52.

Agre, Philip. 1997. *Computation and Human Experience*. Learning in Doing. New York: Cambridge University Press.

Agre, Philip. 1997. "Toward a Critical Technical Practice: Lessons Learned in Trying to Reform AI." In *Bridging the Great Divide: Social Science, Technical Systems, and Cooperative Work*, edited by Geof Bowker, Les Gasser, Leigh Star, and Bill Turner, 131–158. Hillsdale, NJ: Erlbaum.

Agre, Philip, and David Chapman. 1987. "Pengi: An Implementation of a Theory of Activity." In *AAAI-87: Proceedings of the Sixth National Conference on Artificial Intelligence, Seattle, WA, July 13–17, 1987*, edited by Kenneth Forbus and Howard Shrobe, 268–272. Cambridge, MA: MIT Press.

Agre, Philip, and Stanley J. Rosenschein. 1996. *Computational Theories of Interaction and Agency*. Cambridge, MA: MIT Press.

Akrich, Madeleine, Michel Callon, and Bruno Latour. 2006. *Sociologie de la traduction: Textes fondateurs*. Paris: École des mines de Paris.

d'Alembert, Jean Le Rond. (1751) 1995. *Preliminary Discourse to the Encyclopedia of Diderot*, translated by Richard N. Schwab. Chicago: University of Chicago Press.

Almodóvar, Pedro, dir. 2011. *The Skin I Live In*. Madrid: El Deseo Producciones.

Alpaydin, Ethem. 2004. *Introduction to Machine Learning*. Adaptive Computation and Machine Learning Series. Cambridge, MA: MIT Press. Kindle.

Amoore, Louise, and Volha Piotukh. 2016. *Algorithmic Life Calculative Devices in the Age of Big Data*. London: Routledge.

Anders, George. 2017. *You Can Do Anything: The Surprising Power of a "Useless" Liberal Arts Education*. Boston: Little, Brown and Company.

Anderson, Benedict R. O'G. 2006. *Imagined Communities: Reflections on the Origin and Spread of Nationalism*. London: Verso.

Anderson, Chris. 2008. "The End of Theory: The Data Deluge Makes the Scientific Method Obsolete." *Wired*, June. https://www.wired.com/2008/06/pb-theory/.

Anderson, Laurie. 1982. *Big Science*. Burbank, CA: Warner Brothers.

Anellis, Irving H. 2012. "Peirce's Truth-Functional Analysis and the Origin of the Truth Table." *History and Philosophy of Logic* 33:87–97.

Anonymous. 1967. "Dialectic." In *Encyclopedia of Philosophy*. Vol. 2, edited by Paul Edwards, 385. New York: Macmillan and Free Press.

Anonymous. 1992. "Chomsky Is Citation Champ." *MIT Tech Talk* 36, no. 27 (April 15). http://news.mit.edu/1992/citation-0415.

Anonymous. 2017. "Logique." In *Encyclopédie, ou dictionnaire raisonné des sciences, des arts et des métiers, etc.*, edited by Denis Diderot and Jean Le Rond d'Alembert. Chicago: University of Chicago Artfl Encyclopédie Project. http://encyclopedie.uchicago.edu/.

Anonymous. "John Clifford Shaw Papers, 1933–1993: Overview of the Collection." Archives Center, National Museum of American History, Smithsonian Institution. http://amhistory.si.edu/archives/AC0580.html.

Apple. 2015. "Inclusion Inspires Innovation." https://www.apple.com/diversity/.

Ardourel, Vincent. 2015. "A Discrete Solution for the Paradox of Achilles and the Tortoise." *Synthese* 192:2843–2861.

Arendt, Hannah. 1958. *The Human Condition*. Chicago: University of Chicago Press.

Arendt, Hannah. 1990. "Philosophy and Politics." *Social Research: An International Quarterly* 57, no. 1 (Spring): 73–103.

Aristotle. 1950. *Physica*. Edited by W. D. Ross. Oxford: Clarendon Press.

Aristotle. 1954. *Rhetoric*. Translated by W. Rhys Roberts. New York: Modern Library.

Aristotle. 1998. *The Nicomachean Ethics*. Edited by W. D. Ross, J. L. Ackrill, and J. O. Urmson. New York: Oxford University Press.

Arnauld, Antoine, Pierre Nicole, Claude Lancelot, and Petrus Le Mangnier. 1662. *La logique, ou, L'art de penser: Contenant, outre les règles communes, plusieurs observations nouvelles, propres à former le jugement*. Paris: Chez Jean Guignart, Chez Charles Saureux.

Atkinson, Richard C., and William A. Blanpied. 2008. "Research Universities: Core of the US Science and Technology System." *Technology in Society* 30:30–48.

Attfield, S. J., S. K. Hara, and B. L. William Wong. 2010. "Sensemaking in Visual Analytics: Processes and Challenges," International Symposium on Visual Analytics Science and Technology, edited by J. Kohlhammer and D. Keim. Salt Lake City, UT: IEEE.

Auroux, Sylvain. 1994. *La révolution technologique de la grammatisation*. Liège: Pierre Mardaga.

Austin, J. L. 1962. *How to Do Things with Words*. The William James Lectures. Cambridge, MA: Harvard University Press.

Babbage, Charles. (1826) 1961. "On a Method for Expressing by Signs the Action of Machinery." In *Charles Babbage: On the Principles and Development of the Calculator and Other Seminal Writings by Charles Babbage and Others*. Philip Morrison and Emily Morrison, eds., 346–356. Mineola, NY: Dover.

Babbage, Charles. (1832) 2011. *On the Economy of Machinery and Manufactures*. Amazon Digital Services. https://www.amazon.com/dp/B004TS7610/ref=dp-kindle-redirect?_encoding=UTF 8&btkr=1.

Babbage, Charles. (1851) 1961. "Laws of Mechanical Notation." In *Charles Babbage: On the Principles and Development of the Calculator and Other Seminal Writings by Charles Babbage and Others*, edited by Philip Morrison and Emily Morrison, 357–362. Mineola, NY: Dover.

Babbage, Charles. 1961. "Calculating Machines, Chapter XIII, The Exposition of 1851." In *Charles Babbage: On the Principles and Development of the Calculator and Other Seminal Writings by Charles Babbage and Others*, edited by Philip Morrison and Emily Morrison, 322–330. Mineola, NY: Dover.

Babbage, Charles. 1961. "On the Application of Machinery to the Purpose of Calculating and Printing Mathematical Tables." In *Charles Babbage: On the Principles and Development of the Calculator and Other Seminal Writings by Charles Babbage and Others*, edited by Philip Morrison and Emily Morrison, 298–305. Mineola, NY: Dover.

Backus, J. W., F. L. Bauer, J. Green, C. Katz, J. McCarthy, P. Naur, A. J. Perlis, H. Rutishauser, K. Samuelson, B. Vauquois, J. H. Wegstein, A. van Wijngaarden, and M. Woodger. 1963. "Revised Report on the Algorithmic Language ALGOL 60." *Communications of the ACM* 6, no. 1:1–17.

Bacon, Francis. (1620) 1902. *Novum Organum Or True Suggestions for the Interpretation of Nature.* New York: P. F. Collier and Son.

Badiou, Alain. 2008. *Number and Numbers.* Cambridge: Polity Press.

Bailey, David H., Peter B. Borwein, and Simon H. Plouffe. 1997. "On the Rapid Computation of Various Polylogarithmic Constants." *Mathematics of Computation* 66, no. 218:903–913.

Balzac, Honoré de. 1985. *Lost Illusions.* New York: Modern Library.

Barthes, Roland. 1972. *Nouveaux essais critiques.* Paris: Seuil.

Bates, David W. 2002. *Enlightenment Aberrations: Error and Revolution in France.* Ithaca, NY: Cornell University Press.

Bates, David W. 2018. "Automatisation et erreur." In *La vérité du numérique: Recherche et enseignement supérieur à l'ère des technologies numériques*, 29–40, edited by Bernard Stiegler. Paris, France: FYP editions.

Bender, John, and Michael Marrinan. 2010. *The Culture of the Diagram.* Stanford, CA: Stanford University Press.

Bergson, Henri. 1911. *Creative Evolution.* Translated by A. Mitchell. New York: Holt, Rinehart and Winston.

Berlekamp, Elwyn R., John Horton Conway, and Richard K. Guy. 2001. *Winning Ways for Your Mathematical Plays.* 2nd ed. 4 vols. Natick, MA: A. K. Peters.

Berman, Morris. 1981. *The Reenchantment of the World.* Ithaca, NY: Cornell University Press.

Bianchini, Samuel, and Erik Verhagen, eds. 2016. *Practicable: From Participation to Interaction in Contemporary Art.* Cambridge, MA: MIT Press.

Birch, Thomas. 1756–1757. *The History of the Royal Society of London for the Improving of Natural Knowledge, from Its First Rise*, 4 vols. London: Royal Society.

Bloomfield, Leonard. 1931. "Review of 'Was ist ein Satz?' by Johan Ries." *Language* 7:204–209.

Bloomfield, Leonard. 1933. *Language.* New York: Holt.

Bod, Rens, Jaap Maat, and Thijs Weststeijn. 2004. *The Making of the Humanities.* Vol. 1. Amsterdam: Amsterdam University Press.

Bogost, Ian. 2007. *Persuasive Games: The Expressive Power of Videogames.* Cambridge, MA: MIT Press.

Bondarenko, A., P. M. Dung, R. A. Kowalski, and F. Toni. 1997. "An Abstract Argumentation-Theoretic Approach to Default Reasoning." *Journal of Artificial Intelligence Research* 93, nos. 1–2:63–101.

Bonicco-Donat, Céline. 2016. *Une archeology de l'interaction: De David Hume à Erving Goffman.* Paris: Vrin.

Boole, George. 1940. *George Boole's Collected Logical Works, Volume II: The Laws of Thought (1854).* Chicago: Open Court.

Bourquin, Jacques. 1991. "Port-Royal Grammar." In *The Linguistics Encyclopedia*, edited by Kirsten Malmkjaer, 345–351. New York: Routledge.

Boyle, Robert. 1662. "Chapter V: Two New Experiments Touching the Measure of the Force of the Spring of Air Compress'd and Dilated." In *A Defence of the Doctrine Touching the Spring and Weight of the Air*, 57–68. London: Thomas Robinson. https://quod.lib.umich.edu/e/eebo/A28956.0001 .001/1:4.2.5?rgn=div3;view=fulltext.

Brand, Stewart. 1987. *The Media Lab: Inventing the Future at MIT.* New York: Viking.

Bratko, Ivan. 1990. *Prolog Programming for Artificial Intelligence.* 2nd ed. New York: Addison-Wesley.

Breazeale, Daniel, and R. J. Hollingdale. 1997. *Nietzsche: Untimely Meditations.* Cambridge: Cambridge University Press.

Bridgman, Percy Williams. 1938. "Operational Analysis." *Philosophy of Science* 5:114–131.

Bromley, Allan. 1990. "Difference and Analytical Engines." In *Computing before Computers*, edited by William Aspray, 59–98. Ames: Iowa State University Press.

Brown, E. Keith 1991. "Transformational-Generative Grammar." In *The Linguistics Encyclopedia*, edited by Kirsten Malmkjaer, 482–497. New York: Routledge.

Brown, John Seely, and Kurt VanLehn. 1980. "Repair Theory: A Generative Theory of Bugs in Procedural Skills." *Cognitive Science* 4, no. 4: 379–426.

Burack, Benjamin. 1949. "An Electrical Logic Machine." *Science* 109, no. 2842: 610–611.

Burdick, Anne, Johanna Drucker, Peter Lunenfeld, Todd Presner, and Jeffrey Schnapp. 2012. *Digital_Humanities.* Cambridge, MA: MIT Press.

Bury, John Bagnell. 1900. *A History of Greece to the Death of Alexander the Great.* London: MacMillan.

Bush, Vannevar. 1945. "As We May Think." *The Atlantic*, July, 112–124. https://www.theatlantic .com/magazine/archive/1945/07/as-we-may-think/303881/.

Butterfield, Herbert. 1931. *The Whig Interpretation of History.* New York: W. W. Norton.

Callon, Michel. 1986. "Elements of a Sociology of Translation: Domestication of the Scallops and the Fishermen of St Brieuc Bay." In *Power, Action and Belief: A New Sociology of Knowledge?*, edited by John Law, 196–233. London: Routledge.

Callon, Michel, and Bruno Latour. 1981. "Unscrewing the Big Leviathan; or How Actors Macrostructure Reality, and How Sociologists Help Them to Do So." In *Advances in Social Theory and Methodology*, edited by K. Knorr and A. Cicourel, 277–303. London: Routledge and Kegan Paul.

Camp, Tracy. 2001. "Women in Computer Sciences: Reversing the Trend." *Syllabus* 2 (August 2001): 4–26.

Canales, Jimena. 2015. *The Physicist and the Philosopher: Einstein, Bergson and the Debate That Changed Our Understanding of Time.* Princeton, NJ: Princeton University Press.

Canby, Henry Seidel. 1936. *Alma Mater: The Gothic Age of the American College*: Farrar and Rinehart.

Card, Stuart K., Jock Mackinlay, and Ben Shneiderman. 1999. *Readings in Information Visualization: Using Vision to Think.* San Francisco: Morgan Kaufmann.

Carnap, Rudolf. 1937. *The Logical Structure of Language.* New York: Routledge.

Carpenter, B. E., and R. W. Doran, eds. 1986. *A.M. Turing's ACE Report of 1946 and Other Papers.* Cambridge, MA: MIT Press.

Carr, Nicolas G. 2010. *The Shallows: What the Internet Is Doing to Our Brains.* New York: W. W. Norton.

Cassin, Barbara, Emily Apter, Jacques Lezra, and Michael Wood. 2014. *Dictionary of Untranslatables: A Philosophical Lexicon*, edited by Barbara Cassin. Princeton, NJ: Princeton University Press.

Castells, Manuel. 1997. *The Power of Identity.* Information Age. Malden, MA: Blackwell.

Ceruzzi, Paul. 2003. *A History of Modern Computing.* 2nd ed. Cambridge, MA: MIT Press.

Chang, Hasok. 2009. "Operationalism," *The Stanford Encyclopedia of Philosophy* (Fall 2009). https://plato.stanford.edu/archives/fall2009/entries/operationalism/.

Chang, Hasok. 2012. *Is Water H$_2$O? Evidence, Pluralism and Realism.* Boston Studies in the Philosophy of Science 293. Dordrecht: Springer.

Charniak, Eugene, and Drew McDermott. 1985. *Introduction to Artificial Intelligence.* New York: Addison-Wesley.

Chazelle, Bernard. "The Algorithm: Idiom of Modern Science." https://www.cs.princeton.edu/~chazelle/pubs/algorithm.html.

Chomsky, Noam. 1957. *Syntactic Structures.* The Hague: Mouton.

Chomsky, Noam. 1964. "On the Notion 'Rule of Grammar.'" In *The Structure of Language: Readings in the Philosophy of Language*, edited by Jerry A. Fodor, Jerrold J. Katz, and W. V. Quine, 119–136. Englewood Cliffs, NJ: Prentice-Hall.

Chomsky, Noam. 1966. *Cartesian Linguistics: A Chapter in the History of Rationalist Thought.* New York: Harper and Row.

Chomsky, Noam. 1975. *The Logical Structure of Linguistic Theory.* New York: Plenum Press.

Chomsky, Noam. 1977. *Language and Responsibility.* New York: New Press.

Chomsky, Noam. 2004. *The Generative Enterprise Revisited: Discussions with Riny Huybregts, Henk van Riemsdijk, Naoki Fukui and Mihoko Zushi.* Berlin: De Gruyter Mouton.

Chomsky, Noam, and Morris Halle. 1968. *The Sound Pattern of English*. Cambridge, MA: MIT Press.

Chomsky, Noam, and Marcel Schützenberger. 1963. "The Algebraic Theory of Context Free Languages." In *Computer Programming and Formal Systems*, edited by P. Braffort and D. Hirschberg, 118–161. Amsterdam: North-Holland.

Chou, Tracy. 2013. "Where Are the Numbers?," *Medium*, October 13. https://medium.com/@triketora/where-are-the-numbers-cb997a57252.

Church, Alonzo. 1936. "An Unsolvable Problem of Elementary Number Theory." *American Journal of Mathematics* 58, no. 2:345–363.

Church, Alonzo. 1937. "Reviewed Work: On Computable Numbers, with an Application to the Entscheidungsproblem. A. M. Turing." *Journal of Symbolic Logic* 2, no. 1:42–43.

Coleman, Gabriella. 2012. *Coding Freedom: The Ethics and Aesthetics of Hacking*. Princeton, NJ: Princeton University Press.

Colmerauer, A., and P. Roussel. 1993. "The Birth of Prolog." *ACM SIGPLAN Notices* 28, no. 3: 37–52.

Condillac. (1780) 1877. *La Langue des Calculs*. Paris: Sandoz et Fischbacher.

Conniff, Richard. 2015. "How Science Came to Yale." *Yale Alumni Magazine* 78, no. 4 (March–April). https://yalealumnimagazine.com/articles/4066-how-science-came-to-yale.

Consigny, Scott. 1994. "Nietzsche's Reading of the Sophists." *Rhetoric Review* 13, no. 1 (Autumn): 5–26.

Cook, Matthew. 2004. "Universality in Elementary Cellular Automata." *Complex Systems* 15:1–40.

Copeland, B. Jack. 2002. "The Church-Turing Thesis." In *The Stanford Encyclopedia of Philosophy* (Winter 2017 Edition), edited by Edward N. Zalta. https://plato.stanford.edu/archives/win2017/entries/church-turing/.

Coulomb, Charles-Augustin de. 1821. "Résultat de Plusieur Expériences destinées à determiner la quantité d'action que les hommes peuvent fournir pour leur travail journalier, suivant les différentes manières don't ils emploient leur forces." In *Théorie des Machines Simples, en Ayant Égard au Frottement de leurs Parties et à la Roideur des Cordages*, 255–297. Paris: Bachelier.

Courtland, Rachel. 2015. "Gordon Moore, the Man Whose Name Means Progress: The Visionary Engineer Reflects on 50 Years of Moore's Law." Interview. *IEEE Spectrum*, March 30. https://spectrum.ieee.org/computing/hardware/gordon-moore-the-man-whose-name-means-progress.

Couturat, Louis. 1901. *Logique de Leibniz, d'après des documents inédits*. Paris: Félix Alcan.

Cram, David. 2004. "Rhetoric and Music in the Early Modern Period." In *The Making of the Humanities*. Vol. 1, edited by Rens Bod, Jaap Maat, and Thijs Weststeijn, 263–282. Amsterdam: Amsterdam University Press.

Crawford, Sue E. S., and Elinor Ostrom. 1995. "A Grammar of Institutions." *American Political Science Review* 89, no. 3 (September): 582–600.

Cringely, Bob, dir. 1996. *Triumph of the Nerds*. Season 1, episode 3, "Great Artists Steal."

Curley, Robert. 2012. *Scientists and Inventors of the Renaissance*. Encyclopedia Britannica and Rosen Publishing.

Davidson, Arnold I. 1997. *Foucault and His Interlocutors*. Chicago: University of Chicago Press.

Davis, Martin. 1958. *Computability and Unsolvability*. New York: McGraw-Hill. Reprint New York: Dover, 1982.

Davis, Martin. 2000. *The Universal Computer: The Road from Leibniz to Turing*. New York: W. W. Norton.

Davis, Martin. 2001. "The Early History of Automated Deduction." In *Handbook of Automated Reasoning,* edited by Alan Robinson, Andrei Voronkov, 5–15. Amsterdam: Elsevier.

Dawkins, Richard. 1976. *The Selfish Gene*. Oxford: Oxford University Press.

DeLanda, Manuel. 2003. *War in the Age of Intelligent Machines*. New York: Zone Books.

Deleuze, Gilles. 1983. "Plato and the Simulacrum." Translated by Rosalind Krauss. *October* 27 (Winter): 45–56.

Deleuze, Gilles. 1990. *The Logic of Sense*. Translated by Mark Lester and Charles Stivale. New York: Columbia University Press.

Deleuze, Gilles. 1994. *Difference and Repetition*. New York: Columbia University Press.

Deleyre, Alexandre. (1755) 2017. "Épingle." In *Encyclopédie, ou dictionnaire raisonné des sciences, des arts et des métiers, etc.,* edited by Denis Diderot and Jean le Rond d'Alembert. University of Chicago: ARTFL Encyclopédie Project. http://encyclopedie.uchicago.edu/.

Denecker, Marc, and Antonis Kakas. 2002. "Abduction in Logic Programming." In *Computational Logic (Kowalski Festschrift)*, edited by A. C. Kakas and F. Sadri, 402–436. Lecture Notes in Artificial Intelligence 2407. Berlin: Springer-Verlag.

Denning, Peter. 2013. "The Science in Computer Science." *Communications of the ACM* 56, no. 5:30–33.

Deringer, William. 2018. *Calculated Values: Finance, Politics, and the Quantitative Age*. Cambridge, MA: Harvard University Press.

Derrida, Jacques. 1976. *Of Grammatology*. 1st American ed. Baltimore: Johns Hopkins University Press.

Dershowitz, Nachum, and Yuri Gurevich. 2008. "A Natural Axiomatization of Computability and Proof of Church's Thesis." *Bulletin of Symbolic Logic* 14, no. 3:299–350.

Descartes, René. 2006. *A Discourse on the Method: Of Correctly Conducting One's Reason and Seeking Truth in the Sciences*. Translated by Ian Maclean. Oxford World's Classics. Oxford: Oxford University Press.

Devlin, Keith. 2011. *The Man of Numbers: Fibonacci's Arithmetic Revolution*. New York: Bloomsbury. Kindle.

Diderot, Denis. "Art." *Encyclopédie, ou dictionnaire raisonné des sciences, des arts et des métiers, etc.*, edited by Denis Diderot and Jean le Rond d'Alembert. University of Chicago: ARTFL Encyclopédie Project. http://encyclopedie.uchicago.edu/.

Dijkstra, Edsger. 1968. "Go To Statement Considered Harmful." *Communications of the ACM* 11, no. 3:147–148.

Dijkstra, Edsger. 1972. "The Humble Programmer." *Communications of the ACM* 15, no. 10.

Ducheneaut, Nicolas. 2005. "Socialization in an Open Source Software Community: A Sociotechnical Analysis." *Computer Supported Cooperative Work* 14, no. 4:323–368.

Dumit, Joseph. 2000. "Artificial Participation: An Interview with Warren Sack." In *Zeroing in on the Year 2000: The Final Edition*, edited by George E. Marcus, 59–88. Late Editions 8. Chicago: University of Chicago Press.

Dumit, Joseph. 2004. *Picturing Personhood: Brain Scans and Biomedical Identity*. Princeton, NJ: Princeton University Press.

Dumit, Joseph. 2016. "Circuits in the Brain and How They Got There." In *Plasticity and Pathology: On the Formation of the Neural Subject*, edited by David Bates and Nima Bassiri, 219–267. New York: Fordham University Press.

Dung, Phan Minh. 1995. "On the Acceptability of Arguments and Its Fundamental Role in Nonmonotonic Reasoning, Logic Programming and N-Person Games." *Artificial Intelligence* 77:321–357.

During, Elie. 2011. *Bergson et Einstein: La querelle du temps*. Paris: Presses Universitaires de France.

Eagleton, Terry. 1991. *Ideology: An Introduction*. London: Verso.

Easley, David, and Jon Kleinberg. 2010. *Networks, Crowds, and Markets: Reasoning about a Highly Connected World*. Cambridge: Cambridge University Press.

Eco, Umberto. 1995. *The Search for the Perfect Language*. The Making of Europe. Cambridge, MA: Blackwell.

Edwards, Paul N. 1996. *The Closed World: Computers and the Politics of Discourse in Cold War America*. Inside Technology. Cambridge, MA: MIT Press.

Edwards, Paul N. 2010. *A Vast Machine: Computer Models, Climate Data, and the Politics of Global Warming*. Cambridge, MA: MIT Press.

Elders, Fons. 1974. *Reflexive Water: The Basic Concerns of Mankind*. London: Souvenir Press.

Engelbart, Douglas C., and William K. English. 1968. "A Research Center for Augmenting Human Intellect." Paper presented at the AFIPS '68 Proceedings of the Fall Joint Computer Conference (part I), San Francisco, CA, December 9–11.

Ensmenger, Nathan L. 2012. *The Computer Boys Take Over: Computers, Programmers, and the Politics of Technical Expertise*. Cambridge, MA: MIT Press.

Eshghi, K. 1988. "Abductive Planning with Event Calculus." Fifth International Conference and Symposium on Logic Programming, Seattle, August 15–19. Edited by Robert Kowalski and Kenneth Bowen. Cambridge, MA: MIT Press.

Ferreirós, José. 2001. "The Road to Modern Logic—an Interpretation." *Bulletin of Symbolic Logic* 7, no. 4 (December): 441–484.

Fleck, Glen, Office of Charles and Ray Eames, and International Business Machines Corporation. 1990. *A Computer Perspective: Background to the Computer Age*. Cambridge, MA: Harvard University Press.

Floyd, Robert W. 1979. "The Paradigms of Programming: 1978 Turing Award Lecture." *Communications of the ACM* 22, no. 8:455–460.

Flusser, Vilém. 2000. *Towards a Philosophy of Photography*. London: Reaktion Books.

Foucault, Michel. 1969. "Introduction." In *Grammaire générale et raisonnée*, edited by A. Arnauld and C. Lancelot, iii–xxvii. Paris: Republications Paulet.

Foucault, Michel. 1984. "What Is Enlightenment?" In *The Foucault Reader*, edited by Paul Rabinow, 32–50. New York: Pantheon Books.

Foucault, Michel. 2001. *Dits et Écrits: 1954–1988*. Paris: Gallimard.

Foucault, Michel. 2001. "Introduction." In *Dits et Écrits: 1954–1988*, 760–780. Paris: Gallimard.

Foucault, Michel. 2002. *The Order of Things: An Archaeology of the Human Sciences*. New York: Routledge. Kindle.

Foucault, Michel. 2005. *The Hermeneutics of the Subject: Lectures at the Collège de France, 1981–1982*. New York: Palgrave-Macmillan.

Frabetti, Federica. 2014. *Software Theory: A Cultural and Philosophical Study*. Media Philosophy. London: Rowman and Littlefield International.

Franklin, Benjamin. 1735. *Poor Richard's Almanack*. Philadelphia: B. Franklin.

Freud, Sigmund. (1905) 1960. *Jokes and Their Relation to the Unconscious*. Translated by James Strachey. The Standard Edition. New York: W. W. Norton.

Freud, Sigmund. 1950. "The Uncanny (1919)." In *The Standard Edition of the Complete Psychological Works of Sigmund Freud*. Vol. 17, *An Infantile Neurosis and Other Works, 1917–1919*, 217–256. London: Hogarth and Institute of Psycho-Analysis.

Freud, Sigmund. 1950. "Fetishism (1927)." In *The Standard Edition of the Complete Psychological Works of Sigmund Freud*. Vol. 5, *Miscellaneous Papers, 1888–1938,* edited by James Strachey, 198–204. London: Hogarth and Institute of Psycho-Analysis.

Fuller, Matthew, ed. 2008. *Software Studies: A Lexicon*. Cambridge, MA: MIT Press.

Fuller, Matthew, and Sónia Matos. 2017. "Feral Computing: From Ubiquitous Calculation to Wild Interactions." In *How to Be a Geek: Essays on the Culture of Software*, edited by Matthew Fuller, 167–190. Cambridge: Polity Press.

Gandy, Robin O. 1988. "The Confluence of Ideas in 1936." In *The Universal Turing Machine: A Half-Century Survey*, edited by R. Herken, 51–102. New York: Oxford University Press.

Gardner, Howard. 1985. *The Mind's New Science: A History of the Cognitive Revolution*. New York: Basic Books.

Gardner, Martin. 1958. *Logic Machines and Diagrams*. New York: McGraw-Hill.

Garfinkel, Harold. 1967. *Studies in Ethnomethodology*. Englewood Cliffs, NJ: Prentice-Hall.

Gastaldi, Juan Luis. 2014. Une archéologie de la logique du sens: Arithmétique et contenu dans le processus de mathématisation de la logique au XIXe siècle." PhD thesis, École doctorale Montaigne-Humanités en partenariat avec Sciences, Philosophie, Humanités, Université de Bordeaux 3.

Ghallab, Malik, Dana S. Nau, and Paolo Traverso. 2004. *Automated Planning Theory and Practice*. Amsterdam: Elsevier/Morgan Kaufmann.

Gibney, Alex, dir. 2015. *Steve Jobs: The Man in the Machine*.

Gillespie, Tarleton. 2016. "Algorithm." In *Digital Keywords: A Vocabulary of Information Society and Culture*, edited by Benjamin Peters, 18–30. Princeton, NJ: Princeton University Press.

Gillespie, Tarleton, Pablo J. Boczkowski, and Kirsten A. Foot. 2014. *Media Technologies: Essays on Communication, Materiality, and Society*. Cambridge, MA: MIT Press.

Goldin, Dina, and Peter Wegner. 2008. "The Interactive Nature of Computing: Refuting the Strong Church-Turing Thesis." *Minds and Machines* 18, no. 1 (March): 17–38.

Goldstine, Herman, and John von Neumann. 1947. *Planning and Coding for an Electronic Instrument*. Princeton, NJ: Institute for Advanced Study.

Goldstine, Herman H. 1980. *The Computer—from Pascal to von Neumann*. Princeton, NJ: Princeton University Press, 1980.

Golinski, Jan V. 1989. "A Noble Spectacle: Phosphorus and the Public Cultures of Science in the Early Royal Society." *Isis: A Journal of the History of Science* 80:11–39.

Golinski, Jan V. 1994. "Precision Instruments and the Demonstrative Order of Proof in Lavoisier's Chemistry." *Osiris* 9:30–47.

Golumbia, David. 2009. *The Cultural Logic of Computation*. Cambridge, MA: Harvard University Press. Kindle.

Goodman, Nelson. 1954. *Fact, Fiction and Forecast*. London: University of London.

Gramsci, Antonio, Quintin Hoare, and Geoffrey Nowell-Smith. 1972. *Selections from the Prison Notebooks of Antonio Gramsci*. New York: International Publishers.

Green, Cordell. 1969. "Application of Theorem Proving to Problem Solving." In *International Joint Conference on Artificial Intelligence*, edited by Donald E. Walker and Lewis M. Norton, 219–240. New York: Gordon and Breach.

Greenberger, M. 1962. *Management and the Computer of the Future*. Cambridge, MA: MIT Press.

Greimas, Algirdas Julien. 1987. *On Meaning: Selected Writings in Semiotic Theory*. Minneapolis: University of Minnesota Press.

Grier, David Alan. 2005. *When Computers Were Human*. Princeton, NJ: Princeton University Press.

Grosz, Elizabeth. A. 1990. *Jacques Lacan: A Feminist Introduction*. New York: Routledge.

Hacking, Ian. 1975. *The Emergence of Probability: A Philosophical Study of Early Ideas about Probability, Induction and Statistical Inference*. Cambridge Series on Statistical and Probabilistic Mathematics. Cambridge: Cambridge University Press.

Halevy, Alon, Peter Norvig, and Fernando Pereira. 2009. "The Unreasonable Effectiveness of Data." *IEEE Intelligent Systems* 24, no. 2 (March): 8–12.

Hall, Marie Boas. 1958. *Boyle and Seventeenth-Century Chemistry*. Cambridge: Cambridge University Press.

Hall, Stuart. 1982. "The Rediscovery of 'Ideology': Return of the Repressed in Media Studies." In *Culture, Society, and the Media*, edited by Michael Gurevitch, Tony Bennett, James Curran, and Janet Woollacott, 56–90. New York: Routledge.

Hammer, Eric M. 1998. "Semantics for Existential Graphs." *Journal of Philosophical Logic* 27, no. 5 (October): 489–503.

Haraway, Donna Jeanne. 1989. *Primate Visions: Gender, Race, and Nature in the World of Modern Science*. New York: Routledge.

Haraway, Donna Jeanne. 1997. *ModestWitness@SecondMillennium.FemaleManMeetsOncoMouse:Feminism and Technoscience*. New York: Routledge.

Harding, Sandra G. 1991. *Whose Science? Whose Knowledge?: Thinking from Women's Lives*. Ithaca, NY: Cornell University Press.

Harris, Randy Allen. 1995. *The Linguistics War*. Oxford: Oxford University Press.

Harris, Roy. 1987. *The Language Machine*. London: Duckworth.

Harris, Zellig. 1940. "Review of Louis H. Gray, 'Foundations of Language.'" *Language* 16:216–223.

Havelock, Eric Alfred. 1963. *Preface to Plato*. Cambridge, MA: Belknap Press / Harvard University Press. Kindle.

Hayes, Patrick, and Kenneth Ford. 1995. "Turing Test Considered Harmful." In *Fourteenth International Joint Conference on Artificial Intelligence*. Vol. 1, edited by Chris S. Mellish, 972–977. August 20–25, 1995, Montreal. San Mateo, CA: Morgan Kaufmann.

Hemel, Daniel J. 2005. "Summers' Comments on Women and Science Draw Ire: Remarks at Private Conference Stir Criticism, Media Frenzy." *The Harvard Crimson*, January 14. http://www.thecrimson.com/article/2005/1/14/summers-comments-on-women-and-science/.

Herodotus. 2010. *The History*. Translated by David Grene. Chicago: University of Chicago Press.

Hertz, Ellen. 2000. "Stock Markets as 'Simulacra': Observation That Participates." *Tsantsa* 5:40–50.

Hilbert, David. (1899) 1980. *The Foundations of Geometry*. 2nd ed. Chicago: Open Court.

Hilbert, David. 1905. "On the Foundations of Logic and Arithmetic." *The Monist* 15, no. 3:338–352.

Hilbert, David, and Wilhelm Ackermann. (1928) 1950. *Principles of Mathematical Logic* [Grundzüge der Theoretischen Logik]. Translated by Lewis M. Hammond, George G. Leckie, and F. Steinhardt. New York: Chelsea.

Hilbert, David, and Paul Bernays. (1934) 2003. *Foundations of Mathematics*. Vol. 1. Translated by Ian Mueller. Bernays Project Text 12. Pittsburgh: Carnegie Mellon University.

Hilgartner, Stephen. 1990. "The Dominant View of Popularization: Conceptual Problems, Political Uses." *Social Studies of Science* 20, no. 3:519–539.

Hodges, Andrew. 2014. *Alan Turing: The Enigma: The Book That Inspired the Film "The Imitation Game."* Revised ed. Princeton, NJ: Princeton University Press.

Huck, Geoffrey J., and John A. Goldsmith. 1995. *Ideology and Linguistic Theory: Noam Chomsky and the Deep Structure Debates*. London: Routledge.

Huizinga, Johan. 1949. *Homo Ludens: A Study of the Play-Element in Culture*. Boston: Routledge and Keegan Paul.

IEEE. 2008. "754-2008—IEEE Standard for Floating-Point Arithmetic." http://ieeexplore.ieee.org/document/4610935/.

Illich, Ivan, and Barry Sanders. 1988. *ABC: The Alphabetization of the Popular Mind*. San Francisco: North Point Press.

Isaac, Mike. 2015. "Behind Silicon Valley's Self-Critical Tone on Diversity, a Lack of Progress." *New York Times*, June 28. http://bits.blogs.nytimes.com/2015/06/28/new-diversity-reports-show-the-same-old-results/.

Jackson, Allyn. 2008. "Interview with Martin Davis." *Notices of the American Mathematical Society* 55, no. 5 (May): 560–571.

Jameson, Fredric. 1972. *The Prison-House of Language; a Critical Account of Structuralism and Russian Formalism*. Princeton, NJ: Princeton University Press.

Jameson, Fredric. 1981. *The Political Unconscious: Narrative as a Socially Symbolic Act*. Ithaca, NY: Cornell University Press.

Jameson, Fredric. 1987. "Foreword." In *On Meaning: Selected Writings in Semiotic Theory /Algirdas Julien Greimas*. Translated by Paul J. Perron and Frank H. Collins, vi–xxii. Minneapolis: University of Minnesota Press.

Jenkins, Henry, Sam Ford, and Joshua Green. 2013. *Spreadable Media: Creating Value and Meaning in a Networked Culture*. New York: New York University Press.

Johnson, Melvin, Mike Schuster, Quoc V. Le, Maxim Krikun, Yonghui Wu, Zhifeng Chen, Nikhil Thorat, Fernanda Viégas, Martin Wattenberg, Greg Corrado, Macduff Hughes, and Jeffrey Dean. 2016. "Google's Multilingual Neural Machine Translation System: Enabling Zero-Shot Translation." November 14. https://arxiv.org/abs/1611.04558.

Johnson, Melvin, Mike Schuster, Quoc V. Le, Maxim Krikun, Yonghui Wu, Zhifeng Chen, Nikhil Thorat, Fernanda Viégas, Martin Wattenberg, Greg Corrado, Macduff Hughes, and Jeffrey Dean. 2017. "Google's Multilingual Neural Machine Translation System: Enabling Zero-Shot Translation." *Transactions of the Association for Computational Linguistics* 5:339–352.

The Joint Task Force on Computing Curricula of the Association for Computing Machinery (ACM) and the IEEE Computer Society. 2013. *Computer Science Curricula 2013: Curriculum Guidelines for Undergraduate Degree Programs in Computer Science*. New York: ACM, December 20.

Jonze, Spike, dir. 2013. *Her*. Los Angeles: Annapurna Pictures.

Joseph, Miriam. 2002. *The Trivium: The Liberal Arts of Logic, Grammar and Rhetoric*. Philadelphia: Paul Dry Books.

Kadvany, John. 2016. "Pāṇini's Grammar and Modern Computation." *History and Philosophy of Logic* 37, no. 4:325–346.

Kafai, Yasmin B., and Quinn Burke. 2014. *Connected Code: Why Children Need to Learn Programming*. John D. and Catherine T. MacArthur Foundation Series on Digital Media and Learning. Cambridge, MA: MIT Press.

Kakas, A. C., R. A. Kowalski, and F. Toni. 1993. "Abductive Logic Programming." *Journal of Logic and Computation* 2, no. 6:719–770.

Katz, Yarden. 2012. "Noam Chomsky on Where Artificial Intelligence Went Wrong: An Extended Conversation with the Legendary Linguist." *The Atlantic*, November 1. https://www.theatlantic.com/technology/archive/2012/11/noam-chomsky-on-where-artificial-intelligence-went-wrong/261637/.

Kay, Alan C. 1993. "The Early History of Smalltalk." *ACM SIGPLAN Notices* 28, no. 3:69–95.

Keller, Evelyn Fox. 1995. *Reflections on Gender and Science.* New Haven, CT: Yale University Press.

Kelty, Christopher M. 2008. *Two Bits: The Cultural Significance of Free Software.* Durham, NC: Duke University Press.

Kerferd, G. B. 1981. *The Sophistic Movement.* Cambridge: Cambridge University Press.

Kimball, Bruce. *The Liberal Arts Tradition: A Documentary History.* New York: University Press of America, 2010.

Kitchin, Rob. 2014. "Big Data, New Epistemologies and Paradigm Shifts." *Big Data and Society* 1, no. 1 (April–June): 1–12.

Kleene, S. C. 1967. *Mathematical Logic.* New York: Wiley.

Knuth, Donald Ervin. 1966. "Algorithm and Program; Information and Data (letter to the editor)." *Communications of the ACM* 9, no. 9:654.

Knuth, Donald Ervin. 1968. *The Art of Computer Programming.* Vol. 1, *Fundamental Algorithms.* Reading, MA: Addison-Wesley.

Knuth, Donald Ervin. 1968. "Section 1.3: MIX." In *The Art of Computer Programming.* Vol. 1, *Fundamental Algorithms*, 120–181. Reading, MA: Addison-Wesley.

Knuth, Donald Ervin. 1981. *The Art of Computer Programming.* Vol. 2, *Seminumerical Algorithms.* 2nd ed. Reading, MA: Addison-Wesley.

Knuth, Donald Ervin. (1984) 1991. *Literate Programming.* CSLI Lecture Notes. Stanford, CA: Center for the Study of Language and Information.

Knuth, Donald Ervin. 1999. *The Art of Computer Programming.* Fasc. 1, *MMIX.* Reading, MA: Addison-Wesley.

Knuth, Donald Ervin. 2011. *The Art of Computer Programming.* Vol. 1-4A. Boston: Addison-Wesley.

Kolmogorov, Andrey. 1963. "On Tables of Random Numbers." *Sankhyā Series A* 25:369–375.

Kowalski, R. A. 1979. "Algorithm = Logic + Control." *Communications of the ACM* 22, no. 7:424–436.

Kowalski, R. A. 1988. "The Early Years of Logic Programming." *Communications of the ACM* 31, no. 1:38–43.

Kowalski, R. A. 2014. "History of Logic Programming." In *History of Logic.* Vol. 9, *Computational Logic*, edited by Dov Gabbay, Jörg Siekmann, and John Woods, 523–569. Amsterdam: Elsevier.

Kuhn, Thomas S. 1970. *The Structure of Scientific Revolutions.* Chicago: University of Chicago Press.

Lakoff, Robin. 1969. "Review of 'Grammaire générale et raisonnée' by C. Lancelot, A. Arnauld and Herbert H. Brekle." *Language* 45, no. 2, pt. 1 (June): 343–364.

Lancelot, C. 1644. *Nouvelle méthode pour apprendre facilement la langue latine.* Paris: A. Vitré.

Lancelot, Claude, and Antoine Arnauld. 1803. *Grammaire Génerale et Raisonnée de Port-Royale, précedée d'un essai sur l'origine et les progès de la langue française (par M. Petitot)*. Paris: Chez Perlet.

Lassègue, Jean, and Giuseppe Longo. 2012. "What Is Turing's Comparison between Mechanism and Writing Worth?" In *CiE 2012*, edited by S. B. Cooper, A. Dawar, and B. Löwe, 451–462. Lecture Notes in Computer Science 7318. Berlin: Springer-Verlag.

Lasswell, Harold D. 1927. *Propaganda Technique in the World War*. New York: Peter Smith.

Latour, Bruno. 1987. *Science in Action: How to Follow Scientists and Engineers through Society*. Cambridge, MA: Harvard University Press.

Latour, Bruno. 1988. *The Pasteurization of France*. Cambridge, MA: Harvard University Press.

Latour, Bruno. 1993. *We Have Never Been Modern*. Translated by Catherine Porter. Cambridge, MA: Harvard University Press.

Latour, Bruno. 1998. "On Recalling ANT." In *Actor Network Theory and After*, edited by John Law and John Hassard, 15–25. Oxford: Blackwell.

Latour, Bruno. 1999. *Pandora's Hope: Essays on the Reality of Science Studies*. Cambridge, MA: Harvard University Press.

Latour, Bruno. 2008. "The Netz-Works of Greek Deductions." *Social Studies of Science* 38, no. 3:441–459.

Latour, Bruno. 2011. "Some Experiments in Art and Politics." *E-Flux Journal* 23 (March): 1–7.

Latour, Bruno. 2013. *An Inquiry into Modes of Existence: An Anthropology of the Moderns*. Cambridge, MA: Harvard University Press.

Lazarsfeld, Paul. 1947. "Remarks on Administrative and Critical Research." *Studies in Philosophy and Social Science* 9:2–16.

Leach, Arthur Francis. 1911. *Educational Charters and Documents, 598 to 1909*. Cambridge: Cambridge University Press.

Lee, Edward Ashford. 2017. *Plato and the Nerd: The Creative Partnership of Humans and Technology*. Cambridge, MA: MIT Press.

Lehrer, Jonah. 2011. "Steve Jobs: "Technology Alone Is Not Enough." *New Yorker*, October 7. https://www.newyorker.com/news/news-desk/steve-jobs-technology-alone-is-not-enough.

Leibniz, Gottfried Wilhelm. (1685) 1951. *Leibniz: Selections*, edited by Philip P. Wiener. New York, NY: Charles Scribner's Sons.

Leibniz, G. W. 1929. "Machina arithmetica in qua non additio tantum et subtractio set et multiplicato nullo, divisio vero paene nullo animi labore peragantur" (1685). English translation by M. Kormes. In *A Source Book in Mathematics*, edited by D. E. Smith, 173–181. New York: McGraw-Hill.

Levy, Steven. 2000. *Insanely Great: The Life and Times of Macintosh, the Computer That Changed Everything*. New York: Penguin Books.

Lewin, Tamar. 2013. "As Interest Fades in the Humanities, Colleges Worry." *New York Times*, October 31, http://www.nytimes.com/2013/10/31/education/as-interest-fades-in-the-humanities -colleges-worry.html.

Long, Pamela O. 2001. *Openness, Secrecy, Authorship: Technical Arts and the Culture of Knowledge from Antiquity to the Renaissance*. Baltimore: Johns Hopkins University Press.

Long, Pamela O. 2011. *Artisan/Practitioners and the Rise of the New Sciences, 1400–1600*. Corvallis: Oregon State University Press.

Longo, Giuseppe. "Laws of God, Men and Nature." https://www.iea-nantes.fr/en/chercheurs /longo-giuseppe_275.

Lovelace, Ada. 1843. "Sketch of the Analytical Engine Invented by Charles Babbage [by LF Mena-brea, translated and appended with additional notes, by Augusta Ada, Countess of Lovelace]." In *Scientific Memoirs, Selected from the Transactions of Foreign Academies of Science and Learned Societies*. Vol. 3, 666–731. London: Richard and John Taylor.

Lyotard, Jean François. 1984. *The Postmodern Condition: A Report on Knowledge*. Minneapolis: University of Minnesota Press.

Maat, Jaap. 2004. *Philosophical Languages in the Seventeenth Century: Dalgarno, Wilkins, Leibniz*. Boston: Kluwer Academic.

Mackenzie, Adrian. 2017. *Machine Learners*. Cambridge, MA: MIT Press.

MacKenzie, Donald. 1993. "Negotiating Arithmetic, Constructing Proof: The Sociology of Mathematics and Information Technology." *Social Studies of Science* 23, no. 1:37–65.

McCarthy, John. 1960. "Recursive Functions of Symbolic Expressions and Their Computation by Machine, Part I," *Communications of the ACM* 3, no. 4 (April): 184–195.

Mahoney, Michael. 2004. "Finding a History for Software Engineering." *IEEE Annals of the History of Computing* 26, no. 1 (January): 8–19.

Mahoney, Michael S. 1988. "The History of Computing in the History of Technology." *Annals of the History of Computing* 10:113–125.

Mahoney, Michael S. 2011. *Histories of Computing*. Cambridge, MA: Harvard University Press.

Mangalindan, J. P. 2014. "How Tech Companies Compare in Employee Diversity." *Fortune*. http://fortune.com/2014/08/29/how-tech-companies-compare-in-employee-diversity/.

Manovich, Lev. 2001. *The Language of New Media*. Cambridge, MA: MIT Press.

Manovich, Lev. 2016. "Instagram and Contemporary Image." manovich.net.

Markoff, John. 2005. *What the Dormouse Said: How the Sixties Counterculture Shaped the Personal Computer Industry*. New York: Penguin.

Marquand, Allan. 1885. "A New Logic Machine." *Proceedings of the American Academy of Arts and Sciences* 21: 303.

Mateas, Michael. 2005. "Procedural Literacy: Educating the New Media Practitioner." *On the Horizon: Special Issue on Games in Education* 13, no. 2:101–111.

Matiyasevich, Yuri. 2009. "Existential Arithmetization of Diophantine Equations." *Annals of Pure and Applied Logic* 157, no. 2–3: 225–233.

Matiyasevich, Yuri. 2016. "Chapter 2: Martin Davis and Hilbert's Tenth Problem." In *Martin Davis on Computability, Computational Logic, and Mathematical Foundations,* edited by Eugenio Omodeo and Alberto Policriti, 35–54. Switzerland: Springer.

Mattelart, Armand. 2003. *The Information Society: An Introduction.* Thousand Oaks, CA: Sage.

Mays, Wolfe, and D. G. Prinz. 1950. "A Relay Machine for the Demonstration of Symbolic Logic." *Nature* 165 (February 4): 197.

McCulloch, Warren. 1955. "Mysterium Iniquitatis of Sinful Man Aspiring into the Place of God." *Scientific Monthly* 80, no. 1:35–39.

McCulloch, Warren. 1960. "What Is Number, That a Man May Know It, and a Man, That He May Know Number?" *General Semantics Bulletin*, nos. 26–27:7–18.

McCulloch, Warren S., and Walter Pitts. 1943. "A Logical Calculus of the Ideas Immanent in Nervous Activity." *Bulletin of Mathematical Biophysics* 5:115–133.

McDermott, Drew. 1981. "Artificial Intelligence Meets Natural Stupidity." In *Mind Design: Philosophy, Psychology, Artificial Intelligence*, edited by John Haugeland, 5–18. Cambridge, MA: MIT Press.

McDowell, Gayle Laakmann 2015. *Cracking the Coding Interview: 189 Programming Questions and Solutions*. 6th ed. Palo Alto, CA: CareerCup.

McLuhan, Marshall. 1962. *The Gutenberg Galaxy: The Making of Typographic Man*. Toronto: University of Toronto Press.

McLuhan, Marshall, and W. Terrence Gordon. 2006. *The Classical Trivium: The Place of Thomas Nashe in the Learning of His Time*. Corte Madera, CA: Gingko Press.

Meehan, James. 1976. "The Metanovel: Writing Stories by Computer." PhD diss., Computer Science, Yale University.

Menninger, Karl. 1969. *Number Words and Number Symbols*. Cambridge, MA: MIT Press.

Milner, Robin. 1993. "Elements of Interaction." *Communications of the ACM* 36, no. 1:78–89.

Minkel, J. R. 2007. "A New Kind of Science Author Pays Brainy Undergrad $25,000 for Identifying Simplest Computer: But Will It Jumpstart Stephen Wolfram's Scientific Revolution?" *Scientific American*, October 25. https://www.scientificamerican.com/article/simplest-computer-new-kind-science/.

Minsky, Marvin. 1981. "Jokes and Their Relation to the Cognitive Unconscious." In *Cognitive Constraints on Communication*, edited by Lucia Vaina and Jaako Hintikka, 175–200. Boston: Reidel.

Minsky, Marvin. 1986. *Society of Mind*. New York: Simon and Schuster.

Mirowski, Philip. 2002. *Machine Dreams: Economics Becomes a Cyborg Science*. Cambridge: Cambridge University Press.

Monteiro, Stephen. 2017. *The Fabric of Interface: Mobile Media, Design, and Gender*. Cambridge, MA: MIT Press.

Moretti, Franco. 2013. *Distant Reading*. London: Verso.

Morrison, Philip and Emily Morrison, eds. 1961. *Charles Babbage: On the Principles and Development of the Calculator and Other Seminal Writings by Charles Babbage and Others*. Mineola, NY: Dover.

Muggleton, S. 1991. "Inductive Logic Programming." *New Generation Computing* 8, no. 4:295–318.

Muniesa, Fabian. 2014. *The Provoked Economy: Economic Reality and the Performative Turn*. New York: Routledge.

Murtaugh, Michael. 2008. "Interaction." In *Software Studies: A Lexicon*, edited by Matthew Fuller, 143–149. Cambridge, MA: MIT Press.

Nau, D. 2003. "SHOP2: An HTN Planning System." *Journal of Artificial Intelligence Research* 20:379–404.

Naur, Peter, and Brian Randell, eds. 1969. *Software Engineering: Report on a Conference Sponsored by the NATO Science Committee, Garmisch, Germany, 7th to 11th October 1968*. Brussels: Scientific Affairs Division, NATO.

Naur, Peter, Brian Randell, and John Buxton, eds. 1976. *Software Engineering: Concepts and Techniques, Proceedings of the NATO Conferences*. New York: Petrocelli/Charter Publishers, Inc. http://homepages.cs.ncl.ac.uk/brian.randell/NATO/

Netz, Reviel. 1999. *The Shaping of Deduction in Greek Mathematics: A Study in Cognitive History*. Cambridge: Cambridge University Press.

Neumaier, Otto. 1987. "A Wittgensteinian View of Artificial Intelligence." In *Artificial Intelligence: The Case Against*, edited by Rainer Born, 132–173. London: Croom-Helm.

Newell, Allen, Alan J. Perlis, and Herbert A. Simon. 1967. "What Is Computer Science?" *Science* 157, no. 3795:1373–1374.

Newell, Allen, and Herbert A. Simon. 1976. "Computer Science as Empirical Inquiry: Symbols and Search." *Communications of the ACM* 19, no. 3:113–126.

Newton, Isaac. 1687. *Philosophiæ Naturalis Principia Mathematica* [Mathematical Principles of Natural Philosophy]. London: Jussu Societatis Regiæ ac Typis Joseph Streater.

Nietzsche, Friedrich Wilhelm. 1997. "On the Uses and Disadvantages of History for Life." In *Nietzsche: Untimely Meditations*, edited by Daniel Breazeale and R. J. Hollingdale, 57–124. Cambridge: Cambridge University Press.

Nietzsche, Friedrich Wilhelm, and Damion Searls. 2016. *Anti-education: On the Future of Our Educational Institutions*. New York: New York Review Books Classics.

Nofre, David, Mark Priestley, and Gerard Alberts. 2014. "When Technology Became Language: The Origins of the Linguistic Conception of Computer Programming, 1950–1960." *Technology and Culture* 55, no. 1:40–75.

Norberg, Arthur L., ed. 1991. *An Interview with Terry Allen Winograd*. Minneapolis: Charles Babbage Institute, Center for the History of Information Processing, University of Minnesota. December 11. https://conservancy.umn.edu/handle/11299/107717.

Norvig, Peter. "On Chomsky and the Two Cultures of Statistical Learning." http://norvig.com /chomsky.html.

Oleson, Alexandra, and John Voss. 1979. *The Organization of Knowledge in Modern America, 1860–1920*. Baltimore: Johns Hopkins University Press.

Ong, Walter J. 2002. *Orality and Literacy: The Technologizing of the Word*. New York: Routledge.

Palfrey, John, and Urs Gasser. 2008. *Born Digital: Understanding the First Generation of Digital Natives*. New York: Basic Books.

Papert, Seymour. 1980. *Mindstorms: Children, Computers, and Powerful Ideas*. New York: Basic Books.

Peaucelle, Jean-Louis. 1999. "La division du travail: Adam Smith et les éncyclopedistes observant la fabrication des épingles en Normandie." *Gérer et Comprendre, Annales des mines*. No. 57 (September): 35–51.

Peirce, Charles S. (1886) 1993. "Letter, Peirce to A. Marquand." In *Writings of Charles S. Peirce: A Chronological Edition*. Vol. 5, *(1884–1886)*, edited by Christian J. W. Kloesel, Nathan Househ, Marc Simon, André De Tienne, Ursula Niklas, Aleta Houser, Cathy L. Clark, and Max H. Fisch, 421–424. Bloomington: Indiana University Press.

Peirce, Charles S. (1901) 1931–1935. *Collected Papers of Charles Sanders Peirce*, vols. 1–6, edited by Charles Hartshorne and Paul Weiss. Cambridge, MA: Harvard University Press.

Peirce, Charles S. (1901) 1958. *Collected Papers of Charles Sanders Peirce*, vols. 7–8, edited by Arthur W. Burks. Cambridge, MA: Harvard University Press.

Peirce, Charles S. (1901) 1985. "The Proper Treatment of Hypotheses: A Preliminary Chapter, toward an Examination of Hume's Argument against Miracles, in Its Logic and in Its History (MS 692)." In *Historical Perspectives on Peirce's Logic of Science: A History of Science*, edited by Carolyn Eisele, 898–899. New York: Mouton De Gruyter.

Peirce, Charles S. (1903) 1997. "A Deleted Passage." In *Pragmatism as a Principle and Method of Right Thinking: The 1903 Harvard "Lectures on Pragmatism,"* edited by Patricia Ann Turisi, 282–283. Albany: State University of New York Press.

Penny, Simon. 2017. *Making Sense: Cognition, Computing, Art, and Embodiment*. Cambridge, MA: MIT Press.

Pereira, Fernando C. N., and David H. D. Warren. 1980. "Definite Clause Grammars for Language Analysis—a Survey of the Formalism and a Comparison with Augmented Transition Networks." *Artificial Intelligence* 13:231–278.

Perlis, Alan J. 1962. "The Computer in the University." In *Management and the Computer of the Future,* edited by M. Greenberger, 180–219. Cambridge, MA: MIT Press.

Perlis, Alan J. 1982. "Epigrams in Programming." *ACM SIGPLAN Notices*: 6. http://www.cs.yale .edu/homes/perlis-alan/quotes.html.

Perronet, Jean-Rudolphe. 1739. *Explication de la Façon dont on Réduit le Fil de Laiton à Différentes Grosseurs dans la Ville de Laigle* (Manuscript 2384), edited by École Nationale des Ponts et Chaussées. Paris: Archives of the École Nationale des Ponts et Chaussées.

Perronet, Jean-Rudolphe. 1740. *Description de la Façon dont on Fait les Épingles à Laigle en Normandie* (Manuscript 2385), edited by École Nationale des Ponts et Chaussées. Paris: Archives of the École Nationale des Ponts et Chaussées.

Petzold, Charles. 2008. *The Annotated Turing: A Guided Tour through Alan Turing's Historic Paper on Computability and the Turing Machine*. Indianapolis, IN: Wiley.

Pias, Claus. 2015. "Technologies of Simulation." History and Theory of New Media Lecture Series, University of California, Berkeley, October 15.

Picon, Antoine. 1992. *French Architects and Engineers in the Age of Enlightenment*. Cambridge: Cambridge University Press.

Picon, Antoine. 1992. "Gestes ouvriers, opérations et processus techniques: La vision du travail des encyclopédistes." *Recherches sur Diderot et sur l'Encyclopédie, Société Diderot* 13, 131–147.

Plant, Sadie. 1997. *Zeroes + Ones: Digital Women + the New Technoculture*. New York: Doubleday.

Plato. 1963. *The Collected Dialogues of Plato, Including the Letters,* edited by Edith Hamilton, Huntington Cairns, and Lane Cooper. New York: Pantheon Books.

Plato. 1982. *The Republic*. Translated by Allan Bloom. New York: Basic Books.

Plato. 2015. *The Complete Works of Plato* [Annotated]. Translated by Benjamin Jowett. Latus ePublishing. Kindle.

Pliny. 1991. *Natural History: A Selection*. London: Penguin.

Plutarch. 1916. *Plutarch's Lives*. Translated by Bernadotte Perrin. Cambridge, MA: Harvard University Press.

Poincaré, Henri. 1952. *Science and Method*. New York: Dover.

Pollock, Sheldon. 2009. "Future Philology? The Fate of a Soft Science in a Hard World." *Critical Inquiry* 35:931–961.

Post, Emil. 1921. "Introduction to a General Theory of Elementary Propositions." *American Journal of Mathematics* 43, no. 3:163–185.

Post, Emil. 1943. "Formal Reductions of the General Combinatorial Decision Problem." *American Journal of Mathematics* 65, no. 2:197–215.

Powell, Walter W., and Paul DiMaggio. 1991. *The New Institutionalism in Organizational Analysis.* Chicago: University of Chicago Press.

Presburger, Mojżesz. 1929. "Ueber die Vollstaendigkeit eines gewissen Systems der Arithmetik ganzer Zahlen, in welchem die Addition als einzige Operation hervortritt." In *Comptes Rendus du I congrès de Mathématiciens des Pays Slaves,* 92–101. Warsaw, Poland.

Priestley, Mark. 2010. *A Science of Operations: Machines, Logic and the Invention of Programming.* New York: Springer. Kindle.

Prony, Gaspard-Clair-François-Marie Riche de. 1824. "Notice sur les grandes tables logarithmiques et trigonométriques, adaptées au nouveau système métrique décimal, lue à la séance publique du 7 juin 1824." Paper presented at the public meeting of the Académie Royale des Sciences, Paris.

Proust, Christine. 2013. "Du calcul flottant en Mésopotamie." *Société Mathematique de France (SMF) / Gazette des Mathématiciens,* no. 138 (October): 23–48.

Pullum, Geoffrey K. 2011. "On the Mathematical Foundations of Syntactic Structures." *Journal of Logic, Language and Information* 20:277–296.

Quine, W. V. 1976. *The Ways of Paradox and Other Essays.* Revised and enlarged ed. Cambridge, MA: Harvard University Press.

Radway, Janice. 2004. "Research Universities, Periodical Publication, and the Circulation of Professional Expertise: On the Significance of Middlebrow Authority." *Critical Inquiry* 31, no. 1:203–228.

Rajchman, John. 1995. *The Identity in Question.* New York: Routledge.

Rajchman, John. 2000. *The Deleuze Connections.* Cambridge, MA: MIT Press.

Rajchman, John. 2006. *The Chomsky-Foucault Debate on Human Nature.* New York: New Press.

Rapp, Christof. 2010. "Aristotle's Rhetoric." In *The Stanford Encyclopedia of Philosophy*, edited by Edward N. Zalta. Stanford, CA: Stanford University Press. https://plato.stanford.edu/entries/aristotle-rhetoric/.

Reas, Casey, and Ben Fry. 2014. *Processing: A Programming Handbook for Visual Designers and Artists.* 2nd ed. Cambridge, MA: MIT Press.

Reingold, Edward M., and Nachum Dershowitz. 2018. *Calendrical Calculations, The Ultimate Edition,* 4th Edition, Kindle Edition. Cambridge: Cambridge University Press.

Rice, John R., and Saul Rosen. 1994. "History of the Computer Sciences Department of Purdue University." In *Studies in Computer Science: In Honor of Samuel D. Conte, Richard DeMillo and John Rice,* edited by Richard DeMillo and John Rice, 45–72. Dordrecht, Netherlands: Kluwer Academic/Plenum Press.

Rieder, Bernhard. 2012. "What Is in PageRank? A Historical and Conceptual Investigation of a Recursive Status Index." *Computational Culture: A Journal of Software Studies*, no. 3 (September 28). http://computationalculture.net/what_is_in_pagerank/.

Robin, Léon. (1928) 1996. *Greek Thought and the Origins of the Scientific Spirit*. London: Routledge.

Rogers, Richard. 2000. *Preferred Placement: Knowledge Politics on the Web*. Maastricht: Jan van Eyck Akadamie; Amsterdam: De Balie.

Rogers, Richard. 2009. *The End of the Virtual: Digital Methods*. Amsterdam: Vossiuspers UvA.

Rogers, Richard. 2013. *Digital Methods*. Cambridge, MA: MIT Press.

Rojas, Raúl. 1997–1998. *A Tutorial Introduction to the Lambda Calculus*. Berlin: Freie Universitat Berlin.

Rosen, Judith. 2003. "Weighing Wolfram's 'New Kind of Science.'" *Publishers Weekly* 250, no. 2 (January 13). https://www.publishersweekly.com/pw/print/20030113/40516-weighing-wolfram-s-new-kind-of-science.html.

Rosenberg, Daniel. 2013. "Data before the Fact." In *"Raw Data" Is an Oxymoron*, edited by Lisa Gitelman, 15–40. Cambridge, MA: MIT Press.

Rotman, Brian. 1993. *Ad Infinitum … the Ghost in Turing's Machine: Taking God Out of Mathematics and Putting the Body Back In*. Stanford, CA: Stanford University Press.

Rouvroy, Antoinette, and Thomas Berns. 2013. "Gouvernementalité algorithmique et perspectives d'émancipation: Le disparate comme condition d'individuation par la relation? Politique des algorithmes. Les métriques du web." *Réseaux* 31, no. 177:163–196.

Russell, Bertrand. 1903. *The Principles of Mathematics*. Vol. 1. Cambridge: Cambridge University Press.

Russell, Stuart J., and Peter Norvig. 2010. *Artificial Intelligence: A Modern Approach*. 3rd ed. Upper Saddle River, NJ: Prentice Hall.

Sack, Warren. 1996. "Replaying Turing's Imitation Game." Paper presented at Console-ing Passions: Television, Video and Feminism, Madison, WI, April 25–28, 1996.

Sack, Warren. 1998. "Artificial Intelligence." In *The Encyclopedia of Aesthetics*. Vol. 1, edited by Michael Kelly, 123–130. New York: Oxford University Press.

Sack, Warren. 2011. "Aesthetics of Information Visualization." In *Context Providers: Conditions of Meaning in Media Arts*, edited by Margot Lovejoy, Christiane Paul, and Viktorija Vesna Bulajic. Bristol: Intellect.

Sack, Warren, Françoise Detienne, Nicolas Ducheneaut, Jean-Marie Burkhardt, Dilan Mahendran, and Flore Barcellini. 2006. "A Methodological Framework for Socio-cognitive Analyses of Collaborative Design of Open Source Software." *Computer Supported Cooperative Work* 15, nos. 2–3:229–250.

Sapir, Edward. 1921. *Language: An Introduction to the Study of Speech*. New York: Harcourt, Brace.

Sarkar, Palash. 2000. "A Brief History of Cellular Automata." *ACM Computing Surveys* 32, no. 1 (March): 80–107.

Saussure, Ferdinand de. (1916) 1986. *Course in General Linguistics.* Translated by Roy Harris. Chicago: Open Court. Kindle.

Scholz, B. C., and G. K. Pullum. 2007. "Tracking the Origins of Transformational Generative Grammar." *Journal of Linguistics* 43:701–723.

Schopenhauer, Arthur. 1921. *The Art of Controversy, and Other Posthumous Papers.* London: Allen and Unwin.

Searle, John R. 1969. *Speech Acts: An Essay in the Philosophy of Language.* London: Cambridge University Press.

Searle, John R. 1980. "Minds, Brains and Programs." *Behavioral and Brain Sciences* 3:417–457.

Selingo, Jeffrey. 2017. "Six Myths about Choosing a College Major." *New York Times*, November 3. https://www.nytimes.com/2017/11/03/education/edlife/choosing-a-college-major.html.

Serres, Michel. 1974. *Hermès III, la traduction.* Paris: Éditions de Minuit.

Shakespeare, William. 1600. *Merchant of Venice.* http://shakespeare.mit.edu/merchant/full.html

Shakespeare, William. 1623. *Julius Caesar.* http://shakespeare.mit.edu/julius_caesar/full.html.

Shannon, Claude E. 1938. "A Symbolic Analysis of Relay and Switching Circuits." *Transactions of the AIEE* 57:713–723.

Shannon, Claude E. 1948. "A Mathematical Theory of Communication." *Bell System Technical Journal* 27 (July): 379–423; (October): 623–656.

Shannon, Claude Elwood. 1940 (finished in 1937). "A Symbolic Analysis of Relay and Switching Circuits." MS thesis, Electrical Engineering, Massachusetts Institute of Technology.

Shannon, Claude Elwood, and Warren Weaver. 1949. *The Mathematical Theory of Communication.* Urbana: University of Illinois Press.

Shapin, Steven. 1996. *The Scientific Revolution.* Chicago: University of Chicago Press.

Shapin, Steven, and Simon Schaffer. 2011. *Leviathan and the Air-Pump: Hobbes, Boyle, and the Experimental Life: With a New Introduction by the Authors.* Princeton, NJ: Princeton University Press. Kindle.

Shelley, Mary. 1818. *Frankenstein; or, The Modern Prometheus.* London: Lackington, Hughes, Harding, Mavor and Jones.

Shin, Sun-Joo, and Eric Hammer. 2014. "Peirce's Deductive Logic." In *The Stanford Encyclopedia of Philosophy*, edited by Edward N. Zalta. Stanford, CA: Stanford University Press. https://plato.stanford.edu/entries/peirce-logic/.

Sieg, Wilfried. 1999. "Hilbert's Programs: 1917–1922." *Bulletin of Symbolic Logic* 5, no. 1:1–44.

Sieg, Wilfried. 2002. "Calculations by Man and Machine: Conceptual Analysis." In *Reflections on the Foundations of Mathematics: Essays in Honor of Solomon Feferman*, edited by Wilfried Sieg, Richard Sommer, and Carolyn Talcott, 390–409. Natick, MA: A. K. Peters/CRC Press.

Simon, Herbert A. 1996. *The Sciences of the Artificial*. 3rd ed. Cambridge, MA: MIT Press.

Simon, Herbert A. 2000. "Bounded Rationality in Social Science: Today and Tomorrow." *Mind and Society* 1, no. 1:25–39.

Simon, Herbert A., and Allen Newell. 1958. "Heuristic Problem Solving: The Next Advance in Operations Research." *Operations Research* 6, no. 1 (January–February): 1–10.

Singer, Emily. 2008. "Brain Trauma in Iraq." *Technology Review* (May–June). https://www.technologyreview.com/s/409938/brain-trauma-in-iraq/.

Singer, Natasha. 2014. "Intel's Sharp-Eyed Social Scientist." *New York Times*, February 15, https://www.nytimes.com/2014/02/16/technology/intels-sharp-eyed-social-scientist.html.

Smith, Daniel. 2012. "Essay 1: The Concept of the Simulacrum: Deleuze and the Overturning of Platonism." In *Essays on Deleuze,* 3–27. Edinburgh: Edinburgh University Press.

Snow, C. P. 1959. *The Two Cultures and the Scientific Revolution, The Rede Lecture, 1959*. New York: Cambridge University Press.

Soare, Robert I. 1996. "Computability and Recursion." *Bulletin of Symbolic Logic* 2, no. 3:284–321.

Solomonoff, Ray. 1960. *A Preliminary Report on a General Theory of Inductive Inference*. Report V-131. Cambridge, MA: Zator Corporation.

Solomonoff, Ray. 1964. "A Formal Theory of Inductive Inference Part I." *Information and Control* 7, no. 1 (March): 1–22.

Solomonoff, Ray. 1964. "A Formal Theory of Inductive Inference Part II." *Information and Control* 7, no. 2 (June): 224–254.

Sorokin, Pitirim A., and Robert K. Merton. 1937. "Social Time: A Methodological and Functional Analysis." *American Journal of Sociology* 42, no. 5 (March): 615–629.

Spielberg, Steven, dir. 2002. *Minority Report*. 20th Century Fox.

Staal, Frits. 2006. "Artificial Languages across Sciences and Civilizations." *Journal of Indian Philosophy* 34:87–139.

Stern, Howard. 1988. "Logos, Logic, and Logistiké: Some Philosophical Remarks on 19th c. Transformation of Mathematics." In *History and Philosophy of Mathematics*. Vol. 11, edited by William Aspray and Philip Kitchner, 238–259. Minneapolis: University of Minnesota Press.

Sterne, Jonathan. 2012. *MP3: The Meaning of a Format*. Durham, NC: Duke University Press. Kindle.

Stewart, William. "ARPANET—the first Internet." http://www.livinginternet.com/i/ii_arpanet.htm.

Steyerl, Hito. 2016. "A Sea of Data: Apophenia and Pattern (Mis-)Recognition." *E-Flux Journal* 72 (April). https://www.e-flux.com/journal/72/60480/a-sea-of-data-apophenia-and-pattern-mis-recognition/.

Stiegler, Bernard. 1998. *Technics and Time*. Vol. 1, *The Fault of Epimetheus*. Stanford, CA: Stanford University Press.

Suchman, Lucy. 1987. *Plans and Situated Actions: The Problem of Human-Machine Communication*. Cambridge: Cambridge University Press.

Sussman, Gerald Jay, and Guy Lewis Steele, Jr. 1975. "Scheme: An Interpreter for Extended Lambda Calculus (AIM-349)." MIT AI Lab Memo, December.

Swetz, Frank. 1989. *Capitalism and Arithmetic: The New Math of the Fifteenth Century*. Chicago: Open Court.

Takats, Sean. 2011. *The Expert Cook in Enlightenment France*. Johns Hopkins University Studies in Historical and Political Science. Baltimore: Johns Hopkins University Press. Kindle.

Tanenhaus, Sam. 2016. "Noam Chomsky and the Bicycle Theory." *New York Times*, October 31, http://www.nytimes.com/2016/11/06/education/edlife/on-being-noam-chomsky.html.

Terranova, Tiziana. 2000. "Free Labor: Producing Culture for the Digital Economy." *Social Text, 63* 18 no. 2 (Summer): 33–58.

Thomas, James J., and Kristin A. Cook. 2005. "Executive Summary." In *Illuminating the Path: The Research and Development Agenda for Visual Analytics*, edited by James J. Thomson and Kristin A. Cook, 1–18. National Visualization and Analytics Center and IEEE.

Thompson, John B. 1984. *Studies in the Theory of Ideology*. Berkeley: University of California Press.

Thucydides. 1910. *The Peloponnesian War*. New York: E. P. Dutton.

Tomalin, Marcus. 2006. *Linguistics and the Formal Sciences: The Origins of Generative Grammar*. Cambridge Studies in Linguistics. Cambridge: Cambridge University Press. Kindle.

Tomkins, Silvan S., and Samuel Messick, eds. 1963. *Computer Simulation of Personality*. Frontier of Psychological Theory. New York: Wiley.

Tracy, Antoine-Louis-Claude Destutt de. 1800–1815. "Tome I—Chapitre 11: Réflexions sur ce qui précède, et sur la manière dont Condillac a analysé la pensée." In *Éléments d'idéologie*. Paris: P. Didot l'aîné.

Tufte, Edward R. 2001. *The Visual Display of Quantitative Information*. Cheshire, CT: Graphics Press.

Turing, Alan M. 1937. "Computability and λ-Definability." *Journal of Symbolic Logic* 2, no. 4:153–163.

Turing, Alan M. 1937. "On Computable Numbers, with an Application to the Entscheidungsproblem." Paper presented at the Proceedings of the London Mathematical Society, 1936. *Proceedings of the London Mathematical Society*, 2nd ser., 42, no. 1 (January 1): 230–265.

Turing, Alan M. 1950. "Computing Machinery and Intelligence." *Mind* 49:433–460.

Turing, Alan M. 1969. "Intelligent Machinery, National Physical Laboratory Report (1948)." In *Machine Intelligence*. Vol. 5, edited by B. Meltzer and D. Michie, 3–23. Edinburgh: Edinburgh University Press.

Turner, Fred. 2006. *From Counterculture to Cyberculture: Stewart Brand, the Whole Earth Network, and the Rise of Digital Utopianism*. Chicago: University of Chicago Press.

Uspenskii, V. A. 2002. "Arithmetization." In *Encyclopedia of Mathematics*, edited by Ulf Rehmann. Dordrecht: Kluwer Academic.

Uspenskii, V. A. 2002. "Arithmetization of Analysis." In *Encyclopedia of Mathematics*, edited by Ulf Rehmann. Dordrecht: Kluwer Academic.

Vanian, Jonathan. 2016. "Why Data Is the New Oil." *Fortune*, July 11. http://fortune.com/2016 /07/11/data-oil-brainstorm-tech/.

VanLehn, Kurt. 1987. "Learning One Subprocedure per Lesson." *Artificial Intelligence*, no. 31:1–40.

von Ahn, Luis, Manuel Blum, Nicholas J. Hopper, and John Langford. 2003. "CAPTCHA: Using Hard AI Problems for Security." Paper presented at EUROCRYPT 2003: International Conference on the Theory and Applications of Cryptographic Techniques, May 2003.

Waddell, Mark. 2015. *Jesuit Science and the End of Nature's Secrets*. Burlington, VT: Ashgate.

Wardrip-Fruin, Noah. 2009. *Expressive Processing: Digital Fictions, Computer Games, and Software Studies*. Cambridge, MA: MIT Press.

Wark, McKenzie. 2007. *Gamer Theory*. Cambridge, MA: Harvard University Press.

Watts, Duncan. 2013. "Computational Social Science: Exciting Progress and Future Directions." *The Bridge on Frontiers of Engineering (National Academy of Engineering)* 43, no. 4 (December 20). https://www.nae.edu/19582/Bridge/106112/106118.aspx

Weaver, Warren. 1955. "Translation." In *Machine Translation of Languages*, edited by W. N. Locke and D. A. Booth, 15–23. Cambridge, MA: MIT Press.

Weber, Max. (1930) 1992. *The Protestant Ethic and the Spirit of Capitalism*. New York: Routledge.

Weber, Max. 1963. *The Sociology of Religion*. Boston: Beacon Press.

Webster, Charles. 1965. "The Discovery of Boyle's Law, and the Concept of the Elasticity of Air in the Seventeenth Century." *Archive for History of Exact Sciences* 2:441–502.

Wegner, Peter. 1997. "Why Interaction Is More Powerful than Algorithms." *Communications of the ACM* 40, no. 5:80–91.

Weizenbaum, Joseph. 1976. *Computer Power and Human Reason: From Judgment to Calculation*. New York: W. H. Freeman.

Wellmon, Chad. 2015. *Organizing Enlightenment: Information Overload and the Modern Research University*. Baltimore, MD: Johns Hopkins University Press.

White, Hayden. 1973. *Metahistory: The Historical Imagination in Nineteenth-Century Europe*. Baltimore: Johns Hopkins University Press.

Whitehead, Alfred North, and Bertrand Russell. 1910. *Principia Mathematica*. Vol. 1. Cambridge: Cambridge University Press.

Whitehead, Alfred North, and Bertrand Russell. 1912. *Principia Mathematica*. Vol. 2. Cambridge: Cambridge University Press.

Whitehead, Alfred North, and Bertrand Russell. 1913. *Principia Mathematica*. Vol. 3. Cambridge: Cambridge University Press.

Whitehead, Alfred North, and Bertrand Russell. 1925. *Principia Mathematica*. 2nd ed. Vol. 1. Cambridge: Cambridge University Press.

Whitehead, Alfred North, and Bertrand Russell. 1927. *Principia Mathematica*. 2nd ed. Vol. 2. Cambridge: Cambridge University Press.

Whitehead, Alfred North, and Bertrand Russell. 1927. *Principia Mathematica*. 2nd ed. Vol. 3. Cambridge: Cambridge University Press.

Wiener, Norbert. 1948. *Cybernetics: Or Control and Communication in the Animal and the Machine*. Cambridge, MA: MIT Press.

Wiener, Norbert. 1960. "Some Moral and Technical Consequences of Automation." *Science* 131, no. 3410 (May 6): 1355–1358.

Wilkins, John. 1648. "Foreword." In *Mathematical Magick*. Oxford: Rick Baldwin.

Wilson, Curtis. 1993. "Clairaut's Calculation of Halley's Comet." *Journal of the History of Astronomy* 24:1–14.

Wilson, Curtis. 1995. "Appendix: Clairaut's Calculation of the Comet's Return." In *The General History of Astronomy*, edited by Rene Taton and Curtis Wilson, 83–86. Cambridge: Cambridge University Press.

Wing, Jeannette M. 2006. "A Vision for the 21st Century: Computational Thinking." *Communications of the ACM* 49, no. 3:33–35.

Winograd, Terry. 1972. "Understanding Natural Language." *Cognitive Psychology* 3, no. 1 (January): 1–191.

Wittgenstein, Ludwig. 1922. *Tractatus Logico-Philosophicus*. Translated by Frank P. Ramsey. London: Kegan Paul.

Wittgenstein, Ludwig. 1953. *Philosophical Investigations*. New York: Macmillan.

Wittgenstein, Ludwig. 1958. *The Blue and Brown Books: Preliminary Studies for the "Philosophical Investigations."* New York: Harper Torchbooks.

Wittgenstein, Ludwig. 1976. *Wittgenstein's Lectures on the Foundations of Mathematics, Cambridge, 1939*. Chicago: University of Chicago Press.

Wittgenstein, Ludwig. 1978. *Remarks on the Foundations of Mathematics*. Cambridge, MA: MIT Press.

Wittgenstein, Ludwig. 1980. *Remarks on the Philosophy of Psychology*. Vol. 1. Oxford: Blackwell.

Wolfram, Stephen. 2002. *A New Kind of Science*. Champaign, IL: Wolfram Media.

Žižek, Slavoj. 2007. *Enjoy Your Symptom! Jacques Lacan in Hollywood and Out*. New York: Routledge.

Zweben, Stuart. 2013. "Computing Degree and Enrollment Trends: Undergraduate Enrollment Grows for Sixth Straight Year and Ph.D. Production Reaches an All-Time High." http://www.cra.org/uploads/documents/resources/taulbee/CRA_Taulbee_CS_Degrees_and_Enrollment_2012-13.pdf.

Index